Business Opportunities in Indonesia

Titles in the Nanyang Business Report Series

Title	**ISBN**
Business Opportunities in Penang, Malaysia	0-13-267907-8
Business Opportunities in Sichuan Province, China	0-13-267881-0
Business Opportunities in India	0-13-267899-3
Business Opportunities in the Philippines	0-13-267915-9
Business Opportunities in Myanmar	0-13-713208-5
Business Opportunities in the Yangtze River Delta, China	0-13-713059-7
Business Opportunities in Vietnam	0-13-754334-4
U.S.–ASEAN Relations: Implications for Business	0-13-789868-1
Business Opportunities in Indonesia	0-13-080083-X

For further enquiries, information or feedback on the series, please write to the Acquisitions Editor at e-mail: prenhall@singnet.com.sg or Simon & Schuster (Asia) Pte Ltd, 317 Alexandra Road, #04-01 IKEA Building, Singapore 159965.

NANYANG BUSINESS REPORT SERIES

Business Opportunities in Indonesia

Edited by

Tan Teck Meng (Dean)
Low Aik Meng (Vice Dean and Director of MBA Programme)
John J. Williams (Chief Coordinator, Business Study Mission)
Choo Teck Min (Coordinator, Business Study Mission)

Nanyang Technological University
Singapore

Prentice Hall
Singapore New York London Toronto Sydney Mexico City

First published in 1998 by
Prentice Hall
Simon & Schuster (Asia) Pte Ltd
317 Alexandra Road
#04-01 IKEA Building
Singapore 159965

Simon & Schuster (Asia) Pte Ltd
A division of Simon & Schuster International Group

Prentice Hall, Simon & Schuster offices in Asia: *Bangkok, Beijing, Hong Kong, Jakarta, Kuala Lumpur, Manila, New Delhi, Seoul, Singapore, Taipei, Tokyo*

Printed in Singapore

5 4 3 2 1 02 01 00 99 98

ISBN 0-13-080082-1
ISBN 0-13-080083-X (pbk)

Simon & Schuster (Asia) Pte Ltd, *Singapore*
Prentice Hall, Inc., *Upper Saddle River, New Jersey*
Prentice Hall Europe, *London*
Prentice Hall Canada Inc., *Toronto*
Prentice Hall of Australia Pty Limited, *Sydney*
Prentice Hall Hispanoamericana, S.A., *Mexico*

CONTENTS

BANKING AND FINANCIAL ISSUES

MARKETING

FOREIGN INVESTMENT REGULATIONS AND PETROLEUM SECTOR

CONCLUSION

ABOUT THE EDITORS

TAN TECK MENG is Professor and Dean at the Nanyang Business School. Since joining academia in the early 1970s, Professor Tan has combined his university responsibilities with extensive consultancy work, culminating with fellowships in the Australian Society of CPAs, the Institute of Chartered Secretaries and Administrators, and the Institute of Management, U.K., together with an Honorary Ph.D. from Liaoning University in 1996. Professor Tan has been instrumental in nurturing the Nanyang Business School towards world class status with specialised undergraduate business degrees, MBA programmes and the Ph.D. (Business) programmes, leading to a top ten Business School ranking in Asia and Australia by Asia Inc. In addition to other publications, he is responsible for editing the Nanyang Business Report Series (Prentice Hall), and is Editor-in-Chief of the 14-book Singapore Development Series (Addison-Wesley) and the Journal of Enterprising Culture. He holds senior positions on a number of institutional boards and committees in Singapore including the Accounting and Auditing Services Working Group of the Economic Committee, the Public Accountants Board, the Board of Directors of Singapore Reinsurance Corporation Limited, the Institute of Certified Public Accountants of Singapore (ICPAS), the Income Tax Board of Review and the Board of Governors of the Singapore Insurance Institute. Professor Tan is founding Director of the Entrepreneurship Development Centre (ENDEC) and in 1992 was elected to the Board of Governors of the MIT Sloan School of Management Society for Senior Executives.

LOW AIK MENG is Associate Professor and Director of the MBA programme at the Nanyang Business School. He worked for five years as an accountant and an internal auditor before joining academia in 1975. He was Vice Dean of the Faculty of Accountancy and Business Administration at the National University of Singapore until he joined the Nanyang Technological University in 1987. He is currently Vice Dean at the Nanyang Business School and has been the Director of its very successful MBA programme since its inception in 1991. Under his leadership, the MBA programme has been building a network of contacts with businesses and government bodies in Singapore and overseas. He spearheads the thrice-yearly Business Study Missions which are an integral part of the MBA programme. Associate Professor Low continues to be active in the accountancy profession and serves on several committees in the Institute of Certified Public Accountants of Singapore.

JOHN J. WILLIAMS is Associate Professor at the Nanyang Business School and Chief Coordinator of the MBA Business Study Mission programme. He has taught and carried out research projects in several countries including Canada, the U.S., Kenya and Singapore. Throughout the later part of the 1980s, Dr. Williams served as Vice Chairman and Chairman of the Final Accreditation Exam Board for the Society of Management Accountants of Canada, which admitted him as a Fellow in 1992. Although active in consulting for government agencies in the U.S. and Canada during this period, he has published extensively in leading academic and professional journals and he continues to pursue the study of emerging regional economies in the ASEAN region.

CHOO TECK MIN is Senior Lecturer and Deputy Director (Academic) of the MBA programme at the Nanyang Business School. Dr. Choo was the Chairperson of the MBA Business Study Mission to Indonesia. He holds a Ph.D. from the University of Pittsburgh, U.S.A. in accounting and is also a Singapore CPA. He teaches in the areas of accounting, corporate reporting, accounting theory, auditing and judgement and choice at the undergraduate, MBA and Ph.D. levels. His research interests are in the areas of audit judgement, behavioural accounting and management accounting. He has published in local and international journals such as the Singapore Accountant, the Securities Industry Review, the Singapore Management Review and the Managerial Auditing Journal. His current research projects examine the information search and evaluation processes employed by auditors as they perform hypothesis-testing in analytical procedures.

PREFACE

The Nanyang Business School, the largest school in Singapore's Nanyang Technological University, requires every candidate for its Master of Business Administration degree to complete a Business Study Mission (BSM). The main purpose of these organised visits to other countries is to ensure that the MBA participants acquire skills in understanding overseas investment opportunities and evaluating the business climate in which such investments must operate. The Business Study Mission also supports the national economic strategy which, in recent years, has focused on the development of an "external wing" to balance a strong, but relatively small, internal economy.

This volume contains business reports originating from the Business Study Mission to Indonesia in December 1996. Over a nine-day period, 48 participants from the Nanyang Business School MBA programme explored the climate for business enterprises in Jakarta, Surabaya and Yogyakarta located on the major island of Java. Typically, these participants have five years or more of business experience as middle managers in medium-to-large Singapore-based enterprises. During the six months prior to the BSM, participants were engaged in specific lectures and workshops, carried out desk research and interviewed managers who have extensive experience in Indonesia. Following the BSM, the participants transformed their learning experience in Indonesia into the chapters presented here, under the able guidance of their mission supervisors who have expertise in selected functional areas.

As the largest archipelago in the world consisting of over 17,500 islands, covering a land area of 1.9 million square kilometres, and islands that stretch more than one-tenth of the equator between Southeast Asia and Australia, Indonesia has been referred to as the "sleeping giant" in the past. But with a motivated population of approximately 200 million (the fourth most populous nation in the world after China, India and the U.S.) generating GDP growth rates consistently above 7%, and burgeoning foreign investment and trade, Indonesia is now an "awakened giant". Although Java, Sulawesi, Kalimantan and Sumatra are the dominant islands, Java commands the largest proportionate share of domestic and foreign investment. As of mid-1996, Java accounted for 76.4% of total investment projects and 63.5% of total foreign investment valued at US$164.3 billion.

Given the economic importance of Java, the BSM trip focused on Jakarta and Surabaya because of their critical inputs to the political and business climate of Indonesia generally, and also focused on Yogyakarta because it is the cultural centre of Java. This volume, therefore, carefully investigates the macroeconomic and policy context for foreign investment, examines several key sectors of the economy including the vital role of market advertising and distribution, and considers the incredible transformation of the Indonesian banking system and the uncertainty of the rupiah. The objective is to develop and communicate an in-depth understanding of investment opportunities, and the ingredients and behaviours necessary to succeed at doing business in Indonesia.

The Coordinating Minister for Production and Distribution, His Excellency Dr. Hartarto, officially opened the BSM on 8 December 1996 at the Mandarin Oriental Hotel, Jakarta, after opening addresses from Dr. Cham Tao Soon, President of Nanyang Technological University, and Professor Tan Teck Meng, Dean of the Nanyang Business School. The following two days entailed extensive seminar presentations, site visits and discussions with Singaporean businessmen in Jakarta. The first day of seminars centred on guest speakers from the private sector followed by visits to the Jakarta Stock Exchange and P. T. Sassoon Securities Indonesia. The second day of seminars featured prominent guest speakers from the public sector followed by a visit to the Pulo Gadung Special Economic Zone. On the third day, after a privileged closed-door informal discussion with Singapore's Ambassador to Indonesia, His Excellency Mr. Edward Lee, our delegation departed for Surabaya in East Java.

In Surabaya, the Chairman of the Regional Investment Coordinating Board for East Java, Dr. Bambang Koesbandono, delivered the keynote address after opening remarks by Professor Tan Teck Meng. On the following morning, Directors from the Regional Agency National Development and Planning, and the Regional Investment Coordinating Board, provided a rich set of information on economic development and business opportunities in Surabaya and East Java. This was followed by site visits to the Surabaya Industrial Estate, the

Port of Surabaya and several Singaporean companies in Surabaya. Following a delightful bus trip to Tretes and Tanggulangin, our delegation departed for the prestigious cultural centre, Yogyakarta.

The focus of the agenda in Yogyakarta was to gain an understanding of the development issues for infrastructure and small to medium-sized business activities in this beautiful area which is a paramount tourist attraction. Following opening comments by Professor Tan Teck Meng, the keynote address from the Regional Head of the Department of Tourism, Post and Telecommunications in Yogyakarta, Mr. W. J. Pronoto, was delivered. The next day, our delegation visited the spectacular Borobudur site which is classified as one of the "seven wonders" of the world. From there, we proceeded to Malioboro and Kraton, and then visited some batik home industries and the Prambanan Temple. The day was capped with a joyful Andong ride (horse and carriage) to Joyokusuman House for an awesome Ramayana ballet performance followed by dinner. With fond memories and the gracious warmth from all our hosts throughout our sojourn in Indonesia, we reluctantly departed for Singapore the next day.

The knowledge amassed by the MBA participants through this mission to Indonesia is enormous. It is our hope that this book will be insightful for understanding the environment and specific contexts which presently exist throughout Indonesia concerning a variety of business opportunities. To be sure, this book's appeal is global as well as regional: to firms or entrepreneurs eager to provide capital, human resource training or technology; to institutional agencies, public or private, contemplating trade or infrastructure development; to organisations servicing expatriate subsidiary operations in Indonesia; to executives and managers of professional services; and to educational institutions for pedagogical and research purposes.

Editors:
TAN Teck Meng
LOW Aik Meng
John J. WILLIAMS
CHOO Teck Min

ACKNOWLEDGEMENTS

This Business Study Mission to Indonesia would not have been possible without the tremendous support and assistance rendered to us by His Excellency, Dr. Hartarto, Coordinating Minister for Production and Distribution, Republic of Indonesia. The team from his Office that was assembled to assist in the planning and organisation of this Mission was very ably led by Mr. Aizirman Djusan. We are grateful to Pak Aizirman and his team for the time and effort that they put into ensuring that our programme was successful. This entailed contacting numerous government agencies, and even pre-trips to Surabaya and Yogyakarta, to ensure that all arrangements were in order.

The programme officially commenced with the opening banquet and the keynote address by the Guest-of-Honour, His Excellency, Dr. Hartarto. In his address, he dwelt at length on Indonesia–Singapore relations, within the broader context of ASEAN.

Special thanks go to our panel speakers from both the private and government sectors in Jakarta: Mr. Hendrik Suhardiman (Vice President, Tamara Bank), Mr. Kanaka Puradiredja (Managing Partner, KPMG Hanadi Sudjendro and Rekan), Mr. Kok Heng Loong (General Manager, P. T. Sassoon Securities Indonesia), Ms. Ricky S. Nazir (Senior Legal Partner, Ali Budiardjo, Nugroho, Reksodiputro), Ir. Sugihono Kadarisman (Deputy II, Investment Coordinating Board (BKPM)), Dr. Perry Warjiyo (Bank Indonesia), Dr. M. Anwar Wardhani (Bureau of Agriculture and Forestry, Agency of National Development and Planning (BAPPENAS)) and Dr. Mayun Winangun (Department of Finance). The presentations by the speakers and the panel question-and-answer sessions that followed were lively and interesting, and were only constrained by the time available.

Our stay in Jakarta was capped by three engaging site visits. The highlight of the visit to the Jakarta Stock Exchange was the presentation by Mr. D. Cyril Noerhadi, President Director, Jakarta Stock Exchange, who gave a lucid overview of the Exchange's role and function in the Indonesian economy. On the visit to P. T. Sassoon Securities Indonesia, delegates were made to feel at home by the Managing Director, Mr. Mason Tan, who briefed us and showed us the company's broking operations. At the Pulo Gadung Special Economic Zone, delegates were briefed by zone officials before the guided visit of a cooking oil manufacturing plant belonging to P. T. Sinar Meadow International Indonesia.

We are particularly grateful to Tamara Bank for hosting a lunch for us at the Mandarin Oriental Hotel, Jakarta. We would like to express our appreciation to His Excellency, Mr. Edward Lee, Singapore Ambassador to Indonesia, for the support he gave to us by gracing our opening banquet and also addressing us in a closed-door session. We are also grateful to Mr. Peter Chao and Mr. Tommy Kaw of the Singapore Association in Indonesia for arranging a meeting with Singaporean businessmen in Jakarta.

On the second leg of the trip to Surabaya, a special note of thanks goes out to Dr. Bambang Koesbandono (Chairman, Regional Investment Coordinating Board, East Java) for not only officiating at our welcome dinner but also for speaking at our panel session the following day. We also acknowledge the participation of Ms. Nurul Hayati (the Provincial Government of East Java, Regional Development Planning Board) and Ms. Sriwati (East Java Regional Investment Coordinating Board) in the panel session. The speakers provided relevant information and materials on the rapidly growing East Java region. Site visits to the Surabaya Industrial Estate, Rungkut and the Tanjong Perak Harbour proved to be educational and enlightening experiences. For these visits, we thank Dr. Herry Wuwungan (General Manager, Pelabuhan Indonesia III), Mr. Djarwo Surjanto (Technical Director, Indonesia Port Corporation III), Mr. Hartojo Abdulkahar (Director, Marketing and Development, P. T. SIER (Persero)), Mr. Muhammad Shodiq (Finance and General Affairs Director, P. T. SIER (Persero)) and Dr. R. Deddy Prahmono (Regional Investment Coordinating Board) for so warmly receiving us and showing us their operations.

We were privileged to be given access to two companies in Surabaya with substantial Singapore investment. At P. T. Tien Wah Press Indonesia, we are grateful to Mr. Loh Kee Leong, Plant and Factory Manager, for showing us the labour-intensive process of producing a non-standard publication such as a "pop-up" science book. At P. T. Java Pacific Container, we thank Mr. James Khoo, Director, for sharing his insights on the container business and taking us on a walkabout of his manufacturing operations. Special thanks go to Mr. Lee Say Seng from the Singapore Club of Surabaya for arranging a dinner meeting with its members and our delegation. We gratefully acknowledge the assistance provided by Dr. Suprapto, Vice-Governor, East Java province, Surabaya for making the Surabaya sector of this Mission possible.

On the third leg of the trip to Yogyakarta, we are grateful to Professor Boma Wikan Tyoso, Dr. Bambang Sudibyo, Dr. Harsono, Dr. Dumairy and Dr. Basu Swastha Dharmmesta from Gadjah Mada University for the extensive role that they and their University played in hosting us. We appreciate the immense assistance provided by Mr. W. J. Pranoto, Deputy Director General of Tourism, Department of Tourism, Post and Telecommunications, in ensuring that our programme in Yogyakarta was a success.

Many speakers in Singapore prepared us in advance with vital economic, cultural and political information on Indonesia. We are grateful for their substantial contributions to this book. They include Mr. Trijono Marijono (Counsellor (Economic), Embassy of the Republic of Indonesia), Mr. Rachy Rachmat (Third Secretary, Embassy of the Republic of Indonesia), Associate Professor Leo Suryadinata (Department of Political Science, National University of Singapore), Mr. Zaid Hamzah (Khattar Wong and Partners), Mr. Ng Beng Hong (Manager, Economics and Technology Department, Pertamina) and Mr. Ahamed Merican (Economics and Technology Department, Pertamina). We would like to express our gratitude for the substantial contribution from Mr. Chan Ying Lock who was involved in the initial planning and organisation of this Business Study Mission to Indonesia. A special acknowlegement is extended to the diligent supervising efforts of Dr. John Vong, Dr. Krishna Erramilli, Dr. Austin Pullé and Dr. Ashish Lall.

Finally, our sincere thanks to MBA Director, Associate Professor Low Aik Meng, for marshalling together all of the talent and resources necessary to make the BSM a success. Thanks also to the MBA office, to Grace Cheng and Adelene Ang for attending to incredible administrative details; without their efforts the trip would not have worked. Thanks to Linda Chua for her meticulous proofing; to our Publisher, Prentice Hall, for their guidance; and especially to Goh Lai Lay for her painstaking efforts in bringing this book to completion.

INTRODUCTION

Chapter 1

Indonesia: An Awakened Giant

BY
TAN Teck Meng
LOW Aik Meng
John J. WILLIAMS
CHOO Teck Min

INTRODUCTION

THE REPUBLIC OF Indonesia is a composite of over 17,500 islands which stretch from just west of Peninsular Malaysia along the equator some 5,000 kilometres to the northeast coast of Australia. Since 1985, the economy has been growing at more than 7.5% annually. The engines of this growth have been the efforts of approximately 200 million people from over 300 culturally diverse backgrounds, practising four major religions and geared to the fundamental cornerstones of the Indonesian Government which are grounded in unity, tolerance, equality and social harmony (INDIO, 1996).

Indonesia is rich in natural resources and people. And, with the shift in economic development from a heavy reliance on the oil and gas sector to the burgeoning manufacturing sector, nurturing substantial flows of foreign investment and welcoming the transfer of new technologies, Indonesia has awakened on the economic frontiers of the global economy. The Sixth Five-Year Development Plan (*Repelita VI*) unveiled in April 1994 promises to move the country even closer to the competitive standards demanded by the global economy. Nonetheless, there are challenges and issues looming in the distance which investors need to comprehend to take full advantage of the benefits which Indonesia offers. This chapter sketches a few of the major developments which have contributed to Indonesia's current status and then outlines the directions taken in the remaining chapters.

THE HISTORICAL SHAPING OF INDONESIA

Since ancient times, the strategically situated Indonesian archipelago endeared traders searching for spices, gold and prized timber in return for silk, textiles and other commodities from China, India and the Middle East. One of the early foreign influences was Buddhism which flourished in eighth century Srivijaya, South Sumatra, and embraced the Mulawarman kingdom in East Kalimantan and Mataram in southern Central Java by the ninth century. Today, the temples of Borobudur and Mendut are prestigious reminders of the Buddhist influence in Indonesia, both of which were built by King Sonjaya of Mataram in the ninth century.

The next influence making its appearance in the archipelago was Hinduism which thrived in several Javanese kingdoms from the 14th to the 16th centuries. The island of Bali still embraces Hinduism to this day. The advent of Islam first appeared in Acheh in the northern tip of Sumatra around the 14th century. By the 17th century, the Islamic culture had spread to the northern coast of Java and later to the kingdom of Mataram in southern Central Java. Other kingdoms were established in Makasor and Bone, located in South Sulawesi, and regions of Kalimantan. At present, approximately 80% of all Indonesians are Muslim (Kayam, 1996).

The first European intrusion occurred in the Moluccas and other eastern islands of the archipelago, and featured the Portuguese spice traders in the 16th century followed by the Spanish and British traders. With this influence came Christianity and the motive to conquer the spice islands. However, the Dutch ended these intrusions with the formation of the Dutch East India Company in 1605. It survived until 1799 when the Netherlands assumed direct administrative control (Kayam, 1996).

Recent History

The Dutch controlled Indonesia until the Japanese invasion in March 1942. However, Sukarno and Hatta proclaimed independence for Indonesia on 17 August 1945, two days after the Japanese surrendered to the Allied forces. Nonetheless, the Dutch battled for four more years in an effort to reclaim their colonial territory but to no avail. The *Hague Agreement* of 2 December 1949 terminated Dutch control of the archipelago except for the western half of the island of New Guinea. However, the Dutch-held territory of Irian Jaya was transferred to Indonesia on 1 May 1963. Finally, East Timor became Indonesia's 27th province in July 1976, thus ending over 300 years of Portuguese colonial administration (INDIO, 1996). The territory comprising the Republic of Indonesia was complete.

Several months prior to cessation of Japanese control, Sukarno unfolded the five principles of *Pancasila* which govern Indonesian nationhood: belief in one supreme God; justice and civility among the people; democracy through deliberation and consensus; the unity of Indonesia; and social justice for all. These principles have remained unaltered to the present day. Indonesia's political history since 1945 consists of the Old Order and the New Order. The former can be partitioned into the 1945–49 era, which is commonly referred to as the "parliamentary democracy period", while the 1959–65 period is known as the period of Sukarno's "guided democracy". The political focus of these first two decades was dedicated essentially to nation-building rather than economic development. However, a fresh approach to economic development accompanied the New Order Government when General Suharto was elected President of the Republic in March 1968 although he had assumed leadership two years earlier. At the same time, Golkar became the regime's parliamentary vehicle (INDIO, 1996).

THE GIANT EMERGES

Given the bewildering complexity of Indonesian society, it is not surprising that a regulated approach to economic development would accompany the New Order Government. However, by the mid-1980s the economy was in a quagmire from a decade or more of private sector regulations, spiralling inflation for consumers and uncompetitive products on the global front. Export markets were in disarray and domestic inefficiencies in production were rampant. The collapse of oil prices in the mid-1980s strangled the government's subsidisation programmes. There was a desperate need to reform the economy and revitalise the private sector, for the sake of the internal economy and to foster new industries for world markets.

Three initial areas of reform were addressed. First, foreign investment rules were simplified to attract the much needed foreign capital. Secondly, the heavily regulated inter-island shipping industry and steel industry were opened up to new trade reforms. Thirdly, the capital markets were liberalised. All of these reforms emerged under the much heralded *Pakto* liberalisation package in October 1988 and an emerging economic giant was in the making (Schwarz, 1994).

Earlier in 1983, the first steps at improving the banking system were undertaken with the dismantling of interest rate ceilings and revamping of the tax structure in 1984. The rupiah was devalued in 1986 and a tariff structure replaced existing trade barriers. From a single commodity dependent economy in 1981, with oil and gas accounting for over 80% of total trade exports and nearly 71% of the government's receipts, the 1988 reform package permanently shifted Indonesia's economic infrastructure (Schwarz, 1994).

There is virtual unanimity that the financial sector reforms, in particular, contained in the October 1988 reform package were unprecedented and decidedly woke up the "sleeping giant". In a four-year period to 1991, private banks doubled in number, nearly 20 foreign banks emerged and thousands of bank branches appeared across the country. Total bank deposits trebled to US$48 billion; loans increased 250% and state banks became second to private banks in terms of total deposits. More remarkable was the burgeoning Jakarta Stock Exchange which was the world's growth leader in 1989 (Schwarz, 1994). Jakarta was overwhelmed with foreign brokers and fund managers as capital flowed in from all four corners of the globe. The money markets of the world had discovered Indonesia.

INDONESIA'S MAJOR ACHIEVEMENTS

The New Order Government inherited an unenviable economic structure in 1966. Testimony to the problems were the imports of rice and other basic commodities in addition to rampant inflation of 600% per annum (Schwarz, 1994). Thus, the country's First 25-Year Development Plan had no other alternative but to focus on the weak and crumbling economy. And rise to the challenge it did. Gross Domestic Product (GDP) averaged approximately 7% per annum to 1993 with a remarkable 8.3 annual average in the five years preceding 1993 (INDIO, 1996). Since then, there has been continued growth in GDP of 7.5% in 1994, nearly 8.1% in 1995 and a further 7.6% in 1996 when other Southeast Asian neighbours were faring much worse.

A landmark achievement of the Suharto Government has been an economic and social restructuring of the economy, driven by a diversified manufacturing sector and an expanding services sector, and away from the once dominant oil and agriculture sectors. In 1996, the manufacturing sector contributed well over 25% to GDP compared to a meagre 9.2 in 1969. Moreover, from 1975 to the mid-1990s, electricity capacity increased more than 20-fold, telephone lines surged over 8-fold in number and paved roads escalated over 6-fold (Schwarz, 1994). In addition, health care has been a high priority with over 7,000 health care centres and in excess of 20,000 sub-health care centres installed throughout Indonesia by mid-1996. Life expectancy reached 63 years by 1996, up significantly from 43 years in 1970. By the end of 1998, the government expects it to exceed 65 years. Universal primary education is now accessible to all Indonesians, rising to a participation rate of 95% in early 1996 from a paltry 41.4% in 1968 (INDIO, 1996).

These gains in literacy are matching the growing challenges of the labour market. A programme of population control, combined with rising labour productivity and decreased unemployment, have boosted GDP per capita to US$1,023 from US$70 in 1970, an incredible improvement by any standard. Importantly, one of the goals underlying the 25-Year Development Plan was the equitable distribution of development gains and the levels of absolute poor have been reduced to 13.7% in 1993 from over 60% in 1970 (Schwarz, 1994). One could argue that these achievements have allowed Indonesia to herald in the technology age and develop its expanding communications satellite programme. Agriculture has benefited in large ways as well. In the decade to 1986, Indonesia transformed itself from a major rice importer to a self-sufficient nation. The agriculture sector still contributes nearly one-fifth to GDP and absorbs approximately 40 million workers which account for one-half of its workforce (INDIO, 1996). Advanced farming technology, efficient land use, comprehensive pest control programmes and new storage techniques have vaulted Indonesia literally to food self-sufficiency.

AN ATTRACTIVE INVESTMENT CLIMATE

Indonesia's economy experienced strong growth and stable prices in 1996. Estimated growth in output was 7.8% for the year augmented by an inflation rate of 6.5%. Lower inflation seems to have been instrumental in easing interest rates and sparking domestic investment to more than Rp 100 trillion. Output was led again by the private sector which accounted for approximately 80% of total national output, with diversified manufacturing, and oil and gas processing forming the main locomotive of the Indonesian economy (Pacific Economic Cooperation Council, 1997). Domestic trade, financial service, transportation, communication and construction activities are significant components of the tertiary economy as is the tourism sector.

Multilateral and bilateral trade play a pivotal role in Indonesia's economy. Exports have steadily evolved from an agricultural base to the increased growth of oil and natural gas and, more recently, to the dominant manufacturing sector. Table 1–1 shows a healthy trade surplus over the period from 1990 to 1995 with estimates for 1996 pointing to a US$7 billion surplus, despite slower growth in both exports and imports. Indonesia's major external markets are Japan, the U.S., the European Community and ASEAN nations which collec-

TABLE 1–1
Trade Summary: 1990–1996*

Year	Imports	Exports	Trade Balance
1990	21,837.1	25,675.3	3,838.2
1991	25,868.8	29,142.2	3,273.4
1992	27,279.6	33,967.0	6,687.4
1993	28,327.8	36,823.0	8,495.2
1994	31,983.5	40,053.4	8,069.9
1995	40,628.7	45,418.0	4,789.3
1996	42,100.0	49,000.0	6,900.0

* 1996 data are estimates.
Source: Investment Coordinating Board (1996a).

tively account for approximately 75% of total exports (Investment Coordinating Board, 1996a). The current account deficit has moved from US$3.5 billion in 1994 and 1995, respectively, to just under US$9 billion in 1996 largely because of interest payments on debt (Pacific Economic Cooperation Council, 1997).

The government has been instrumental in designing trade incentives to stimulate exports. In June 1996, the government cut import tariffs on 1,497 items. It has promised further reductions to a maximum of 10% by 2003. In addition, regulations for expatriate workers have been liberalised and more export processing zones have been established (INDIO, 1996). Finally, the much debated general elections were held in May 1997. President Suharto won by a clear mandate of 70.2% which ensures the country of continued political stability for another five years. Investors have responded by continuing to pour billions of dollars into the Indonesian economy.

FOREIGN DIRECT INVESTMENT TRENDS

Indonesia has been attracting foreign capital at an increasing rate and as at mid-1996 it totalled US$153 billion excluding the petroleum and financial sectors (see Table 1–2). With deregulation and more

TABLE 1–2
Foreign Investment: 1967–1996*

Year	Number of Projects	Capital Invested (US$ billion)
1967–1986	782	23.2
1987	130	1.5
1988	145	4.4
1989	294	4.7
1990	432	8.8
1991	376	8.8
1992	305	10.3
1993	329	8.2
1994	449	23.7
1995	799	39.9
1996	546*	20.9
Total	**4,587**	**154.4**

* To 30 June 1996.

Source: Investment Coordinating Board (1996a).

reforms enacted since 1993, the growth over that last several years has been stunning. Foreign investors have been particularly active in the manufacturing sector with the chemicals and pulp and paper industries attracting 66.2% of cumulative foreign investment between 1967 and mid-1996 (see Table 1–3). In the services sector, utilities and hotels and restaurants have secured 26.4% of cumulative foreign investment (INDIO, 1996).

TABLE 1–3
Leading FDI Sectors: 1967–1996*

Sectors	Number of Projects	Investment Value (US$ billion)
Chemicals	600	47.7
Paper	83	22.7
Metal Goods	840	13.0
Utilities	21	12.4
Hotels	173	9.5
Transportation	116	7.9
Basic Metals	92	7.1
Mining	121	6.4
Textiles	490	6.2
Property	104	6.0

* To 30 June 1996.
Source: INDIO (1996).

Table 1–4 gives the top ten foreign investors in Indonesia by country. In terms of investment value, Japan is the leader with 19.5%, followed by the U.K., Hong Kong and Singapore with 17.4%, 11.1% and 8.1%, respectively. Japan also leads in the number of projects followed by Singapore and Taiwan (Investment Coordinating Board, 1996b). These latter two countries are less involved in major infrastructure projects but prefer instead the tertiary and service sectors of the economy. Approximately 25% of FDI in Indonesia is arranged through joint ventures among countries.

By far, the majority of FDI in Indonesia is located on the islands of Java and Madura which account for 64.6% of the total investment value. The island of Sumatra is next with 18.7% followed by Kalimantan and Sulawesi with 5.9% and 5.2%, respectively (INDIO, 1996).

TABLE 1–4
Leading Foreign Investors in Indonesia: 1967–1996*

Countries	Number of Projects	Capital Invested (US$ billion)
Japan	871	31.8
U.K.	195	27.4
Hong Kong	346	18.2
Singapore	545	13.2
U.S.	242	12.3
Netherlands	148	10.4
Taiwan	474	9.1
South Korea	395	7.1
Australia	226	6.1
Germany	96	5.1

* To 30 June 1996.
Source: Investment Coordinating Board (1996b).

ORGANISATION OF BOOK

Given the vast richness and diversity of the Indonesian economy, it is an ominous task to cover all aspects of the business opportunities which are available. More importantly, the rapid pace of critical reforms and regulations underpinning the incredible growth of this country requires distillation for making judicious investment decisions. Thus, the contents of this book have been designed to provide potential investors with an understanding of major transitional changes at the macro level, new reforms across several industrial and financial sectors, and issues associated with the important functional area of marketing, as a pre-requisite for doing business in Indonesia. The remainder of this book contains four sections plus a concluding chapter. Although each section is devoted to a particular business focus, considerable diversity remains among the specific chapters. Therefore, a synopsis chapter concludes each section with the express purpose of synthesising the major themes of each chapter. In doing so, these synopsis chapters are intended to be more critical, and somewhat opinionated, of the chapters under review, offering extended views and additional information where appropriate.

The section on Trade and Manufacturing focuses on several major macroeconomic reforms and policies related to trade. Since the manufacturing sector has assumed such a prominent role in Indonesia's economic restructuring, and given its linkage to privatisation and deregulation generally, it is appropriately included in this section. Chapter 2 commences with an overview of Indonesia's sixth phase of planned economic development, *Repelita VI*. Chung *et al.* then review Indonesia's performance via several economic indicators including trade, the current account balance, foreign debt and exchange rate policy. The analysis then turns to issues of macroeconomics stability, non-tariff barriers, trade liberalisation and Indonesia's role in several major world trade organisations. In Chapter 3, Nallappan *et al.* examine Indonesia's privatisation efforts and deregulation measures. The latter focus on key deregulation packages introduced by the government from May 1994 through June 1996 and their impact on the economy. Chapter 4 shifts attention to the manufacturing sector where Tham *et al.* discuss a number of industries. Related issues within this sector are examined including employment, manpower development, wages, productivity, manufacturing zones, taxes and incentives, and emerging challenges. Lall concludes this section in Chapter 5 with a candid assessment of Indonesia's liberalisation efforts.

The next section, Banking and Finance, begins with Li *et al.* tracing the financial reforms in the banking industry and describing the characteristics of the Indonesian financial system. They also delve into the problems and challenges facing Indonesian banks. The latter part of the chapter includes their analysis of nine selected banks in terms of five generally accepted performance indicators. This is followed by Gan *et al.*, in Chapter 7, who discuss project financing and then evaluate three major infrastructure projects. Chapter 8 details the recent developments surrounding Indonesia's monetary and exchange rate policies. Lim *et al.* describe the rupiah intervention band and recent trends of the currency before dealing with various hedging alternatives. Chapter 9 concludes this section with Vong summarising a number of the top banks, outside sources of funding for infrastructure development and future movements in interest rates and the rupiah exchange rate.

Turning to the section on Marketing, Chapters 10, 11 and 12 provide a detailed coverage of distribution issues, advertising and market research. In Chapter 10, Chan *et al.* describe the typical Indonesian distribution system for consumer products in tandem with the retail market structure. The authors also examine the demographic structure and geographical distribution of consumers throughout the country. Finally, Chan *et al.* consider some specific challenges for foreign companies and various ways of entering the Indonesian market. Chapter 11 pursues recent developments impacting the advertising and promotion media in Indonesia. Cheong *et al.* discuss a variety of advertising controls and constraints before analysing and evaluating various advertising media. Chin *et al.*, in Chapter 12, deal with the very important area of market research in Indonesia, including surveys, language, the reliability of secondary data and problems in gathering primary data. Chapter 13, by Erramilli, concludes this section and it adopts a unique question and answer approach in dealing with some poignant issues about Indonesian marketing.

The last major section turns attention to several topics embedded in legal and regulatory developments. Foreign direct investment is addressed in Chapter 14 and Ng *et al.* discuss the deregulation process unfolding in Indonesia along with new laws, foreign investment issues and legalities pertaining to a foreign entity investing in Indonesia. The oil and gas industry is the subject matter of Chapter 15 where Susastra *et al.* present an overall profile of Pertamina's role in the petroleum sector, including production sharing contracts, as well as upstream and downstream industries, their problems and investment opportunities. In Chapter 16, de Souza and Karolewski review Indonesia's legal structure and business laws. Of crucial importance to investors, the authors then describe dispute resolution procedures followed by the technicalities associated with domestic and foreign arbitration. Pullé, in Chapter 17, succinctly addresses new reforms impacting foreign investors and discusses the wider implications of the new, but as yet untested, *Company Law*.

In Chapter 18, Williams concludes the book with some emerging developments and what the future may hold for business opportunities in Indonesia. Finally, there are considerable references throughout the book to various regions, provinces and cities located throughout the sprawling Indonesian archipelago. To facilitate an understanding of relative locations, a territorial map of Indonesia is presented in Figure 1–1.

FIGURE 1–1
Map of Indonesia

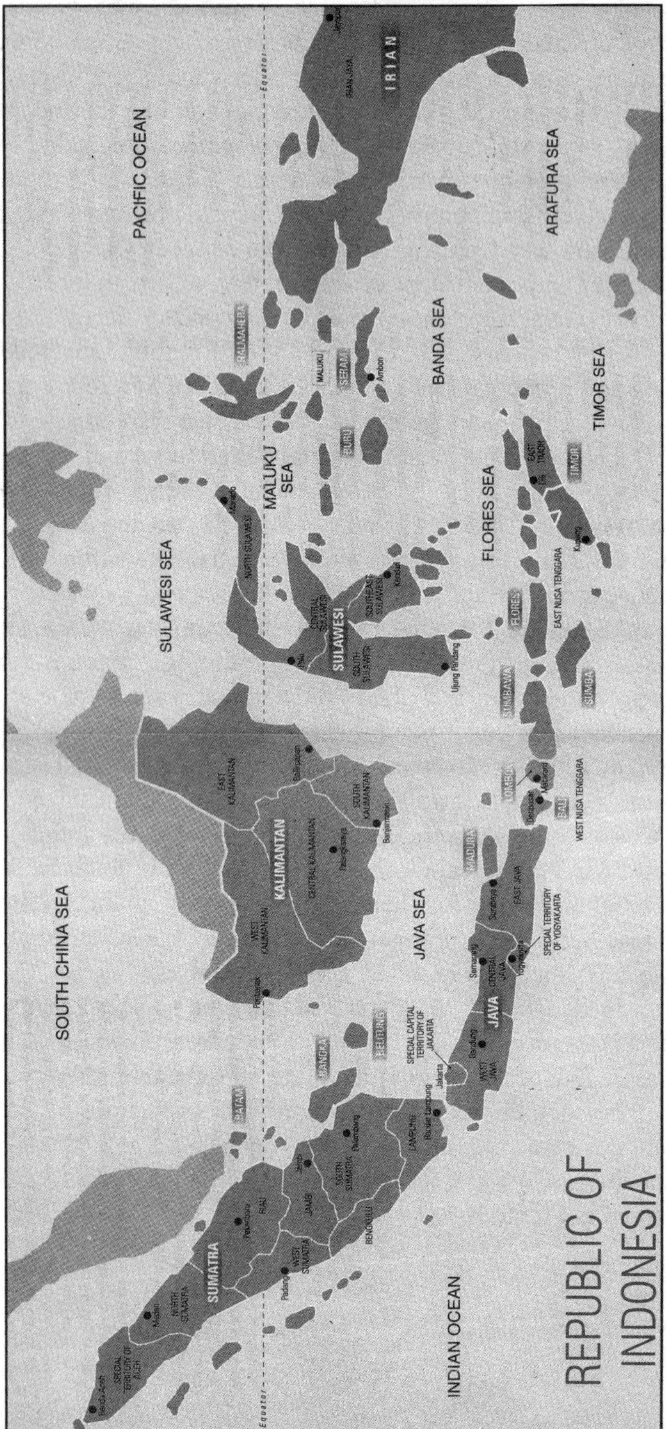

Source: INDIO (1996).

REFERENCES

Investment Coordinating Board, *Indonesia: A Brief Guide for Investment*, Ministry of Investment, Jakarta, 1996a.

Investment Coordinating Board, *Indonesia: Investment Statistics*, Ministry of Investment, Jakarta, 1996b.

INDIO, *Indonesia Source Book 1996*, Jakarta, 1996.

Kayam Umar, "On Foreign Influence: The Indonesian Case", *The Indonesian Quarterly*, Vol. 24, No. 3, pp. 214–20.

Pacific Economic Cooperation Council, *Pacific Economic Outlook*, The Asia Foundation and Arthur Anderson, Washington, D.C., 1997.

Schwarz Adam, *A Nation in Waiting: Indonesia in the 1990s*, Allen & Unwin, Australia, 1994.

TRADE AND MANUFACTURING

Chapter 2

Trade Policy: Challenges and Issues*

BY
CHUNG Sang Pok
TAN Hock Yew
Daniel GOH
YANG Chin Chung

INTRODUCTION

INDONESIA'S ECONOMIC PROGRESS over the past 30 years has been impressive. It includes strong economic growth, resilience to major external shocks, implementing substantial structural reforms that have diversified the economy, expanding the role of the private sector, reducing the reliance on oil, building an export-oriented economy and reducing poverty. Indonesia's annual GDP growth has averaged 6.9% over this period, placing it among the fastest growing economies in the world (Kraar, 1993). The World Bank recognises it as the fourth best performer over this period among countries with a population of more than 30 million. A middle class of 17 million people has emerged and investors who aim for Indonesia's huge domestic market have a lot to gain from the rising affluence of this group and continued economic prosperity (Astbury, 1995a).

Yet beneath all these achievements and promises lie economic and social problems that are equally staggering: a current account deficit foreign debt, instability of the currency, maintaining macroeconomic stability to sustain

* We wish to thank Dr. Ashish Lall for his comments and guidance.

foreign investment growth, social inequality, unstable political climate, economic uncertainties associated with President Suharto's changeover (Astbury, 1995b) and so forth. Economists point out that current macroeconomic problems faced by Indonesia, especially the trade deficit, seem very similar to those encountered by Mexico before its currency crisis. Foreign investors have a big stake in Indonesia; in aggregate, they have pledged a record US$39.9 billion worth of investments in 1995 alone. At the same time, Indonesia needs to strive for overall macroeconomic stability to continue attracting foreign investment, especially since the country still has an outstanding foreign debt amounting to US$58.2 billion and a current account deficit which stood at US$7.5 billion as of 1996 (INDIO, 1996a, pp. 42–5). These issues will have a major impact on inflows of foreign capital.

This chapter examines Indonesia's current account deficit in a macroeconomic framework and tries to determine if there is really cause for concern. It also focuses on current trade policy issues dealing with non-tariff barriers. Finally, Indonesia's liberalisation programme is examined within the context of the global move towards a more open international trading environment.

DEVELOPMENT PLANS: INDONESIA'S VISION

Indonesia is presently in its sixth phase of planned economic development, *Repelita VI*. This phase is from 1994 to 1999 and it originally aimed for an average GDP growth of 6.2% per annum. Over the five years to 1993, the actual growth rate was estimated at an annual average of 8.3%, followed by 7.5% in 1994 and just under 8.1% in 1995. President Suharto, in his Independence Day speech on 17 August 1995, announced that the government had revised the projected GDP growth for 1996 upwards to 7.1%. The country's aim is to raise per capita income to US$1,280 by 1999 (Soesastro, 1996b).

Since the fifth plan, *Repelita V*, the government has been emphasising structural adjustments to reduce the dependence on oil revenue and enhance the flexibility of the economy. Development of the export-oriented manufacturing industry is encouraged in particular. *Repelita VI* calls for a continuation, extension and intensification of policies which have proved successful in the past and, yet, they must be implemented with sufficient flexibility to allow for adjustments to changing circumstances and new challenges (Soesastro, 1996b).

Indonesia hopes to attain the status of a newly industrialising country by the year 2019. Among other things, this involves quadrupling the current per capita GDP to US$4,092 over the next 25 years. Three decades of steady economic growth have created an increasingly visible middle class. Economists predict that 10.5% of Indonesia's population will earn an annual income of US$3,600 by the year 2000. The domestic market clearly has attractive growth potential.

To sustain such robust growth, Indonesia expects US$52 to US$55 billion in industrial exports by the end of *Repelita VI.* It aims to attract US$300 billion in investments in the same period, with 73.4% coming from the private sector and the balance from public investments. At least 50% of the private sector investment is expected to come from foreign direct investment (Soesastro, 1996a). Improvement in the quality of life will be realised through a declining rate of population growth, enhanced educational opportunities, increased employment, and improved health and welfare provisions.

AN OVERVIEW OF TRADE

Indonesia's membership in world and regional trade bodies, such as the World Trade Organisation (WTO), the ASEAN Free Trade Area (AFTA) and the Asia-Pacific Economic Co-operation (APEC), reflects the vital role that multilateral and bilateral trade plays in the country's economy. Indonesia's exports have evolved from an initial base of agricultural products, through the extended growth of oil and natural gas exports, to the latest phase of manufactured products which have grown to become the largest source of export earnings.

Indonesia's current strategy for economic development is primarily oriented towards promoting non-oil exports, especially manufactured goods, in order to achieve the triple goals of earning foreign exchange, domestic job creation, and technology transfer and development. The share of manufactured exports in total export earnings grew from less than 12% in 1982 to 64.6% in 1995 (INDIO, 1996c).[1]

Total merchandise exports reached US$45.4 billion and imports were US$40.6 billion as of 1995. Indonesia still registered a mer-

---

[1] Fact sheets obtained at the MBA BSM Seminar, Mandarin Oriental Hotel, Jakarta, on 10 December 1996.

chandise trade surplus of US$5.3 billion. However, the growth of imports of 25.7% was significantly higher than the 13.4% growth of exports. Growth in imports of consumption goods, and of raw materials and capital goods to meet the needs of the rapidly growing economy, were the main contributors to the surge in imports which were greater than expected. In addition, the service account registered a deficit of US$12.8 billion. With the service deficit offsetting the merchandise trade surplus, Indonesia's current account deficit widened by 150% over the previous year to US$7.5 billion in 1995 (Central Bureau of Statistics, 1996).

On the export side, oil and gas exports remained stable over the period from 1991 to 1995 (see Table 2–1). The share of manufactured exports in total exports increased from 51% in 1991 to 64% in 1995, reflecting the dynamics of the manufacturing sector and the government's efforts to boost manufactured exports.

TABLE 2–1
Exports by Sector: 1991 to 1995
(US$ million)

	1991	1992	1993	1994	1995
Agriculture	2,282	2,212	2,644	2,818	2,889
Mining	889	1,453	1,464	1,800	2,691
Manufacturing	15,068	19,613	22,944	25,702	29,328
Other	8	18	25	39	46
Total non-oil/gas	18,247	23,296	27,077	30,359	34,954
Oil/gas	10,895	10,671	9,746	9,694	10,464
Total exports	**29,142**	**33,967**	**36,823**	**40,053**	**45,418**

Source: INDIO (1996c).

Table 2–2 shows that in 1995, auxiliary goods consisting of raw materials, spare parts, and food and beverages formed the largest component (72.8%) of the total imports followed by capital goods (21.4%). The growth in consumption imports from 1994 to 1995 was 64%, the highest of all the categories of imports.

The major export markets in 1995 were Japan (27.1%), the U.S. (13.9%), the EC (14.6%) and ASEAN (13.4%). The principal import markets were Japan (22.7%), the EC (19.5%), ASEAN (12.4%) and the U.S. (11.7%) (Central Bureau of Statistics, 1996).

TABLE 2–2
Imports by Main Category: 1991 to 1995
(US$ million)

	1991	1992	1993	1994	1995
Auxiliary goods	14,924	16,585	17,724	20,709	26,676
Capital goods	7,677	7,367	7,091	7,420	8,642
Consumption goods	958	1,213	1,342	1,430	2,350
Total non-oil/gas	23,559	25,165	26,157	29,559	37,718
Petroleum products	2,310	2,115	2,171	2,424	2,911
Total imports	**25,869**	**27,280**	**28,328**	**31,983**	**40,629**

Source: INDIO (1996c).

ANALYSIS OF CURRENT ACCOUNT DEFICIT, EXCHANGE RATE AND FOREIGN DEBT

Current Account Deficit

Indonesia, like Malaysia and Thailand, has a large current account deficit. The current account deficit was US$7.5 billion for the year 1995 as compared to US$3 billion in the previous year (see Table 2–3). The current account deficit as a percentage of GDP increased from 1.6% in 1993 to 1.85% in 1994, and jumped to 3.9% in 1995.

TABLE 2–3
Current Account (US$ billion)

	1990	1991	1992	1993	1994	1995
Oil and gas	5.6	5.0	3.8	2.5	3.5	3.5
Exports	11.9	11.4	10.5	9.5	9.9	10.3
Imports	-3.2	-3.3	-3.4	-3.8	-3.6	-3.7
Services	-3.1	-3.1	-3.3	-3.2	-2.9	-3.1
Non-oil and gas	-8.8	-9.4	-6.9	-4.8	-6.4	-11.0
Exports	14.9	18.2	23.3	27.0	30.3	35.6
Imports	-18.2	-21.5	-23.4	-24.5	-28.7	-36.9
Services	-5.5	-6.1	-6.8	-7.3	-8.0	-9.7
Total	**-3.2**	**-4.4**	**-3.1**	**-2.3**	**-3.0**	**-7.5**

Source: INDIO (1996a).

The deterioration of the current account deficit over the past several years has been a concern for the government because the deficit has more than doubled from 1994 to 1995 and is estimated to increase to US$7.9 billion in 1996 (*The Straits Times*, 14 April 1996). The deterioration of the current account deficit in 1995 was due to a significant increase in non-oil imports (28.6% increase in one year as compared with an export growth of only 17.5%), with consumption goods registering the largest percentage increase of 64.3%. This trend may continue given the rising affluence of Indonesia's middle class. However, the deficit is not consumption driven but is a by-product of high growth and spending.

Maintaining non-oil export growth is of crucial importance to the economy's future prospects as Indonesia faces stiffer competition in the international market. The government's efforts are being geared towards boosting competitiveness through tariff cuts, provision of incentives for key export industries, and attracting additional export-oriented foreign investments (*Jakarta Post*, 14 May 1996). Capital goods and raw material imports registered healthy and steady growth, reflecting a robust manufacturing sector. Offsetting the current account deficit were the substantially greater inflows of capital which not only enabled Indonesia's balance of payments to remain in surplus but to more than double from the previous year (see Tables 2–4 and 2–5). The increase in foreign direct investment (FDI) of more than 100% in 1995 is a very encouraging sign. Capital inflows in the form of FDI covered more than 50% of Indonesia's current account deficit. Therefore, it is crucial for Indonesia to maintain its competitiveness in terms of foreign investment.[2]

Economists and government officials have different views on whether the current account deficit has reached a crisis level. Economists point out that the debt service ratio of 32% is a danger signal (*The Straits Times*, 18 December 1996a). This means that one-third of total export revenue has to be set aside to repay and service the debt. However, government officials are less concerned about the ballooning current account deficit. They point out that the trade deficit is covered by capital inflows in the form of foreign direct investment which is long term in nature. Such foreign investments, they argue,

---

[2] Interview with Dr. Tubagus Feridhanusertawan, Department of Economic Affairs, Centre for Strategic and International Studies, Jalan Tanah Abang III/23-7, Jakarta 10160, Indonesia, on 11 December 1996.

should eventually translate into higher exports and, hence, reduce the deficit (*Jakarta Post*, 22 March 1996).

TABLE 2–4
Capital Account (US$ billion)

	1990	1991	1992	1993	1994	1995
Official capital and transfer	4.5	5.6	5.8	6.0	5.7	5.7
Debt repayment	-3.9	-4.2	-4.7	-5.3	-5.4	-5.3
Direct investment	1.1	1.5	1.8	2.0	2.1	4.6
Other private and miscellaneous capital	3.0	2.9	3.6	3.2	1.6	4.0
Total	**4.7**	**5.8**	**6.5**	**5.9**	**4.0**	**9.8**

Source: INDIO (1996a), p. 44.

TABLE 2–5
Balance of Payments (US$ billion)

	1990	1991	1992	1993	1994	1995
Current account	-3.2	-4.4	-3.1	-2.3	-3.0	-7.5
Capital account	4.7	5.8	6.5	5.9	4.0	9.8
Bal. of payments	1.5	1.4	0.4	3.6	1.0	2.3
Errors and omission	-0.6	-0.2	-1.6	-2.9	0.2	0.7
Total movement	**0.9**	**1.2**	**1.8**	**0.7**	**0.8**	**1.6**

Source: INDIO (1996a), p. 45.

As mentioned earlier, the deficit reached 3.9% of GDP in 1995 compared with 1.85% GDP and 1.6% GDP in 1993 and 1994, respectively. However, International Monetary Fund economist Morris Goldstein pointed out that if the deficit is greater than 5% of GDP, then the problem is a cause for concern (*The Straits Times*, 31 August 1996). Although Indonesia's current account deficit is within this limit, it still falls short of the government's target of 2% of GDP.

Despite the current account deficit problem, the Indonesian government states that its overall macroeconomic and trade policies are geared toward attaining long term economic growth rather than merely fixing the deficit problem because short term solutions may cause other distortions. But efforts to lower, or at least to contain the current account deficit, and to maintain macroeconomic stability will always be priority items in formulating economic policies.[3] Measures to tackle the deficit problem include promoting non-oil exports, reviewing investments that rely heavily on imported supplies and depreciating the rupiah to boost the competitiveness of exports (Fadjar, 1996). The government has assured investors and the people that it will closely monitor the deficit situation and make the necessary adjustments from time to time.

Foreign Debt[4]

Related to the current account deficit issue is Indonesia's staggering foreign debt. Data on Indonesia's external debt vary depending on the source. World Bank data show that by the end of 1993, Indonesia's total external debt outstanding (excluding undisbursed) amounted to US$89.6 billion. This consisted of public debt of US$52.5 billion and private debt of US$37.1 billion which included about US$20 billion in short term debt. A local source suggested that outstanding government external debt was US$58.2 billion at the close of financial year 1995/96 (INDIO, 1996a, p. 58).

From 1981 to 1986, external public debt growth outpaced private foreign debt. Since 1986, however, the pattern of growth has been reversed. The reason is that the investment boom commencing in the late 1980s led to a surge in foreign borrowing by the private sector. The tight monetary policy adopted by the government to cope with an overheating economy led to this increased foreign borrowing by the private sector. For those investors having access to offshore loans, this is a more attractive source of funds because the interest rate is lower (*Jakarta Post*, 21 June 1996).

To prevent the government debt from growing uncontrollably, Indonesian state-owned enterprises are fully responsible for all the loans they assume unless indemnity is expressly given by the government. It is the government's policy not to guarantee such debt and, to date, no indemnity has been given. Reducing the debt has always been one of the government's fiscal priorities and, in recent years, the

---

3 Panel discussion with the Bank of Indonesia at the MBA BSM Seminar, Mandarin Oriental Hotel, Jakarta, on 10 December 1996.

4 This section is based on an interview with Dr. Tubagus Feridhanusertawan, an economist with the Centre for Strategic and International Studies, Jakarta, on 10 December 1996.

government has accelerated the repayment of high interest bearing loans utilising a combination of government receipts from privatisation of state assets and budget surpluses (INDIO, 1996a, pp. 58–9). This is a wise strategy because the proceeds will reduce the government's external debt as well as preventing expansionary effects from absorbing the proceeds.

Indonesia had a windfall of additional revenue due to higher oil prices in 1996 and the government is placing emphasis on repaying expensive external debt. External debt from multilateral, bilateral and export credit sources with interest rates of more than 9% are to be paid-off first (Praginanto, 1996).

A substantial portion of the Indonesian government's borrowing is in Japanese yen. This partly explains why there is a jump in government debt whenever the yen appreciates. The Bank of Indonesia has announced that 35% of its official reserves are in yen. This should cushion the effect somewhat of the yen's appreciation (Manning and Jayasuriya, 1996).

The continuing rapid growth of private sector borrowing is a concern if the funds are not used to finance the production of tradables. This can be avoided if the deregulation process continues. The concern about the private sector relying too much on foreign borrowing led the government to set up an agency called the Foreign Commercial Borrowing Coordinating Team (*PKPLN*) to monitor foreign loans from the commercial sector (Fadjar, 1996).

Exchange Rate Policy

Indonesia follows a managed floating exchange rate policy where the central bank sets the value of the rupiah around which it will intervene. The Bank of Indonesia widened the intervention band from 3% to 5% in June 1996 to maintain monetary stability, to discourage speculative short-term capital inflows, as well as to provide room to manoeuvre while simultaneously encouraging the development of an inter-bank foreign exchange (forex) market. In September 1996, the bank surprised the forex market by widening the rupiah-U.S. dollar intervention band from 5% to 8% thus allowing the rupiah a larger fluctuation against the U.S. dollar. At the same time, it raised the reserve requirements of commercial banks from 3% to 5%, effective from 16 April 1997. The Bank of Indonesia stated that its intentions were to control inflation, reduce speculative trading in the forex market and allow more room for the market mechanism to operate in the forex market (Fadjar, 1996).

Indonesia has a history of devaluing its currency, presumably for boosting exports to ease the current account deficit. Both the Ministry of Finance and the Bank of Indonesia do not openly admit that there is an "official policy" of devaluation. But there is a widely held belief that Indonesia's currency management is based on a policy of devaluing the rupiah at an average of 5% per annum against the U.S. dollar. The Bank states that it is aiming for the rupiah's effective rate against a basket of currencies. Furthermore, the Bank is striving for an overall macroeconomic equilibrium through a proper policy mix instead of simply boosting exports by devaluation. However, policy makers generally agree that allowing the rupiah to depreciate faster against the dollar was one of the government's policies to stimulate exports. In nominal terms, the rupiah depreciated against the U.S. dollar by 3.83% in mid-1995 and 2.74% in September 1996. During the same period, the rupiah appreciated against the yen by 10.27% (Fadjar, 1996).

According to the Bank of Indonesia's assessment, the long term real exchange rate of the rupiah is relatively stable. However, since mid-1995, the real exchange rate against a basket of currencies has been appreciating and it reached 8.56% in September 1996. There has been concern about a potential overvaluation of the rupiah leading to a weakening of Indonesia's export competitiveness. According to the Morgan index shown in Figure 2–1, the real effective exchange rate appreciated by just over 8% between August 1995 and April 1996, mainly after the first widening of the band in December. This happened despite the targeted devaluation of the nominal exchange rate to compensate for inflation rate differentials with trading partners in order to maintain the real exchange rate (Manning and Jayasuriya, 1996).

Many factors can affect the real exchange rate but, given the current situation, recent large capital inflows may be the main cause of this appreciation. The long term appreciation of the real effective exchange rate may be a sign of economic success. However, the adverse effect on the trade sector from this appreciation may be costly given that Indonesia is striving for non-oil manufactured export growth.

FIGURE 2–1
Real Effective Exchange Rate (vertical axis) of Indonesia (1990 = 100)

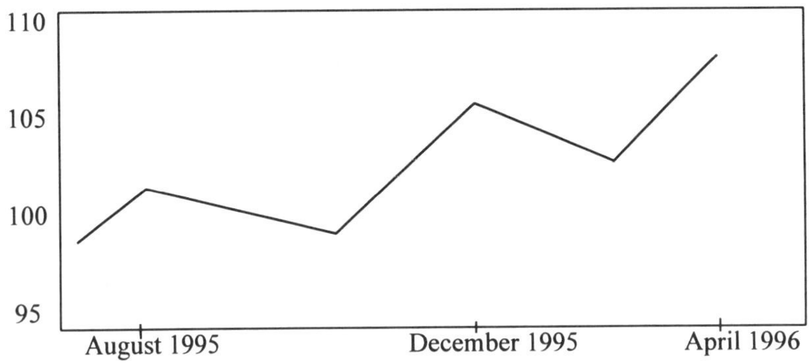

Source: Manning and Jayasuriya (1996), p. 14.

MAINTAINING MACROECONOMIC STABILITY

Macroeconomic stability is a fundamental condition for sustained growth. However, the current account deficit, domestic inflationary pressure and large capital nflows, especially the short term type, pose quite a challenge to the policy makers (*Jakarta Post*, 18 June 1996).

The inflow of capital creates inflationary pressure. Indonesia is a favourite destination for speculative capital inflow because of the high yields in its currency and stock markets. Since these capital movements are volatile, a sudden and significant reversal of flows causes problems in the capital market. This reaction has been manifested previously during a political crisis or fear of one (INDIO, 1996b).

To counter speculative capital inflows, the primary policy response from the Bank of Indonesia is to use sterilisation. The efficacy of this measure has been questioned by economists since Indonesia had an open capital account which allowed capital to flow in and out with little restriction. Raising interest rates to curb inflation would increase the inflow of capital which counteracts the tight monetary policy. The government acknowledges that the long term solution to capital volatility lies in a more efficient capital market. As the bond and equity market become more developed, the economy will be more capable of absorbing funds effectively. Other factors that create a strong inflationary pressure include supply side and cost push factors, nominal depreciation of the rupiah against foreign currencies that adds to imported inflation, the strong growth of consumer demand and investment, and the strong credit growth.[5]

The Bank of Indonesia has addressed the problem of money supply through open market operations, reviewing the private banks' credit programmes, cautioning banks not to over extend credit to risky sectors and raising the banks' reserve requirements from 2% to 3% after 1996 (Fadjar, 1996). The government's efforts to control inflation appear focused on the demand side through a tight monetary policy and a conservative fiscal policy. These efforts may not be adequate since the problems lie on the supply side. To ease the supply side constraints, the government will have to expedite deregulation and adopt a more coordinated monetary and fiscal policy.[6]

NON-TARIFF BARRIERS

Intellectual Property Rights

Since 1989, Indonesia has been on the "watch list" under the "special 301" provisions of the 1988 U.S. *Trade Act* as a result of inadequate intellectual property protection offered to foreign trading partners and investors (http:webmaster@USTR,1996). In the area of patents, some new concerns include compulsory licensing provisions, a relatively short protection time of 14 years, and a provision which allows unauthorised importation of 50 specific products by third parties. It is uncertain whether the enforceability of the new patent law, which is intended to bring Indonesia into Trade Related Intellectual Property Rights (TRIPs) compliance, will address these concerns (Pangestu, 1996b).

In the area of copyright protection, the government has demonstrated its resolve to stop piracy and is willing to work with copyright holders to achieve this end. Enforcement of the ban on illegal copying has been reasonably satisfactory. But court rulings involving cases of

---

5 Interview with Dr. Tubagus Feridhanusertawan, Department of Economic Affairs, Centre for Strategic and International Studies, Jakarta, on 11 December 1996.

6 Panel discussion with the Bank of Indonesia at the MBA BSM Seminar, Mandarin Oriental Hotel, Jakarta, on 10 December 1996.

intellectual property rights remain unpredictable and this has made enforcement of intellectual property rights laws less effective. Substantial improvement came in the form of a new copyright law intended to bring Indonesia into TRIPs compliance. Similarly, in trademarks, a new law to counter trademark counterfeiting activities has been enacted to offer protection for trademarks, servicemarks and collective marks while bringing Indonesia into compliance with TRIPs (Tabalujan, 1996).

Services[7]

Although the June 1994 *Presidential Decree No. 20* opened many areas to 100% foreign-owned companies, service trade entry barriers still exist in many sectors. For example, foreign accounting firms must operate through technical assistance arrangements with local firms, and citizenship is a requirement for licensing as an accountant. Foreign agents and auditors may only act as consultants but they cannot sign audit reports. Also, foreign law firms are not allowed to establish a practice in Indonesia and attorneys are admitted to the bar only if they have graduated from an Indonesian law faculty or an equivalent institution.

Foreign firms and joint ventures with a majority foreign share are not allowed to distribute products in the domestic market unless the foreign company manufactures the products in Indonesia. Even then, they can distribute only to the wholesale level, and only for goods produced domestically. An Indonesian agent or distributor must be engaged for wholesale distribution if the foreign company does not manufacture in Indonesia.[8] U.S. firms are concerned that these restrictions will increase costs and impede their ability to effectively market and service their products in Indonesia.

In financial services, foreign participation in insurance is allowed subject to a minimum Indonesian ownership of 20%. These joint ventures must be capitalised up to five times the level of domestic operations but Indonesia has offered to phase this requirement out over time under WTO negotiations. A 1992 law allowed the insured to freely choose the insurer except for social insurance programmes.

---

7 Interview discussion with Dr. Tubagus Ferihanusertawan, Economist, Department of Economic Affairs, Centre for Strategic and International Studies, Jakarta, on 11 December 1996.

8 Panel discussion with the Bank of Indonesia at the MBA BSM Seminar, Mandarin Oriental Hotel, Jakarta, on 10 December 1996.

Turning to banking, foreign participation is limited to a maximum of 85%. The capital requirement of foreign joint venture banks is US$49 million, twice the requirement for domestic banks. However, this will be raised to US$66 million by the year 2001 regardless of local or foreign joint venture banks. In the case of securities firms, the same local participation rate applies as for banks. Foreign joint ventures are also subject to differential capital requirements that are twice those of local firms (http:webmaster@USTR,1996).

Agriculture and Food Sector

Trade in the agriculture and food sector is under the control of a small group comprising the state logistics agency (BULOG), state trading enterprises and some private companies. Import control is mainly exercised by restrictive import licensing. BULOG has the exclusive right to import wheat, sugar, rice, flour, corn, soybeans and soybean meal. Two state trading enterprises, Kerta Niaga and Tjipta Niaga, have import rights of other food items. Reforms leave much to be desired in this sector. Items which had the non-tariff barriers removed were subject to higher surcharge levies. Nevertheless, cotton and refined vegetable oil were removed from the restricted licence category and added to the general importer category which allows private companies to import without any restrictions.

Although the objective of BULOG is to stabilise products and consumer prices through import licensing as well as to achieve economies of scale, this is generally viewed as political. In the case of imported wheat and soybeans, it seems that the aim of licensing is to protect domestic monopoly producers who have political connections (Pangestu, 1996a).

Export bans have also been on the rise. The rationale is to increase the processing of raw materials and resources (Pangestu, 1996a). It seems that this policy has spurred the success of the plywood industry. Trade associations form cartels to regulate the industry. However, the benefits to consumers are debatable since the high cost of imported machinery, the cost of subsidised credit and environmental costs may offset any gains in foreign exchange and employment.

The main obstacle to deregulation in the agricultural sector is the potential negative effect on farmers. The monopoly profits of licence holders are large but the net loss is spread over a large group of consumers. The impact, therefore, is not so great on consumers that they have a desire to lobby the government. On the other hand, government agencies and private companies form a concentrated and powerful lobby group. Overall, the higher cost to consumers needs to be carefully evaluated against the implications of being less competitive internationally (*Jakarta Post*, 14 June 1996).

Manufacturing Sector

The engineering sector is still subject to non-tariff barriers. This sector mainly comprises motor vehicles, aircraft and vessels. The motor vehicle subsector does not include just the assembly of vehicles but includes the whole integrated industry from engine manufacturing to components and assembly. This sector is dominated by a few large groups who form a powerful lobby. Any reduction in trade protection will need to carefully evaluate the impact on the upstream producers linked to this sector. However, some rationalisation is possible in the motorcycle industry which is thought to be competitive (Pangestu, 1996a).

The national car policy, which dominated economic news in the second quarter of 1996, has been the subject of much controversy (*Jakarta Post*, 11 April 1996). In addition, there are complaints from American, European and particularly Japanese trading partners who stand to lose the most due to their large share of the local car market. The criticism is that the policy which discriminated against other local car assemblers is against the WTO non-discriminatory principle. The national car, Timor, is assembled by a joint venture company P. T. Timor Putra Nasional. The company is 70% owned by Hutomo Mandala Putra, President Suharto's son, and the remaining 30% is owned by KIA, one of the smaller Korean car manufacturers. Prices of the car are 30% or more below those of competitors in the same vehicle size category (*Far Eastern Economic Review*, 14 March 1996). The Timor is exempt from luxury tax and import duties (*Business Week*, 8 July 1996). In return, P. T. Timor must meet the domestic content requirement of 20% by the end of the first year, 40% by the end of the second year and 60% by the end of the third year (*Jakarta Post*, 26 July 1996). To meet these requirements, Indonesia sent Indonesian workers to KIA in Korea and parts were shipped from Indonesia to Korea. The reason for these actions was that plant facilities were not ready in time for production (*The Straits Times*, 16 September 1996).

The government's motives for the national car project were: to become self-reliant in car manufacturing, to benefit local consumers and to reduce the current account deficit. To appease its foreign trading partners, the government announced in June 1996 that all companies that achieved the 60% local content requirement would be exempt from the 35% luxury tax on cars. The car manufacturers' responses were that they would not be able to reach the 60% target in the next three years. Nevertheless, Indonesia's international reputation was damaged and investors are looking cautiously at the capriciousness of the decisions surrounding the national car (*The Straits Times*, 16 September 1996). Further interventions in favour of P. T. Timor seem likely and industry sources believe that the company is unlikely to meet domestic content requirements on time. The success of the national car hinges on whether P. T. Timor can compete for value and quality in the eyes of consumers. More trade protection will probably lead to higher prices.

The aircraft and vessel subsectors are protected because these industries are viewed as being of strategic importance. It seems unlikely that there will be a reduction of trade protection in these subsectors.

Customs Reform

In addition to trade reform and deregulation, which have been crucial in promoting trade flows, increased exports and improved economic competitiveness, customs reform in Indonesia is a crucial instrument in smoothing trade activities. Since the 1985 customs reform, Indonesia has been using the efficient, corruption-free pre-shipment inspection system. This system has been operated by the Geneva-based Societe Generale de Surveillance (SGS). In 1991, P. T. Surveyor Indonesia (owned 76% by the Indonesia Government, 20% by SGS and 4% by another state-owned firm, P. T. Sucofindo) was established to gradually take over the duties of pre-inspection (INDIO, 1996a, p. 166). Importers like this arrangement and in August 1995, the government decided that the pre-shipment inspection system would be maintained. An additional two-year contract was signed with P. T.

Surveyor and the firm also extended its technical assistance agreement with SGS.[9]

Trade activities are expected to be smoother with the enforcement of the 1995 *Custom Law* beginning on 1 April 1997. The flow of goods through Indonesia's customs is also expected to be facilitated by the enforcement of this law. This new law replaces the one inherited by Indonesia from the former Dutch administration. The law provides for a firmer legal foundation for increasingly globalised trading activities. Among other measures, the law provides for less restrictive regulations on exports than imports. While imported goods will continue to be subjected to physical examination under the pre-inspection system, checking related to most exports will be confined to the associated documentation rather than focusing on the goods themselves. However, the new customs law will introduce a post-audit import system and return the inspection authority to the Director-General of Customs and Excise (*Jakarta Post*, 5 December 1996).

In summary, custom reform in Indonesia has created smoother trading activities since 1985. The new 1995 *Custom Law* will provide less restrictive regulations for trading activities. However, there is some scepticism about the return of the inspection authority to the Director-General of Custom and Excise in April 1997. Customs officials are allaying fears by assuring the business community that they will exercise their authority efficiently and effectively, and that they will be able to guarantee the smooth flow of imports (*Jakarta Post*, 12 December 1996).

TRADE LIBERALISATION AND TRADE ORGANISATIONS

Trade bodies such as the World Trade Organisation (WTO) and the Asean Free Trade Area (AFTA) have played, and will continue to play, an important role in Indonesia's trading system. Indonesia's trading activities are very much affected by the WTO at the multilateral level while AFTA plays a critical role in enhancing regional trade.

---

[9] Currently, the government has not decided whether the pre-shipment inspection system will continue or be terminated but it has decided to end its inspection contract with P. T. Surveyor Indonesia on 1 April 1997 (*Jakarta Post*, 12 December 1996).

World Trade Organisation (WTO)

Indonesia's membership in the WTO reflects the vital role that multilateral trade plays in the country's economy. The WTO, established on 1 January 1995, is successor to the General Agreement on Tariffs and Trade (GATT). It is the legal and institutional foundation of the multilateral trading system and it provides the principal contractual obligations for determining how governments frame and implement domestic trade legislation and regulations. It is also the platform through which trade relations among countries evolve through collective debate, negotiation and adjudication. Among other important functions, the WTO administers and implements the multilateral and plurilateral trade agreements which make up the WTO agreement. The WTO now has 126 member countries and another 28 countries are seeking membership including China, Russia, the Ukraine and Saudi Arabia.

Indonesia has been an active participant in the WTO. One of the issues facing Indonesia is the demand made by the U.S. and France to introduce a "social clause" into the WTO's mandate. In 1994, the U.S. threatened that the Generalised System of Preferences (GSP) facility would be removed if Indonesia did not recognise more than the one government sanctioned labour union. Indonesia, along with other ASEAN member nations and many other developing economies, opposed the demands to include the social clause in the mandate of the WTO (Pangestu, 1996b). Specifically, Indonesia was sticking to its position that core labour standards should be dealt with by the International Labour Organisation and not the WTO. Other trade-related issues affecting Indonesia relate to environment, investment, competition policy and information technology (IT) issues.

On the other hand, at the recent WTO Ministerial Conference held in Singapore in December 1996, trade ministers from 28 countries, including Indonesia, reached a landmark deal at the WTO meeting to support the elimination of tariffs on computer and communication products by the year 2000. Specifically, an agreement was signed by 28 countries representing 85% of the global IT trade. The agreement will eliminate all tariffs on semiconductors, telecommunications and computer equipment as well as computer software. Companies will be allowed access to markets such as the European Union (EU) where tariffs range from 6% to 14%. Indonesia mentioned that it would be ready to open fully its IT product market by the year 2005 (*The Straits Times*, 18 December 1996b). This action highlights Indonesia's deepening commitment to the objectives and rules of the WTO.

The ASEAN Free Trade Area (AFTA)

As a trading nation, Indonesia stands firmly committed to the opening up of regional trade. This commitment is reflected in its membership and active participation in the agreements and accords within AFTA.

In 1992, ASEAN agreed to form a free trade area called AFTA. Initially, the agreement provided for the tariffs on goods with 40% or more ASEAN content to be reduced to a maximum of 5% by the year 2008, with the exception of certain sensitive items critical to different members' economies. At the 1994 ASEAN Economic Ministers Meeting (AEM) in Chiangmai, Thailand, the timetable for completion was brought forward five years to 2003.

The WTO and AFTA have complimented the trading policies of Indonesia. They should be viewed as positive factors in the opening-up of regional and multilateral trade for Indonesia and providing mutual benefits for Indonesia and other countries. More importantly, the WTO and AFTA will enhance multilateral and regional trade which has a vital role in Indonesia's economy.

CONCLUSION

Indonesia is undergoing a greater economic transition than at any time in the past 20 years. The economy was once dominated by oil and commodity related activities. Now, diversified manufacturing, oil and gas processing form the main engine of growth for the Indonesian economy. The government realises that it can no longer rely on its past strategies for continued growth. Therefore, it has embarked on comprehensive economic reforms and deregulation, and the move is gaining momentum. Despite its huge current account deficit, foreign debts and interim adjustment problems, Indonesia seems to be on the right track for more robust growth in the future.

As a trading nation, Indonesia stands firmly committed to the opening up of regional and multilateral trade. This commitment is reflected in its memberships and active participation in the agreements and accords with AFTA, APEC and WTO. This is evident in several rounds of across-the-board tariff and non-tariff reductions, the gradual liberalisation of its restricted and regulated domestic market, and customs reform. These actions are laudable but greater transparency in the market and trading system is required to enhance investors' confidence further.

Maintaining macroeconomic stability is a continuing challenge. The Indonesian government will strive for the coordination of monetary exchange rate, fiscal and trade policy to achieve a delicate balance that rectifies any trade imbalance but without seriously compromising overall economic growth. This balancing act between seemingly incompatible economic objectives will continue to be a significant feature of Indonesia's economic strategy.

REFERENCES

Astbury Sid, "Indonesia: The Signals Ahead", *Asian Business*, Vol. 31, No. 12, December 1995a.

Astbury Sid, "Indonesia After Suharto", *Asian Business*, Vol. 31, No. 12, December 1995b, p. 20.

Australian National University, "Indonesia Project", *Bulletin of Indonesian Economic Studies*, Vol. 32, No. 2, August 1996, p. 14.

Business Week, "A Furious Flap Over Favoritism", 8 July 1996, pp. 14–5.

Fadjar Ending, *Economic and Monetary Development in 1996*, Economic and Monetary Statistics Department, Bank of Indonesia, December 1996.

Far Eastern Economic Review, "All in the Family", 14 March 1996, pp. 50–1.

Far Eastern Economic Review, "Power Steering", 20 June 1996, pp. 60–1.

http:Webmaster@USTR, "1996 National Trade Estimate – Indonesia", 1 April 1996.

INDIO, *Indonesia Source Book 1996*, Indonesia National Development Information Office, Jakarta, 1996a.

INDIO, *Sustaining Economic Growth with Macroeconomic Stability*, Indonesia National Development Information Office, Jakarta, February 1996b.

INDIO, Central Bureau of Statistics, *Indonesia Facts, 1996*, Indonesia National Development Information Office, 1996c.

Jakarta Post, "Account Deficit Worries House", 22 March 1996.

Jakarta Post, "Econit Criticises Government Over New Car Policy", 11 April 1996.

Jakarta Post, "Estimate of Current Account Deficit Revised Upwards", 14 May 1996.

Jakarta Post, "RI's Non-Tariff Barriers Remain High", 14 June 1996.

Jakarta Post, "Stability of RI's Macroeconomy Uncertain: Econit", 18 June 1996.

Jakarta Post, "Indonesia's Foreign Debt Called Critical", 21 June 1996.

Jakarta Post, "Interest Rates May Decrease One Point", 26 July 1996.

Jakarta Post, "Macroeconomic Stability Vital for Investment", 9 August 1996.

Jakarta Post, "Importers Prefer Pre-shipment Inspection System", 5 December 1996.

Jakarta Post, "Customs Officers Return", 12 December 1996.

Kraar Louis, *Fortune International*, "Indonesia on the Move", 20 September 1993.

Manning Chris and Jayasuriya Sisira, "Survey of Recent Developments", *Bulletin of Indonesian Economic Studies*, Vol. 32, No. 2, August 1996, pp. 15–6.

Pangestu Mari, "Economic Reform, Deregulation and Privatization: The Indonesian Experience", Centre for Strategic and International Studies, Jakarta, 1996a.

Pangestu Mari, "Social Clause and International Trade", *The Indonesian Quarterly*, Vol. 24, No. 2, Centre for Strategic and Business Studies, Jakarta, 1996b, pp. 128–39.

Praginanto, "Indonesia Moves Closer to the Black with Extra Petrodollars", *The Straits Times*, 4 December 1996.

Soesastro Hadi, *Indonesian Perspectives on APEC and Regional Cooperation in Asia Pacific*, Centre for Strategic and International Studies, Jakarta, 1994.

Soesastro Hadi, "Challenges to AFTA in the 21st Century", *The Indonesian Quarterly*, Vol. 24, No. 2, Centre for Strategic and Business Studies, Jakarta, 1996a.

Soesastro Hadi, *Indonesia Assessment 1995: Development of Eastern Indonesia*, Institute of Southeast Asian Studies and Australian National University, Singapore, 1996b.

Tabalujan Benny, Minter Ellison and Makarim, and S. Taira, *Doing Business in Indonesia*, Minter Ellison, 1996.

The Straits Times, "Large Current Account Deficits No Cause for Alarm", 14 April 1996.

The Straits Times, "Continued Prudence Needed, World Bank Tells Indonesia", 18 May 1996.

The Straits Times, "Could Asian Economies Go the Way of Mexico?", 31 August 1996.

The Straits Times, "Indonesia's Timor Car Targets 40% Market Share", 16 September 1996.

The Straits Times, "Indonesia's Deficit at Alarming Levels Says Ex-Minister", 18 December 1996a.

The Straits Times, "Indonesia Will Open up Its Market by 2005", 18 December 1996b.

Chapter 3

Privatisation and Deregulation: Policies, Implications and Opportunities*

BY
Kunaciilan NALLAPPAN
ONG Beng Hong
TEE Song Jue

INTRODUCTION

MANY ASIAN COUNTRIES have experienced radical political and economic reforms in recent years. These reforms have been fueled partly by globalisation which enhances the mobility of capital and technology flows. Developing countries, in particular, have been introducing policies to deregulate their domestic economies in order to facilitate trade with other nations. Indonesia also has been trying to align its economic policies with these changes to attract foreign direct investment.

This chapter examines the macroeconomic impact of privatisation and deregulation in Indonesia. The first section defines privatisation and deregulation from an economic development point of view. The next two sections consider Indonesia's privatisation policies and the government's effort in deregulating various sectors of the economy, respectively. The final section examines the future impact of the current privatisation and deregulation policies on the economic development of the country. De-

* We thank Dr. Ashish Lall for his comments and assistance.

tailed chronological information on various reforms is provided in Appendix 3–1.

THE ESSENCE OF PRIVATISATION AND DEREGULATION

Privatisation

Privatisation is a process which reduces the role of government while increasing the private sector's role in economic activities and asset ownership. In practice, it may include "load shedding" or divestiture; the replacement of budgeted public activity by private market mechanisms such as consumer cooperatives or coproductions; and various public/private sector partnerships. Privatisation covers state management contracts, such as monopoly franchises for the private supply of public services, user charges, lease-purchase arrangements, and even tax reduction, intended to stimulate private sector investment (Gayle and Goodrich, 1990).

The expected economic benefits of privatisation include higher output, better quality, reduced unit costs of production, higher employment as well as growth opportunities over the longer term and the generation of new technologies. When accompanied by liberalisation, privatisation encourages the emergence of managers who are willing to champion an entrepreneurial, risk-taking culture. Privatisation can assist in balancing the national budget, reducing government expenditure, financing capital investment programmes, decreasing foreign debt, lowering consumer prices, broadening share ownership across a society and altering public attitudes toward business. In summary, the rationale is that most goods and services produced by the government might be more economically produced in the private sector (Gayle and Goodrich, 1990).

Deregulation

Deregulation reduces or eliminates specific governmental rules and regulations that apply to private businesses. Regulation may be either industry specific, where costs and benefits can usually be estimated, or nation-wide, with virtually unlimited scope for expansion. It may provide significant competitive advantages for specific firms through certification, or permit and licensing systems, that raise entry barriers. Consequently, many companies have strongly supported at least some of the socioeconomic regulations governing them. Within regulated markets experiencing rapid technological change, corporate interest groups frequently seek continued regulation and selective deregulation simultaneously (Gayle and Goodrich, 1990).

Deregulation is often accompanied by efforts to encourage corporate self-regulation by means of company codes, social audits and industry codes. Competition is seen as the ultimate guarantor of corporate performance. However, insufficient industry specific regulation may facilitate corporate fraud (Gayle and Goodrich, 1990).

The argument for deregulation is that government restrictions on corporate activities, products, and location decrease the range of options available to consumers and artificially increase prices by limiting competition. Such protection reduces the incentive for regulated firms to minimise current costs. It also reduces their need and desire for innovation and efficiency. Both privatisation and deregulation imply expanded private sector activity and a corresponding contraction in public sector size to embrace productive efficiency (Gayle and Goodrich, 1990).

PRIVATISATION EFFORTS

The process of privatisation started in 1989 and since then it has gained in momentum and achievement which have transformed Indonesia's social and economic fabric. This quest for privatisation comes from two concerns: the need to shake up the inefficient state sector and raising much needed funds to repay foreign debt which was nearly US$100 billion at the beginning of 1996 (*Euromoney*, February 1996). Privatisation is also making the state sector more transparent and efficient.[1]

Spinning off inefficient state enterprises is intended to counter falling oil revenues and help the government to build more infrastructure under the current five-year plan. This can lay the foundation for a vibrant private sector (*Asiamoney*, July/August 1994). Other objectives for the privatisation of state-owned enterprises (SOEs) include raising capital to expand and pay debt, increasing the distribu-

1 Interview with Mr. D. Cyril Noerhadi, President and Director, Jakarta Stock Exchange on 9 December 1996.

tion of share ownership and further developing the domestic capital market. Privatisation can also help to expand the domestic investor base and boost stock market liquidity (IBC Online, 1996).

Privatisation of SOEs

In 1989, a Presidential decree ordered the privatisation of 50 state companies within three years. Two years later, the listing of P. T. Semen Gresik (a cement manufacturer) was a disaster, its share price plunged from Rp 7,000 to Rp 2,580 (*Asiamoney*, July/August, 1994). This was bad timing because stock market sentiment was poor at that time. The government tried to revitalise its privatisation programme in 1992 with the launch of another state company, P. T. Semen Tomasa (a cement producer). However, it was later scrapped due to poor demand (*Asiamoney*, July/August 1994). The decision by the Ministry of Finance to list 35% of P. T. Indonesia Satellite Corp. (Indosat) was the first success. The government raised US$1.16 billion from the share issue. Indosat was the first Indonesian corporation to seek an international listing. To date the initial public offering (IPO) of state-owned companies, such as P. T. Semen Gresik, P. T. Indosat, P. T. Tambang Timah and P. T. Telkom, has netted the government and the companies about US$3.1 billion (IBC Online, 1996).

With the positive results from the early privatisation programmes, such as Indosat, more SOEs are queuing up to be privatised. P. T. Krakatau Steel, P. T. Perusahaan Listrik Negara, P. T. Aneka Tambang and P. T. Jasa Marga are scheduled to float their shares in 1996/1997. P. T. Bank Negara Indonesia was floated in December 1996 with a market capitalisation of US$2.37 billion. In addition, P. T. Telkom's second offering involved 15% of its share capital.

The government has pushed privatisation by pursuing a series of joint ventures among state companies and private firms under the *Kerjasama Operasi* (KSO) scheme. This approach enabled the government to pursue infrastructure projects without increasing its foreign debt (BKPM).[2] For example, P. T. Telkom signed three revenue-sharing agreements in 1993 under which Bakrie Electronics would

---

2 Remarks made by Ir. Sugihono Kadarisman, Deputy II, BKPM on 10 December 1996 during a speech made at the NTU MBA Business Study Mission Seminar in Jakarta.

supply 133,000 telephone lines. Toll road projects have been awarded to private operators on build, operate and transfer (BOT) terms. Power projects are being carried out with foreign joint venture partners (*Asiamoney*, July/August 1994).

The future pace of privatisation will depend on how fast and efficiently the SOEs can restructure to be viewed favourably by investors. Their performance has been promising thus far. Investors who bought Telkom's IPO shares have gained 60% and the share price of P. T. Telkom is presently 90% above its listing level (IBC Online, 1996). The proposed privatisation schedule for other SOEs from 1997 to the year 2000 is shown in Table 3–1.

TABLE 3–1
Privatisation Schedule of SOEs

Company Name	Type of Business	Estimated Listing Date
P. T. PLN	Electricity	1997
Garuda Indonesia	Airline	1998
Pertamina	Oil and Gas	1998–1999
P. T. Pelindo	Port Operator	1999
P. T. Aneka Tambang	Mining	1999–2000
P. T. Tambang Batubara	Mining	1999–2000

Source: Business Monitor International Ltd. (1996).

Impact of Privatisation

Not so long ago, privatisation was a shunned word in Indonesia. In a country that had suffered a bad colonial experience under the Dutch and whose private sector was already dominated by Indonesians of Chinese descent (i.e., 3% of the population controlling 70% of the economy), the idea of selling state companies to foreigners and non-indigenous locals was unthinkable (*Asian Business*, March 1996). After years of pushing for privatisation and deregulation, the results have been promising. Small investors have begun to buy shares in SOEs on a stock market that hardly functioned prior to 1990. In 1996, 250 companies with a capitalisation of US$89 billion were listed on the stock market compared with 53 companies with a capitalisation of US$9.6 billion at the end of 1989. By August 1995, more than US$8 billion had been invested since the opening of the Jakarta Stock Exchange (JSX) in 1989 (*Euromoney Supplement*, August 1995). Market capitalisation grew by 100% over the period from 1994 (103.83 trillion rupiah) to the end of November 1996 (204.41 trillion rupiah).[3, 4] Foreign investors now regard the Indonesian stock market as one of the most attractive in the region.

The privatisation programme has changed the nature of business in Indonesia. With the dismantling of the state sector, the perceived dominance of companies owned by ethnic Chinese is receding. Foreign partners, once keen to do business with Chinese conglomerates, now favour the *pribumi* (the indigenous people) groups because of their rising status (*Asian Business*, March 1996). This shift has had a positive impact on the social stability of the country. The population will feel that the country's resources are being more fairly distributed with indigenous businesses involved in more major projects and contracts (*Asian Business*, July 1995).

The pribumi enterprises are concentrated mainly in infrastructure or related sectors such as cement, power, roads and telecommunications. They are also active in heavy industry, banking, finance, retail, property, broadcasting and entertainment. Collaboration with multinational foreign firms should boost the expertise and professionalism of the Indonesian companies involved (*Asian Business*, July 1995).

Privatisation has improved the transparency of SOEs whose accounts are not usually published. They have been pressured by powerful political insiders for many years into taking actions or making deals that are disadvantageous to their operations (*Asian Business*, March 1996). The strict rules required by stock exchange regulators worldwide and the risk to Indonesia's reputation if any malpractices were to be revealed have both made a big difference. Professional managers of publicly listed SOEs can now operate without political interference (*Asian Business*, March 1996).

Future Challenges And Opportunities

The Indonesian capital market needs more listings of SOEs for expanding the domestic investor base and boosting market liquidity. Thus far, only five SOEs have been listed on the domestic exchange. They account for about 26.5% of JSX's market capitalisation which is US$89 billion.

---

[3] Interview with Mr. D. Cyril Noerhadi, President and Director, Jakarta Stock Exchange on 9 December 1996.

[4] The exchange rate of US$1 was approximately 2,383 rupiah in November 1996.

Although privatisation was intended to boost the participation of domestic investors, it is foreign investors that will continue to play an important role in the market. A common denominator of successful privatisation programmes is a large capital ownership by individuals rather than institutions. The future challenge, therefore, is to get more domestic investment in listed SOEs. This can happen only if confidence is enhanced further (*Euromoney Supplement*, August 1995).

Risk taking by domestic investors is minimal given high interest rates in the region of 15% to 18%. Nearly 85% of a local pension fund is invested in high-yield but risk-free time deposits (*Euromoney Supplement*, August 1995). Liquidity will remain a problem until the population becomes more familiar with risk taking. Currently, only 0.22% of the population own shares compared with 20% of the Malaysian population (P. T. Sassoon, 1996, p. 21). Moreover, there is still a need to educate the public about share ownership.[5]

DEREGULATION IN INDONESIA

The Need for Deregulation

Indonesia's deregulatory measures have been introduced in anticipation of tougher competition in the era of trade liberalisation (Gayle and Goodrich, 1990). A reduction of the cost of both final and intermediate imported goods is needed. Reducing the latter will reduce production costs across the board and make Indonesian exports more competitive in the world market.

The government is trying to improve national efficiency through deregulating a number of key sectors. Competition is seen as the ultimate guarantor of corporate performance (Gayle and Goodrich, 1990). Moreover, Indonesia is responding in part to changes in neighbouring countries which are all competing to attract foreign capital.

The Investment Deregulation Initiative

The May 1994 and 1995 deregulation packages indicate a consistent policy by the government. In addition, *Badan Kondinasi Penanaman*

---

[5] Speech made by Mr. Kok Heng Loong, P. T. Sassoon Securities Indonesia, on 9 December 1996 to the NTU MBA Business Study Mission participants in Jakarta.

Modal (BKPM), Indonesia's Investment Coordinating Board, stated that the 23 May 1995 deregulation package was the first to introduce a schedule of tariff reductions up to the year 2003. The package reduces import restrictions, opens up ten previously closed sectors to foreign investment, reduces tariffs on 6,030 items, simplifies licensing procedures and facilitates traded goods in export processing zones.

The World Bank disclosed that the tariff cuts would reduce anti-trade bias by one-third (*Indonesian Commercial Newsletter*, 10 June 1996). Although these packages accelerate scheduled cuts in tariff and non-tariff barriers, the World Bank believes that the deregulation agenda is far from finished. The unfinished agenda includes removing the tariff protection on vehicles, opening up of the strategic industries to import competition, removing of domestic subsidies, removing export taxes on forest products and removing non-tariff barriers on agricultural commodities.

The unfinished agenda for reducing import restrictions consists of removing non-tariff barriers, notably on rice, sugar, wheat and soybean, and the associated restrictions that protect wheat flour milling. The state's National Logistics Agency (BULOG) has the sole right to import these items. The deregulation package sent confusing signals because ten sectors were removed from the restricted investment list but there was no deregulation of trade in key commodities (Business Monitor International, 1996).

On 26 January 1996, the government introduced another deregulation package. Its purpose was to boost export competitiveness through reducing tariffs on imported goods used in manufacturing export products, facilitating imports of capital goods and raw materials, and opening export and import business to foreign firms (INDIO, 1996). According to Tunkey Ariwiboro, the Indonesian Minister of Trade and Industry, the January package targeted government efforts to stimulate the nation's non-oil exports, thus giving export-oriented companies more room to manoeuvre in foreign markets (*International Herald Tribune*, 13 May 1996).

According to the World Bank, Indonesian trade policy has an anti-trade bias. This means that domestic production is favoured in import-competing sectors, and domestic sales are favoured over exports. Import protection tariffs and non-tariff barriers account for two-thirds of the anti-trade bias while export restriction accounts for the remainder (*Indonesian Commercial Newsletter*, 10 June 1996).

Indonesian exports remain subject to considerable restrictions which cover one-half of total non-oil exports and affect nearly 2,000 products. The export restrictions cover mainly agricultural products which include export bans, regulated exports by exporters approved by the Ministry of Industry and Trade, supervised exports (requiring approval by the Ministry of Trade and Industry) and export taxes. The key elements of the January 1996 deregulation package are shown in Table 3–2 (INDIO, 1996).

TABLE 3–2
January 1996 Deregulation Package

Key Elements	Changes
VAT	Removal of VAT on imports of fishing and other commercial vessels, and shipping related services.
Monitoring Fees	Abolition of monitoring fee previously imposed on firms exporting textiles and related products to countries imposing quotas.
Export Taxes	Export taxes eliminated for a number of products.
Bonded Zone	Private firms are allowed to develop and manage bonded zones from April 1996.
Firm Ownership	Wholly-owned firms are allowed to establish export houses and import firms for further processing of export and re-exports.
Duty Exemption	Imports of machinery and plant equipment by automobile firms are exempted from duties to boost component manufacturing and save on imports.
Import Tariff	Import tariffs reduced by 5% to 20% on 428 items.

Source: INDIO (1996).

The 4 June 1996 deregulation package (*Indonesian Commercial Newsletter*, 10 June 1996) contained 11 main items (see Table 3–3 for an abbreviated summary). In addition, the package supported the continuation of the import policies drafted on 23 May 1995. It reduced 1,497 out of 7,288 tariff lines. The tariff lines are divided into two groups. The first group is scheduled to reach an import duty rate not higher than 5% by the year 2000. The other group is to reach an import duty rate not higher than 10% by the year 2003 (see Table 3–4). Surcharges will be removed after the application of the June 1996 deregulation. The government also removed import restrictions for

TABLE 3–3
June 1996 Deregulation Package

Key Elements	Changes
Import duties	• Continuation of reduction schedule. • Change in duty rate for capital goods. • Elimination of surcharge. • Streamlining of import mechanism. • Anti-dumping stipulation.
Export facilitation	• Streamlining of licensing mechanism. • Operation of bonded warehousing.
Manufacturing sector	• Relaxation of import and export activities by manufacturing companies. • Simplification of import procedure of industrial waste for raw material used in domestic industries.

Source: *Indonesian Commercial Newsletter*, 10 June 1996.

TABLE 3–4
Schedule Tariff Reduction to 23 May 1995 Deregulation Package

Before May 1995	1995	1996	1997	1998	1999	2000	2001	2002	2003
5%	*	*	*	*	*	Max. 5%			
10%	5%	*	*	*	*	Max. 5%			
15%	10%	*	5%	*	*	Max. 5%			
20%	15%	*	10%	*	5%	Max. 5%			
25%	20%	15%	*	10%	*	*	*	*	Max. 10%
30%	25%	20%	*	15%	*	10%	*	*	Max. 10%
35%	30%	25%	*	20%	*	15%	*	10%	Max. 10%
40%	30%	25%	*	20%	*	15%	*	10%	Max. 10%

* Unchanged.
Source: *Indonesian Commercial Newsletter*, 10 June 1996.

nine commodities by allowing general importers to replace producer-importers. This was intended to facilitate the import of capital goods and raw materials (*Indonesian Commercial Newsletter*, 10 June 1996).

The new deregulation package specifies that there will be no ceiling on a single party's share ownership of publicly listed Indonesian companies (*Business Times*, 23/24 November 1996). It also abolishes the need for foreign companies to reduce their equity stakes in Indonesian companies to 49% after 20 years. Foreign companies are permitted to assume a 95% maximum stake in wholly-owned companies or joint ventures. Foreign-owned companies are now allowed to operate anywhere in Indonesia without minimum capitalisation limits. Their 30-year licences are renewable for another 30 years. The deregulation package abolishes the compulsory examination of export commodities by Sucofindo, a government appointed surveyor. The policy simplifies procedures to obtain a certificate of origin (Business Monitor International, 1996). The major features of the May 1995 deregulation package on investment are shown in Table 3–5.

Impact of Deregulation

Deregulation can only be implemented successfully via a supportive domestic policy. Successful deregulation requires a legal code that adequately addresses issues such as asset ownership and property rights. The benefits could include substantial employee ownership of firms, increased job stability and expanded employment opportunities (Gayle and Goodrich, 1990). As of 1 January 1997, seven major sectors have been deregulated including banking, finance, real estate, transportation, telecommunications, airlines, petrochemical and automotive.

The Indonesian government has handled deregulation with great care to avoid nationalists' claims that the control of critical economic sectors is being assumed by foreign interests. This sentiment was expressed by both Budi Hardjono, of the Home Commission V on Communication and Public Works, and Bomer Pasaribu, House of Representatives Commission on State Budget Affairs.[6]

---

6 "At present we can see that there is no strong basis for Indonesia to be optimistic in the face of the coming free trade era" and "... Indonesia should manage its economy cautiously in the face of WTO rules on such sensitive issues as labour, investment, trade liberalisation and openness in trade policies" (*The Straits Times*, 16 December 1996).

TABLE 3–5
Change of Investment Rules

Investment Rules: Indonesia Before and After May 1995 Deregulation Package		
Item	**Before**	**After**
Foreign equity	Maximum of 85% for investors in Bali and Java, and 100% ownership only for ventures worth Rp 50 million or more in outlying islands.	Foreign investor decides but 100% foreign firm allowed to operate anywhere in the country except in areas closed to foreign investments.
Minimum Indonesian equity requirement	20%	5%
Divestment	Reduce foreign share-holding to 51% after 20 years.	Reduce to 15 years but no limit set, 1% Indonesian ownership is acceptable.
New areas opened	NA	Partial foreign ownership is allowed but no minimum set for nuclear power, mass media, ports, telecommunications, railways, aviation.
Validity of foreign licence	20 years.	30 years and renewable for another 30.

Source: *Southeast Asia Business Omnibook* (1995).

The government is aware that implementing programmes of deregulation without sufficient regard for the long term implications will invite new charges of policy failure. This was the case with banking deregulation in the late 1980s. Indonesian state banks encountered significant competition for the first time and many did not fare well (*International Herald Tribune*, 13 May 1996). Deregulation reduced the source of cheap funds from liquidity credits and forced state banks to compete with private banks for deposit funds. This increased their awareness of competition and led to increased efficiencies (Pangestu, 1996).

The tariff reduction schedules in the May 1995 deregulation package provide businesses with a high degree of certainty. Furthermore, they are in compliance with the country's tariff commitment under the ASEAN Free Trade Area (AFTA), the General Agreement on Tariffs and Trade (GATT) and the Bogor Declaration of the Asia Pacific Economic Cooperation (APEC) forum (*International Herald Tribune*, 13 May 1996).

All domestic interest groups do not benefit equally from policies of privatisation and deregulation. However, higher investment has created more production and employment which could support medium term growth (Gayle and Goodrich, 1990). For the cash-strapped Indonesian government, foreign participation offers the best access to both technology and international capital markets (*Asiamoney*, 7 September 1993).

Indonesia needed an overall strategy in response to falling petroleum prices which led to a fall in foreign exchange earnings. Furthermore, around 60% of the government's revenue came from taxes on petroleum corporations. The shortfall in revenue caused by lower oil prices will affect development expenditures (Pangestu, 1996). From the environmental perspective, one study indicated that Indonesia could reduce its carbon dioxide emissions without considerably suppressing the growth of its economy by deregulating energy prices and improving different levels of taxation of fossil fuels (*Energy Policy*, December 1991).

Deregulation has succeeded in diversifying the economy and reducing its heavy dependence on the petroleum sector (*Global Trade*, August 1992). The largest inflows of private foreign capital in the latter part of the 1980s were clearly due to the deregulation in both foreign investment regulations as well as the capital markets. The economic reforms and adjustments undertaken since then have created a better business environment for overall investment (Pangestu, 1996).

The deregulation of foreign investment rules has sparked increased interest in the Jakarta property market (Ford, 1997). Under the deregulation package of 4 June 1996, companies operating in an industrial estate are no longer required to have a special permit if the Capital Investment Board (BKMS) has granted the necessary final permit. Foreign companies are now allowed to import complementary products from their affiliated companies abroad. They are also allowed to sell their products and the imported complementary products in the domestic market. The procedure of importing industrial waste has been streamlined and simplified (*Indonesian Commercial Newsletter*, 10 June 1996). A summary of major reforms affecting the Indonesian economy from 1983 to 1996 is presented in the Appendix 3–1.

The pace of liberalisation has occurred at a faster rate than other changes in the related laws. This has led to inconsistencies between regulations and legislation. Problems arising from interpretations and implementation will contribute to greater uncertainty regarding the government's commitment to the reform process (Pangestu, 1996). The deregulation agenda is still far from finished since some essential obstacles have not been addressed including monopoly, oligopoly, restrictions on the import and export of certain goods, wrong targets for incentives, high interest rates and high valued added taxes (*Indonesian Commercial Newsletter*, 10 June 1996).

The government's deregulation drive has been hampered by politics. Lately, investors have expressed unhappiness about presidential decrees that provide protection to industries that are dominated by the President's friends and family (*The Asian Wall Street Journal*, 12 August 1996). Major areas that require deregulation, such as monopolies and oligopolies in upstream production as well as non-tariff levies in the domestic production and distribution system, are likely to remain untouched (*International Herald Tribune*, 13 May 1996). Macroeconomic policies will remain virtually unchanged although changes to foreign investment regulations will continue to be forthcoming (*Business Asia*, 7 June 1993).

CONCLUSION

Deregulation encourages small enterprises to operate efficiently in preparation for tougher competition. It will take companies five to ten years to adjust to deregulation. Deregulation should also foster a middle income group to bridge the gap between the rich and the poor. The pace of deregulation will be driven by the higher expectations of the younger generation.[7]

The rate of privatisation depends on how quickly the SOEs can become profitable. The timing of privatisation is important for the stock market to absorb the additional business/liquidity. The government will have to ensure that local companies are ready to face external competition before opening protected sectors to foreigners to ensure a level playing field for all companies. This requires that local enterprises and SOEs become transparent in their dealings, adapt to the latest technological innovations and operate on a slim budget.[8]

The increasing frequency of liberalisation and deregulation packages announced in 1996 confirms the government's commitment to create a more efficient market. At the same time, there are signs that the government is improving the environment for fair competition and enhancing anti-trust type regulations. Foreign direct investment in infrastructure is encouraged in the less developed areas of the country.

Some of the obvious hindrances to implementing reforms are bureaucratic delays and political resistance. This arises from the connection of prominent businessmen to present political leaders. However, pressures from world trade bodies and global investors will continue to push Indonesia to open its markets more and to create a more transparent and efficient economy. The present reforms are unlikely to be reversed because there is too much at stake. The pace of reforms and the ability of the people to adapt to the new world order will determine Indonesia's economic success.

---

7 Extracted from interview notes with Professor Harsono of Gadjah Mada University during a dinner hosted by the NTU MBA Business Study Mission, Yogyakarta, 14 December 1996.

8 Interview with Mr. Kanaka of KPMG Hanadi, Sudjendro and Rekan on 10 December 1996, Jakarta, during the NTU MBA Business Study Mission.

APPENDIX 3–1
Summary of Major Reforms Affecting the Indonesian Economy

Reforms	Main Contents	Effects
Financial 1 June 1983: Banking deregulation	• Remove interest rate control for state banks. • Reduce liquidity credit.	• Rise in deposit rate. • Some fall in intermediation costs. • Liquidity credits increase.
October 1986	• Remove ceiling on central bank swap.	
27 October 1988	• Open up licences for new banks, including JVs. • Lending limits regulation. • Reserve requirement lowered. • Deregulation of capital markets. • Reduce government role in stock market. • Foreigners can buy stock.	• Opening up of new banks and JVs. • Competition between banks. • Rising interest rates and falling spreads.
December 1988	• Capital market deregulated further. • Deregulation in insurance industry. • Rationalisation of financial services sector.	• Sharp increase in capital market activity and index. • Major SOEs and private companies went public.
Fiscal April 1984: Tax reform	• Remove withholding tax and introduce VAT. • Rationalisation of income and sales tax.	• Increased government revenues.

APPENDIX 3–1 (cont'd)

Reforms	Main Contents	Effects
Investment May 1986	• 95% foreign ownership possible for export-oriented FDI. • Export-oriented firms allowed to distribute domestically. • JVs can participate in government export credit scheme.	• Improve investment climate and encourage exports.
July 1987	• Deregulation of investment and capacity licensing. • Broad banding. • Closed sectors opened to export-oriented firms.	• Improve investment climate.
November 1988	• JVs allowed to distribute own products domestically.	
May 1989	• Removal of priority scale list for investment through Board of Investment. • Introduction of negative list.	• Improve investment climate and ease investment application.

APPENDIX 3–1 (cont'd)

Reforms	Main Contents	Effects
October 1993	• Simpler procedures for obtaining investment licences. • 100% foreign ownership (FDI) extended from 5 to 10 years. • Lifting of ban on used machinery to encourage relocation of plants to Indonesia. • Exempting duty on 92 categories of goods and lowering it on 27 others.	• Improve investment climate and reduce bureaucracy.
23 May 1995	• New business sectors previously closed were open. • Tariff reductions and trading of goods in export processing zones (EPZ). • Simplified business licensing procedures.	• Improve investment climate and trade facilitation.
January 1996: Deregulation package	• Foreign companies allowed to provide services to support exports and to own 100% equity in such ventures. • Private sector allowed to develop special EPZ zones. Foreign owners can participate in these zones as long as finished goods are for export.	• Improve investment climate and increase exports.

APPENDIX 3–1 (cont'd)

Reforms	Main Contents	Effects
May 1996: Deregulation package	• Allow foreigners to establish 100% foreign-owned company or a JV with Indonesian partner. • Reduction of corporate tax from 35% to 25%. • Streamlining of approval process and improved IPR protection laws. • Opening up of a number of strategic sectors to offshore investors for JVs (e.g., telecoms, toll roads, shipping).	• Improve investment climate.

Source: Adapted from Pangestu (1996).

REFERENCES

Asia, Inc., "The Cukong Cover Their Assets", July 1995.

Asiamoney, "Answering the Call for Growth", Vol. 4, 7 September 1993.

Asiamoney, "P. T. Indosat Sets the Trends", July/August 1994, pp. 39–45.

Asiamoney, "Yen for Privatisation", April 1995, p. 5.

Asian Business, "Indonesia – Indigenous Companies Flourish", Vol. 31, July 1995, pp. 12–4.

Asian Business, "Privatisation Benefits Apparent", March 1996, pp. 40–3.

Asian Wall Street Journal, "Suharto Favors Ownership Cap on Listed Firms", 20 November 1996.

Badan Kondinasi Penanaman Modal (BKPM), *Brief Guide to Investing in Indonesia*, Jakarta, 1996.

Business Asia, "Indonesia: No Sign of Free Market Mania", 7 June 1993, p. 5.

Business Monitor International, *Indonesia 1996–1998*, London, 1996.

Business Review Southeast Asia, Indonesia, "Southeast Asia Business Omnibook", Singapore, 1995, pp. 95–156.

Central Bureau of Statistics, *Indonesian Economic Indicators Handbook*, Indonesia, 1996.

East Asian Executive Reports, 15 January 1996, pp. 9–15.

Economic and Business Review Indonesia, "High Marks for Indonesia's Privatisation Program", IBC Online (Indonesia.clever.net/company/ebri/eb_news.htm), 21 August 1996.

Energy Policy, December 1991, pp. 970–7.

Euromoney Supplement, "And Now for the Hard Part", August 1995, pp. 1–14.

Euromoney, "Lessons in Privatisation", February 1996, pp. 93–4.

Far Eastern Economic Review, "Policy Making; Deregulation; Tariffs", Vol. 158, No. 23, 8 June 1995, p. 5.

Ford Maggie, "Indonesia–Property Boost Follows Rule Change", www.asia1.com.sg/timesnet/data/ab/docs/ab036a.html, 1997.

Gayle, J. Dennis and N. Johnathan Goodrich, *Privatisation and Deregulation in Global Perspective*, Chapter 1, Quorum Books, New York, 1990.

Global Trade, "Executive Summary of May 1995 Deregulation Package", August 1992, pp. 34–8.

INDIO, "Sustaining Economic Growth with Macroeconomic Stability", *Indonesia Economic Brief*, Indonesia National Development Information Office, Jakarta, February 1996.

Indonesian Commercial Newsletter, Edition 197, 10 June 1996.

Institutional Investor, "Greater Emphasis on the Private Sector", December 1994.

International Herald Tribune, "Indonesian Telecommunication Industry, Data Consult on Line", 13 May 1996.

Makarim & Tairas Legal Consultants, *Doing Business in Indonesia*, Jakarta, February 1996.

P. T. Sassoon Securities Indonesia, *Sassoon Stock Commentary, Indonesia July 1996*, Paagestum, Jakarta, 1996.

Pangestu Mari, *Economic Reform, Deregulation and Privatisation. The Indonesian Experience*, Centre for Strategic and International Studies, Jakarta, 1996.

The Asian Wall Street Journal, "Diversification and Deregulation Draw Massive Investments to Fuel Growth", 12 August 1996, p. 10.

The Business Times, "No Ceiling to Ownership of Listed Indon Firms: Minister", 23–24 November 1996.

The Straits Times, "Government Action Needed to Remove Hindrances to Efficiency", 16 December 1996.

The Straits Times, "Indonesia Plans to Sell 15% Stake in Telkom to Public", 22 November 1996.

The Straits Times, "Indonesia: No Plans to Curb Share Ownership", 23 November 1996.

The Straits Times, "Suharto Said to Favour Limit on Equity", 20 November 1996.

Chapter 4

Manufacturing in Indonesia*

BY
Andrew THAM
Robin HE
LIM Seng Hoo
Eugenio REYES
Simon DUTTA

INTRODUCTION

INDONESIA IS A developing country rich in natural resources. Yet, approximately 15% of the 200 million population live below the poverty line.[1] One urgent challenge is creating enough good jobs for about three million people reaching working age each year.[2] The manufacturing sector has replaced the more traditional natural resource industries as the major component of the economy and source of new jobs. This shift in emphasis is due to the pro-development policies of the Suharto era which started in 1967 and the realisation that natural resources are non-renewable. Economic

* Our Business Study Mission (BSM) team would like to express our sincere appreciation to Dr. Ashish Lall, the Trade Development Board and the Indonesian Embassy in Singapore for their valuable advice and assistance.

1 Per official Indonesian estimates. The World Bank in 1996 estimated that 30% to 40% of the population can be classified as poor (Business Monitor International Ltd., 1996, p. 3).

2 Indonesian Embassy officials in Singapore gave an estimate of three million. The actual number may be more and it is on the increase. The Economist Intelligence Unit, 3rd Quarter 1996, and the Capital Investment Coordinating Board (BKPM) provided estimates of 2.3 million and 2.4 million, respectively, but these are net job increment figures which harmonise with the roughly 1.0 million retiring or exiting each year.

policy in Indonesia has often been ad hoc and without clear focus. Recently, however, government introduced several initiatives to deregulate sectors of the economy, and to reduce tariff and non-tariff barriers in line with commitments made at the World Trade Organisation (WTO), Asia Pacific Economic Cooperation (APEC) and the ASEAN Free Trade Area. Although these set the tone for a clearer direction, events still occasionally happen that conflict with the broader goals. But these occurrences simply reflect the size and diversity of Indonesia.

This chapter first traces the growth and development of the manufacturing sector. It discusses the sub-sectors of the automotive, food, textile and electronics industries, and the size-distribution of manufacturing firms. Next, it examines employment, manpower development, wages and productivity. This is followed by a discussion of manufacturing investment in Indonesia with a focus on foreign direct investment (FDI). The chapter finally considers broader issues relating to the manufacturing environment such as the location of manufacturing zones, infrastructure and taxation, and concludes by highlighting the challenges facing Indonesia.

GROWTH, DEVELOPMENT AND PROFILE OF MANUFACTURING

The manufacturing sector has grown rapidly in relation to other sectors as shown in Table 4–1. Manufacturing's GDP share increased from 9.2% in 1969 to almost 25% of GDP by 1995. The contributions of agriculture and mining-quarrying have declined over the years but the latter remained the prime export earner up to 1991. The government projects that by the start of *Repelita X* in 2014 (near the end of the second 25-year plan, PJP II), the contribution of non-oil manufacturing to GDP will be 32.5%.

The early development of manufacturing activities took place in a mixed economy where the government, in addition to regulatory and supervisory roles, actively intervened and invested in industry. Activities such as the production of fertiliser and steel are controlled by state-owned enterprises and so are paper manufacturing and cement plants. In recent years, however, there have been efforts at deregulation and privatisation, and this trend is expected to continue as emphasis switches towards exports and the development of more efficient market mechanisms. A breakdown of manufacturing output by sector for 1995 is given in Table 4–2 while Table 4–3 shows the composition of manufactured exports.

TABLE 4–1
GDP by Sectors (Selected Years)*

	1984		**1990**		**1995**	
	Rp (bn)	**%**	**Rp (bn)**	**%**	**Rp (bn)**	**%**
Agriculture, forestry & fisheries	20,420	21.9	22,604	19.6	61,637	16.1
Mining & quarrying	16,939	18.1	17,538	15.2	35,145	9.2
Manufacturing	**13,113**	**16.3**	**22,277**	**19.3**	**91,929**	**24.0**
Utilities	354	0.5	726	0.6	4,281	1.1
Construction	4,757	5.1	6,679	5.8	29,191	7.6
Transportation & communications	5,051	5.2	6,392	5.5	27,148	7.1
All others (trade, hotel, financial, etc.)	25,068	32.9	39,265	34.0	133,720	34.9
Gross Domestic Product	85,702	100.0	115,481	100.0	383,051	100.0

* 1983 constant rupiah.
Sources: United Nations (1996a); Investment Coordinating Board (BKPM) (1996).

Food Processing and Packaging[3]

Food processing and packaging is the largest manufacturing industry and it has been growing rapidly due to the size and rising incomes of the local population. The industry is dominated by large firms, such as the IndoFood Group, although there are smaller players. While the early orientation was primarily domestic, the industry is starting to make increasingly successful export thrusts. This is supported by production economies on a global scale which allow for the implementation of some modern processing and packaging technologies

---

3 Material for this section on the food sector was compiled from the following sources: http://www.indonesianet.com/hilight/manu2.html 28 December 1996; http://caticsuf.csufresno.edu:70/et/agtrade/mktplans/asia/indonesi, 25 November 1996; http://ffas.usda.gov/faspublication.or-rep/food-mar-over/indones.html, 23 November 1996; http://www.tradepia.or.jp/indo/ma211.html, 25 November 1996; and http://yazhou.asiainfo.com.sg/weis/research/research.html dated 9 May 1996, "P. T. IndoFood Sukses Makmur".

combined with the availability of low cost raw materials, land and labour. Major foreign food companies have invested in processing facilities in Indonesia for export purposes. Thus, processed food exports grew to US$1.9 billion, or 6.5% of manufactured exports in 1995, and is expected to increase further.

TABLE 4–2
Output of Manufacturing Industries: 1995

Major Industries	Output (US$)	%	Orientation
1. Food, beverages and tobacco	37,188	40.5	Domestic, starting to export
2. Transport equipment	10,681	11.6	Domestic
3. Fertilizers, chemicals & rubber goods	10,498	11.4	Domestic and exports
4. Petroleum & gas manufacturing	10,131	11.0	Domestic and exports
5. Textile, leather products & footwear	8,045	8.8	Largest export sector
6. Wood products & other wood products	5,698	6.2	Domestic and exports
7. Paper & paper goods	3,442	3.7	Domestic and exports
8. Iron & steel basic industries	2,915	3.2	Exports and domestic
9. Cement & non-metallic mineral	2,853	3.1	Domestic
10. Others	479	0.5	
Total	**91,930**	**100.0**	

Sources: United Nations (1996a); Investment Coordinating Board (BKPM) (1996).

TABLE 4–3
Export of Manufactured Products: 1995

Manufacturing Sector	Exports (US$ million)	Share
Textile/garments	6,218	21.2%
Wood products	4,986	17.0%
Electrical apparatus	2,786	9.5%
Processed rubber	2,200	7.5%
Footwear	2,053	7.0%
Processed food/oils	1,906	6.5%
Steel/metal articles	1,789	6.1%
Pulp/paper products	1,026	3.5%
Chemicals	528	1.8%
Others	5,836	19.9%
Total	**29,328**	**100.0%**

Source: INDIO (1996b).

Subah Indah, IndoFood and ABC are the largest manufacturers and distributors of food products. All three firms have strategic alliances or joint ventures with foreign food firms allowing access to advanced food and packaging technology, products, brands, and supply of formulations and ingredients. In several cases, these joint ventures provide access to export markets.

Poultry processing, seafood and instant noodles are among the more significant activities. Poultry processing has grown rapidly with modern technology, stock imports and lower feed costs, coupled with increasing consumer demand. There is also a growing export component led mainly by U.S. companies. Processing of seafood products, such as canned tuna and frozen shrimp, are led by Japanese ventures which export these to the region and to Japan. IndoFood is the largest and fastest growing instant noodle supplier in the world and dominates 90% of the Indonesian market. Other manufactured food products include vegetables and fruit processing, packaging (baby corn and pineapple), snacks and confectionery, biscuits and bakery, juices, dairy items, meat products, sauces and condiments. Certain ingredients, such as fruit concentrates for juices and soybeans for *tofu* and *tempe*, are imported extensively.

IndoFood Sukses Makmur is a dominant producer that was incorporated in August 1990. With 1995 net sales of Rp 2,091 billion and net income of Rp 305 billion, it is the country's largest food, foodstuffs and consumer products company. The company is divided into five divisions: noodles, snack foods, food seasonings, baby foods and beverages. Instant noodles accounted for 87.8% of the turnover in 1995 but the other divisions are being actively developed. In snack foods, IndoFood has teamed up with PepsiCo Food's Frito-Lay division and it leads the industry with 30% market share compared to the nearest competitor at 8.2%. Given that this business is still young, growth potential is expected to be high.

IndoFood's manufacturing and distribution includes a network of 23 manufacturing plants and 300 distribution depots employing 2,400 sales personnel with 1,000 vehicles, reaching over 150,000 retail outlets throughout the country. In addition, the company exports to nearly 30 countries and has manufacturing facilities in Jeddah (Saudi Arabia), Nigeria and China. The strength of IndoFood is in part due to government concessions and monopoly privileges granted in certain sectors, coupled with successful and effective marketing programmes. The recent government liberalisation towards a freer and more open market[4] will mean increased domestic competition but IndoFood has a strong headstart. In 1995, the company continued its expansion and productivity improvement programmes and invested Rp 250 billion in capital assets. Some milestones achieved by the company include the adoption of freeze-drying technology to improve quality standards and obtaining the ISO 9002 certification in 1994. Operations have been integrated to enhance efficiency and powerful computers were installed for tracking daily sales, production and costs. IndoFood was ranked sixth in 1995 among Indonesian companies on overall management quality (*Far Eastern Economic Review*, 16 May 1996).

Transport Equipment

Transport equipment is the second largest manufacturing sub-sector with the automotive and aerospace industries the most dominant. The automotive industry was the early target for import-substitution and it is now relatively well developed. Sales in the 1990s are depicted in Table 4–4. In 1972, the government disallowed imports of completely built-up (CBU) cars to force local assembly of completely knocked-down (CKD) vehicles. The policy, however, did not result in the local manufacture of parts until 1978. Initial progress was slow and engines parts have been produced locally only since 1989. A prime effect of the policy was that direct and indirect taxes, on car imports, ownership and use provided a major portion of government revenues in the 1970s and 1980s, and they continue to be important today (INDIO, 1996a).

Table 4–4
Automobile Sales (thousand units)

1990	1991	1992	1993	1994	1995	1996*
275	265	170	210	320	380	315

* Estimate.
Source: INDIO (1996a).

---

4 In July 1995, four instant noodle expansion proposals were rejected by BKPM, due to a new policy to limit monopolistic and cartel activities for companies holding market shares greater than 50%, unless the new plant capacities are for export production.

Japanese auto-makers were early investors in the automotive industry and have carved out the leading market share. This was due partly to Japan's proximity to Indonesia. But the Japanese were also more flexible and adaptable to the conditions and circumstances required for local automotive production. Hence, they were able to introduce appropriate production processes at a time when no supporting industrial infrastructure existed. With the supporting industries fairly well established and the market developed, European, U.S. and Korean auto-makers are anxious to gain a share of the market.

All the automotive plants are essentially joint ventures set up with major foreign producers. The biggest group is Astra, founded as an independent private enterprise by William Soeryawidjaya. It has become the country's most admired and best managed business. However, a setback[5] in 1992 allowed control to pass into the hands of a consortium considered to be close to the President, led by Bob Hasan,[6] Prajogo Pangetsu, Putera Sampoerna, Anthony Salim and others. Astra is comprised of two key divisions: Toyota Astra, which manufactures and distributes Toyota in Indonesia; and Astra Mobil which manufactures and distributes for Daihatsu, BMW, Peugeot, Nissan Diesel, Isuzu and Honda motorcycle (Solomon and MacBeth, 1996; Shari *et al.*, 1996).

The other important automotive group is the Salim-owned IndoMobil Group which is tied up with Suzuki, Mazda, Volvo, Ford, Nissan and Hino. Other automotive manufacturers in Indonesia include German Motors (Mercedes Benz), Dan Motors (Kawasaki and Vespa), Tiga Berlian (Mitsubishi cars, vans and trucks), Imora (Honda cars), Bimantara (Hyundai) and Humpuss (Timor/Kia). A number of new projects led by European auto-makers are in the planning stage.

The birth and development of the industry has been traumatic. In the early 1980s, four assembly plants closed down during a recession coinciding with tax penalties for non-compliance with government deadlines for local content. This led rival Japanese joint venture firms to support vendor development in 1987 aimed at producing more local automotive parts. As a result, production now encompasses en-

---

5 Due to the collapse of P. T. Bank Summa run by the eldest son which the family had to bail out despite the principle of limited liability. The Government was considering sedition charges should the collapse result in protests and riots by depositors.

6 Bob Hasan runs the Nusamba Group, a holding company which is 80% controlled by the President.

gines, from die-casting engine blocks to machining and final assembly. The next target is to localise the production of transmissions systems that entails complex gear mechanisms (Economist Intelligence Unit, 1996a).

Achieving a high portion of local content under existing government definitions is not easy. To illustrate, 100% of the body, 47% of the engine, 40% of the transmission system, 30% of the steering system, 28% of the axle, 40% of the suspension and 20% of the electricals (alternators, ignition, etc.) of a typical Astra car are produced locally.[7] Given this input, the car is considered to be only 42% local because the power drive train is defined as comprising 45% of the content value of the entire car. Presently, none of the companies are planning local production of power trains because this entails very advanced technology which is mastered by only a few firms worldwide (INDIO, 1996a).

Another consideration is that local value added production remains low. For a made-in-Indonesia Daihatsu car engine which cost Rp 3,400,000 to produce in 1996, the actual value added may be as low as 7%! Other than labour, everything else is imported including the machine tools, steel and even the cutting oil. The significance of local content was felt when the government suddenly announced a National Car Project in early 1996. P. T. Timor Putra Nasional, the brainchild of Hutomo "Tommy" Mandala Putra, youngest son of the President, was granted tax exemptions from import and luxury taxes, although their cars were wholly imported from their joint venture partner, Kia of Korea. This led to a 17% fall in the sales of four-wheel drive vehicles in the first nine months of 1996 (MacBeth and Thornton, 1996; Rahul, 1996).

The four taxes affecting car prices in 1996 were a 10% VAT, 2.5% sales tax, 60% luxury tax and 100% import tax. The import tax is waived if 40% local content is achieved and many car makers have qualified for this waiver. Following the ensuing Timor Putra controversy, the government offered to waive the luxury tax for cars with engine capacities of 1600cc or less if they satisfy the 60% local content, putting these on a similar footing, but this is a tall order yet.

The overall pace of development for the industry should remain intact for the following reasons. First, these events may prove to be a blessing in disguise resulting in faster tax reductions for the industry.

---

7 This information was obtained during an interview with officials while on a site visit to an Astra plant on 10 December 1996.

Secondly, there is still significant potential for the development of automotive component manufacturing for exports under a series of ASEAN complementation schemes. These are designed to allow for the duty-free intra-ASEAN trade of complementary components that can be used for the production of whole products. One scheme is called "brand to brand" which is designed to help manufacturers overcome high break-even volume investment barriers by allowing for the specialisation of component manufacturing among member countries (INDIO, 1996a). Thirdly, the Indonesian Government is an effective negotiator and, with rising GNP per capita and an increasing domestic market, foreign direct investments in the sector can be expected to resume soon. Whether Indonesia will ever successfully export a fully made-in-Indonesia car is a separate question that is yet unanswered.[8]

The motorcycle industry has powered ahead strongly, with sales and production increasing rapidly. Honda has about 49% of the market share and production increased from 590,000 units in 1995 to 760,000 units in 1996, and it is expected to reach 900,000 units in 1997. These increases are expected to continue as GDP per capita surpasses US$1,000, making motorcycles more affordable to a larger segment of the population.

There is talk of a national motorcycle project but such an undertaking requires a pool of highly skilled engineers and designers that are not currently available. A local director of a Honda motorcycle plant argued that Taiwan took many years to develop its indigenous capabilities and, over a period of 20 years, sent many engineers to the U.S. for training and exposure. Indonesia may have to do the same or develop more realistic aspirations.

The aircraft industry forms the balance of the transport equipment sector. The country's interest in air transportation stems from its being an archipelago of islands. Indonesia has become the first Southeast Asian manufacturer of aircraft. This accomplishment is credited to the Minister of Research and Technology, Bacharuddin Habibie, who also founded Industri Pesawat Terbang Nusantara (IPTN), the national aircraft industry company based in Bandung (Clifford, 1993).

---

[8] There could be differences in opinions on the viability of an Indonesian car. At the official opening of a Japanese die-casting plant on 23 November 1992, for example, the Coordinating Minister of Production and Planning offered the view that it would be more viable to build up an export sector for car components than to produce an Indonesia car.

IPTN is involved in several joint ventures with foreign aircraft producers such as British Aerospace (BAe) and Casa of Spain. In co-operation with these firms it produces the CN235 transport aircraft. Under offset deals on commercial and military aircraft purchases negotiated by the government, IPTN gained contracts and technology transfers to assemble a range of helicopters and produce aircraft parts. It recently made a bid for the assembly of the Hawk trainer fighter aircraft in Indonesia.

IPTN's high point was the August 1995 demonstration flight for the 50-seater CN250, slated as the first commercial aircraft designed and built entirely in Indonesia. Following this event some purchase options were announced.[9] IPTN now plans to produce commuter aircraft ranging from 20 to 130-seaters and hopes to become the "Toyota of aerospace". IPTN, however, has its critics and industry sources have often questioned the rationale for many unprofitable ventures which consume huge financial resources that may have been better utilised elsewhere to provide urgently needed jobs (Business Monitor International, 1996).

Fertilisers, Chemicals and Rubber

This is the third largest sub-sector in manufacturing. Fertiliser production is state-controlled and output is geared for domestic consumption by the agriculture and forestry sectors. Production of chemicals and pharmaceuticals, on the other hand, is mostly under foreign joint ventures and licences. The government is providing incentives to this industry with the intention of promoting exports (Economist Intelligence Unit, 1996b). Indonesia is also a major rubber producer. The emphasis is now shifting towards the production of finished products such as tyres for cars, motorcycles and bicycles. In 1993, the production of car and motorcycle tyres was 9.66 million units and 21.34 million units of bicycle tyres (Business Monitor International, 1996).

Oil and Gas

This industry has a major impact on the economy due to backward

---

9 The announcements were controversial. Apparently, the sales options of some aircraft to Malaysia were tied to the import of Proton cars. Over at Merpati Airlines, the CEO was removed because he questioned some terms of the lease purchase agreements for aircraft from IPTN.

linkages with exploration activity and forward linkages with petroleum refining. This makes oil and gas the fourth largest sub-sector in manufacturing. Manufacturing activities are carried out by foreign oil companies and joint ventures, mostly as subcontractors to Pertamina, which controls and monopolises this industry as well as the nation's network of gas stations (INDIO, 1996a).

Textile and Garments

The first four sub-sectors discussed above are largely geared towards the domestic market but the fifth largest sub-sector, textile and garments, is the country's leading export contributor. This is a change from earlier years when the textile industry was developed as an alternative to import substitution. But product life cycle changes and the gradual ending of the General System of Preference (GSP) privileges for neighbouring countries resulted in shifting textile manufacturing to Indonesia and other countries affording lower manufacturing costs (INDIO, 1996a).

Indonesia has a large pool of low cost (mostly female) labour and a tradition of handicraft production. This sub-sector is now the largest employer in the manufacturing sector and workers are usually paid the minimum daily wage of Rp 4,000. Production is located mainly in the greater Jakarta area, Bandung and Bali (INDIO, 1996b).

Exports have registered high growth since the late 1980s and comprised 21.2% of all manufactured exports by 1995. However, international competition has greatly intensified in recent years, especially from China, India and Vietnam, and has placed severe pressure on profit margins in the industry. This has led major textile producers, such as the Texmaco Group, to diversify into automotive engines and components manufacturing. The challenge for the industry is to move into higher value added ready-to-wear garments (INDIO, 1996b).

Wood and Related Products

In the early 1980s, the government banned the export of raw timber in order to develop the indigenous wood processing industries and, hence, to retain the value added benefits in the country. This strategy seems to have worked and exports of finished wood products, including plywood and furniture, grew to US$4.98 billion or 17% of manufactured exports in 1995 (INDIO, 1996a).

Paper and Printing

Like the wood products industry, this industry has also thrived due to government policies. It is the sixth largest component of manufacturing. In 1995, the output of this sector was valued at US$3.44 billion and slightly over US$1.0 billion was exported. Scandinavian paper, and wood-making equipment and technology were among the imports that helped improve the quality of products (INDIO, 1996a).

Iron and Basic Metals

This title may be misleading as this sub-sector includes the electronics industry which has recently been earmarked for special attention. Initial development was centred in Bandung and comprised the production of consumer durables (TV sets, radios, refrigerators, fans, etc.) for domestic consumption. Now the industry produces audio and video equipment, telecommunication equipment, data processing, medical equipment and electronics components.

A major shift in electronics has occurred. New investment laws allow 100% foreign ownership coupled with tax incentives. Special bonded zones for electronics in Jakarta and Batam can be set up to promote exports. The initial foreign investors were the Japanese and Koreans, investing in low cost manufacturing and exporting to Japan and the U.S. Early results have been promising. Total output grew at an annual average of 52.4% from 1990 to 1995 and exports grew from US$1.4 billion in 1993 to US$2.5 billion in 1995 (*Far Eastern Economic Review*, 16 May 1996). It is too early to know if the country will be as strong in electronics as Penang in Malaysia or the Philippines; both have grown just as fast but started from a higher base.

Domestic-oriented producers have had to overcome bureaucratic limitations. A case in point is Sony, which has two plants side by side, one producing for export and the other for domestic consumption.[10] The former enjoys relatively high efficiency while the latter is plagued by customs delays, sometimes up to one month long, and bureaucratic inefficiencies. This problem, together with the absence of domestic suppliers of precision components and moulds, prevented the adoption of just-in-time and lean manufacturing techniques in the domestic producing plants. As a result, the older P. T. Sony Manufacturing Indonesia factory only employs 600 workers while the newer export-oriented P. T. Sony Electronics Indonesia is an efficient

---

[10] The authors made a site visit to Sony in Cibitung, Bekasi, on 10 December 1996.

operation employing 6,000 workers (*The Asian Wall Street Journal*, 12 August 1996a; 12 August 1996b).

Investors have cited under-developed support industries such as tool, die and mould-making, as well as the lack of local component suppliers, as limitations. Tool and die making requires a high level of technology which the country does not have while component manufacturing requires volume production which current volumes do not justify. Hence, these are imported mainly from Japan, Thailand, Singapore and Malaysia. However, the scenario is gradually changing and a number of Japanese and South Korean firms have plans to source more parts locally through new plant investments. These include recent investments by Samsung, Asahi Glass and Nippon Electronic Glass in cathode ray TV tube production facilities in Indonesia (P. T. Ekamasni Consultants, 1996).

One other initiative expanding beyond the Special Bond Zone for Electronics (EPTE) envisaged by Mr. Widjaja, Chairman of the Indonesian Electronics Industry Association, is to develop special duty-free technology parks such as LIKE (an Indonesian acronym for Special Zone for Electronics Components Industry) which will provide one-stop tax, immigration, customs, licensing services and other facilities including a technical college for further systematic development of the industry (INDIO, 1996a).

Cement Production

This is the ninth and smallest sub-sector of manufacturing. Nonetheless, production reached a high of US$2.85 billion in 1995. In the late 1980s and early 1990s, there was a shortage of cement in Indonesia due to urbanisation and infrastructure development (*Dow Jones International News*, 1995). The government banned cement exports in order to meet domestic needs. The ban may be lifted in 1998 or 1999 when the country is expected to be self-sufficient in cement production (*Dow Jones International News*, 1996). In the meantime, new investments in production capacity have been approved and the shortfall has been made up via importing (mostly from Mexico) as much as one million tons of cement and clinker per year since 1994 (Borsuk, 1995).

Ownership and Participation Structure

The government is committed to encouraging and developing small scale enterprises to expand employment opportunities, and redistribute income and wealth (ISEAS, 1996). At the end of 1993, these were 2,353,600 household firms employing an average of 1.7 workers each, and 125,000 small scale enterprises employing an average of 7.6 workers each. The latter were engaged in food processing, handicrafts, clothing, leather and wood processing which accounted for US$2.67 billion of exports (Soetijipto *et al.*, 1996).

In contrast, the share of large and medium scale industries (LMIs) in manufacturing has increased since 1984 and accounted for 68.4% of total manufacturing activities in 1994. LMIs are defined by a government census first introduced in 1975 as enterprises with 20 or more employees. Table 4–5 summarises the number of establishments and workers as well as output by industries for selected years up to 1994. During these years, textiles provided the highest growth in employment, followed by metallic products and wood.

EMPLOYMENT, MANPOWER DEVELOPMENT, WAGES AND PRODUCTIVITY

The manufacturing sector accounted for 23.3% of GDP in 1994 and employed only 13.2% of the nation's workforce. Agriculture, on the other hand, accounted for 16.7% of GDP and 45.6% of employment in 1994 (see Table 4–6). Only about 37.7% of the manufacturing workforce are employed by LMIs and they account for 68.4% of output. This unequal distribution is one reason why wages in Indonesia are among the lowest in Asia despite the growth of manufacturing. Tables 4–7 and 4–8 show hourly manufacturing wages in 1995 and monthly wages by skill levels in 1995, respectively.

The low share of agriculture and small scale industry output combined with their high share of employment indicates that labour productivity is low.[11] Increased foreign investment in manufacturing and faster deregulation of sectors directly supporting manufacturing may allow workers in agriculture and small scale industries to switch to more productive and better paying jobs. They would also be exposed to better training and technology transfer. These actions lead to faster economic growth, help alleviate social inequalities and increase support for the government.

---

[11] Employment in agriculture has fallen from 42 million in 1993 to 39 million in 1994. The trend should be encouraged via continued restructuring.

TABLE 4–5
LMI Economic Activities and Share of Total Employment Output[12]

	1984			1989			1994		
Industries	No. of Firms	No. of Workers	Total Output (Rp billion)	No. of Firms	No. of Workers	Total Output (Rp billion)	No. of Firms	No. of Workers	Output (Rp billion)
Food	4,839	542,066	2,411.19	5,201	666,920	4,801.95	5,180	790,039	12,491.64
Textile	3,526	427,708	1,053.32	4,082	714,253	3,391.95	4,747	1,342,008	13,174.78
Wood	1,426	218,270	542.61	2,253	397,482	2,746.98	2,669	563,400	5,413.90
Paper	687	59,193	223.47	787	89,039	885.34	894	141,584	2,862.33
Chemical	1,749	236,560	1,076.65	213	342,760	3,017.94	2,400	474,622	8,048.62
Non-metallic	1,411	86,381	313.80	1,501	121,178	670.86	1,721	167,710	2,403.37
Basic metal	78	21,708	404.46	112	32,034	1,852.12	162	49,995	4,328.22
Metallic product	1,326	178,443	859.76	1,771	251,679	3,086.63	2,226	467,287	12,561.08
Other	158	11,577	18.98	280	24,703	280.93	412	79,680	457.40
LMI total:	15,200	1,781,906	6,904.24	16,200	2,640,048	20,734.70	20,411	4,076,325	61,741.34
Total mfg:		5,573,000	13,113.00		7,335,000	30,323.00		10,824,000	90,207.00
LMI share:		32.0%	52.65%		36.0%	68.38%		37.7%	68.44%

Source: Central Bureau of Statistics (1996).

12 Statistics for the number of household and small scale establishments are not published regularly as they are for LMIs. Figures for total manufacturing employment for 1994 are obtained from official figures while those for 1984 and 1989 are extrapolated from growth trend figures in surrounding years where official employment figures were found.

TABLE 4–6
Employment in Indonesia
(Based on 1994 GDP and Employment Data)

	Employment (millions of workers)	Share of Employment (%)	GDP Contribution (%)
Agriculture	38.94	45.6	16.7
Manufacturing	11.27	13.2	23.3
Trade, hotel and restaurant	14.60	17.1	16.7
Mining	9.22	10.8	8.7
Others	11.36	13.3	34.5

Source: INDIO (1996a).

TABLE 4–7
Average Hourly Manufacturing Wages: 1995

Selected Countries	(US$/hr)	Selected Countries	(US$/hr)
Japan	20.26	Hong Kong	4.66
Europe	16.88	Malaysia	1.30
U.S.	13.44	Thailand	1.10
Korea	6.17	Philippines	0.80
Singapore	6.07	China	0.35
Taiwan	5.39	Indonesia	0.33

Source: United Nations (1996a).

TABLE 4–8
Monthly Wage Rates by Skill Level: 1995

Classification	US$/Month After Tax
Unskilled labour	60–80
Skilled labour	100–200
Factory supervisor	200–400
Factory manager	1000–2500
Clerk and typist	150–250
Senior English speaking secretary, senior acountant, marketing manager, personnel manager	400–600
Production manager	600–1500
Financial controller	1200–2500

Source: Investment Coordinating Board (BKPM) (1996).

Table 4–9 provides a comparison of adult literacy, education indices and the percentage of cohort enrolment in secondary schools for selected Asian countries. The low enrolment rate in Indonesian secondary schools is of concern since it adversely affects labour productivity. More resources are needed in education to prepare the populace to meet the challenges of transforming the country into the manufacturing age as stipulated in *Repelita VIII* to *IX*. The number of students taking the nation-wide test for entry into the 43 state universities declined 8% in 1996. More students are opting for shorter courses that provide practical workplace skills. Even so, competition for university entry remains tough with about 379,000 students vying for a 70,000 enrolment cap.

TABLE 4–9
Literacy and Education Indicators: 1992

	Adult Literacy Rate (%)	Education Index	Percentage Enrolled in Secondary Education
China	79.3	0.71	51
India	49.9	0.52	44
Indonesia	**82.5**	**0.75**	**38**
Malaysia	81.5	0.74	58
Philippines	94.0	0.88	74
Singapore	99.0	0.93	90
South Korea	97.4	0.91	90
Thailand	93.5	0.81	33

Sources: United Nations (1996b); Business Monitor International Ltd. (1996).

Due to the shortage of human resource skills at middle and senior management levels, the number of expatriates occupying senior positions within Indonesian firms continues to rise (see Table 4–10). Foreign firms in Indonesia have difficulties in obtaining employment passes for expatriates and this translates into difficulties at the operational level. This shortage thwarts attempts to switch to higher value added manufacturing industries and processes.

The All Indonesia Labour Federation (SPSI) established in 1973 is the umbrella trade union representing 21 different industrial sectors. Membership in unions is not compulsory and labour strikes are not prohibited. Strikes have taken place in protest against companies not complying with minimum wages set for various districts or because of extremely poor working conditions. However, there have been few strikes demanding higher wages due to high unemployment.

TABLE 4–10
Issuance of Work Permits for Expatriates

Industry	1994/95		1995/96		Increase
	Number	%	Number	%	%
Mining	6,166	24.3	6,348	23.6	3.0
Processing industries	4,563	18.0	5,019	18.6	10.0
All others	14,680	57.8	15,579	57.8	6.1
Total	**25,409**	**100.0**	**26,946**	**100.0**	**6.0**

Source: Economist Intelligence Unit (1996c).

SOURCES OF MANUFACTURING INVESTMENT

In the past, Indonesia relied more on domestic investment than foreign investment because of the orientation and development of the manufacturing industry. Recently, there has been a shift towards exports which has meant opening up the economy to foreign investment (Halverson, 1996). The majority of foreign direct investment (FDI) initially went to the oil and gas sector and it was difficult to attract large investments into manufacturing. The turning point was 1994 when Indonesia hosted the APEC Summit which ended with strong affirmations for economic co-operation and speeding up tariff reductions. FDI commitments in 1994 reached US$23.4 billion, with a further record-breaking US$39.9 billion in 1995. Out of the latter, US$26.9 billion was committed to manufacturing. Earlier FDI commitments from 1980 to 1993 were low compared to those for China, Mexico and the Asian Newly Industrialised Countries (NICs) (*The Economist*, 26 October 1996).

Investment commitments in 1996 were lower than in 1995. It is widely held that the recent and somewhat controversial Timor Putra national car project may have an adverse effect on FDI. The rationale for the national car project was to ensure indigenous car production capabilities, independence and freedom to export vehicles. The project sent shock waves through the automotive industry and observers claim that it is a reversal of the spirit of the 1994 APEC agreements.[13] The U.S., European Union and Japan have lodged protests at the WTO. The Japanese auto-makers were the most severely affected despite being the earliest investors.

Doubts have surfaced about how much of the investment commitments made in 1994 and 1995 will be realised (Golub, 1996). The Capital Investment Coordinating Board (1996) calculates the ratio of realised to approved investment by comparing projects implemented by a given date with the volume and value of approvals for the previous two years. On this basis, 74% of the domestic projects approved in 1994 and 1995, and 44.6% of their investment value had been realised by June 1996. For foreign investments, 71.3% of the approved projects had been realised for an investment value equal to 55.2% of the cumulative approved value.

Lower than expected 1996 figures for imported capital goods and machinery may point to lower realisation rates for the 1994–1995 investment approvals (P. T. Sassoon Securities, 1996). Some large projects were cancelled, such as a planned investment by Ford and GM decided to locate a large scale plant in Thailand rather than in Indonesia.[14] Observers cited increasing social unrest due to rising income inequalities as additional factors that may affect project proposals.[15]

Currently, the largest foreign investors are Japan, U.K., Hong Kong, Singapore and the U.S. while the major investors in manufacturing are Japan, Taiwan and South Korea. South Korean manufacturers were latecomers but they are now making strong headway with about 500 companies in Indonesia (an increase of 100% over the past five years) employing 300,000 workers. Along with Taiwanese companies, the South Koreans have a stake in almost all of Indonesia's large textile and shoe companies and they are now targeting the growing electronics industry currently dominated by the Japanese. Lucky Goldstar is leading this challenge with plans to invest US$1 billion

---

[13] Indonesia may be thinking that under the two-track process, it has until the year 2020 to remove all tariff barriers and this is sufficient time to establish a national car project.

[14] This was announced by GM during the opening ceremony of their new plant in Thailand in September 1996.

[15] Government Ministers such as Ginandjar Kartasasmita, Chairman of the National Development Planning Board, have openly stated that corruption is out of control and must be dealt as the root cause of social inequalities (*Jakarta Post*, 30 October 1996).

by the year 2000 (*The Asian Wall Street Journal*, 1996c). Table 4–11 shows the number of projects and the value of approved foreign direct and domestic investments in the manufacturing sector from 1991 to 1995 while Table 4–12 shows the rankings of the ten leading countries in FDI.

TABLE 4–11
Approved Manufacturing Investments: 1991 to 1995

	FDI		Domestic Investment		Total Investment	
Year	No. of Projects	US$ billion	No. of Projects	US$ billion	No. of Projects	US$ billion
1991	277	3.97	476	13.87	753	17.84
1992	190	5.67	232	9.25	422	14.92
1993	182	3.42	282	11.39	464	14.81
1994	293	18.74	405	14.51	698	33.25
1995	410	26.89	312	18.78	722	45.67

Source: Investment Coordinating Board (1996).

TABLE 4–12
Total FDI by Country
(January 1967 to June 1996)

Ranking	Country	No. of Projects	Investment Value (US$ m)
1	Japan	986	31,846.9
2	U.K.	264	27,444.8
3	H.K.	447	18,239.1
4	Singapore	675	13,186.7
5	U.S.	290	12,258.2
6	Netherlands	177	10,380.1
7	Taiwan	525	9,094.2
8	South Korea	421	7,065.9
9	Australia	259	6,119.1
10	Germany	110	5,083.4

Source: Investment Coordinating Board (1996).

Research on Indonesia has shown that for developing countries with a large pool of low-skilled labour, the transfer of investments and technology from intermediate or less developed countries (LDC) such as Taiwan and South Korea, could be more effective than from advanced industrialised countries (Halverson, 1996). It was found that companies from LDCs tend to transfer technology which places greater reliance on labour, these conforming better to the host country's needs. The companies from developed countries are more attuned to state-of-the-art automated technologies which reduces the involvement of labour. This could pose problems for car manufacturers which plan to enter Indonesia if they do not factor in the need to adapt manufacturing processes to the local situation. However, second generation technologies from Asian producers could be both easier to implement and absorb.[16]

Sectors Closed to Investments

A Presidential decree in 1995 categorised four lists of sectors closed to investment.[17] The first two lists contain activities closed in whole or in part to foreign investors. The next two lists are activities closed generally, or absolutely, to all investments. In addition to these lists, there is an appendix listing sectors that are reserved for small scale industries which may co-operate with LMIs. The trend, however, has been for these lists to get shorter, and further liberalisation and deregulation may follow as the country develops (Economist Intelligence Unit, 1996c).[18]

LOCATION OF MANUFACTURING ZONES

The major manufacturing investments are centred in the western region of Indonesia with West Java, Jakarta and East Java accounting for 60%. This concentration is natural since foreign manufacturers tend to cluster together. Labour tends to move to where there are jobs and manufacturing activities tend to be located where there are workers. Thus, the western regions have become very densely populated.

The government has tried to balance this concentration by offer-

---

16 Site visits by the authors to Japanese Automotive JV factories indicated that the Japanese are sensitive to this issue and have been able to transfer a mix of other technologies and some automation of carefully selected processes such as aluminium die casting.

17 *Decree of the President of the Republic of Indonesia Number 31* of 1995.

18 At times there are reversals such as the May 1995 Deregulation Package when eight sectors were added back to the negative investment list.

ing additional incentives for investments in the eastern and outlying areas but investments continue to concentrate in the west. The eastern regions remain largely dependent on natural resource-based activities such as agriculture, forestry, fisheries and mining. These locations are also the poorer regions in terms of health care, education and wage levels.[19] Table 4–13 shows cumulative foreign investment approvals in the major regions as of 31 March 1995.

The government is trying to encourage migration through developing export processing zones further away from Java, and especially form Jakarta. The success of Batam shows that the government's efforts are not in vain.

INFRASTRUCTURE SUPPORTING MANUFACTURING

The majority of manufacturing activities are located in Jakarta, and east and West Java and traffic congestion is a major problem, especially in Jakarta.[20] Surfaced streets account for only 4% to 5% of Jakarta. It has insufficient road space to accommodate the growing number of vehicles which, in turn, are testimony to the local automotive manufacturing success.

Jakarta's government has articulated an ambitious project which includes the towns of Bogor to the south, Tangerang to the west and Bekasi to the east, to form Jabotabek (an acronym). The megapolis comprises more than 7,500 square kilometres and will help to alleviate space problems. In conjunction with this project, major industries have been encouraged to relocate outside Jakarta. The areas vacated in the process, such as the industrialised Sunter area not far from the city, will be developed for residential use (Business Monitor International, 1996).

Indonesia has 350,000 kilometres of roads and 35% are classified as in good condition, 30% in moderate condition and the balance needs repair. There is continuous construction of new roads and toll

---

[19] For a further treatise on the east–west divide, see "Indonesia Assessment 1995 – Development in Eastern Indonesia" published jointly by the Institute of Southeast Asian Studies and the Australian National University.

[20] As per official figures, the population of Jakarta is 8 million. Unofficial estimates put this figure at 10 to 12 million during the day (INDIO, 1996a).

TABLE 4–13
Cumulative FDI Approvals by Location: March 1995

Location East	Investment Value (US$m)	Percentage	Location West	Investment Value (US$m)	Percentage
West Nusa Tenggara	81.9	0.1	West Java	28,653.1	27.1
East Nusa Tenggara	19.1	0.0	Jakarta Capital Territory	17,511.0	16.6
South Kalimantan	2,800.7	2.6	East Java	16,917.6	16.0
East Kalimantan	2,514.5	2.4	Central Java	4,304.1	4.1
Central Kalimantan	267.8	0.3	North Sumatra	4,755.0	4.5
West Kalimantan	122.6	0.1	West Sumatra	340.4	0.3
Irian Jaya	3,955.7	3.7	South Sumatra	1,449.7	1.4
Central Sulawesi	840.4	0.8	Bali	2,478.4	2.3
North Sulawesi	432.6	0.4	Yogyakarta	115.7	0.1
South Sulawesi	2,758.3	2.6	Riau	9,434.7	8.9
Southeast Sulawesi	75.3	0.1	Aceh	4,579.1	4.3
Maluku	116.6	0.1	Jambi	39.6	0.0
East Timur	0.0	0.0	Bengkulu	93.3	0.1
			Lampung	1,101.2	1.0
Total	**13,985.5**	**13.2**	**Total**	**91,772.9**	**86.8**
Grand total				**105,758.4**	**100.0**

Source: Adapted from ISEAS (1996).

highways which are privatised[21] and the older highways have been improved. Priority has been given to Java, Bali and Sumatra, and major towns are connected to good main roads or secondary roads that are linked to Jakarta.

A 14.5-kilometre subway project has been proposed in Jakarta, starting from Block M in downtown south Jakarta to Kota in west Jakarta. This line will be extended later with another two 40-kilometre lines. Bambang Trihatmodjo, one of the President's sons, is masterminding the project with a consortium of Japanese and European investors. An overland light railway system connecting a number of suburbs in south Jakarta is scheduled for completion in 1998.

There is a shortage of telephone lines because of the large population. Obtaining a telephone may take a year and it is also expensive.[22] Investments are being enhanced to improve telecommunications. The advent of cellular telephone helps to ameliorate some of these difficulties but, because of the cost, only a small minority can afford this alternative. It is projected that 20 million lines will be needed by the year 2005 to achieve the target of ten phones per 100 persons. Joint public-private consortia have been formed to expand the network given the large investment required (Business Monitor International, 1996).

By the year 2004, Indonesia plans to have a power-generating capacity of 39,000 megawatts which will require an investment of about US$60 billion. Due to state budget limitations, the private sector is involved and 12 power plants have been approved for the first phase of power plant development estimated at US$8.9 billion. Eight additional projects involving foreign funding have been proposed. In the meantime, many larger manufacturers have installed factory power generators as well as voltage stabilisers to reduce the risks from brown-outs and voltage fluctuations.

Finally, the quality of tap water in Jakarta and most parts of the country is poor. It is not drinkable and most residents drink spring mineral water supplied in bottles. The water quality is a problem for certain electronics manufacturing processes that require high purity

---

[21] There are complaints about high toll fees, and the fact that the concessionaire is Citra Marga Nusaphala Persada, a company controlled by Siti Hardiyanti Rukmana, the President's eldest daughter.

[22] Although the official rate is around Rp 900,000 per line at business sites and Rp 700,000 for home connections, waiting times are very long, sometimes six months to several years. Thus, landlords of buildings with ready lines often charge a deposit of US$1,500 per line.

water. Tables 4–14 and 4–15 summarise the state of Indonesia's infrastructure and related government expenditures.

TABLE 4–14
Indonesia's Infrastructure: Key Facts as of 1995

Roads	350,000 kilometres of roadways of which 200,000 are paved. There were 475 kilometres of tollroads operating in November 1995.
Rail	Approximately 6,900 kilometres of track with 13,000 passenger kilometres and 15 million tonnes of cargo rail traffic annually.
Power	Total 1995 capacity is estimated at 13,500 megawatts, generated by the state-owned electricity company Perusahaan Listrik Negara.
Telephones	2.76 metres telephone lines in June 1995 (1.5 lines per 100 people).
Seaports	349 ports for ocean-going and inter-island shipping, the largest of which is Tanjung Priok in Jakarta, currently being expanded to handle up to 2.5 million TEU container per annum by 2000.
Airports	140 airports, of which 49 have regular flight services. International airports include Jakarta, Bali and Medan. The total service network encompasses 240 routes covering the provinces throughout the archipelago and several countries.

Source: Economist Intelligence Unit (1996c).

The government has set aside land resources for establishing industrial estates, free-trade zones and bonded warehouses to accommodate manufacturing operations and foreign investments (*The Asian Wall Street Journal*, 12 August 1996d). Three export processing zones (EPZs) have been established in the Jakarta area in addition to Batam,[23] and more are in the pipeline.

A reform package announced in June 1996 has simplified licensing procedures for firms operating within industrial estates so that no additional permits will be required once an investment permit has been granted by the Investment Coordinating Board.[24] With the completion of expansion projects in successful industrial estates (such as those in Karawang, which will contribute almost 50% of the new

[23] A free trade zone established in co-operation with Singapore to develop the Singapore–Johor–Batam growth triangle.

[24] Typically, as many as 20 permits are required to be fully operational.

TABLE 4–15
Central Government Expenditure on Infrastructure

	Budget (Rp billion)	1994/95 %	Outrun (Rp billion)	1994/95 %	Budget (Rp billion)	1995/96 %	Budget (Rp billion)	1996/97 %
Infrastructure:	**9,774**	**35.67**	**11,910**	**40.84**	**12,671**	**41.16**	**14,039**	**40.69**
Energy	3,154	11.51	3,806	13.05	3,800	12.34	3,996	11.57
Transportation	4,260	15.55	5,583	19.14	5,864	19.06	6,735	19.51
Post and telecommunications	673	2.46	775	2.66	965	3.13	991	2.90
Water resources	1,687	6.15	1,746	5.99	2,042	6.63	2,317	6.71
Human resources:	**4,446**	**16.23**	**4,276**	**14.49**	**4,789**	**15.57**	**5,736**	**16.62**
Manpower, education and training	3,125	11.40	2,943	10.00	3,437	11.16	4,043	11.72
Population planning	290	1.07	273	0.95	300	1.00	328	0.94
Social welfare and health	1,031	3.76	1,060	3.54	1,052	3.41	1,365	3.96
Regional development	**4,458**	**16.27**	**5,676**	**19.14**	**5,114**	**16.61**	**5,388**	**15.62**
Others	**8,720**	**31.83**	**7,301**	**25.03**	**8,209**	**26.66**	**9,340**	**27.07**
Total expenditure	**27,398**	**100.00**	**29,163**	**100.00**	**30,783**	**100.00**	**34,503**	**100.00**

Sources: State budget documents and *Repelita VI*; Economist Intelligence Unit (1996c).

supply in 1997 and 1998), the net take-up of land is expected to increase and put upward pressure on prices.

The concept of techno-parks has been introduced and the first one, Bumi Serpong Damai in Tangerang, was completed in December 1996. Industrial land prices as at June 1996 were US$37.50 to US$45.00 per square metre (psm) in Tangerang and Serang; US$45.00 to US$55.00 psm in Karawang; US$65.00 to US$85.00 psm in Bekasi and US$150.00 to US$160.00 psm in Jakarta. A list of industrial estates under development is given in Table 4–16. Standard factory buildings are also available at industrial sites such as the one at Pulo Gadung in Jakarta. Sizes range from small (600 sqm), medium (960 sqm) and large (1,800 sqm) at monthly rentals ranging from Rp 4,500 to 7,500 per square metre, excluding VAT.

TABLE 4–16
Industrial Estates Under Development

Project	Status	Location
Delta Silicon Industrial Park (Lippo Cikarang)	Expansion	Bekasi
MM2100	Expansion	Bekasi
Karawang International Industrial City	Expansion	Karawang
Mitra Karawang Industrial Estate	Expansion	Karawang
Suryacipta City of Industry	Expansion	Karawang
Modern Cikanda Industrial Estate	Expansion	Serang
BSD Techno Park 1	New	Tangerang

Source: Economist Intelligence Unit (1996c).

GOVERNMENT TAXES AND SUPPORT INCENTIVES

Corporate income tax in Indonesia is fixed at 30% except that the first Rp 25 million is taxed at 10% and the next Rp 25 million is taxed at 15%, excluding manufacturing companies operating in one of the EPZs. Taxes are paid monthly based on monthly returns that companies are required to submit to the Revenue authorities. The government intends to change the tax regime to improve the overall business environment. Under a new regulation (No. 45/1996 issued on 8 July 1996), certain newly-established resident companies are eligible for tax incentives. Industries qualifying will be determined by the President based on proposals prepared by the various ministries. These incentives will be for a maximum of ten years. Projects outside of Java and Bali may have the incentives extended by a further two years.

In a January 1996 deregulation package, import tariffs on machinery intended for industrial restructuring were eliminated together with reductions on 428 other items. In July 1996, an agreement supplementary to the U.S.–Indonesia Income Tax Treaty was signed which eliminates withholding taxes previously levied at 15%, on interest, branch profits of permanent establishments and royalties. A similar agreement with Singapore reduces withholding taxes from 15% to 10%. Article 23 related to mining reduces withholding taxes on support services and rents, and other income to 4.5% and 6%, respectively. Other reductions and simplifications have also been made to taxes on investment funds and interest, VAT on import and shipping services, and local tax on expatriates.

Investors hope that this trend will continue with further tax rationalisation harmonised in tandem with the simplification of bureaucracy and the deregulation of closed sectors. For example, despite the removal of import taxes on machinery, machine tools and measuring equipment are still more expensive in Indonesia which indicates inefficient distribution. Distribution is classified as retail trade and, thus, closed to foreign investments although local distributors are lagging behind in technical competence. Opening up highly technical distribution areas to foreign specialists should perhaps be considered to boost Indonesia's advance into higher technology-based manufacturing. This will create an open machine tool market to supply the latest technologies at competitive prices and allow the rapid development of supporting industries.

CONCLUSION

The manufacturing sector in Indonesia has been developing faster than all the other sectors of the Indonesian economy. This is in accordance with the government's target of making manufacturing the prime mover of the country's future economic growth.

Manufacturing firms appear to have adjusted to the Indonesian business environment but many of them desire greater transparency, more deregulation, and better coordinated and more consistent policies. Indonesia is facing increasingly intense global competition and there is an urgency of removing self-imposed road blocks to domestic competitiveness. However, manufacturing offers opportunities to alleviate some of these uncertainties by providing better paying and more satisfying jobs. The urgency to shift the present economic structure towards a more open and competitive one is greater than ever before. Government authorities have recognised these concerns and agree that more transparency is required. In his welcome speech to the BSM group, His Excellency, Minister Hartarto,[25] remarked that for further growth to take place Indonesia must continue to debureaucratise and attract more foreign investments, reduce social inequalities by creating more employment to redistribute wealth, and reduce the "east–west" divide by encouraging more investments and development in the eastern regions. Manufacturing is vital to these objectives and it must rank as a prime sector for welcoming FDI and receiving the support of government.

REFERENCES

Alatas Ali, "Indonesia's Path Toward World Prominence through Economic and Social Harmony", *Asia Pacific Economic Review*, Vol. 2, No. 4, 1995.

Borsuk Richard, "In Jakarta: Cement Stocks Are Solid Bets, Analyst Say", *The Asian Wall Street Journal*, 30 June 1995, p. 15.

Business Monitor International, *Indonesia 1996–1998*, London, 1996.

Business Review Southeast Asia, "Southeast Asia Business Omnibus", 1995, pp. 95–156.

Central Bureau of Statistics, *Indonesia Economic Indicators*, Jakarta, June 1996.

Clifford Mark, "Promises, Promises: Indonesia's Habibie Draws Increasing Fire", *Far Eastern Economic Review*, 29 July 1993, p. 58.

Dow Jones International News, "Focus/Indonesia/Cement/Gresik-2: Undersupply Importance", 27 December 1995.

Dow Jones International News, "Emerging Markets Report – Indonesia Cement Sector as a Whole Said Looking Good", 29 June 1995.

Economic & Business Review Indonesia, "The Astra Saga: Is It a Takeover?", 6 November 1996.

[25] Indonesia's Coordinating Minister for Production and Distribution.

Economic & Business Review Indonesia, "Tale of Two Brothers: Building a National Car", 12 June 1996.

Economist Intelligence Unit, *Indonesia: Country Profile 1995–1996*, U.K., 1996a.

Economist Intelligence Unit, *Indonesia Forecast*, U.K., 3rd Quarter, 1996b.

Economist Intelligence Unit, *Business Report: Indonesia*, U.K., 3rd Quarter, 1996c.

Far Eastern Economic Review, "Report on Indonesia", 16 May 1996, p. 45.

Golup Philip, "Foreign Direct Investment Outstrips Trade", *Asia Times*, 26 September 1996.

Halverson Karen, "Foreign Direct Investment in Indonesia: A Comparison of Industrialised and Developing Country Investors", *Law and Policy International Business*, Vol. 22, 1996, pp. 75–105.

Hamlin Kevin, "Indonesia Car Monopoly Threat to Other ASEAN Manufacturers", *Asia Times*, 8 May 1996.

INDIO, *Indonesia: Source Book*, Jakarta, 1996a.

INDIO, *Indonesia: Facts*, Jakarta, July 1996b.

INDIO, *Sustaining Economic Growth With Macroeconomic Stability*, Jakarta, February 1996c.

Investment Coordinating Board (BKPM), *A Brief Guide for Investment*, Ministry of Investment, Jakarta, February 1996.

ISEAS, *Indonesia Assessment 1995 – Development in Eastern Indonesia*, Institute of Southeast Asian Studies and the Australian National University, Singapore, 1996.

Jakarta Post, Editorial, 30 October 1996.

MacBeth John and Emily Thornton, "Power Steering: Jakarta's National Car Angers Auto Makers Again", *Far Eastern Economic Review*, 20 July 1996, p. 60.

P. T. Ekamasni Consultants (Business Information Division), "Indonesian Business Trend", TBI/EMC No. 36, 20 August 1996, pp. 18–20.

P. T. Sasson Securities, *Indonesia Economic Focus*, Jakarta, 11 October 1996.

Rahul Jacob, "Like Father Like Son: Indonesia's Proposed National Car Has Plenty of International Critics – And a Familiar Face at the Helm", *Time International*, 6 October 1996, p. 40.

Shari Michael, Edith Hill, Catherine Lee and Keith Naughton, "A Furious Flap over Favouritism", *Business Times*, 7 August 1996, p. 14.

Solomon J. and John MacBeth, "A Whole New Astra: But Many Wonder What the New Owners Are Up To?", *Far Eastern Economic Review*, 21 November 1996, p. 70.

Soetjipto H., W. A. Karamoy and M. S. Wuryani, *Indonesia 1995: An Official Handbook*, Department of Information, Directorate of Foreign Information Services, Perum Percetakan Negara, Indonesia, 1996.

The Asian Wall Street Journal, "Indonesia", 12 August 1996.

The Asian Wall Street Journal, "Sony Knows the Tricks of the Trade", 12 August 1996a, p. 15.

The Asian Wall Street Journal, "Electronics Industry Needs Components to Stay Competitive", 12 August 1996b, p. 15.

The Asian Wall Street Journal, "Diversification and Deregulation Draw Massive Investments to Fuel Growth", 12 August 1996c.

The Asian Wall Street Journal, "Infrastructure Offers Opportunities", 12 August 1996d.

The Business Times, "Top Astra Shareholders Say No Management Changes Likely", 28 November 1996.

The Economist, "UNCTAD Report", 26 October 1996, p. 152.

The Straits Times, "Indonesia Looks East", 10 November 1996.

United Nations, *Statistical Yearbook for Asia and the Pacific*, New York, October 1996a.

United Nations, "International Marketing Data and Statistics", *U.N. World Population Prospects*, (20th edition), New York, 1996b.

Chapter 5

Indonesia: The Rewards of Liberalisation

BY
Ashish LALL

INTRODUCTION

REAL GDP GROWTH in Indonesia averaged 6.5% per annum over the period 1980 to 1996.[1] Over the same period, inflation declined consistently as did real interest rates. Foreign exchange reserves, on the other hand, increased four-fold over the period 1979 to 1996. Economic growth over the last quarter of a century has been partly attributed to structural change in both the domestic and export sectors. The contribution of the manufacturing sector to GDP now stands at about one-quarter.[2]

The diversification of the domestic economy and the reduced reliance on primary and resource-based industries are also reflected in the trade sector. Thirty years ago, non-oil exports accounted for about 20% of the total value of exports. Today, their share is over 90%. Manufactured goods now account for between 75% and 80% of non-oil exports. Thus, the overall shift from agriculture to manufacturing is also mirrored in the export sector. Though the value of imports of consumer goods increased by 70% in 1995 and 35% in 1996, this merely reflects rising per

[1] All macroeconomic data including forecasts for 1997 are based on Nomura Singapore Ltd., 20 December 1996.

[2] See Table 4–1 in Chapter 4.

capita incomes. Capital goods, raw materials and auxiliary goods continue to account for over 90% of the value of imports.

Forecasts of major economic indicators suggest that real GDP growth in 1997 will be 7.8%, or 30 basis points higher than in 1996. Inflation in 1997 is expected to be 7%, which is one percentage point lower than in 1996.[3] Though the current account deficit is expected to increase to US$9.8 billion in 1997, foreign direct investment is expected to be higher by US$2 billion. Since this is twice the anticipated increase in the current account deficit, financing the deficit does not appear to pose a problem.[4] This is consistent with past trends which show a widening current account deficit, but increasing foreign exchange reserves. As a result, Indonesia's ability to pay for its imports has only been affected marginally.[5]

The two areas of concern continue to be the widening resource gap and the increasing foreign debt.[6] Insofar as the former is concerned, while the ratio of savings to GDP has remained at approximately 25% over the last ten years, gross fixed capital formation as a percentage of GDP has increased consistently since 1993 and is forecast to be 29.8% in 1997. The 1997 forecast for external debt is US$100 billion which represents a five-fold increase over the 1980 figure. While Indonesia's ability to service the external debt has deteriorated somewhat since 1994, the bigger picture suggests a substantial improvement over the past ten years. Maintaining fiscal prudence and keeping the current account deficit in check will prevent this from becoming a problem in the future.

Chapters 2 through 4 discuss various aspects of the Indonesian economy. While Chapter 2 is devoted to trade policy issues, Chapters

---

3 This is the annual change in consumer prices rather than in the implicit GDP deflator.

4 Chapter 2 indicates that although the government has allowed the Indonesian rupiah to depreciate at a rate of 5% per annum against the US dollar, the real effective exchange rate has increased over the years. The worsening terms of trade could be responsible for the declining surplus on the merchandise trade account.

5 Indonesia is expected to have sufficient foreign exchange reserves to finance 4.2 months of merchandise imports in 1997. This figure has fluctuated only marginally during the 1990s.

6 A third area of concern, and much speculation, is the possible increase in political risk over the next couple of years. Nomura is of the opinion that this is not a source of concern. See Nomura Singapore Ltd., 18 October 1996.

3 and 4 concentrate on domestic issues. Chapter 3 examines the domestic policy environment while Chapter 4 provides an extensive discussion of what has become the most important sector in the economy – the manufacturing sector.

THE MANUFACTURING SECTOR

The process of economic development involves a decline in the contribution of primary sectors to total output and an increase in that of the secondary and tertiary sectors. The shift in output is accompanied by shifts in employment due to increases in productivity in the agricultural sector. Though the share of the agricultural sector in total output has declined, the decline in employment in agriculture has been less pronounced. In 1995, the share of the manufacturing sector in total GDP was 24% while that of agriculture was 16%.[7] About 14% of the workforce was employed by manufacturing and 45% by the agricultural sector, indicating that labour productivity continues to be low in the latter.

In 1995, the food, beverage and tobacco industries accounted for 40% of manufacturing output. Transport equipment, fertilizers and chemicals, and petroleum and gas manufacturing each accounted for about 11% to 12% of manufacturing output. These four sectors are largely geared towards serving the domestic economy. Textiles, on the other hand, accounted for 8% of manufacturing output but 20% of the value of manufactured exports.[8] This industry has also seen the highest growth in employment over the period from 1984 to 1994. In part, this can be attributed to the relocation of labour intensive industries from neighbouring countries to Indonesia, since workers in this industry are primarily women who are paid the minimum wage. In 1995, the average hourly wage in the manufacturing sector in Indonesia was US$0.33 compared with US$1.10 in Thailand and US$1.30 in Malaysia.

Until recently, Indonesia followed a strict import substitution strategy, prohibiting exports of items such as raw timber and cement, and imports of finished products such as automobiles. At present, all imported cars still have to be completely knocked-down units, which

---

7 Data referred to in this section are from Chapter 4.

8 The wood products industry is similar. It accounted for 6.2% of manufacturing output and for 17% of the value of manufactured exports in 1995.

are then assembled locally. Cars are also subject to a variety of taxes such as a value-added tax, sales tax, luxury tax and a 100% import duty, which may be waived if certain local content requirements are met. Indonesia's policy toward the automobile sector is controversial for two reasons. Firstly, local content requirements violate the agreement on trade-related investment measures (TRIMS) and, secondly, the national car project provides tax exemptions only to P. T. Timor Putra Nasional and not to other producers.[9]

While the government seeks to promote small scale enterprises, many industries in the manufacturing sector are highly concentrated. Three large firms, one of which owes its position to government concessions, dominate the largest industry which is food and beverages. In fact, the share of large and medium enterprises (LMEs) in total manufacturing output has been increasing over the years. In 1994, LMEs accounted for 68% of the output and 38% of the employment in manufacturing.

As of late, there has been a shift in the domestic policy environment towards more private sector involvement, both domestic and foreign, export orientation and deregulation. For example, the government allows 100% foreign ownership of electronic companies, and is providing tax incentives and setting up special bonded zones to promote exports. Foreign direct investment has increased substantially in the last few years and stood at about US$40 billion in 1995. Approximately US$27 billion of the total inflow was invested in manufacturing.[10] The private sector is also involved in the construction of new infrastructure facilities, since agglomeration effects have led most investment to be located in western Indonesia. The high population density in this region combined with the increased economic activity is straining existing infrastructure. The liberalisation of the domestic economy is discussed further in the following section. This policy shift is timely and is in the spirit of the recent multilateral agreements that seek to improve market access.

---

9 Even though eventually the Timor will be manufactured in Indonesia, for the time being, the government is allowing luxury and import tax exempt imports from Timor's joint venture partner – Kia of South Korea. Since most joint ventures in this sector are with major Japanese producers, Japan is most concerned about this policy.

10 Japan, South Korea and Taiwan are the major investors in the manufacturing sector.

PRIVATISATION AND DEREGULATION

The economic rationale for the public provision of goods and services is typically based on arguments that allude to market failure. Thus, the government usually provides public goods such as national defence. In addition, the divergence between private and social costs and benefits at the margin, justifies government funding for education, health care, and research and development activity. Moreover, natural monopoly characteristics and the existence of positive network externalities may warrant government ownership of telecommunications, postal services and electric utilities. In general, however, agency theory suggests that private firms are more efficient than state-owned firms. Privatisation, therefore, enhances productive efficiency.

Deregulation, on the other hand, promotes competition and contributes to both productive and allocative efficiency. In Indonesia, one of the aims of deregulation is to allow both the domestic and foreign private sector to assume a larger role in generating economic activity. Privatisation complements this initiative and also allows the government to reduce its mounting external debt. Efforts to deregulate the economy started more than a decade ago and, over the years, new measures have been introduced almost annually. Recently, the pace has picked up, with three initiatives being announced in 1996.

Many of the early initiatives over the period 1983 to 1988 were directed toward the financial sector. These included removing interest rate controls on state banks, issuing licences for new banks (including joint venture banks) and reducing restrictions on stock ownership by foreigners. These initiatives have resulted in increased competition in the financial sector. More recent measures seek to reduce investment impediments. They include reductions in corporate income tax rates, strengthening of intellectual property laws, deregulation of investment and capacity licensing, streamlining investment approval procedures, relaxing constraints on foreign ownership, particularly in export-oriented sectors, and allowing joint venture firms to distribute their own products domestically. In addition, the government has opened up sectors such as transportation, infrastructure, telecommunications and banking to foreign investors.

Both deregulation and privatisation have allowed Indonesia to move away from its traditional import substitution model of economic growth and brought it in harmony with the export-oriented approach that has brought considerable prosperity to some of its

ASEAN neighbours. The privatisation of Indosat in October 1994 was the first major success. It raised US$320 million on the Jakarta Stock Exchange and US$800 million on the New York market.[11] As of December 1996, the government had raised about US$3.1 billion through privatisation. By the turn of the century, it plans to further divest its interest in the state-owned electric utilities, airlines, oil and gas, and mining companies. Privatisation has boosted the market capitalization of the Jakarta Stock Exchange. In 1989, there were 53 listed firms with a market capitalization of US$9.6 billion. These figures increased to 250 and US$89 billion, respectively, in 1996. Deregulation has probably contributed to the recent surge in foreign direct investment. The government also reduced both tariff and non-tariff barriers which has improved market access. These are discussed next.

TRADE POLICY

Since the mid-1980s, deregulation initiatives have sought not only to liberalise the domestic economy but, also, to reduce tariff and non-tariff barriers. In 1989, the agricultural sector, in general, and food crops, in particular, were subject to a high degree of import licensing. In the manufacturing sector, food, beverages and tobacco, and engineering industries were subject to high non-tariff barriers. The effective rates of protection were 174% and 142%, respectively.[12] In May 1995, and January and June 1996, the government announced a tariff reduction schedule up to the year 2003. Tariffs greater than 20% at the time of announcement are to be reduced to 20% or less by 1998 and to 10% or less by the year 2003. Those tariffs that were at 20% or less at the time of the announcement are to be reduced to 5% or less by the year 2000. Some industries, such as the automobile industry, are not covered under this schedule and, in fact, tariffs on sedans, jeeps and minibuses may be approximately 60% by the year 2003. As was pointed out in Chapter 2, this schedule is more ambitious than Indonesia's commitments under the ASEAN free trade area common effective preferential tariff scheme.

---

[11] Data referred to in this section are from Chapter 3.

[12] Data referred to in this section are from Chapter 2.

Despite these positive steps, trade in agricultural commodities continues to be controlled by state agencies that have exclusive rights to import staples such as wheat, rice, corn and soybean. In the manufacturing sector, motor vehicles, aircraft and vessels production continue to be subject to non-tariff barriers. In the services sector, there are barriers to entry for foreign accounting firms and law firms.

CONCLUSION

The three chapters reviewed here suggest that there is a definite shift in Indonesia's economic policy. The government is committed to allowing greater opportunity to both the domestic and the foreign private sector. This has been accompanied by reductions in tariffs based on an announced schedule, and "tariffication" of non-tariff barriers. While there is some concern about Indonesia's large foreign debt and deteriorating current account balance, liberalisation of both the domestic and traded goods sector will, in the long run, help redress these problems.

REFERENCES

Nomura Singapore Ltd., *Indonesia: Will Political Risk Swamp Economic Success?* 18 October 1996.

Nomura Singapore Ltd., *Indonesia 1997 Outlook*, 20 December 1996.

BANKING AND FINANCIAL ISSUES

Chapter 6

Indonesian Banking: Marriage or Perish*

BY
LI Wei Jie
LIU Lei
TONG Wee Li

INTRODUCTION

THE BANKING SECTOR in Indonesia dominates the financial sector, accounting for about 90% of its assets. Despite a budding capital market, industry and commerce rely heavily on banks for their financial needs through loans or similar arrangements. Scandals in the Indonesian banking industry in the early 1990s shook the confidence of investors. However, in 1995, the banking industry had an outstanding performance with the 22 listed banks showing a profit growth of 32%. But the authorities decided to cool Indonesia's economic growth rate by limiting credit expansion. On top of this, the lending and deposit markets are becoming highly competitive which cuts into the lending margins of banks. The performance of the banking industry over a five-year period beginning in 1992 is shown in Table 6–1. It was envisaged that market pressures, coupled with increasing regulatory measures, would limit the profitability of Indonesian banks (*Bankwatch*, June 1996, p. 1).

Historically, reforms displaced market processes by placing increasingly more of the financial sector under government control. Re-

---

* We are grateful to Dr. John Vong for his comments and guidance.

form measures included a thorough restructuring of the banking system in accordance with the 1967 *Banking Act*. This was followed by 15 years of consolidation and development whereby the banking industry grew in size and sophistication. However, extensive and restrictive central bank controls were imposed during this period. A significant shift in this pattern of tightly supervised development occurred in the wake of the oil price cuts agreed to by the Organisation of Petroleum Exporting Countries (OPEC) in 1983. It was recognised that over-regulation of the banking system would restrain the mobilisation of domestically generated development funds which were needed because of reduced oil and gas revenues. To overcome this constraint, the financial sector has been subjected to liberalising reforms ever since 1 June 1983 when a number of special regulations governing dominant state-owned commercial banks were removed.

TABLE 6–1
Financial Profile of the Banking Industry in Indonesia

Performance Indicators	1992	1993	1994	1995 (estimate)	1996 (estimate)
Earning assets/total assets	92.0	92.0	93.0	94.0	93.0
Loans/earning assets	77.0	73.0	76.0	78.0	79.0
Loan growth	11.4	40.4	42.6	25.9	21.2
Deposit growth	22.4	37.2	33.0	25.2	20.6
Asset growth	24.9	39.5	31.4	26.5	18.6
Average CAR	9.0	9.0	9.2	8.9	9.7
ROAA	1.3	1.2	1.4	1.2	1.5

Source: Adapted from *Asia Money*, July/August 1996.

This chapter considers the characteristics of the Indonesian financial system, and the challenges and opportunities faced by Indonesian banks. The main objective is to inform potential investors about the competitiveness of the Indonesian banking industry and the need for mergers by some banks to compete effectively.

Financial Reforms

The process of financial liberalisation initiated in 1983 reached a climax in late 1988 with the introduction of a wide-ranging reform package on 27 October (see Appendix 6–1). The package, generally known by its Indonesian acronym *Pakto*, consisted of 47 different decrees and regulations. This package increased financial competitiveness by removing most of the entry barriers. New banks, and joint venture and domestic banks, could be set up with capital requirements of Rp 50 billion (US$21.08 million) and Rp 10 billion (US$4.22 million), respectively, and successful private banks were eligible for a foreign exchange licence.

Financial liberalisation changed the market structure and the competitive situation facing the banking sector. The number of commercial banks increased from 124 in 1988 to 240 as of March 1996. Table 6–2 shows the annual growth in the number of commercial banks by year from 1988 to 1996. Relaxing branch requirements and competition led to a dramatic increase in the number of bank offices. There was also a "mad scramble" for qualified human resources. The financial sector had entered into a state of intense flux during this period which triggered a dramatic and ongoing expansion in the number and variety of financial institutions and services.

CHARACTERISTICS OF THE INDONESIAN FINANCIAL SYSTEM

Prior to October 1988, Indonesia had a system of functional specialisation among the various financial institutions. These specialisations included the central bank, the commercial banks, development banks, saving banks, secondary banks, finance banks and other non-financial intermediaries. In 1992, the new banking law reclassified the institutions formerly belonging to the saving and development banks category to commercial banks. Before the change, the financial system was centred around the banks; state-owned banking institutions played a dominant role; the system favoured bank loans over equity finance; and the banks channelled loans to highly protected and well-connected big firms in preference to medium and small scale enterprises.

The core of the Indonesian financial sector is the banking system in terms of total assets. It consists of Bank Indonesia (BI) and 34 commercial banks, with 7 state-owned and 27 owned by provincial governments. Other financial institutions, such as leasing companies and insurance firms, are relatively small. The capital market is in the early developmental stage. The dominance of the banks is evident in

TABLE 6–2
Number of Commercial Banks

Year	State Banks	Private National Banks	Regional Development Banks	Foreign and Joint Venture Banks	Non-Bank Financial Institutions	Total Commercial Banks
1988	7	66	27	11	13	124
1989	7	90	27	21	13	158
1990	7	109	27	28	13	184
1991	7	129	27	29	13	205
1992	7	144	27	30	13	221
1993	7	161	27	39	0	234
1994	7	166	27	40	0	240
1995	7	165	27	41	0	240
March 1996	7	165	27	41	0	240

Source: Suhardiman (December 1996).

the heavy reliance on debt financing which makes the banks and debtors vulnerable to internal and external shocks. The rise in interest rates from the currency realignment in the late 1980s combined with slower growth in the early 1990s strained the cash flows of companies because of their debt leveraging. These two factors, in turn, impacted the liquidity of lending banks.

The financial reforms in 1988 addressed the unhealthy structure of the banking system and the concentration of lending. Increasing the range of activities undertaken by financial institutions and lowering barriers to market entry greatly improved competition. Big companies turned to the bond, equity and international financial markets for funds which forced banks to lend more to medium and small enterprises.

The World Bank Report on Indonesia in 1996 commented that "A healthy financial system is a prerequisite for a modern economy. Enforcement of the programmed increase in bank capital and the existing related group lending limits, along with support from the highest political level to collect overdue loans from state banks, would increase confidence in the financial system and reduce domestic interest rates" (*Economic & Business Review Indonesia*, 29 May 1996). The report points to the system's high risks as the major cause of high interest rates. Factors such as low capital, high group exposure and light penalties for breaking the rules increase the riskiness of lending. Lenders and depositors react to these factors by demanding higher rates of return which, in turn, translate into higher domestic interest rates.

As of March 1996, there were 240 commercial banks operating in Indonesia. They include the 7 state banks, 165 private commercial banks, 27 development banks, 31 joint venture (JV) banks and another 10 foreign banks (see Table 6–2). Bank Indonesia has various functions. It is the central bank and manages Indonesia's monetary policy and supervises all banks and financial services (Suhardiman, 1996).

Commercial Banks

(i) ***State-owned Commercial Banks***: Commercial banking is dominated by the seven state-owned banks established under separate banking acts. They traditionally have served as the primary source of development funds for economic development and, hence, are not profit-oriented. This feature rendered them inefficient in the past but with emerging privatisation they must adopt a commercial profile.

(ii) ***Private Commercial Banks***: For much of the past decade, Bank Indonesia has endeavoured to strengthen the financial position of private commercial banks through various measures including mergers. Several of the weaker privately held banks have been weeded out of the banking system through closure or the cancellation of licences. The *Pakto* reform package of October 1988, however, provided for granting operating licences to new commercial and development banks after an interval of several years. Since 1988, the number of commercial banks has doubled and assets have increased ten-fold. There were 165 private commercial banks in operation by March 1996, with many of them small but more efficient than the state-owned commercial banks. A significant number of these private commercial banks are owned by, or associated with, large business groups and are forced to extend credit beyond the regulatory limits. They do not have the government support that the state banks enjoy (*Bankwatch*, June 1996).

Development Banks

Development banks fall into three categories: the Development Bank of Indonesia (Bank Pembangunan Indonesia – BAPINDO); the regional development banks; and the private development bank (Bank Pembangunan Industri).

(i) ***Development Bank of Indonesia***: It is the sixth largest state-owned bank and was set up to promote internal development projects.

(ii) ***Regional Development Banks***: There were 27 regional development banks in operation at the end of March 1996. These are owned by local authorities, or jointly owned by local authorities and private parties. They offer medium-term loans for the acquisition of fixed assets or for working capital financed through BAPINDO.

(iii) ***Private Development Bank***: This is a small privately-owned development bank, established in 1962, which provides investment and development services. Until the mid-1980s, it had only one branch and had not started functioning as a long-term lender and investment promoter. Since then, it has expanded modestly.

By the end of March 1996, it had six branches and three of them were opened during that year.

Savings Banks

Savings banks in Indonesia have the word *Tabungan* in their names. By the middle of the 1980s, the number of savings banks were reduced to the state savings bank, Bank Tabungan Negara BTN, and a small privately-owned savings bank, P. T. Bank Tabungan Himpunan Saudara based in Bandung, West Java. During the 1986/87 fiscal year which ended on 31 March 1987, a second private savings bank, Bank Tabungan Pensiun Nasional was licensed. It is a pension saving bank with 27 branches. The operations of these two private banks are modest, however; and the savings bank sector is dominated by BTN which obtains the majority of its funds from government sponsored savings schemes. The majority of its loans are for middle and low income housing mortgages (*Bankwatch*, June 1996).

Other Banking Institutions

In addition to the major banks, Indonesia has a multitude of relatively small banking institutions organised to meet the needs of market retailers and farmers. These institutions comprise market or *pasar* banks, village or *desa* banks, *paddy* banks, employees' banks, co-operative banks and other similar banks which operate in the rural areas. Bank Rakyat Indonesia, which is under the direction of Bank Indonesia, supervises and controls their activities. Matters concerning co-operative activities are under the jurisdiction of the Department of Co-operatives (McLeod, 1995).

Foreign Banks

The provisions for foreign banks relating to the location, operation and procedures for licence application are contained in *Government Regulation No. 3* (1968) concerning foreign banks, and the *Letter of Decision* from the Minister of Finance on 20 February 1968. These provisions cover the legal forms of foreign banks, regulate their capital and personnel requirements and regulate their right to transact business as general commercial or development banks. The branches of foreign banks in Jakarta are now permitted to establish sub-branches in six major provincial cities (Bandung, Semarang, Surabaya, Medan, Ujung Pandang and Denpasar). However, export credits must account for at least 50% of their total credit portfolio within one year of their establishment (KPMG, 1995, p. 51). Despite this restriction, foreign banks now are taking advantage of the newly granted opportunities to expand their operations outside of Jakarta. Several of them have opened sub-branches in Surabaya.

The objective of permitting foreign banks to open branches was to enable them to participate in foreign investments, finance import and export business, and assist in the development of domestic industries and production. Although their numbers and assets have expanded rapidly, foreign banks only account for a tiny portion of the industry. Generally, they focus on foreign exchange-related business and provide financial services to foreign-venture companies (*Bankwatch*, June 1996).

PROBLEMS FACED BY INDONESIAN BANKS

Problem Loans

Bad debts in Indonesian banks are common. The stringent Indonesian bank secrecy laws make it almost impossible to determine the true extent of the problem. It is difficult to know who is in trouble and what banks might be guilty of showing little prudence in providing credit, especially to companies within their own business group. Bank Indonesia deemed that bad debts should be written off for the health of the entire industry. Theoretically, this is a good move but it is difficult to achieve in practice. As of April 1996, the total non-performing loans were Rp 9.02 trillion (US$3.8 billion), representing 3.19% of the total credit provision by all the banks. This figure only refers to the loans which are truly beyond redemption. Approximately 3.04% of the total credit provision belongs to the *kurang lancar* category which means "less than fluid" and 4.52% belongs to the *diragukan* category which means "doubtful". Hence, only 89.25%, or Rp 252.65 trillion (US$106.5 billion), are considered *lancar* with repayment as scheduled.

State banks have been criticised for their bad debts. Given the importance of many borrowers, more collections are likely to require support from the highest political level. A lasting solution to this problem requires a change in the culture and privatisation would ensure appropriate incentives for the owners, managers and borrowers. As of June 1996, 70.7% of these problem loans applied to state banks and represented Rp 6.38 trillion (US$2.69 billion); 17.2%

applied to private banks and represented Rp 1.55 trillion (US$0.65 billion); 6.1% applied to regional banks and represented Rp 0.55 trillion (US$0.23 billion); and 6% applied to foreign and joint venture banks, representing Rp 0.54 trillion (US$0.227 billion). Table 6–3 shows a summary of the bad debts from 1994 to 1996. (*Economic & Business Review Indonesia*, 11 September 1996).

The enforcement of measures against debtors is problematic. Banks do insist on collateral when they lend, and Bank Indonesia (BI) penalises banks if they do not obtain it. But the actual value of the collateral is negligible and the problem is not with overvalued collateral but with non-performance. BI's measures have concentrated on regulatory mechanisms. It has established an early warning system for problems arising from the on-site bank audits.

Management

The bad debt problem can be attributed to corruption, fraud, embezzlement, the weakness in borrower selection, and the state banks' inability to administer and supervise loans and to recover overdue repayments. When Bank Pacific's management was discovered to have made bad property loans to affiliates, it was replaced immediately and put under BI's supervision. It was revealed that 70 banks in 1996 had violated the legal lending limit – up from 44 in 1995 (*Euromoney*, April 1996). Many of the problem loans were caused by poor bank management and improper credit assessment which resulted from strong competition in the banking sector following the introduction of deregulation measures (McLeod, 1995, p. 167).

Security

The internal security procedures of some local banks are not up to international standards. In one incident, fraudulent faxes containing secret key codes were sent over from large European banks to the Jakarta branch of Hongkong and Shanghai Banking Corporation. The bank was asked to transfer cash totalling Rp 165 billion (US$69.6 million) to several small banks in Jakarta. Some of these faxes were actually processed and, subsequently, millions of dollars were handed over to fraudsters. The case exposed the difficulties created by Indonesia's still inadequate legal system (*Euromoney*, April 1996).

TABLE 6–3
Summary of Bad Debts

Source	1994 (Rp trillion)	1994 % of Industry Bad Debts	1995 (Rp trillion)	1995 % of Industry Bad Debts	1996 (Rp trillion)	1996 % of Industry Bad Debts
State banks	6.18	71.4	6.39	72.6	6.38	70.7
Private banks	1.63	18.8	1.43	16.3	1.55	17.2
Regional banks	0.41	4.8	0.48	5.5	0.55	6.1
Foreign & JV banks	0.43	5.0	0.49	5.6	0.54	6.0

Source: *Economic & Business Review Indonesia*, 11 September 1996.

Highly Concentrated Lending

The problem loans of state and private banks are concentrated in large firms and conglomerates. Land is the main form of collateral for bank loans in Indonesia. Therefore, the health of the banking system is dependent on the capability and willingness of these companies to repay overdue loans, and on the legal status and value of land used as security (McLeod, 1995, p. 152).

OPPORTUNITIES FACING INDONESIAN BANKS

Indonesian banks recently experienced accelerating growth due to new business and new products. In 1996, business volume increased 30.4% compared to 15.6% in 1995. This growth was due to higher fund mobilisation and loan extensions in conjunction with rising economic activity. Profitability in the banking sector rose from 0.6% of revenue in 1994 to 1.8% in 1995. Banking efficiency, measured by the ratio of operating cost to operating income, improved to 92.2% in 1995, down from 95.3% in 1994 (*The Indonesia Times*, 19 July 1996).

Privatisation

Infrastructure lending used to be dominated by the state banks but this was opened to private participation in 1993 and to foreigners in 1995. Projects structured on build-operate-transfer (BOT) terms are now common. The government's privatisation programme is generating more business for private banks because state companies have been released from their obligations to support state banks. Large deposits are now flowing into private banks from privatised firms such as P. T. Telkom (*Euromoney*, April 1996).

Going Public

Stock listing is becoming a strategic imperative. Banks can find asset growth by tapping into the capital market for long term funds. The flexibility and ability to respond swiftly to changes in the market will determine the banks that expand and contract relative to others.

CHALLENGES FACED BY THE BANKS

In June 1996, Moody's concluded that the health of the Indonesian banking system was improving but the regulatory, accounting and legal infrastructures were still weak. Moody's assigned ratings from Ba1 to Ba2 to Bank Bali, Bank Dagang Nasional Indonesia, Panin Bank, and Bank Danamon which are all listed banks. The growth of the private banks over the last five years has outstripped that of the state-owned banks. The asset quality and capital levels of the rated private banks appear strong in comparison to the state banks. Rapid growth in lending over the last two years, however, may have a negative impact on future asset quality. The growth in lending has outstripped deposits in the system, thus forcing banks to rely on short term borrowing from interbank markets and foreign sources (*Economic & Business Review Indonesia*, 19 June 1996).

New Regulations

The central bank's decision to increase the commercial bank reserve requirement has put banking shares under pressure. On 11 September 1996, Lippo Bank fell Rp 175 (US$0.074) to Rp 3,376 (US$1.423). Bank Danamon shed Rp 50 (US$0.02) to Rp 1,625 (US$0.685) and Bank International Indonesia was down Rp 125 (US$0.053) to Rp 5,300 (US$2.234). Bank Indonesia raised the reserve requirement of commercial banks from 3% to 5% effective 16 April 1997. The central bank indicated that this move was in line with its policy of containing an overheated economy, reducing speculative trading in financial markets and strengthening the central bank's ability to control fluctuations.

The reason for increasing the reserve requirement was because banks surpassed the 17% target of credit growth. Besides P. T. Panin Bank, which has reserves at BI in excess of the current minimum 3% requirement, all listed banks are affected by the new reserve requirement which will increase their cost of funds. The new reserve requirement will force banks to increase their interest rates in an effort to maintain liquidity. Although the banks will try to pass this increase on to customers, this will take time and it will squeeze profit margins in the short term. Tighter restrictions are likely to curb private banks' lending growth and profitability for 1996. Lending growth for small banks slowed to 14% in 1995 from 25% in 1994. However, the larger banks maintained growth levels of 25% or more in 1995 (*Economic & Business Review Indonesia*, 25 September 1996).

Attracting Good Customers

With more than 240 banks competing and with the high prevailing lending interest rates of 20% to 22%, most Indonesian banks have found the maintenance of loan quality difficult (*Euromoney*, April 1996). New credit worthy borrowers are difficult to find as well. BI expressed concern over the rising proportion of loans to the property sector given the high interest rates and a slow real estate market. This combination of factors increases the risk of bad loans. The level of credit to the real estate sector was 26% of total loans between January and September in 1996 compared with 16% for the same period in 1995. Analysts claim that the level of loans to real estate companies should be only 17% (Dewi, 1996).

There are various reasons that banks continue lending funds to property developers. First, costs often are marked up well above the actual project cost and the interest rate applied to the loan is well above the market rate. The bank official and the developer benefit from the deal but the bank, which has to carry the bad loans, suffers considerably. Secondly, even though the risk is large, banks still provide loans to the real estate sector because the situation in other industries is less attractive. Therefore, so long as the potential profits in the property sector are higher than in other sectors, the bankers and business interests in the property sector will find ways to circumvent the rules (Dewi, 1996).

Capital Market

The ability of the capital market to substitute for banks depends crucially on the relative inability of the latter to provide long-term financing to borrowers on attractive terms. The banks have been facing a strong challenge from the Jakarta Stock Exchange. The number of listed companies rose from a mere 24 in 1988, with a capitalisation of Rp 449 billion (US$189.2 million), to a respectable 250 firms by November 1996, with a capitalisation of Rp 204.4 trillion (US$86.17 billion) (P. T. Bursa Efek Jakarta, 1996). Prominent companies have begun to raise funds in the capital market which enables them to grow rapidly. To make things worse, a significant portion of the funds raised were used to repay bank loans. Banks dealing with the corporate sector were forced to search for different market segments because of the corporate preference for the capital market.

Government Policies

The government's recent decision to protect a domestic car manufacturer may have a negative impact on the domestic banking industry. The new automotive policy has lowered the demand for cars because the public is expecting car prices to fall. This should increase the risk in providing automotive credit. If the car market continues to worsen, then many banks could suffer huge losses due to the decreasing value of automobile collateral. This is problematic because automotive credit is one of the fastest growing credit sectors. Many car buyers prefer to buy on credit rather than in cash (*Economic & Business Review Indonesia*, 27 March 1996).

The Absence of Legal Redress

The lack of legal redress is causing banks to be extremely careful in their lending policies. In Indonesia, there is no concept of negative equity. If car or house prices fall, then consumers can vacate their homes or return their cars to the bank and stop the loan payments. Following the announcement of the national car policy, new car prices are expected to plunge because the national car (assembled in Korea) is exempt from import duties and taxes for three years. Banks are concerned about existing loans if car prices across the board should fall (*Euromoney*, April 1996).

Interest Rate

Bank Indonesia is exercising a tight monetary policy in the face of strong liquidity and the need to limit the supply of credit to prevent an overheated economy. The most effective monetary device for doing this is a high interest rate. The bank also has tried to put a cap on overall credit growth.

Indonesia's interest rates are among the highest in the region with deposit rates ranging from 12% to 17% and with lending rates at about 21%. Bank Indonesia does not control the interest rate directly but manages it through various financial instruments such as the *Sertifikats Bank Indonesia* (SBI) and the *Surat Berharga Pasar Uang*

(SBPU).[1] At the end of June 1995, Bank Indonesia introduced the Jakarta Inter-Bank Offer Rate (JIBOR) which is based on the interest rates of 24 commercial banks. High interest rates have meant fewer bank loans to big companies (*Bankwatch*, June 1996).

Foreign Exchange Licence

In September 1995, Bank Indonesia issued a decree imposing stricter controls and restrictions on banks with a foreign exchange licence. This policy affected the large banks and those seeking foreign exchange bank status. It required foreign exchange banks to have paid-up capital of Rp 150 million (up from Rp 50 million) and to reach a capital adequacy ratio of 12% by September 2001. Banks have to raise their capital levels much sooner to maintain their loan growth rates (*The Banker*, May 1996, p. 38).

BANK MERGERS

Bank Mergers in East Asia

The state-controlled banking systems of many Asian countries can no longer meet the financial services demanded by the fast growing trade and industrial sectors. The basic problem is the inefficient use of capital. Asian countries require modern and efficient banking systems to channel domestic savings and foreign capital into infrastructure projects. The need for upgrading the infrastructure is acute for developing countries such as China, Thailand, Malaysia and Indonesia. Several Asian countries have deregulated their financial sectors to facilitate a more sophisticated range of services for infrastructure projects.

One result of deregulation is the strong wave of mergers and acquisitions of banks in Southeast Asian countries. The Philippine central bank announced on 28 November 1996 that commercial banks must raise their minimum capital to 4.5 billion pesos from 2.5 billion

[1] SBI is a rupiah denominated bearer certificate issued under a discount system by Bank Indonesia as a short term debt instrument. SBPU is a money market security. One type is the promissory note which can be issued in connection with credit extended by a bank to finance a specific transaction or in the framework of inter-bank borrowing. The second type is a trade bill which is drawn by one party and accepted by another party in connection with a specific transaction.

pesos to initiate consolidation in the banking industry. There was too much competition and many banks in the Philippines are looking for partners to stay competitive. The Malaysian government announced that it would encourage bank mergers to deal with increasing competition and that it had no plans to issue new banking licences (*The Indonesia Times*, 5 November 1996). Singapore's Finance Minister Richard Hu indicated that as global financial markets opened up, the Association of Southeast Asian Nations (ASEAN) banks might not be able to compete on their own. Some co-operative alliances could possibly sharpen their competitive edge. Larger established international banks are increasingly expanding into the ASEAN region and generating more competition for domestic banks (*The Indonesia Times*, 19 July 1996).

Bank Mergers in Indonesia

The rapid expansion of banks following the 1988 deregulation package was beyond expectations and now there are too many banks and they have grown too quickly. Given the large number of banks, the structure of the Indonesia banking industry is not efficient for reasons discussed above. This predicament prompted the government to consolidate the banking industry for increased efficiency.

There has never been mergers among the large or medium-sized banks in Indonesia. Instead, mergers occurred only among unprofitable banks and small banks. To expedite the merger of these unprofitable small banks, the government is encouraging and providing incentives. In 1996, the acquisition of smaller banks by industrial groups stagnated but 1997 appears more promising for mergers among smaller banks. Indra Kesuma, the *Direktur Utama Bank Bukopin*, believes that these should be based on the complementary and strategic strengths of the smaller banks (Kesuma, 1996).

Bank Indonesia's Regulatory Efforts

Regulatory measures are used by the government in an effort to strengthen the banking industry. The objective is to make it more efficient for globalisation purposes. Therefore, consolidation of the banking industry is strongly encouraged and tax incentives are offered for mergers. Bank Indonesia can have better control and supervision if there are fewer branches. To promote these mergers, the capital adequacy ratios will be raised from 6% to 12% by the year 2001. The bank reserve requirement has been increased from 2% to 3% and the amount of money that a bank can lend to an affiliated company has been limited. These measures are forcing banks to raise additional capital and there is a current flurry of bank equity and debt issues. Many smaller banks will be unable to meet these new requirements and, consequently, merger activity should intensify as the year 2001 approaches (*Asia Money*, July/August 1996, p. 60).

Reasons for Mergers

Since the introduction of deregulation, the large banks have become richer while the small banks have remained small. Asset growth for the top 20 banks has averaged 28% per annum over the last five years. Large players have picked up new borrowers, such as corporate customers requiring venture and working capital, through their extensive branch networks. They have built up their deposit base by focusing on a thriving consumer market. Larger banks listed on the Jakarta Stock Exchange are preparing for the 2001 deadline by turning to their stockholders for funds. Several banks have announced rights issues in 1996 including Bank Danamon, Lippo Bank, Bank Bira, Bank Umum Nasional and Ficorinvest Bank. Three other banks, BDNI, BII and Bank Niaga, are preparing rights issues for 1997 (*Asia Money*, July/August 1996, pp. 57, 60) .

Smaller banks are beginning to discover that they have no real niche. They have trouble raising funds because they cannot access the capital market. They have no option but to merge. For eight years since *Pakto*, banks have flourished by providing funds to businesses and consumers that had limited sources of financing. Now that Indonesia's capital market is flourishing, the banking sector is headed for consolidation. According to the World Bank representative in Jakarta, Dennis de Tray: "It is going to take some tough people to regulate and manage the banking system. The notion of imposing heavy penalties on those who violate banking regulations is still gaining ground here. Once it is achieved, we will see some banks close and others merge" (*Asia Money*, July/August 1996, pp. 57, 60).

THE PRESENT STUDY

Bank Indonesia's regulatory measures are aimed at slowly "tightening the screws" on the banks. Hence, a steady imposition of the limits is happening rather than a sudden ultimatum which would imperil the common depositors. In the short term, small and unhealthy banks will be forced to merge by the central bank through the various regulatory measures and incentives. Banks which are unable to fulfil Bank Indonesia's requirements by the target dates will be managed by the bigger and healthier banks followed by acquisition, as in the case of Bank Delta's acquisition by Bank Danamon. Over the long term, the trend will be for large and healthy banks to merge in order to compete internationally.

The focus of the present study is to evaluate a set of performance indicators of nine selected banks. The banks hold a wide portfolio of businesses such as consumer and corporate banking, trade finance, merchant banking and businesses in the middle market, retail middle market and fixed-income fee business. They are considered to be sound banks by Merrill Lynch (Merrill Lynch, 28 October 1996, pp. 10, 11).

Criteria

(i) ***Capital Adequacy Ratio (CAR)***: The principal objective of a bank's capital adequacy requirement is to ensure that an adequate level of capital is maintained for withstanding any losses which may result from "credit risk". The risk-based capital adequacy framework is consistent with the international standards of the Basle Committee on Banking Regulations and Supervisory Practices. The framework has three basic aspects; the capital base elements, the required capitalisation level and the risk weighted regime.

The capital base for regulatory purposes comprises two elements, namely, Tier 1 and Tier 2 capital after making certain deductions. The Tier 1 ratio is equal to the core capital divided by risk adjusted assets. The Tier 2 ratio is equal to the total capital divided by risk adjusted assets.

Tier 1 capital includes paid-up ordinary capital, paid-up non-cumulative irredeemable preference shares, retained earnings and reserves (other than asset revaluation reserves) less goodwill and other intangible assets. If future income tax benefits are greater than deferred income tax liabilities, then the net future income tax benefit is deducted from Tier 1 capital. This condition did not exist at 30 September 1995 and, therefore, no adjustment was required.

Tier 2 capital includes assets revaluation reserves, the general provision for doubtful debts, hybrid debt/equity instruments and subordinated term debt with an original maturity of at least seven years. In order to determine the capital adequacy ratio, all assets are weighted to provide a broad indication of relative credit risk. There are five risk weightings (0% – no risk, 10%, 20%, 50%, 100% – standard risk).

(ii) ***Asset Quality***: Asset quality is usually measured in terms of total loans and other receivables. Bankers must manage their loan levels very closely given capital constraints, new and increasingly stringent legal lending limits, and the requirement to expand small business loans relative to total loans. Some banks are even structuring their loans so that they are tradable. One way to do this is by ensuring that the loan documentation includes a loan assignment clause. This allows banks to assign their loans to other banks, thus reducing their total loan levels. Although still limited in volume, these "asset sales transactions" are becoming more common.

With asset growth constrained by various requirements, the catchword for many banks is "free business", a term that encompasses any revenue generating activity that does not require the recording of an asset on a bank's balance sheet. These activities include foreign exchange purchases and sales, fees for guarantees, letter of credit business, cash management, custodian and trust services, for example.

(iii) ***Net Interest Margin (NIM)***: One of the primary objectives of asset/liability management is to reduce the interest rate risk, thereby sustaining a desired level of profitability. The net interest margin is utilised since volume is significant in asset/liability management. Improvement in the NIM requires careful management of rates, volumes and mix criteria within the asset/liability portfolio.

(iv) ***Earnings (net income)***: The two most common ratios used in determining banking performance are return on equity (ROE) and return on assets (ROA), which are expressed as net income to stockholder's equity and net income to total assets, respectively. Higher ratios of ROE and ROA mean more efficient and profitable operations.

(v) ***Loan to Deposit Ratio (LDR)***: A bank's liquidity needs consist of immediate obligations, such as deposit withdrawals or legitimate loan demands, that the bank must meet to be recognised as an ongoing financial intermediary. LDR is generally expressed in terms of total loans divided by total bank deposits. In May

1993, BI allowed capital to be included in the LDR's denominator. It is important to note that most Indonesian banks lend above their deposit level, depending on externally, and more expensive sources of funds. However, it must remain attentive to always have an attractive and competitive source of funds. Liquidity risk is high because of Indonesian banks' dependence on exterior funding (McLeod, 1995).

RESULTS

Tables 6–4 and 6–5 show the average score for each performance indicator for the nine banks. Those banks whose performance indicators are generally below these benchmarks will be considered to be in relative danger of being edged out of competition in the long run. Since the methodology adopted is based on averaging the performance of the nine banks which are considered relatively healthy by Indonesian banks standards, it makes sense that the benchmarks have to be dynamic and change with time. The analysis attempts to give the foreign investors an idea as to what constitute competitive Indonesian banks and what constitute merger imminent banks.

CONCLUSION

Indonesia is geared towards liberalisation and providing a comfortable climate for investment. To do this it is imperative for the central bank to rejuvenate the banking industry. Bank Indonesia has been partially successful in strengthening the market entry requirements, enforcing regulations and amplifying the quality of the banking industry. Banks have been encouraged to formulate long-term growth strategies, including restructuring, while Bank Indonesia is tightening the issuance of new permits for national banks and encouraging inter-bank mergers to salvage less successful banks and increase their competitiveness (*The Banker*, May 1996, p. 39). The next five years should witness the merger of small and unhealthy banks through the various regulatory measures and incentives.

Past experience suggests that the value of banks are likely to increase in the merger process. It has been predicted that overhead costs could fall by 20% if two banks merge (Kesuma, 1996, p. 77). In Indonesia, foreign investors may acquire a maximum of 49% of the issued stock of listed companies. Thus, the bank merger trend could provide ample opportunities for investors.

TABLE 6–4
Bank Comparative Matrix 1

Banks	Rating	Competitive Position	Loan Portfolio	Asset Quality
Bank Bira	D-1-1-7	Second-tier bank	over 80% earning asset	NPL 1.2%, provision 92% NPL
Bank Bali	D-3-2-7	6th largest private bank	75% earning asset	NPL 1.9%, provision 100% NPL
BDNI	D-2-3-8	3rd largest private bank	85% earning asset	NPL 0.2%, provision 100% NPL
Bank Danamon	Rstr	2nd largest private bank	over 90% earning asset	NPL 1.9%, provision 75% NPL
BII	D-2-1-7	4th largest private bank	70% earning asset	NPL 1.8%, provision 140% NPL
Bank Lippo	D-2-2-7	5th largest private bank	77% earning asset	NPL 1.7 % provision 110% NPL
Bank Niaga	D-3-2-7	7th largest private bank	77% earning asset	NPL 2.7%, provision 70% NPL
Bank Panin	D-2-2-7	9th largest private bank	56% earning asset	NPL 1.7%, provision 170% NPL
Bank Tiara	D-3-1-7	Second-tier bank	92% earning asset	NPL 1.0%, provision 120% NPL
Average	Nil	Nil	78% earning asset	NPL 1.7%, provision 209% NPL

Source: Merrill Lynch, 28 October 1996.

The impending merger wave should create a wider reach of the branch network which would certainly be beneficial to investors interested in retail businesses (it is a closed sector to foreigners at the moment). Foreign banks and non-bank financial institutions could form joint ventures with Indonesian banks. This yields mutual benefits because the Indonesian partners can then access the international capital markets while the foreign partner can penetrate the Indonesian market.

As Indonesia's banks go through the painful process of transformation with mergers and acquisitions, customers should benefit from the heightened competition. Bank services have improved dramatically and will continue to do so since many banks have invested heavily in information systems over the past few years. Some banks have chosen to differentiate and concentrate on specific market segments by offering specialised services. In the future, Indonesia's banking industry will have fewer participants offering a wider variety of services after the wave of mergers and acquisitions.

TABLE 6–5
Bank Comparative Matrix 2

Banks	CAR (%)	LDR (%)	NIM (%)	ROE (%)	ROA (%)
Bank Bira	15.0	90.7	6.0	19.2	3.0
Bank Bali	11.8	82.0	4.7	20.7	1.8
BDNI	8.7	90.9	3.1	17.1	1.2
Bank Danamon	10.3	95.7	4.2	13.0	1.3
BII	9.3	73.9	4.7	23.4	1.9
Bank Lippo	12.1	84.7	5.3	16.5	1.7
Bank Niaga	9.5	91.1	4.9	20.7	1.3
Bank Panin	15.0	65.7	4.4	16.2	1.9
Bank Tiara	12.8	99.0	7.0	17.6	2.8
Average	11.6	86.0	4.9	18.3	1.9

Source: Merrill Lynch, 28 October 1996.

APPENDIX 6–1
Important Milestones of Financial Reforms

June 1983	• Elimination of asset ceilings for all banks.
February 1984	• Reintroduction of *Sertifikat Bank Indonesia* (SBIs).
January 1985	• Introduction of *Surat Berharga Pasar Uang* (SBPU).
July 1987	• Introduction of managed auction system for issuing SBIs and purchasing SBPUs.

APPENDIX 6–1 (cont'd)

October 1988	• Removal of most restrictions on entry for foreign and domestic banks and domestic branching. • Permitting banks and NBFIs to raise equity capital in the stock markets. • Reducing bank reserve requirements from 15% to 2%. • Improvement in other aspects of soundness requirements.
September 1989	• Foreign investors permitted to buy up to 49% of issued securities of companies listed on the stock exchange.
December 1990	• New prudential rules, capital requirements and standards for capital market participants introduced.
February 1991	• Requiring banks to strengthen their capital base in accordance with Bank for International Settlements recommendations.
November 1991	• Imposition of ceilings on public sector-related offshore borrowing.
December 1991	• Privatisation of the Jakarta Stock Exchange.
December 1992	• Promulgation of new Banking, Insurance and Pension Fund Law.
May 1993	• Modification of banking prudential standards to stimulate lending in the short run.

Source: Adapted from McLeod (1995), pp. 156–7.

REFERENCES

Asia Money, "Survival of the fittest", July/August 1996.

Bankwatch, "Banking System Report Indonesia", June 1996.

Dewi Pudyanti Loveard, "Bad Debt Risks Worry Bank Indonesia", *Asia Times*, 20 November 1996.

Economic & Business Review Indonesia, "New Automotive Policy Affects Banking Industry", 27 March 1996.

Economic & Business Review Indonesia, "World Bank Report 1996: A Call for Quality Growth", 29 May 1996.

Economic & Business Review Indonesia, "Moody's: Indonesian Banking System Improving", 19 June 1996.

Economic & Business Review Indonesia, "Bad Debt Write-offs: BI's Mandatory Solution", 11 September 1996.

Economic & Business Review Indonesia, "New Reserve Requirement Dogs Banking Shares", 25 September 1996.

Economic & Business Review Indonesia, "Reserve Requirement Hike May Spur Interest Rates", 9 October 1996.

Euromoney, "Banks Refocus on Making Profits", September 1993.

Euromoney, "Private-Sector Banks Must Lead the Recovery", April 1996, http://www.emwl.com/contents/pu..em.96.04/em.96.04.29.html.

Kesuma Indra, Editorial, *InfoBank*, No. 204, December 1996.

KPMG, "Investment in Indonesia", KPMG Peat Marwick, Chartered Accountants, Jakarta, 1995.

McLeod Ross H., *Indonesia Assessment 1994: Finance as a Key Sector in Indonesia's Development*, Research School of Pacific and Asian Studies, Australian National University, Canberra and Institute of Southeast Asian Studies, Singapore, 1995.

Merrill Lynch, *Indonesian Banks*, Jakarta, 28 October 1996.

P. T. Bursa Efek Jakarta, *Jakarta Stock Exchange Activity, 1977–November 1996*, Jakarta Stock Exchange, 1996.

Suhardiman Hendrik, Vice President Director of P. T. Tamara Bank, "Highlights of Indonesia Monetary Policy and Banking Development", Seminar Paper, MBA Business Study Mission to Indonesia, Jakarta, 9 December 1996.

The Banker, "Family Business", May 1996.

The Indonesia Times, "ASEAN Banks Told to Forge Pacts to Face Competition", 19 July 1996.

The Indonesia Times, "Malaysia's Government Presses Banks to Merge", 5 November 1996.

Chapter 7

Project Financing in Indonesia: Critical Factors*

BY
GAN Tion Chin
Jimmy KHOO
LIM Hun Meng
WONG Poh Seng

INTRODUCTION

DEVELOPING NATIONS IN the Asia-Pacific region are undergoing massive economic expansion and, as a result, infrastructure project opportunities abound. Nowhere is this more obvious than in Indonesia which needs US$330 billion of project financing over the next few years to boost its global competitiveness (Business Review Southeast Asia Publishing Service, 1995). Like other developing countries, Indonesia is looking increasingly towards the private sector for financing, building and operating these infrastructure projects.

The signing of the 30-year power purchase agreement (PPA) for the US$2.6 billion 1,320 megawatt Paiton I power plant in February 1994, was an important event for the Indonesian banking industry. It signalled the go-ahead for banks to strike new deals and to revive a string of old projects that were put on hold in 1991 after President Suharto's clamp- down on offshore debt (*Project Finance International*, November 1994). However, the number of projects actually available to foreign investors is uncertain. With the liberalisation of foreign investment regulations, foreign investment is

* The authors are grateful for the assistance provided by Dr. John Vong.

now allowed in power generation, telecommunications, water supply and transport (McMeckan, 1995).

Indonesia has just completed its fifth phase of planned economic development called *Repelita V* (1989 to 1994). This programme emphasised structural adjustments to enhance the flexibility of the economy. *Repelita VI* is the country's sixth five-year plan and it began in April 1994, with growth projections of 6% to 6.5% per annum which will require investments of US$335 billion. Indonesia hopes to achieve newly industrialised country-hood status by the year 2019. Indonesia also expects to have US$52 billion to US$55 billion in industrial exports by the end of *Repelita VI* in 1998. It aims to attract US$300 billion in investments over this same period, with 73.4% coming from the private sector and the balance from public investments. At least 50% of the private investment is expected to come from foreign direct investments (Business Review Southeast Asia Publishing Service, 1995).

THE DEMAND FOR INFRASTRUCTURE

The investment required in Indonesia for infrastructure development is enormous and the government must turn to private financing in order to develop the needed infrastructure. But Indonesia's private sector cannot provide all of the necessary funds and the government, therefore, is encouraging foreign investors to participate in developing its needed infrastructure.

Infrastructure developments in transportation, electricity and telecommunications are vital for achieving the government's plans under *Repelita VI.* It needs to spend in excess of US$65 billion on infrastructure over the next five years. More than US$25 billion is needed for power generation, US$13 billion for transportation, US$7.8 billion for water supply and US$6 billion for telecommunications. Also, Indonesia is planning the construction of 10,000 kilometres of new roads at a cost of US$10.2 billion (Business Review Southeast Asia Publishing Service, 1995).

(i) ***Power***: In 1994, Indonesia signed its first build-operate-transfer (BOT) power plant located at Paiton, Java. This move is in line with the government's efforts to raise the electricity generating capacity by 41 gigawatts over the next ten years. The project's expected cost is US$37 billion (Minter *et al*., 1996).

Outside of the major cities, Indonesia's households remain largely without electricity. According to the Central Bureau of Statistics, about 61% of the rural population use kerosene and other non-electrical means as a source of light whereas it is only 10% in urban areas. Nationally, electricity illuminates the homes of 55% of the population. At most, 70% of the country's electricity is generated by Perusahaan Listrik Negara (PLN), a state-owned utility, while private companies produce the remainder using "captive" generators. These generators serve individual factories or estates but not the public grid. The World Bank forecasts Indonesia's demand for electricity to grow by about 12% per year between 1994 and 1999 (*Business Asia*, 22 May 1995). Plans for electricity supply during *Repelita VI* include the construction of nearly 18,500 kilometres of transmission lines and 300,000 kilometres of distribution lines (INDIO, 1996). Some of the power and distribution targets are shown in Table 7–1.

TABLE 7–1
PLN Electric Power Targets for *Repelita VI*

Type	Units	1999*	1994
Installed capacity	Megawatt	13,568	9,522
Steam	Megawatt	4,690	2,660
Combined cycle	Megawatt	3,411	3,344
Diesel	Megawatt	2,119	404
Hydroelectricity	Megawatt	2,178	948
Geothermal, gas turbine, barge mounted	Megawatt	2,166	1,170
Transmission	Kilometre-cable	18,500	10,548
Distribution			
Medium voltage	Kilometre-cable	225,000	133,317
Low voltage	Kilometre-cable	275,000	196,741
Rural electrification villages	Kilometre-cable	30,000	18,619

* Cumulative for five years.
Source: INDIO (1996).

(ii) ***Transportation***: The government has estimated that Rp 57,346 billion is needed for the development of the land transportation sub-sector, out of which Rp 24,695 billion is needed for the construction and maintenance of roads. Development for the sea transportation sub-sector is estimated to be Rp 15,824 billion. Most of this amount is for vessel procurements and the funding is expected to come from private investors (Transportation Industry, 1996). Table 7–2 summarises the investment requirements for the development of the transportation sector in *Repelita VI*.

TABLE 7–2
Investment Requirements for Transportation Sector

Transportation Sub-sectors	Investment Requirement (Rp billion)
Road	24,695
Road support facilities	486
Rail road	2,962
River transports and crossing facilities	1,207
Sea transport	15,824
Air transport	10,817
Meteorology, etc.	1,355
Total	**57,346**

Source: Transportation Industry (1996).

(iii) ***Telecommunications***: In the telecommunications sector, Indonesia is lagging behind many other countries. This is reflected in its low telephone density compared to other ASEAN countries. It is estimated that the demand for telephone lines will reach 8 million line units by the end of 1999. To meet this demand, the government is planning to install 5 million telephone line units so that the telephone density will be 3.2 telephones per 100 people. The expectation of the private sector playing a greater role has forced the government to open up this sector. The government's current monopoly cannot be sustained any longer because the growing demand for a wider range of telecommunication services requires multiple operators (Telecommunication Industry, 1996).

PROJECT FINANCING

Definition

Project financing deals with funding a project independently of the sponsor companies. Consequently, a project needs to be technically, commercially and financially viable. Therefore, its projected cash flows must be sufficient to cover all operating costs, provide debt servicing and provide an adequate return on investment. The fundamental difference between project financing and conventional corporate financing is the issue of recourse by the lenders. After a project is completed and operating according to plans, recourse to the sponsors or borrowers under project financing is usually limited to the assets and cash flows of the project. This means that project financing is conservatively assessed and structured.

Project financing has four key characteristics. The first is risk sharing. A large project involves huge sums of money, has a long time frame and is often subjected to several types of operational risks. It is advantageous for several parties to jointly administer a project in order to share the risk. Moreover, banks/lenders do not normally extend financial packages to a single customer. Part of the reason for this restriction is that banks cannot lend more than a specified percentage of their capital base to a single customer.

The second characteristic is risk segregation. Risk is removed from the party (called the sponsor) that makes the project proposal. If the project fails, then a sponsor's loss is limited to the invested amount. Therefore, project financing is a means for separating the risk from a sponsor by creating a separate business to undertake the project. If a project is unsuccessful, the sponsoring company remains intact.

Thirdly, there are tax advantages in project financing. Depending on a country's tax code where a project is located, it is possible to take maximum advantage of the tax incentives given to new projects. Capital allowances for new equipment, tax holidays, special relocation allowances and export grants are some of the tax incentives available in Indonesia. Finally, debt capacity can be maximised because more funding can be obtained when several parties sponsor a project since the banks are afforded increased security. This increased financial strength is very important in the initial negotiations, and in determining the size and pricing of the debt package.

Bank Indonesia, the central bank, manages international reserves, regulates and directs the nation's banking system. Although there is a capital market in Indonesia, most businesses still rely heavily on the banks for financing. There are many offshore financial products and services which foreign investors can utilise including private banking, working capital lines, trade financing, syndicate loans, capital market products, foreign exchange, money markets and leveraged fixed deposits. Generally, there are no restrictions on offshore financing by companies although the Indonesian authorities may decide not to approve commercial loans from foreign banks if the interest rates are above a specified limit. Foreign investors may obtain debt financing from local banks without requiring prior approval, except for importing and exporting rupiah. Also, foreign investors can obtain financing through inter-company loans. While there are no restrictions on this type of financing, the tax authorities require an arm's length transaction before allowing interest deductions.

Evaluating Risk Exposure

The ultimate goal of project financing is to arrange borrowing for a project which benefits a sponsor on a non-recourse basis and does not affect its credit standing or balance sheet. Indeed, project financing is sometimes called off-balance sheet financing. However, there is considerable room for disagreement among lenders and borrowers as to what constitutes good project financing. Borrowers prefer their projects to be financed on a 100% non-recourse basis. Lenders, on the other hand, are not in the venture capital business nor are they equity risk takers. Lenders want to feel secure that they are going to be repaid by the project, a sponsor or an interested third party. Generating this security is the challenge of project financing. Thus, the key for successful project financing is structuring the financing with as little recourse as possible to the sponsor while simultaneously providing sufficient credit support (through guarantees, undertakings of a sponsor or a third party) for lenders to satisfy their credit risk. There really is no magic in project financing.

Before potential lenders invest in a project, they normally evaluate its credit risk. If the credit risk is unsatisfactory, then they will not proceed until the problem of unsatisfactory risk exposure is resolved. In financial markets, there are many tools used by lenders to perform this risk evaluation task. The Stanchart (Standard Chartered

Bank) checklist is one of the tools often used in the industry. It is a checklist which is typically used by Stanchart to evaluate the feasibility of financing a project and consists of five major criteria which are described below.

(i) ***Completion***: Completion risks are sometimes assumed by a lender when it is not possible to complete a project or facility on schedule and/or within budget. If the problem is due to a scheduling overrun, then the risk can be handled with minimal additional exposure to the lender. However, the loan terms may have to be extended because actual production is lower than what was anticipated in the original financial projections. Incentives or penalty clauses are typically built into the agreement to entice early completion and discourage scheduling overruns. With cost overruns, sponsors normally have a lump sum fixed price contract with their main contractors/vendors to limit their risk exposure.

(ii) ***Production/Operations***: Once a project is completed and operating according to specifications, a project assumes the characteristics of an established operating company. Lenders now must depend on the operating company to maintain its operations and generate sufficient revenue for debt repayment. Several considerations which are very important during this phase include the operating contract, reputation of the operator, the supporting infrastructure maintenance programme agreement and other financial or non-financial undertakings.

(iii) ***Market***: The financial success of many investment projects depends on future markets for any products or services produced by the project. Pricing strategies must ensure cash flows to meet the profit objectives of providing capital. Marketing surveys can provide a basis for the anticipated volume and price of the various products or services. If a project is producing a commodity for sale on the open market rather than under a long term contract, then the lender must appraise this future market and assess whether the price projections are realistic.

(iv) ***Feedstock***: Supply sources and contracts for feedstocks or raw materials needed by a project should be assured at costs consistent with the financial projections. When the price and quality of raw materials are used in the underlying financial projections, the reliability of the supplier is a key consideration. In the event of non-performance by the supplier, enforceability of the contract is critical and potential substitutes must be considered. Another important issue is the duration of the raw material supply contract. A long term contract allows a sponsor to eliminate some uncertainty in the financial projections. However, this arrangement has both advantages and disadvantages since a sponsor is locked into a mutually agreed upon price and quality. The supply of raw materials is particularly acute for processing plants, notwithstanding the forgoing risks.

(v) ***Foreign Exchange***: So long as capital expenditures, operating expenses, revenues and debts are denominated in the same currency, there is no exchange risk. However, in the case of foreign investment and any expenditures outside the home country, there is exposure to foreign exchange risk. These risks will have to be appropriately covered by indexing the payments under the contractual agreement to a freely convertible currency. In addition it is necessary to guarantee the convertibility of local currency into hard currency to ensure that foreign currency payment obligations under the various contracts can be honoured.

While these five criteria are relatively straightforward, it is more meaningful to place them in the context of *de facto* infrastructure projects. Accordingly, three major infrastructure projects are examined in the next section. The intention is to provide a brief background of the need for each project and the manner in which the major interests in each project were structured. In the process, the complexity of project financing is highlighted and the scenario developed in each situation serves as a basis for evaluating the projects' risks using the Stanchart criteria.

SELECTED INFRASTRUCTURE PROJECTS

Paiton I in the Power Sector

In April 1995, Paiton Energy Company became the first private foreign investment company to obtain a BOT contract for a 2×615-megawatt power plant in East Java which will cost US$2.5 billion. The concession period of the contract is 30 years. The name of the power plant is Paiton I which was initially known as Paiton 5 and 6.

Paiton I is a coal-fired base load plant to supply the Java-Bali grid. PLN, the state-owned electric utility, will purchase capacity and energy from the Paiton Energy Company but it will not have an equity investment in the project (*Project Finance International*, 8 June 1995). The power project is due to begin operations in the second quarter of 1998, with full capacity on stream in the third quarter (*Project Finance International*, 18 February 1994).

The equity stakes in Paiton Energy Company are divided amongst Mission Energy (32.5%), Mitsui & Co. (32.5%), General Electric Capital Corporation (20%) and P. T. Batu Hitam Perkasa (15%). Each shareholder is a leader in their respective fields: Mission Energy is the largest private power supplier in the U.S.; Mitsui is one of the biggest trading houses in Japan; GE will supply the turbines in the project; and Batu Hitam has a coal mine close to the project (*Project Finance International*, 5 February 1993).

The success of this project will depend on whether Paiton Energy can raise the required US$1.9 billion in offshore financing. Crucial to accessing funds for the project is the Power Purchase Agreement (PPA) and the level of participation of export credit agencies. The tariff is structured to overcome interest rate fluctuations and exchange rate risks. The long term of the loan (around 12 to 13 years) complicated commercial bank participation. On the other hand, the long term meant that there was less stress on the tariff structure and initial prices would not be higher (Wuigfield, 1994). However, the proceedings of the whole negotiation were a long and difficult process which took two years to complete according to Mr. Toru Nakagawa, senior deputy general manager of the project engineering department at IBJ, and Mr. Paul Fyke, managing director and regional head of global power and project finance at Chase Manhattan in Hong Kong. IBJ and Chase Manhattan are the financial advisers and lead arrangers for Paiton Energy Company because the Indonesian authorities have had no experience in independent power projects (IPPs) and have had no framework to work with since IPPs are a recent phenomenon in Asia. The negotiations were lengthy and difficult because the PPA is the document that fixes the price for the power produced (*Euromoney*, September 1995).

The price that consumers will pay for privately generated power is a politically sensitive issue. According to Mr. Fyke, 18 months were spent "talking to the government about whether it really wanted private power and what it involved and what it didn't involve". A major factor in the protracted discussions was the absence of a regulatory framework or guidelines for independent power producers to work on. The sponsors and their advisers in this case were basically setting the standards and, indeed, the Paiton project was intended to be the model which would govern later IPPs (*Project Finance International*, 21 July 1994).

One important factor high on the consortium's list was protection against devaluation of the rupiah. This was a point of some debate. From the outset, Japanese financing accounted for approximately one-half of the total requirement and was provided on the assumption that the rupiah to yen rate would be locked in. For every 100 megawatts of power, a standard yen payment would be given by PLN. Jexim, the Japanese agency, had always financed on these terms. However, in 1993, the Indonesian Government watched the yen appreciate from 132 per U.S. dollar to around 105. Understandably, it was reluctant to lock in a yen exchange rate. Finally, a compromised dollar-to-rupiah rate was arrived at (*Euromoney*, September 1995).

Political concerns, raw material supply, environment and technology were not big risk factors. Indonesia has a long record of honouring its agreements with foreigners. Furthermore, coal as the basic raw material will be supplied by P. T. Batu Hitam's mine in southern Kalimantan which is very near to the Paiton power plant (*Project Finance International*, 18 February1994). The coal is classified as ultra-clean burning fuel which contains low sulphur called envircoal. This coal has emission levels that are within the standards set by the World Bank and Indonesia. This environmentally friendly feature is likely to win support from multilateral agencies as well. Also, the technology used in the power plant is well-proven for its high performance efficiency and environmental friendliness (*Project Finance International*, 21 July 1994; *Power in Asia*, 19 September 1994). In addition to these, the issues of plant operator and plant maintenance were resolved. Mission Energy which is the largest power supplier in the U.S. will operate the plant and its wholly-owned subsidiary Mission Operation and Maintenance Inc. will operate and maintain the project (*Project Finance International*, 25 May 1995).

The risks associated with construction and equipment suppliers are minimal since construction is being undertaken on a fixed sum turnkey basis by a group of experienced multinationals renowned in their fields. Mitsui and Toyo Engineering are the primary construction contractors. The equipment and services suppliers are General Electric, Combustion Engineering, Duke/Fluor Daniel and Burns & Roe Enterprises (*Project Finance International*, 2 March 1995; *Project Finance International*, 8 June 1995).

In early August 1993, the Minister of Mines and Energy, I. B. Sudjana, claimed that the original estimated construction cost of US$2.5 billion was too high and he pressed for a reduction to US$1.5 billion, noting that the decision to reduce the final figure would hasten negotiations (*Project Finance International*, 13 September 1993). After further re-evaluation and assessment, the consortium finally managed to justify their original proposal and convince the Indonesian Government. On 12 February 1994, the PPA was signed. This was a critical milestone in the whole project.

Under the PPA, Paiton Energy Company will charge tariffs based on a three-tier structure: 8.56 U.S. cents per kilowatt hour for the first six years; 8.41 U.S. cents per kilowatt hour for the following six years; and 5.54 U.S. cents per kilowatt hour for the remaining 18 years (*Power in Asia*, 19 September 1994). In addition to this, capacity fees will cover debt service, equity return, fixed operating costs and taxes payable in Indonesia. Payments will be adjusted for inflation as well as any changes in operating and fuel costs. Sources said that the PLN has agreed to make U.S. dollars available to Paiton Energy if the latter cannot convert the rupiah. PLN also has agreed to accept a tariff adjustment if any government action increases Paiton's costs (*Project Finance International*, 29 September 1994).

After signing the PPA, forming a loan syndication to finance the project was another big challenge. The project financing took an additional 14 months. Chase Manhattan considered this to be quick since financing a project of this size in the U.S. can take up to 18 months. The eight arrangers are Chase Manhattan, IBJ, Bank of America, Barclays, Credit Lyonnais, Fuji, Sakura and UBS who collectively underwrote the required US$1.9 billion. This amount was subsequently reduced to US$1.82 billion. Finally, a syndicate of 37 banks participated in the project financing: 14 Japanese banks; 8 non-Japanese, Asian and Australian banks; 10 European banks; and 5 North American banks. The maturity of the loan is 16 years (*Project & Trade Finance*, January 1996).

The presence of government agencies in this agreement was essential. Jexim of Japan took US$540 million of the loan. It also guaranteed the construction risk, for the first time ever, on a US$360 million commercial loan that included non-Japanese banks. U.S. Exim was prohibited from guaranteeing any construction risk but it gave a political risk guarantee on US$540 million of commercial bank lending. On the project's completion, it will refinance this debt with a U.S. Exim 12-year loan thus extending the debt to the required 16 years. There was a US$200 million facility from the U.S. Government agency OPIC and US$180 million of pure commercial bank risk (*Project Finance International*, 27 April 1995). Finally, there was a US$93.75 million contingent facility for any project cost overrun (*Project Finance International*, 8 June 1995).

Paiton was the first project for U.S. Exim's project finance team and analysts said that this caused difficulties. Jexim's experience was wide but it was concerned with the issue of inter-creditor voting. Jexim had always made the Japanese banks in the syndicate surrender their votes. However, the non-Japanese banks refused to surrender their votes. This dilemma led to prolonged negotiations. Jexim eventually agreed, for the first time, to allow voting on the basis of one vote per one dollar which means that it could be outvoted. Bankers commented that countless intricacies such as this one had to be resolved (*Euromoney*, September 1995).

The financing negotiation went right to the deadline and in the best project finance tradition, everyone worked non-stop for the final 36 hours. An ominous constraint was the PPA expiry date of 21 April 1995. Bankers feared that if the PPA expired it would take at least six months to re-negotiate and may be even impossible to do so (*Euromoney*, September 1995).

U.S. Exim was concerned about the support letter that the Indonesian Government had signed. The language left it ambiguous as to whether the lenders had any legal recourse against the government. There was also a dispute over whether the Paiton private power company would own the land on which it was building. The prospective lenders asked the government to give some clear guarantees (*Euromoney*, September 1995). On 20 April 1995, the government responded that its letter of support was sufficient and that the lenders should be satisfied with this comfort. Meanwhile, the sponsors of the project pushed for a signing. But U.S. Exim became cautious and went to its board to seek approval. The board said that greater risk should be reflected in the pricing and so the banks raised their fees. The deal was finally signed on 21 April 1995.

This date has become a landmark for the first private power plant being successfully negotiated through project financing (*Euromoney*, September 1995). There is no further support other than the government's letter and the cost overrun facility. To attract banks' commitment, lenders will receive attractive yields with margins ranging from 175 basis point to 237.5 basis point depending on the facility (*Project Finance International*, 25 May 1995). About 30 banks have responded to Paiton Energy's call for extended lead managers by booking their interest with co-ordinating banks, Chase Manhattan Bank and IBJ. The replies were described as "overwhelmingly enthusiastic", reflecting the strong confidence financial institutions have in the project (*Project Finance International*, 1 September 1994). The commercial syndication for the financing of Paiton I was signed on 2 July 1995. The loan agreement provides for repayment over 16 years, a four-year grace period and an average interest rate of 9% (*Power in Asia*, 10 July 1995).

P. T. Pramino Ikat Nusantara in the Telecommunications Sector

Indonesia has one of the lowest telephone densities among ASEAN countries. To support its economic growth, Indonesia (under *Repelita VI*) has created the *Kerjasame Operasi* (KSO) scheme. This scheme encourages private sector operators and investors to enter joint ventures with P. T. Telkom, the state-owned telecommunications operator, under build-operate-transfer (BOT) arrangements. The five-year *Repelita VI* plan calls for the installation of two million lines at a cost of nearly US$3 billion by March 1999. The objectives of KSO are to improve P. T. Telkom's efficiency and standards by bringing in experienced telecom operators, and to finance the construction and integration of two million new lines across the five KSO regions identified which include Sumatra, West Java, Central Java, Kalimantan and east Indonesia (*Project Finance International*, 25 September 1996).

P. T. Pramino Ikat Nusantara (Pramino) won the tender in 1995 to build and finance 520,000 lines in the Sumatra region for US$450 million. The joint venture company consists of Indonesia companies P. T. Astratel Nusantara (59.5%), P. T. Intertel Pratamamedia (3.5%) and Primkopparpostel (2%) and an overseas partner, France Telecom

(35%) (*Project Finance International*, 8 May 1996). The tender was awarded even though there was no financing guarantee from Telkom or any other government agencies (*Project Finance International*, 30 March 1995).

The KSO structure was new and unfamiliar to the market at its launch time given the two-tier structure of the KSO unit. At the KSO unit level, a licensee would take over the existing Telkom setup and staff, and then expand the network to be designed, supplied, financed and owned by a private sector investor. At the company level, private investors would supply the operating management as well as build and finance the KSO unit. Private investors would only receive income distributed by Telkom in agreed proportions after deducting the operating expense and minimum Telkom revenue (MTR) during the 15-year revenue sharing scheme (*Project Finance International*, 25 September 1996).

Banks that examined the telephone deals highlighted foreign currency risks and tariff increases as their key concerns. Since revenues are in rupiah, sponsors must resolve the foreign currency problem in order to repay the U.S. dollar debt. In the concession agreement, P. T. Telkom is allowed to review the tariffs every three years although any increases are subject to approval by the Indonesian Government (*Project Finance International*, 11 October 1995). In the initial stage, Pramino as the first consortia had to settle issues such as the calculation of the revenue split between itself and Telkom because of the connection and intersection of KSO lines with existing Telkom phone lines. A sponsor also had to resolve the tax issues because P. T. Telkom is VAT-exempt. If it had to pay any VAT on the Telkom asset being assumed, the issue was whether these charges could be passed on to the customers. As the first of its kind in Indonesia, Pramino also needed to decide whether completion guarantees or other forms of similar support were needed to boost the confidence of financial investors (*Project Finance International*, 25 October 1995).

Pramino engaged ING Barings as its financial adviser. Chase Manhattan, BNP, Societe Generale and Fuji Bank comprised the lead arrangers. Pramino also approached the International Finance Corporation (IFC) to assist in its technical and financial needs. The shelter provided by the World Bank and the prestige attached to the IFC involvement would serve to enhance the comfort level of the deal (*Project Finance International*, 31 January 1996). Besides the IFC involvement, pricing of the deal was also set at 187.5 basis points which was satisfactory to most banks. The debt package was divided into US$100 million rupiah denominated tranches and an offshore US$350 million direct loan. A road show was conducted on 7 February 1996 to offer the US$350 million debt package in two tranches. Tranche A consisted of the standby letter of credit facility of up to US$150 million which will support the sponsors' guarantee issue to P. T. Telkom for the MTR payment. Tranche B was the standard commercial co-financing loan through a participation agreement with the IFC as the lender of record (*Project Finance International*, 14 February 1996). The full details are indicated in Table 7–3.

TABLE 7–3
Tranche Information

	Tranche A	**Tranche B**
Facility	NA	IFC "B" Loan
Amount	Up to US$150 million	Up to US$350 million
Tenor	8 years	8 years
SBLC fees	162.5 bp	NA
Margin	NA	187.5 bp
Repayment	In 12 semi-annual instalments after a three-year grace period	In 12 semi-annual instalments after a three-year grace period

Source: *Project Finance International*, 14 February 1996.

The business plan and financial model for the telecoms network were based on forecasts. There were no offtake agreements nor any series of structured contracts to support the revenue and expense assumptions. Also, there was no completion guarantee by the sponsors. Nonetheless, given the reputation of the sponsors, the economic prospects for Indonesia, the IFC involvement and the attractive pricing, financing was oversubscribed with 26 banks committing a total of US$485 million (*Project Finance International*, 13 March 1996). The final allocations that were made are as shown in Table 7–4.

On 29 July 1996, the US$400 million (inclusive of IFC's direct loan of US$50 million) financing package for Pramino was signed. This marked the conclusion of the first financing structure under the KSO scheme. The signing has set the benchmark for the remaining consortia to negotiate their financing structure and arrangement. As for Pramino, the progress of telephone installation has been encouraging and it increased installations by 33% to 100,000 lines by December 1996. France Telecom's Group Executive Vice President, Jean Yves Gouiffes, said that progress was ahead of schedule for the next two years (*Project Finance International*, 25 September 1996).

TABLE 7–4
Offshore Debt Package to Finance Pramino's 520,000 Lines in Sumatra

Roles ($ per participant)	Participants	US$ (millions)
Arrangers (US$18.5 million)	BNP, Chase Manhattan, Fuji Bank, Societe Generale.	74.0
Co-arrangers (US$15 million)	Banque Paribas, Hypobank, Credit Lyonnais, LTCB, Bank of Tokyo-Mitsubishi, WestLB.	90.0
Co-arrangers (US$10.5 million)	Keppel Bank, Toronto Dominion Bank.	21.0
Lead managers (US$13 million)	Banque Indosuez, Royal Bank of Scotland, Bayerische Landesbank.	39.0
Lead managers (US$10.5 million)	BFCE, Cho Hung Bank, Credit National, IBJ, Rabobank, De Nationale Investerings Bank, Sakura Bank, Sumitomo Trust, Union Europeene CIC.	94.5
Managers (US$7 million)	Banque Worms, Generale Bank, Toyo Trust.	21.0
Co-managers (US$3.5 million)	Credit Commerciale de France, Korea Exchange Bank, Seoul Bank.	10.5

Source: *Project Finance International*, 11 April 1996.

Chandra Asri in the Petrochemicals Sector

On 16 September 1995, Chandra Asri Olefin Petrochemical Complex (CAPC) which was inaugurated by President Suharto, became the first of its kind in Indonesia. The complex is sited at Cilegon, Serang, West Java. It was constructed at a cost of US$1.6 billion. Since the opening of this complex coincided with the fiftieth anniversary of Indonesia's independence, the completion ceremony of the two plants within the complex was included as part of the commemorative celebration.

The Indonesian P. T. Chandra Asri Group was established in late 1994 after the project was finally approved in 1993. It is 75%

owned by Indonesian investors (the Bimantara group, the Napan group, and Prajogo Pangestu of the Barito Pacific group) and 25% by Japanese companies including Marubeni (20%) and Showa Denko KK (5%) (Toyo Engineering, December 1995).

The process from the project's inception to its inauguration was a long and arduous one for all concerned. It all started when the Chandra Asri consortium leapfrogged Shell's advanced plans to build a plant at Cilacap (near Jakarta) by snaring the naphtha that it needed as feed-stock from Pertamina, the Indonesian state oil company in late 1990 (*Asia Money & Finance*, July/August, 1992). Then in November 1991, a sudden clampdown on all foreign borrowings was imposed under *Presidential Decree 39 (PD39)*. The aim was to arrest the rapid build-up in Indonesia's foreign debt by creating a priority queue for all new projects.

Despite CAPC's strong political connections, the clampdown on foreign borrowing affected it badly. The new rules torpedoed its plan to tap international markets for US$1.1 billion to supplement the US$500 million in equity and US$800 million in locally raised debt and working capital that was expected to be needed for the US$2.4 billion complex. Moreover, before project approval was given, work on the project had already begun with incurred costs estimated at US$263 million. Abandoning the project at that point would have meant huge losses for all concerned. The major problem underlying this project is the large upfront fees that the sponsors have built into the project. They are so significant that they may endanger the economic feasibility of the project. Despite the large capital outlay, it is widely believed that a full feasibility study was not done on the project because of its complexity (*Asia Money & Finance*, July/August 1992).

The construction of the olefin complex marked an important step towards Indonesian self-sufficiency in this area, particularly those products related to the plastics industry. By cutting the dependence on imported petrochemical products, the government hoped that its trade deficit would be further reduced (Phillip Townsend Associates, May 1996). However, in order to remain competitive in the market and to obtain a yield of 10% return on this project, CAPC proposed a 15% tariff on these imports. The idea of protection for CAPC upset Indonesia's technocrats who spent the 1980s cutting tariffs because of their contribution to Indonesia's high cost and low competitive economy (*Asia Money & Finance*, July/August 1992).

Meanwhile, the increasing domination of the project consortium by Marubeni, one of Japan's strongest trading companies and a member of the powerful Fuyo group of companies (including Fuji Bank), helped to rally support for the project from other equity investors. Marubeni's eagerness was based on its long term expansion strategy in Indonesia. It finally committed up to 40% of the US$500 million of equity needed for the plant. This was considerably higher than normal for a Japanese trading company in such a project.

However, there was scepticism about two other planned elements of the CAPC financing scheme. One was the US$550 million offshore syndicated loan and the other was a US$550 million deferred letter of credit payment from the Export Import Bank of Japan (Jexim) to replace an irrevocable letter of credit (ILC) issued by the state-owned Bank Bumi Daya. The project will be able to call on no more than US$300 million of first ranking bank project debt (*Asia Money & Finance*, July/August 1992).

In April 1992, a new rule was implemented to allow 100% foreign investment in large projects. The rationale of this abrupt change in policy was unclear but it was expected to revive some of the large projects suspended when PD39 was introduced in November 1991. CAPC immediately re-formulated their proposal to meet the "purely private" requirements of the April ruling and re-submitted this to the government for approval (*Asia Money & Finance*, July/August 1992). In January 1993, the project was approved, nearly two years after the idea was conceived. The project has since been converted into a foreign-owned entity with a reduced investment volume to circumvent restrictions on foreign borrowings (*Project Finance International*, 22 January 1993).

In March 1993, Marubeni Corp, Showa Denki and Indonesia's Barito Pacific group garnered more than US$600 million in loans for the US$1.6 billion project. The Exim Bank of Japan granted loans of more than US$400 million to the two Japanese companies. The two Japanese companies borrowed a total of US$190 million from 10 to 12 banks against corporate guarantees. Apparently, the Japanese companies tapped on credits already available to them and there was no syndication of the bank loans (*Project Finance International*, 30 April 1993).

In early 1995, the Indonesia P. T. Chandra Asri group asked the government to impose a 40% levy on imported ethylene and propylene. This caused resentment among the established corporations with downstream operations that depend on ethylene as a raw material. These firms include Shell, BP, Mitsubishi and Mitsui, which now find themselves pitted against newcomers such as Marubeni, BTR Nylex of Australia and Himmont Inc. of the U.S. All of them would welcome import tariffs to protect their recent investments. On the other hand, local plastic manufacturers expressed resistance to import levies by pointing out that these may raise production costs, thus reducing their competitive edge in exporting finished plastics products (*Petrochemicals*, October 1995). A few days before the inauguration ceremony, Industry Minister Tungky Ariwibowo reiterated that the government would not give tariff protection, tax incentives or special trade regulations to support the CAPC. The request was rejected because it contravened Indonesia's commitment to free trade (*Indo Business*, September 1995).

However, in February 1996 the decision was reversed and a 20% to 25% import surcharge was levied on both products. The Indonesian Government has committed itself to reduce tariffs to 10% by the year 2003. But analysts feel that protection will continue to be provided to certain sectors such as automobiles, petrochemicals and agriculture (*Euromoney*, April 1996).

In preparing the economy for advanced industrialisation, Indonesia's planners have recognised the need for a critical mass of industrial and technological capacity to reach higher levels of productivity and to prevent economic flight in the competitive and turbulent environment that lies ahead. Securing the most modern petrochemical facilities is recognised as the catalyst for growth in the various sectors of the Indonesian economy, including the plastics industry, a sector in which the country has lagged until now. Indonesia's planners believe that Indonesia will gain enormously from an economically viable petrochemicals sector. More than US$1 billion is expected to be saved annually on imports; new spin-off enterprises will emerge; Indonesians will gain in know-how from the new technologies; and thousands of new jobs will be created. A profitable industry is expected to contribute taxes to the government exchequer and thus broaden development. Consequently, the petrochemicals sector is destined to sustain growth in the foreseeable future (INDIO, 1996).

RISK ANALYSIS

The Stanchart checklist was used to analyse the risk exposure in the three scenarios described in the previous sections. A risk analysis matrix summarising the rating of the risk components and overall project risk rating is tabulated in Table 7–5.

TABLE 7–5
Risk Analysis Matrix

	Projects		
Risk Components	**Paiton I**	**Pramino**	**CAPC**
Completion	L	L	L
Production/operation	L	L	L
Market	L	M	L
Feedstock	L	N/A	L
Foreign exchange	L	H	L
Project risk rating	L	M	L

L – low risk exposure
M – middle risk exposure
H – high risk exposure
N/A – not applicable

Paiton I

The construction and equipment suppliers' risk can be considered low as construction is undertaken on a fixed sum turnkey basis by a group of experienced multinationals that are renowned in their field. Mission Energy, a partner of Paiton Energy, has vast experience in operating and maintaining power plants. Hence, the production and operation risks are considered low. PLN has signed a contract to purchase all the capacity and energy produced by Paiton Energy Company. This reduces the market risk to a minimum level. The risk level for feedstock is low because the supply of the coal feedstock is provided by P. T. Batu Hitam which is also a partner of the Paiton Energy Company. The coal is also an ultra-clean burning fuel with low environmental effects and, thus, is well accepted by the Indonesia government. In the PPA, the capacity fees including debt service, equity return, fixed operating costs and taxes are borne by Indonesia. Also, payments to Paiton Energy Company have been adjusted to include tariffs and inflation due to changes in operations and fuel costs. PLN has also agreed to make U.S. dollars available to Paiton Energy Company if the latter cannot convert the rupiah. Hence, the foreign exchange risk is classified as low.

Pramino KSO

The Pramino KSO was the first among the five consortia to complete the financing arrangement. Since the KSO structure was new, unfamiliar to the market and somewhat complex given the two-tier structure, there was no precedence as far as risk evaluations were concerned. As a new privately funded telecommunications project, a completion guarantee was deemed to be important to investors but the sponsors decided not to provide one. However, the completion risk was not a real concern among the investors because the reputation of the sponsors, France Telecom and P. T. Astratel, was strong. With France Telecom's experience, the technology risk during the implementation was low. Although there was no guarantee of completion, investors were comfortable with the sponsors' abilities to complete the project on time and within budget. Investors were also confident with the sponsors' abilities to manage operations and production but concern was raised on meeting the US$150 million MTR guarantee. This was resolved by IFC's due diligence study. The study showed a positive correlation between the higher level of MTR (which could signify a larger network taken over from Telkom) and subsequently higher distributable KSO revenue in the early years for Pramino, thus reducing the need to finance capital expenditures with external debt (*Project Finance International*, 25 September 1996).

The business plan and financial model for a telecommunications project are usually based on a forecast of the futures market. There were no offtake agreements, or series of structured contracts, to support the revenue and expense assumptions. Investors could only rely on the realism of the forecast and the assumptions used in the financial planning and projections, combined with the knowledge of Indonesia's economic growth and the low telephone penetration in Sumatra. Whether these positive aspects outweighed the market risks is a moot point from an investor's perspective. Feedstock risk evaluation did not apply in this scenario. As for foreign exchange risk, Pramino collects its revenue in rupiah but needs to repay the external debt in U.S. dollars; thus, it is subject to foreign exchange risk exposure. This risk will remain as a challenge for the sponsors.

CAPC

Completion risks resulting from construction, equipment suppliers and foreign exchange were minimal for CAPC since the project was undertaken on a fixed sum turnkey basis by a group of experienced multinationals that are renowned in their respective fields. Toya Engineering Corporation (TEC) was the primary construction contractor for both the ethylene and polyethylene plants in the petrochemical complex under the supervision of TEC President Sonoda. All transactions in the project, including the purchase of feedstock and the sale of end products to customers, are denominated mainly in U.S. currency. Hence, the foreign exchange risk is kept to a minimum (Toyo Engineering, December 1995).

Production and operating risk are low because the company has experience in operating such plants. Indonesia has a large pool of both skilled and semi-skilled labour to support the manufacturing industry. CAPC is strategically located to take advantage of the large labour base and the growing industrialisation (growth rate of 7%) of the country (Phillip Townsend Associates, May 1996). There is also minimal risk in the supply of feedstock because CAPC has struck an agreement with Pertamina, the state oil company, to purchase the vital naphtha feedstock originally intended for the Shell complex (*Asia Money & Finance*, July/August 1992). The ethylene plant was designed to produce about 510,000 tonnes per year of ethylene and 240,000 tonnes per year of propylene. However, the output from the complex is not expected to meet domestic demand. To make up the shortfall, Indonesia still has to import more than US$2 billion in upstream petroleum products each year. Hence, market demand for its products is not an issue (*Indo Business*, September 1995).

In this analysis, all the Stanchart components (except feedstock) were considered by the investors. Although not all the risks could be overcome, they were minimised. The threshold level of risk to be taken depends on the investors' experiences in project financing and understanding of the business.

CONCLUSION

Indonesia has liberalised its foreign investment policy to enable the private sector to play an increasingly important role in the financing of infrastructure projects. Investors are advised to understand the underlying critical success factors of project financing in Indonesia in order to minimise their risk exposure.

REFERENCES

Asia Money & Finance, "Shell and Chandra Asri Resume the Olefin Race", July/August 1992, pp. 45–9.

Business Asia, "Indonesia Overview – Filling Potholes", 22 May 1995, p. 6.

Business Review Southeast Asia Publishing Service Inc., *Southeast Asia Business Omnibook – Indonesia*, Jakarta, 1995.

Euromoney, "Indonesia's Protracted Power Project", September 1995, pp. 260–1.

Euromoney, (http://www.euromoney.com/contents/publications/euromoney/em.96/em.96.04/em.96.04.29.html), April 1996.

INDIO, *Indonesia Source Book 1996*, Jakarta, 1996.

Indo Business, "Indonesia's First Olefin Plant Inaugurated", (http://www.indobiz.com/company/ebn/eb950930.htm#W3), 30 September 1995.

McMeckan J., "Infrastructure Developments in Indonesia", *Macquarie*, Spring 1995, pp. 18–9.

Minter Ellison and Makarim & Tairas, Legal Consultants, *Business Opportunities: Doing Business in Indonesia*, Jakarta, February 1996.

Petrochemicals, "SE Asian Melee Bleeds Investment from Vietnam" (http://www.serve.vet/vietnam/pages/viet0219.htm), October 1995.

Phillip Townsend Associates Inc. (http://www.pla1.com/~townsend/newslet/may96×1.html), Vol. 28, May 1996.

Power in Asia, "Paiton Power Station to Use Ultra Clean Coal", 19 September 1994, p. 13.

Power in Asia, "Commercial Syndication for Paiton I Closes", 10 July 1995, pp. 15–6.

Project and Trade Finance, "Indonesia's Power First", January 1996, p. 29.

Project Finance International, "Foreign Investments Reach Record Volume", 22 January 1993, p. 15.

Project Finance International, "Projects Await Paiton Completion", 5 February 1993, pp. 7–8.

Project Finance International, "US$600 Million Loans Set Olefins on Its Way", 30 April 1993, p. 13.

Project Finance International, "Paiton Energy Company Covers Project Cost", Issue 31, 13 September 1993, p. 11.

Project Finance International, "PPA Puts Paiton Back on Banks' Live List", Issue 42, 18 February 1994, p. 8.

Project Finance International, "Eight Banks Lead Paiton", Issue 53, 21 July 1994, pp. 10–1.

Project Finance International, "Paiton Gives Strong Support", Issue 55, 29 September 1994, pp. 11–2.

Project Finance International, "Paiton Overwhelms", Issue 55, 1 September 1994, p. 11.

Project Finance International, "The Bucks Stop Here", November 1994, pp. 45–7.

Project Finance International, "US Exim Agrees to Paiton Deal", Issue 67, 2 March 1995, p. 11.

Project Finance International, "Singapore Telecom, BTU Online for Award", Issue 69, 30 March 1995, p. 10.

Project Finance International, "Paiton Secures Landmark Funds", Issue 71, 27 April 1995.

Project Finance International, "Long-term Deals Priced from 125 bp", Issue 73, 25 May 1995, pp. 9–10.

Project Finance International, "The Paiton that Would Not Die", Issue 74, 8 June 1995, pp. 8–10.

Project Finance International, "KSO Rings in Phone Funds", Issue 82, 11 October 1995, pp. 2–3.

Project Finance International, "KSO's Cross Lines", Issue 83, 25 October 1995, p. 10.

Project Finance International, "KSO Lines Buzz", Issue 89, 31 January 1996, p. 8.

Project Finance International, "KSO's Ring and Tell", Issue 90, 14 February 1996, p. 12.

Project Finance International, "KSO Lines Bunch Up", Issue 92, 13 March 1996, p. 13.

Project Finance International, "Pramino Ikat Statistics", Issue 94, 11 April 1996, p. 10.

Project Finance International, "KSO Sponsor Boost", Issue 96, 8 May 1996, p. 11.

Project Finance International, "P. T. Pramino Ikat", Issue 105, 25 September 1996, p. 12.

Project Finance International, "Pramino Breaks New Ground in Asian Telecom's Financing", Issue 105, 25 September 1996, p. 42.

Telecommunication Industry (http://www.idola.net.id/dc/tele.htm#summary), October 1996.

Toyo Engineering (http://www.toyo-eng.co.jp/NewHome/Overview/TECInformation/Dec95/suharto-e.html), December 1995.

Transportation Industry (http://www.idola.net.id/dc/trans.htm#summary), October 1996.

Wuigfield T., "The Competitive Edge", *Project and Trade Finance*, May 1994, pp. 43–4.

Chapter 8

Hedging the Rupiah's Risk*

BY
LIM Ay Ling
ONG Pang Huat
GOH Yew Soong
Steven CHIN Vui Hiung

INTRODUCTION

THERE WERE TWO significant devaluations of the rupiah in the 1980s and the fear of its devaluation again re-surfaces from time to time. While this possibility is small, it is an important consideration for prospective foreign investors considering Indonesia. This chapter summarises the recent history of monetary and exchange rate management in Indonesia as well as its present exchange rate management system. The trends of the rupiah's value and the available hedging instruments in Indonesia are discussed.

MONETARY AND EXCHANGE RATE MANAGEMENT

Central Bank

Indonesia has implemented its monetary policy through a central bank since the early stages of its independence in 1945. In 1946, Indonesia established *Bank Negara Indonesia* to act as the central bank. However, it was not active until 1950 due to Indonesia's continuing struggle against the Dutch even after it proclaimed independence. In 1951, the Indonesia government nationalised *De Javasch Bank*. It subse-

* We appreciate the comments and guidance from Dr. John Vong.

quently converted *De Javasch Bank* into its central bank under a new name, Bank Indonesia, based on the *Central Bank Act* of 1953. Bank Negara Indonesia was then converted into a commercial bank (Suhardiman, 1996).

By the *Presidential Decree* of 1965, Bank Indonesia, together with four other state-owned banks, were integrated into a new bank named Bank Negara Indonesia. The *Central Bank Act* of 1968 subsequently reinstated Bank Indonesia as the central bank of Indonesia (Binhadi, 1995).

As the central bank of Indonesia, Bank Indonesia implements monetary policy and is responsible for regulating and supervising the banking system. It is the sole issuer of currency. The central bank sets the value of the rupiah on a daily basis and influences the markets through the purchase and sale of foreign currency (The Chase Manhattan Bank, 1996).

Historical Development

Before December 1964, the Indonesia government had adopted a tight foreign exchange control system introduced by the Dutch in 1940. All foreign exchange transactions were prohibited unless they were explicitly allowed. The government required the surrender of all privately earned foreign exchange proceeds to the central bank. The allocation of foreign exchange for various purposes was based on a rationing system, using a multiple exchange rate. Under the multiple exchange rate system, the government varied the official rate from time to time based on the need to support exports and to restrain imports. The official rate also varied according to the categories of exports or imports (Binhadi, 1995).

In December 1964, Indonesia implemented a new *Foreign Exchange Act*. Under this Act, the central bank, private companies and individuals had the right to keep foreign exchange proceeds. However, the government still held full control on the use of foreign exchange with regard to import of goods and services (Binhadi, 1995).

In 1967, the government established a foreign exchange bourse following its abolition of the regulation that required the government's permission for the use of foreign exchange. The establishment of the foreign exchange bourse provided a place where foreign currencies could be traded. This was also the first time since the existence of an exchange control that foreign currencies could be legally traded against the rupiah. The foreign exchange bourse assumed the responsibility for determining the foreign exchange rates. The foreign exchange bourse participants consisted of the central bank, foreign exchange banks and other legalised companies considered appropriate by the central bank to be bourse members (Binhadi, 1995).

Also in 1967, the government enacted a new *Banking Act* which allowed foreign banks in Indonesia to function as foreign exchange banks. These banks were required to actively develop Indonesia's international trade, broaden the international market for Indonesian exports and encourage foreign investment in Indonesia (Binhadi, 1995).

Since 1969, the government has further authorised some of the private national banks to operate as foreign exchange banks. These particular private national banks must meet the eligibility criteria of the central bank to be upgraded to foreign exchange banks. The criteria includes the implementation of sound management and operation systems as well as possession of financial and technical capabilities (Binhadi, 1995).

During the period 1970 to 1978, there were further changes to both the foreign exchange trading mechanism and foreign exchange rates. With effect from 1970, the holding, sale and purchase of foreign exchange were no longer subject to restrictions. However, exporters were still required to surrender the export proceeds to a foreign exchange bank. The foreign exchange banks, in turn, were required to sell the acquired foreign exchange to the central bank. On the other hand, importers and others who needed foreign exchange were required to buy it from a foreign exchange bank. In this context, a foreign exchange bank could purchase and sell foreign exchange. The foreign exchange transactions between any bank and the central bank were done through the foreign exchange bourse (Binhadi, 1995).

After August 1971, the foreign exchange rate was no longer determined at the foreign exchange bourse. It was determined solely by the central bank using the principle of pegging the rupiah to the U.S. dollar. At the same time, the rupiah was devalued by about 10% so that the rupiah middle rate was set against U.S. dollar at Rp 415 for US$1 (Suhardiman, 1996).

A fundamental change in the exchange rate system occurred between 1978 and 1982. In 1978, the method of determining the exchange rate was changed from pegging to the U.S. dollar to pegging the rupiah to a basket of currencies of Indonesia's main trading partners. Before making this change, the government devalued the rupiah by 33.6% against the U.S. dollar because of high inflation and the loss of external competitiveness. With this new system, it was expected that Indonesia would increase exports and foreign exchange revenues in addition to stimulating foreign capital investments (Suhardiman, 1996).

Between 1982 and 1992, there was further deregulation in the foreign exchange market mechanism. During this period, the government abolished nearly all foreign exchange restrictions. Beginning in 1982, for example, exporters and importers were free to move funds in and out of the country. They could freely buy or sell rupiah through foreign exchange banks. From 1988 onwards, joint venture banks formed by foreign and local banks are allowed to function as foreign exchange banks (Binhadi, 1995).

In 1989, the government abolished the foreign exchange bourse and decided that transactions between the central bank and a foreign exchange bank must be done through the dealing room. Since then, the exchange rate determined by the central bank is not the daily compulsory rate. This means that the exchange rate in the foreign exchange market can fluctuate in accordance with developments in the domestic and international markets. The central bank can intervene to adjust this rate. The government has allowed the establishment of brokerage firms since 1992 to encourage the development of the foreign exchange market (Binhadi, 1995).

In the mid-1980s, a series of external shocks weakened Indonesia's economy. Among them were a severe decline in oil prices, a sharp rise in international interest rates and a depreciation of the U.S. dollar against the Japanese yen. The government consequently devalued the rupiah by 28% in 1983 and by 31% in 1986 (The Chase Manhattan Bank, 1996).

After 1986, Indonesia implemented a managed floating exchange rate to prevent possible speculation in the foreign exchange market arising from foreign exchange deregulation and rumours of a further rupiah devaluation. The central bank also pursued a policy of depreciating the rupiah against the U.S. dollar by 4% to 5% a year. This action reduces the need for a large one-off devaluation of the rupiah and boosts the competitiveness of the country's non-oil exports (*The Banker*, 1996). In August 1996, Indonesian Finance Minister Mar'ie Muhammad reconfirmed the continuation of this policy by pointing out that an undervalued rupiah against the U.S. dollar was preferred (*The Business Times*, 9 August 1996).

The Intervention Band

Since 1986, the central bank has targeted a steady real exchange rate by allowing the nominal exchange rate to depreciate in line with the differential between the domestic and U.S. inflation rates. To achieve this target, the central bank quotes the value of the rupiah daily against a basket of foreign currencies including a heavily weighted U.S. dollar.[1] It sets an intervention band around these daily quoted mid-rates and sells or buys U.S. dollars against the rupiah accordingly to ensure the intended depreciation. The value of the rupiah is allowed to fluctuate within the intervention band. The central bank intervenes when the spot rate falls outside of the band (The Chase Manhattan Bank, 1996).

The central bank has attempted to raise the flexibility of the rupiah exchange rate in order to discourage speculative capital inflows, in particular short-term capital, and to dampen pressures on the rupiah exchange rate. It has done this by repeatedly widening the intervention band seven times from Rp 6 (0.3% maximum fluctuation rate) in September 1992 to Rp 192 in September 1996 (8% maximum fluctuation rate) as shown in Table 8–1. The intervention bands of the rupiah from 1991 to 1996 are shown in Table 8–2 and Figure 8–1.

TABLE 8–1
The Widening Band of the Rupiah from 1992 to 1996

Date	Buying rate Rp	Selling rate Rp	Intervention Band
16 September 1992	2,045	2,055	Rp 6 – Rp 10
3 January 1994	2,112	2,132	Rp 10 – Rp 20
5 September 1994	2,166	2,196	Rp 20 – Rp 30
30 June 1995	2,224	2,268	Rp 30 – Rp 44
29 December 1995	2,286	2,352	Rp 44 – Rp 66
13 June 1996	2,378	2,496	Rp 66 – Rp 118
11 September 1996	2,412	2,604	Rp 118 – Rp 192

Source: Bank Indonesia (May 1996).

THE TRENDS OF THE INDONESIAN RUPIAH

Trends Over the Last Five Years

The central bank discouraged speculative capital inflows by widening the intervention band. In theory, widening the band increases the uncertainty in exchange rate movements. Wider intervention bands should increase the currency risk of holding rupiah assets and thereby

---

1 This information was obtained with permission from private sources in Singapore, December 1996.

TABLE 8–2
The Intervention Band of the Rupiah
(exchange rate per US$1)

	1991		1992		1993		1994		1995		1996	
	Buy	Sell	Buy	Sell	Buy	Sell	Buy	Sell	Buy	Sell	Buy	Sell
January	1,909	1,915	2,001	2,007	2,060	2,070	2,112	2,132	2,192	2,222	2,322	2,388
February	1,917	1,923	2,007	2,013	2,062	2,072	2,126	2,146	2,197	2,227	2,333	2,399
March	1,929	1,933	2,014	2,020	2,066	2,076	2,134	2,154	2,204	2,234	2,344	2,410
April	1,936	1,942	2,019	2,125	2,069	2,079	2,139	2,159	2,212	2,242	2,353	2,419
May	1,944	1,950	2,024	2,030	2,074	2,084	2,145	2,165	2,221	2,251	2,365	2,431
June	1,951	1,957	2,030	2,036	2,083	2,093	2,150	2,170	2,224	2,268	2,378	2,496
July	1,956	1,962	2,032	2,038	2,091	2,101	2,159	2,179	2,234	2,278	2,387	2,505
August	1,962	1,968	2,031	2,037	2,097	2,107	2,165	2,185	2,244	2,288	2,399	2,517
September	1,965	1,971	2,033	2,043	2,103	2,113	2,166	2,196	2,254	2,298	2,412	2,604
October	1,974	1,980	2,045	2,055	2,101	2,111	2,171	2,201	2,263	2,307	2,426	2,618
November	1,982	1,988	2,054	2,064	2,101	2,111	2,178	2,208	2,274	2,318	2,345	2,537
December	1,989	1,995	2,057	2,067	2,100	2,120	2,185	2,215	2,286	2,352	2,359	2,551

Sources: Bank Indonesia (1996); Central Bureau of Statistics (1995) and (1996b).

FIGURE 8–1
Intervention Band of the Rupiah (December 1991 to December 1996)

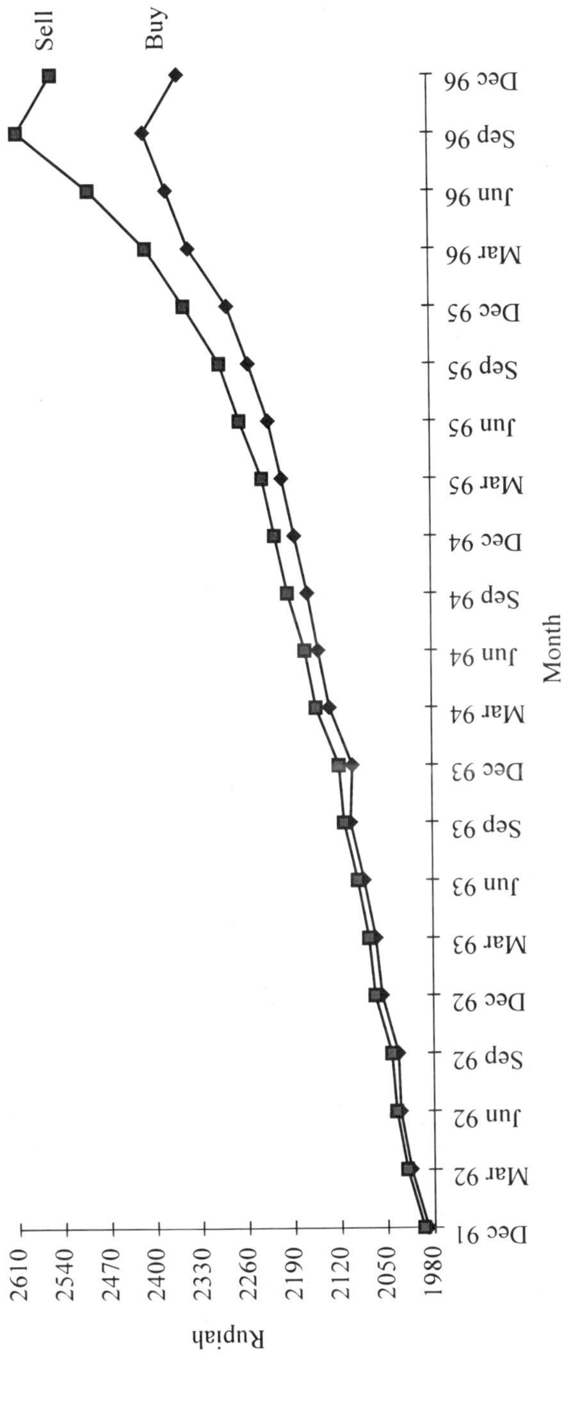

Sources: Bank Indonesia (1996); Central Bureau of Statistics (1995) and (1996b).

dampening the demand for these assets. However, with local three-month interest rate spreads of almost 1,000 basis points over U.S. dollar rates and a known currency downside of only 4% to 5% per year, the currency risk is worth taking. Thus, rupiah assets continue to attract substantial capital inflows. This inflates the money supply and undermines domestic monetary policy, providing support for the rupiah. Every time the central bank widens the intervention band, the rupiah is likely to collide with the strong side of the intervention band within the next ten days. The rupiah has appreciated, rather than depreciated.

Despite widening the currency bands, the central bank has achieved an average annual rupiah depreciation of almost 5% since 1988. The average exchange rate of the rupiah to each U.S. dollar from 1991 to 1996 continues to weaken as shown in Table 8–3.

TABLE 8–3
The Average Exchange Rate of the Rupiah Against the U.S. Dollar: 1991 to 1996

Year	1991	1992	1993	1994	1995	1996
January	1,912	2,004	2,066	2,122	2,207	2,322
February	1,920	2,010	2,067	2,136	2,212	2,333
March	1,932	2,017	2,071	2,144	2,219	2,344
April	1,939	2,022	2,074	2,149	2,227	2,353
May	1,947	2,027	2,079	2,155	2,236	2,365
June	1,954	2,033	2,088	2,160	2,246	2,378
July	1,959	2,035	2,096	2,169	2,256	2,387
August	1,965	2,034	2,102	2,175	2,266	2,399
September	1,968	2,038	2,108	2,181	2,276	2,412
October	1,977	2,050	2,106	2,186	2,285	2,418
November	1,985	2,059	2,106	2,193	2,296	2,441
December	1,992	2,062	2,110	2,200	2,308	2,455

Sources: Bank Indonesia (1996); Central Bureau of Statistics (1995) and (1996b).

Future Trends

The rupiah market continues to be rife with speculation over a further widening of the intervention band from the current level of Rp 192 (Private sources, Singapore, 1996). The expectation is that the value of the rupiah is unlikely to deviate very much in the short term from its historical trend. In January 1997, an established financial institute in Singapore forecasted the future trend of the rupiah against the U.S. dollar as shown in Table 8–4.

TABLE 8–4
Rupiah Versus U.S. Dollar (end of period)

1996 Estimate	1997 Forecast	1998 Forecast
2,363	2,450	2,535

Source: Private sources, Singapore, 1997.

HEDGING

Events and Political Factors

The central bank's implementation of a managed floating exchange rate has contributed to the extremely low volatility of the rupiah. The rupiah's movements against the U.S. dollar are the least volatile of any Asean currency, using the standard deviation as a measure of daily volatility in exchange rate movements. By comparison, the Malaysian ringgit and the Singapore dollar are estimated to be 2.3 times more volatile than the rupiah as shown in Table 8–5 (The Chase Manhattan Bank, 1996).

TABLE 8–5
Average Daily Volatility
from January 1993 to February 1996

Currency	Daily Volatility (%)
Indonesian rupiah	0.0995
Thai baht	0.1003
Singapore dollar	0.2336
Malaysian ringgit	0.2289

Source: The Chase Manhattan Bank (1996).

While the rupiah's movements against the U.S. dollar have been generally stable, it is susceptible to event risk. For example, there was doubt over Indonesia's ability to service its debt obligation when Mexico's financial crisis took place in early 1995. The same uncertainty existed when the yen appreciated steeply against the U.S. dollar in March 1995 (The Chase Manhattan Bank, 1996).

Political factors appear to have contributed to the rupiah's exchange risk. Indonesian financial markets were hurt twice in June 1996 on false rumours that President Suharto was in ill health (*The*

Business Times, 20 September 1996). Further, the financial markets tumbled in the wake of the riots and a crackdown on the opposition headquarters of the Indonesian Democratic Party in July 1996 (*The Business Times*, 29 July and 3 August 1996).

The rupiah closed at a stable 2,333 on Friday, 26 July 1996 but tumbled to 2,360 on Monday, 29 July 1996 after police stormed the Indonesian Democratic Party headquarters in Jakarta on Saturday, 27 July 1996 (*The Business Times*, 30 July 1996). The rupiah, however, was well on its way to recovery on Friday morning, 2 August 1996, after investor confidence was buoyed by the easing of tension (*The Straits Times*, 3 August 1996).

Economic Factors

The major risk to the rupiah is a sudden change in the exchange rate policy (The Chase Manhattan Bank, 1996). The increased frequency of widening the intervention band has led to the perception of a forthcoming free float to dampen speculation and discourage short term capital inflows. A move to a free float could result in initial currency volatility, with speculators playing on the misfounded fears of the rupiah devaluating.

Derivative Products

The derivative products that can be used to hedge against exchange rate risk are numerous. In general, these products can be classified as options, forward contracts, futures and swaps (Bank Indonesia, 23 September 1996).

An option is a contract between a buyer and a seller that gives the buyer the right, but not the obligation, to purchase or sell a foreign currency at a later date at an exchange rate agreed upon today. The option buyer pays the seller a certain amount of premium. The option seller stands ready to sell or buy according to the contract terms if and when the buyer so desires (Chance, 1989).

A forward contract is an agreement between a buyer and a seller to purchase or sell a foreign currency at a later date at an exchange rate agreed upon on the agreement. A forward contract is like an option. However, an option carries the right, not the obligation, to go through with the buy or sell transaction. If the exchange rate of the underlying foreign currency changes, then the option holder may decide to forgo buying or selling at the fixed rate. On the other hand, the two parties in a forward contract incur the obligation to ultimately buy and sell the foreign currency (Chance, 1989). A forward contract is commonly used for known exposures to currency risk.

Unlike option markets, forward markets have no physical facility for trading. Forward markets operate through informal communication channels among major financial institutions instead of organised exchanges (Chance, 1989).

Forward contracts are often used to hedge the risk of holding a certain asset (or liability). This allows the contract owner to "lock-in" the price and, so, to fix the revenue from the future asset sale at the time the contract is made. It is also commonly used for known exposures (Anderson, 1993).

A futures contract is an agreement between a buyer and a seller to buy or sell a foreign currency at a future date. The contract trades on a futures exchange and is subject to a daily settlement procedure. In essence, futures contracts are like liquid forward contracts. Unlike forward contracts, however, futures contracts trade on organised exchanges which are called futures markets (Chance, 1989).

With organised exchanges, the buyer of a futures contract, who has the obligation to buy a foreign currency at a later date, can sell the contract in the futures market which relieves the obligation to purchase the foreign currency. Likewise, the seller of the futures contract, who is obligated to sell a foreign currency at a later date, can buy the contract back in the futures market which relieves the obligation to sell the foreign currency. Futures contracts differ from forward contracts in that they are subject to a daily settlement procedure. In the daily settlement, investors pay losses every day to other investors who make a profit (Chance, 1989).

A swap is an agreement between two parties to switch one currency with another currency at a fixed interval. Swap contracts are similar to forward contracts. However, swap contracts are available for longer maturities. Currencies are swapped initially through a normal spot foreign exchange transaction. In this way, each party involved has full availability of the currencies they are seeking. Each of the parties pays the other one the interest obligation in accordance with the swap agreement throughout the life of the two obligations. At maturity, the currencies are swapped back to the original currencies through a forward foreign exchange transaction (Anderson, 1993).

Because Indonesia's trade has grown substantially, quotes for the rupiah against major currencies such as the U.S. dollar and Deutschmark can now be obtained in other regional centres such as Singapore and Hong Kong. Trading volumes in the spot and forward markets in Indonesia have risen rapidly in recent years. The average daily turnover for the rupiah is estimated at US$10 billion to US$12 billion for the spot and forward transactions (The Chase Manhattan Bank, 1996).

The average transaction size for the spot market is US$5 million. The forward markets generally are liquid up to one year. The majority of market liquidity falls in the shorter period of up to six months, although deals have been agreed for up to five years. The average transaction size is estimated at between US$10 million and US$20 million, with forward bid-offer spreads of about Rp 1 to Rp 2 for one to three-month forwards, Rp 2 for three to six-month forwards, and Rp 3 to Rp 8 beyond six months. At times of liquidity squeezes, spreads can be widened substantially for periods over six months (The Chase Manhattan Bank, 1996).

Regulations

To deter speculative activities in derivative contracts, the authorities limited the net open position and net forward position of commercial banks to 25% of their capital. Exposure to a single currency cannot exceed 25% of the total exposure (The Chase Manhattan Bank, 1996).

The central bank introduced provisions on derivative transactions through the *Decree of the Board of Managing Directors of Bank Indonesia* on 29 December 1995. They are designed to provide banks with minimum guidelines to limit the risks that may be incurred from derivative transactions. There are several key points to the provisions. First, the derivative transactions conducted for customers without fund movement must meet a margin deposit of at least 10% of the transaction ceiling, unless the margin deposit has been specifically set. If the margin deposit reaches 50% of the original balance, then the customer must bear the difference. Secondly, the loss for derivative transactions conducted for a bank's own position must not exceed 10% of its capital. Thirdly, banks are required to submit a weekly report on derivative transactions to the central bank. The report must cover gains or losses on derivative transactions, either realised or unrealised, in the interest of the bank or customers (Bank Indonesia, 23 September 1996).

Implications of the Rupiah's Risk for Foreign Investors

Hedging the rupiah's risk increases business costs of foreign investors in Indonesia. On the other hand, the overall profit of foreign investors is squeezed to the extent that any significant rupiah devaluation takes place and there is no hedge.

Although there are a number of hedging instruments available, their use by foreign small or medium-sized enterprises (SMEs) are limited for several reasons. First, forward, option and swap contracts involve creditworthiness. SMEs may not be perceived as having adequate creditworthiness for using these hedging instruments without complications. Secondly, SMEs may have difficulty raising the required upfront premiums on certain types of hedging instruments such as forward contracts. Thirdly, SMEs may lack the knowledge underlying the strategic use of hedging instruments. Nonetheless, SMEs with small or medium amounts of capital that have not hedged against the rupiah's risks are in serious jeopardy if the rupiah is devalued.

CONCLUSION

Indonesia's economic growth is buoyant and it has committed to deregulation and free trade. Today, it offers one of the best regulatory and economic environments for foreign business. Foreign investors in Indonesia, like in many other countries, may face the exchange rate risk of the currency of the host country. This risk, however, can be hedged against with proper use of the available derivative products.

REFERENCES

Andersen Torben Juul, *Currency and Interest Rate Hedging: A User's Guide to Option, Futures, Swaps and Forward Contracts*, 2nd edition, New York Institute of Finance, New York, 1993.

Bank Indonesia, *Indonesian Financial Statistics*, Vol. 24, No. 5, Jakarta, May 1996.

Bank Indonesia, *Report for the Financial Year 1995/1996*, Jakarta, 1996.

Bank Indonesia, "Weekly Report No. 1940", Jakarta, 23 September 1996.

Binhadi, *Financial Sector Deregulation, Banking Development and Monetary Policy: The Indonesian Experience (1983–1993)*, Indonesian Bankers Institute, Jakarta, 1995.

Chance Don M., *An Introduction to Options and Futures*, 3rd edition, Dryden Press, Chicago, 1989.

Central Bureau of Statistics, *Foreign Exchange Rates and Gold Prices in Jakarta 1994*, Indonesia, 1995.

Central Bureau of Statistics, *Economic Indicator May 1996: Monthly Statistical Bulletin*, Indonesia, 1996a.

Central Bureau of Statistics, *Foreign Exchange Rates and Gold Prices in Jakarta 1995*, Indonesia, 1996b.

Suhardiman Hendrik, "Highlight of Indonesia Monetary Policy and Banking Development", P. T. Tamara Bank, Jakarta, 9 December 1996.

The Banker, "Indonesia Widens Band", February 1996.

The Business Times, "Stock Market, Rupiah Expected to be Hit Today", 29 July 1996.

The Business Times, "Indonesian Stocks, Rupiah Tumble in Aftermath of Riots", 30 July 1996.

The Straits Times, "Jakarta Markets Recover from Turmoil", 3 August 1996.

The Business Times, "I Prefer Rupiah to be Undervalued, says Indon Finance Minister", 9 August 1996.

The Business Times, "Rupiah Recovers after Govt says Suharto is Well", 20 September 1996.

The Chase Manhattan Bank, "Indonesian Rupiah", *Asiamoney*, Hong Kong, November 1996.

Chapter 9

The Awakened Giant: Implications for Indonesia's Banking and Financial Sector

BY
John VONG

INTRODUCTION

BUSINESS TRAVELLERS, INVESTORS and holiday makers complain endlessly about clogged roads, an unreliable power supply and congested telephone lines. But they keep coming back to Indonesia. Business travel is growing by leaps and bounds, and investment capital keeps on increasing. There is also foreign investment flowing into Kalimantan, Borneo. Travel and tourism are major industries in the country judging from the number of five-star hotels. The allure of both business opportunities and sight-seeing keeps capital flowing in unabated. For potential investors, the clogged roads represent opportunities in infrastructure development; the sporadic power supply indicates a need for power projects; and, finally, the congested phone lines spell a boon for the telecommunications industry.

Businesses have witnessed the impact of *Pakto 1988* which signalled the start of the financial deregulation process, seen the fall of Bank Summa and analysed the scandal of Bapindo, the state bank for industrial development. But these episodes are mere teething problems of an awakened giant compared to opportunities for investors who are ready and prepared. This chapter provides an overview of the established banking institutions, their ownership structures, their depth of market penetration for the bank's financial services which they offer, the impact of monetary policy on the rupiah and, finally, the economic sectors that have the largest project financing opportunities.

FINANCIAL INSTITUTIONS AND THEIR FINANCIAL SERVICES

By design, Li *et al.* discuss the larger banking sector in Chapter 6. Their analysis begins with the important financial reforms introduced by the Indonesian Government on 27 October 1988. Next they turn their attention to some basic characteristics of the Indonesian financial system.

Chapter 6 notes that at the end of 1996 there were 240 banks in the Republic, including 165 private commercial banks (75 with foreign exchange licences), 31 joint venture banks, 27 development banks, 10 foreign banks, and 7 state banks (see Table 9–1). In addition, there were 160 finance companies. Prior to *Pakto 1988*, Indonesia had only 124 licensed banks. But the Indonesian banking sector is undergoing a metamorphosis. Intensified competition and the stipulation of stringent regulations by Bank Indonesia, the central bank, have constrained smaller banks that are under-capitalised. Moreover, it is now more common for bigger corporations to seek funding through the capital market.

TABLE 9–1
Banking Industry in Indonesia:
Market Share (%) as at December 1995

Type of Bank	Number of Banks	Assets (%)	Equity (%)	Deposits (%)
State	7	45.2	34.2	40.3
Private	165	43.4	49.8	50.7
Development	27	2.7	3.2	3.3
Joint venture	31	5.2	9.2	1.8
Foreign	10	3.5	3.6	3.9

Source: Bank Indonesia (1996).

Private banks have increased their loans and advances two-fold since 1995. This trend is likely to continue especially since the seven state banks need to have a greater level of efficiency in enhancing economic development. Some banks have realised the potential of information technology (IT) and have pursued a consistent level of investment in delivery and support systems while others have found niche markets to be very lucrative. Given the voluminous size of the financial sector, the following subsections focus on the more established banks listed on the Jakarta Stock Exchange (JSE), their ownership characteristics and the strength of their financial services. The top 16 banks in terms of market share are shown in Table 9–2. Eight of these are addressed specifically below as well as two tier-2 banks that are performing very well. This macroanalysis was not covered in Chapter 6.

TABLE 9–2
Top Banks by Market Share:
Assets and Profits as of 1995

Name	Assets (%)	Net Profit (%)	Management
Bank Negara Indonesia	8.5	8.3	State
Bank Dagang	7.8	4.8	State
Bank Rakyat	7.5	5.2	State
Bank Central Asia	7.0	3.6	Salim Group
Bank Bumi Daya	6.9	1.5	State
Exim Bank	5.9	4.2	State
Bank Danamon	3.7	3.9	Admadjaja family
Bapindo	3.7	0.3	State
Bank International	3.4	5.6	Sinar Mas Group
BDNI	3.3	4.1	Gajah Tunggal Group
Bank Tabungan	2.5	3.2	State
Bank Lippo	2.0	2.4	Riady family
Bank Niaga	1.7	1.9	Tahija family
Bank Bali	1.7	2.8	Riady family
Bank Umum Nasional	1.6	1.6	Not available
Bank Panin	1.1	1.5	Gunawan family

Source: The Association of Indonesian Private Commercial Banks (1996).

Bank Negara Indonesia (BNI)

BNI is the largest bank in Indonesia with an asset base of Rp 32,175 billion as at December 1995. Its profit accounted for 8.3% of the total profits of the banking sector. It is a state-owned bank and was listed on the JSE in November 1996. Most observers in the financial markets believe that it will continue to be a solid performer because of its market share in deposits and loans, with the former at 7.0% and the latter at 8.5%, respectively. Market optimism was reflected in the initial public offering when the shares were oversubscribed by 350%, with a strong demand from foreign investors.

With 489 branches, BNI has one of the largest branch networks in the country. This penetration is primarily due to its role as an agent of national and economic development. It allocates funds to many rural co-operatives to finance their operations. Nearly 76% of its lending is directed to domestic operations while 24% is for international business lending.

One of BNI's priorities is management development because of the need for more skilled personnel. There are more than 10,000 employees worldwide (Bank Negara Indonesia, 1995) and both the number and management quality are expected to increase. Executive development is carried out by local and foreign universities. BNI has an abnormally high level of personnel costs in relation to operating expenses and restructuring its operations could increase efficiency. Bad loans are a pressing issue in Indonesian banking and BNI should be admired for making a loan loss provision of 2.6% of its gross loans. The nature of BNI's operations are focused on domestic trade and business sectors rather than international operations. However, it intends to concentrate more on the foreign arena in the immediate term.

Bank Danamon (BD)

BD is the second largest private bank with 4% of total assets in the banking sector but it ranks seventh among all banks in asset terms as at the end of 1995. It has been growing rapidly and has a domestic network of around 300 branches. The main shareholder of the bank is Usman Admadjaja.

BD's low provision for doubtful loans is a reflection of its aggressive lending and credit expansion in 1995. Because of a focus on lending, it has relatively few avenues for fee-based income. The non-interest income is earned from trade financing and foreign exchange services. BD intends to develop into a large consumer bank because of its high market share in deposits at 4.6%.

BD's investment in IT since the early 1990s to drive consumer banking has been profitable given the relatively high and stable interest margins. During 1995, it implemented on-line branch applications and expanded ATM services. There are some concerns over possible non-performing loans because of the high growth in loans. With Indonesia's economic and industrial growth expectations, this exposure may not be an insurmountable problem.

Bank Internasional Indonesia (BII)

BII is the banking arm of the Sinar Mas Group and its strategic direction is largely determined by President Director Indra Widjaja. It was the ninth largest bank in 1995 but ranked third as a private bank. BII's profits accounted for 5.6% of the banking sector's total profit (see Table 9–2). Its strength in the market place traditionally has been foreign exchange services and trade finance. Its treasury team is reputedly one of the best in the country and is known to be a market maker. BII is well placed to service corporate clients with international operations.[1] The spin-offs from corporate banking are corporate finance activities including project finance, loans syndication and initial public offerings.

In consumer banking, BII has a substantial share of the credit card business which adds to the high interest margins and fee income. A greater expansion of its consumer business is expected in the short run. In Indonesia, this means more ATMs, branches and increased branch automation.

BII is focusing on five areas over the next three years. First, it intends to enhance the core business of lending and corporate banking. Secondly, with the rapid growth of the capital market, BII intends to establish its strength by assisting Indonesian state-owned enterprises to privatise. Thirdly, cost control and profitability will be closely monitored. Fourthly, the equity base will be expanded. Finally, investment in staff training and technology will trigger customer service.

Bank Dagang Nasional Indonesia (BDNI)

BDNI is the fourth largest private bank based on assets reported in 1995 and it is part of the Gajah Tunggal Group, with vested control in the hands of the owner Sjamsul Nursalim. There is a focus towards increased profitability and productivity as part of its strategic plan, evidenced by branch automation implementation programmes, market repositioning and new product offerings. The branch automation includes plans to link up all branches by satellite. BDNI is one of the few banks to have a local area network in each of its branches. The cost of transactions is expected to decrease when the automation plan is completed.

Market repositioning focuses on BDNI's liabilities. Senior man-

---

[1] The international strategic partners of BII are Fuji Bank, Credit Lyonnais and Lend Lease Corporation Australia.

agement realises the overdependency on time deposits as a source of funding. It is reported that time deposits and certificates of deposits account for 80% of its total deposit base. This explains the emphasis on service quality improvement in branch banking so as to attract less costly forms of deposits.

To market a wide range of financial services in the shortest possible time, BDNI has entered into various institutional relationships. The names of their foreign partners[2] indicate that BDNI intends to build its investment management services in the region. The customer segment where BDNI has a foothold is the middle market, primarily in trade and commerce, unlike other banks where the manufacturing sector is the largest recipient of funding.

Lippo Bank (LB)

LB is a major component of the Lippo Group controlled by the Riady family. LB is professionally managed and has a strong reputation. Although there were some concerns in 1995 because of the links with Lippoland's transactions, it has received fresh capital injections since then and dispelled most of the adverse comments. It ranked twelfth in terms of assets among all banks but it is the fifth largest private bank.

LB has one of the highest net interest margins at 5.3%. This is the result of a large, stable and low cost retail deposit base coupled with middle market loans which traditionally contribute to higher interest revenues. The consumer markets will be targeted to increase fee-based income. Presently, most of its non-interest income is derived from trade finance[3] which is not expected to yield dramatic improvement because the utilisation of trade facilities by the middle market pales in comparison to the corporate market.

As noted in its *Annual Report 1995*, LB is organised into four service sectors in response to the needs of manufacturers, wholesalers, retail commercial traders and individual consumers. This strategy is regarded as market penetration through customer synergy. One customer segment is related to another via a supply chain of goods and services beginning with manufacturers and ending with individual consumers.

---

2 They are DBS Securities, Daiichi Kangyo Bank and Prudential Asset Management.

3 International partnerships of LB include the Tokai Bank, Banques National de Paris and General Motors Acceptance Corporation (GMAC).

Bank Niaga (BN)

Starting out as a one branch bank four decades ago, BN now has 57 branches and ranks sixth as a private bank in terms of assets. Controlled by the Tahija family group, it has a prudent approach and is professionally managed. Unlike many other established banks, it intends to be a dominant player in corporate finance and merchant banking. The corporate and merchant banking divisions provide a wide range of financial services to premier private, state-owned and multinational corporations. BN is fairly active in fund raising through loan syndications, and debt and equity issues. In addition, it has a presence in project finance[4] and trade finance. Based on the financial thrust of the bank, there is an emphasis on fee-based income.

The private banking division was recently set up to cater for the high net worth clients who come from their corporate base. To offer services at an appropriate level to this market, BN decided to move quickly towards electronic banking. This accounts for their increased IT investment. The Niaga Visa which started in 1994 now has a card membership of 35,000. Greater efficiency is another IT investment goal.

Bank Bali (BB)

Historically, BB has served large and medium-sized corporations but, recently, it has moved towards consumer banking. In asset terms, it ranks seventh among private banks. The management is vested with the Ramli family which is a major shareholder. BB is conservative but well managed, with a strong market reputation.

BB is a forerunner in IT investments spurred on by its push into consumer banking. It is one of the few banks that has introduced "direct banking". Software applications to support lending operations, trade finance business and funds transfers are continuously being developed. By the end of 1995, all branches were linked together on line. To improve efficiency, electronic mail was introduced to share information. The mainframe system runs on an open system application with client server architecture. In the near future, further market penetration into credit cards and personal mortgages can be expected. BB is the only bank to offer co-branded credit cards together with two of the largest supermarket chains in Indonesia.

---

[4] Their global strategic partners are the Sumitomo Bank, Barclays Zoete Wedd, Cigna Insurance, International Finance Corporation and Indover Bank.

Panin Bank (PB)

As one of the earliest banks to be listed on the JSE, PB has maintained a stable earnings record. Bank analysts view it as an excellent bank, cost efficient and well managed although there appears to be an under-utilisation of its deposit and capital base. It is the ninth largest private bank in asset terms.

PB's revenue includes a strong fee to gross income ratio of 35%. Avenues for fee income include trade finance, foreign exchange and investment banking.[5] Given its high liquidity, PB is a dominant force in the money market and targets medium-sized corporations. It is expected to grow gradually by focusing on middle market loans and money market transactions.

Bank Bira and Bank Tiara

These two tier-2 category banks are excellent niche market players. Bank Bira focuses on investment banking and possesses entrepreneurial flair. Loan syndication and note issuance activities generate fee income. Bira is a highly profitable bank and has tried to enter the trade finance and foreign exchange arena.

Bank Tiara, which is part of the Ometraco Group, concentrates on medium-sized companies. Its 7% net interest margin is the highest among all banks. However, this rate of profitability is highly dependent on the interest spread between the cost of funds and lending rates; its fee income is negligible. There is some concern over its loan portfolio in the event of an economic downturn.

PROJECT FINANCING OPPORTUNITIES

The Asia-Pacific region is experiencing massive economic development and expansion which is reflected in the growth of infrastructure projects. The Asian Development Bank (ADB) based in Manila estimates that about US$2.5 trillion worth of investments is required for infrastructure in the region over the next decade. According to the latest industry study by the Political and Economic Consultancy Group in Hong Kong, the projected Asian infrastructure spending between the years 1994 and 2000 is US$155 billion. The distribution

---

[5] Its global partners include the Australia New Zealand Bank, International Finance Corporation, Nippon Credit Bank, Credit Lyonnais, AMP Society and Schroeders plc.

of this spending among countries in percentage terms is shown in Table 9–3.

Many of the infrastructure projects have huge funding requirements and are immensely complex. Asian governments are increasingly using alternative sources of project financing in order to reduce public borrowing and reserves. In many countries, infrastructure investment requirements have been turned over to private sector joint ventures which have been successful in raising both equity and debt capital in large amounts and over long periods of time. Similar to many of its Asian neighbours, Indonesia openly announced plans to increase private sector participation in infrastructure development (*The Business Times*, 18 October 1994).

TABLE 9–3
Share of Asian Infrastructure Spending (1994–2000)

Country	Percentage
China	34
India	23
Indonesia	9
Korea	9
Thailand	6
Malaysia	5
Taiwan	4
Others	10
Total	**100**

Source: Political and Economic Risk Consultancy (1996).

Given this opportunity and governmental support, it is more than appropriate for Gan *et al.*, in Chapter 7, to have considered the critical factors associated with project financing in Indonesia. One message that emerged is the enormous demand for infrastructure developments in transportation, electrical power and telecommunications. However, before dealing with these sectors, Chapter 7 appropriately explained the nature of project financing and the five criteria related to the critical task of evaluating the risk exposure linked to any particular project.

To give a sense of the complexity which can envelop the financing of a project, Gan *et al.* analysed the crucial details surrounding three *de facto* projects dealing with power, telecommunications and petrochemicals. Then, using the Stanchart checklist which they described earlier, the authors generated a summary of this risk analysis for these three projects. However, Chapter 7 did not examine the government's role in the Indonesian power industry nor the impact of several laws which govern this sector. The power sector is singled out because it is one of the most important sectors for infrastructure development.

The projects in Indonesia that are being funded by ADB (*Business Opportunities*, February 1997) total US$111.4 billion. These are shown in Table 9–4. It is advisable for potential partners, supply contractors and project consultants to concentrate on those sectors or related sectors along the supply chain. Given that power projects have the largest support from aid agencies, the remainder of this section deals with this sector.

TABLE 9–4
ADB Loans for Indonesia

Sector	Loan Amount (US$ million)	Division in Charge
Power	250.0	Perusahan Perseroan (Persero)
Education	180.3	Ministry of Religious Affairs
Airports	150.0	Director-General, Air Communications
Urban housing	100.0	Director-General, Human Settlements
Ports & ships	100.0	Director-General, Sea Communications
Agriculture	100.0	Ministry of Agriculture
Fisheries	85.0	Indonesian Institute of Science
Health	81.1	Director-General, Communicable Disease
Water supply	65.0	Director-General, Public Administration

Source: Asian Development Bank, February 1997.

Power projects are the most common form of privatised infrastructure projects offered by host governments in Asia. Power is one of the most critical prerequisites for industrialisation among all other infrastructures such as highways, ports and telecommunications. Rapid growth in industrialisation which, in turn, leads to economic growth is extremely difficult in the absence of energy. Frequent blackouts in the Philippines and Indonesia, for example, have hindered foreign investment in these countries for many years.

The Indonesian power industry is governed by the Department of Energy. Prior to 1991, the state-owned electricity company, Perusahan Umum Listrik Negara (PLN) held a monopoly on both electricity generation and distribution. The company generates about one-half of the total installed power capacity in Indonesia. The growth in electricity demand is expected to average 15.5% over the next decade. The aggregate investment in the capacity for electricity generation and distribution is projected at US$35 to US$46 billion over the next ten years. It is unlikely that the financial resources of PLN can meet these funding requirements.

The Indonesian authorities have recently unveiled plans to float two subsidiaries of PLN. One of them will operate existing PLN plants in West and Central Java, while the other will take over facilities in East Java and Bali. The government is looking towards independent power projects (IPPs) to increase the power capacity and supply. Since PLN is the sole transmitter and distributor of the power supply, IPPs are required to sell their power to the national body. But in places where PLN does not have transmission facilities, they are allowed to sell power directly to the consumers. However, private power prices must reflect the cost and must be approved by the Ministry of Mines and Energy.

The Indonesian Government is pursuing a programme to encourage power generation, with support and technical assistance funded by international aid agencies such as the World Bank. A host of financial and non-financial incentives await a foreign investor. There are attractive incentives such as the waiver of import duty on capital goods and tax holidays.

Power projects in Indonesia can be categorised as solicited or unsolicited projects. The former are based on the results of a tender, with participation by investors who have been pre-qualified by the Indonesian Government. Investors are invited by the government to participate in the pre-qualification selection via announcements in both the national and international media. The latter are proposals submitted and examined by PLN and the Director-General of Electricity. Once approved, a preliminary approval letter is issued and the company can then apply for an investment licence. Construction work in both categories must begin, at the latest, within 180 days after the date of issuing the investment licence.

Although Indonesia's basic electricity law (*Law 15*, 1985) states that "in so far as the interests of the government are not harmed, the widest possible opportunity shall be given to co-operatives and other enterprises to provide electricity", there is no specific legal authorisation for the PLN to purchase power from private suppliers. However, *Presidential Decree No. 37* (1992) provides for private power projects to supply electricity directly to PLN "where PLN cannot satisfy the demand for electricity" and expresses the government's preference that such projects should be developed on a build-own-operate basis. This means that the private power company can build the power plant, own it and operate it without the condition of transferring the plant to the government at a later date.

Decree No. 37 makes power producers responsible for their own fuel supply and, thus, appears to prohibit conversion contracts where PLN would supply the fuel. The decree mandates that top priority be given to domestic fuel suppliers. Although Indonesia remains a net exporter of oil, the regulations discourage the use of oil as a fuel source. Most of the private power projects proposed thus far are dependent on coal or gas. The country has large coal reserves and there are several private coal suppliers in addition to the state-owned Tambang Natubara Bucket Asam. The only domestic source of gas is Pertamina, the state-owned oil company.

The Decree, together with the Ministry of Mines and Energy, both require electricity sold to PLN to be priced in rupiah. This means that exchange rate risk must be dealt with through provisions in the power project agreement. This provision adjusts a portion of each monthly power sales invoice to take into account changes in the Rp/US$ rate. With respect to this portion, the rupiah amount paid by PLN is determined by the rate at which the electricity vendor is able to enter into foreign exchange contracts to convert rupiah into U.S. dollars. In the event that the vendor is unable to do so, PLN is obliged to pay that portion of the invoice in U.S. dollars.

For projects involving foreign investment, this requires establishing a project management company under the *Foreign Investment Law*. Although it has been amended to allow such companies to be 100% foreign-owned, they must be organised as a joint venture and, therefore, must have at least 5% Indonesian ownership. The *Foreign Investment Law* grants foreign investors the right to compensation in the event of nationalisation, and investors are allowed to arbitrate any disputes with the government concerning the terms of the investment before the International Center for Settlement of Investment Disputes (ICSID) in Washington, D.C. The project management company has the right to convert rupiah into foreign currency and repatriate it.

A critical risk in any power project is a potential change in the law. But under the change-in-law provision, an investor is entitled to an equitable increase in electricity price to compensate the company for material cost increases resulting from a change-in-law or from governmental acts undertaken against the project "without justifiable cause". However, the price is subject to a downward revision if a change in the law materially reduces the vendor's operating costs. If there is a new environmental law enforced which requires the power plant to be shut down for a period of time to upgrade the air pollution control system, then the vendor is entitled to receive capacity payments during such shutdowns and is entitled to recover, as an adjustment to the electricity price, both capital cost and increased operating costs attributable to the upgrade.

Private power investors in Indonesia should also take note of the enforceability of the terms in their agreements. The fear is that a foreign investor is placed at a distinct disadvantage in the Indonesian courts in case of a dispute with PLN or other local power purchasers. To mitigate this particular risk, an investor should ensure the inclusion of a clause stating that disputes are to be resolved by international arbitration. Indonesia is a party to the *New York Convention* on the Recognition and Enforcement of Foreign Arbitral Awards. Although successful enforcement may not be guaranteed, international legal firms have recommended the inclusion of such a clause.

MONETARY POLICY, INTEREST RATES AND THE RUPIAH

Indonesia has one of the fastest growing GDP rates in the world, averaging 7.5% per annum for the last decade (see Table 9–5). Because of this rapid growth, it faces formidable challenges in implementing the monetary policy. Since the 1980s, BI, the central bank, has had only limited success. Lim *et al.*, in Chapter 8, explain the evolution of monetary policy in Indonesia beginning with the establishment of Indonesia's central bank. Following this historical overview, the authors describe the intervention band mechanism designed to stem speculation in the rupiah and stabilise its exchange rate. This policy has produced a steadily declining rupiah relative to the U.S. dollar. Moreover, it has necessitated a continual widening of the band as the authors clearly note. This action theoretically increases the risk exposure to exchange rate fluctuations and, thus, Lim *et al.* discuss the hedging options which are available to investors. However, several additional comments on the government's monetary policy are necessary.

In the early 1990s, interest rates sky-rocketed when BI attempted to dampen economic growth by using a tight monetary policy. This move was blamed for the business failures that occurred at that time. This affected the property sector sufficiently enough to lead to the fall of Bank Summa, the nation's second largest private bank, which was exposed heavily to this sector. Also, the rupiah strengthened as money flowed in from other financial centres in search of higher interest rates. This was unintended since BI's policy was to depreciate the currency gradually.

TABLE 9–5
Key Economic Indicators (percentage)

	1994	1995	1996 (estimate)	1997 (forecast)
GDP	7.5	8.1	7.6	7.5
Capital investment	13.8	12.9	10.0	12.7
Private consumption	5.8	6.3	6.5	6.3
Govt. consumption	2.3	3.4	7.0	4.5
Exports	9.0	4.3	12.3	12.9
Imports	14.5	24.5	6.8	12.8
Manufacturing output	17.6	16.8	16.0	18.0
SBI 30-day (% yield)	12.8	13.5	12.0	11.0
Exchange rate* (Rp/US$)	2,198	2,294	2,370	2,488

* Absolute value.
Source: Merrill Lynch (1996).

Since 1984, BI has assumed the role of lender of last resort. Two discount facilities were started to assist state and private banks facing liquidity problems. First, the BI certificates *Sertifikats Bank Indonesia* (SBIs) are an avenue for the excess short term funds of the banks. They have varying maturities and can be used in interbank trading. Secondly, the *Surat Berharga Pasar Uang* (SBPUs) are promissory notes issued to bank customers and trade bills endorsed by financial institutions with maturities ranging from 70 to 180 days. They provide additional liquidity to the money market. Since introducing these two instruments, BI has been active in trading SBIs and SBPUs through daily auctions. This intervention has given BI better control of market liquidity and, hopefully, a more effective tool in monetary policy management.

For many years, BI tried encourage the use of the SBI rate as the prime rate but it has not had much success. The industry complained that the rate calculated by BI is inconsistent with what is determined by the market. In response, it started a base lending rate developed from the lending rates of 24 commercial banks: ten are privately-owned, seven are state-owned and seven are foreign-owned. The rates are updated daily by Reuters, Telerate and BI's own online system.

The rates come with an overnight maturity, 7-day, 30-day, 90-day and 360-day maturities.

Interest rates in Indonesia are the highest in the ASEAN region. Deposit rates range from 12% to 17% while lending rates are at least 4% higher. Analysts think that there is an underlying pressure for the rupiah interest rate to decrease. As long as BI resists any cut in interest rates, it will have to accept the continued high growth in the money supply from offshore arbitrage, or allow the rupiah exchange rate to strengthen to a point where overvaluation will discourage arbitrageurs.

BI has had a managed float policy since the mid-1980s. This policy was invoked after devaluations in 1983 (28%) and 1986 (31%). Since 1986, the rupiah has been devalued at a rate of 4% per annum. However, BI has tried to prevent outflows of speculative money by a further widening of the Rp/US$ band to 8% (or Rp 192) from 5% (Rp 118). This is the seventh move in the last three years, when the band then stood at Rp 6. The foreign exchange market is continuing to reflect strong economic fundamentals which has kept the rupiah at the high end of the new band.

The rupiah is freely convertible into all major currencies without limits on the amount to be transferred in and out of the country. Thus, there are few regulations pertaining to capital transfers and profit repatriation. There are no restrictions on holding rupiah or foreign currency by residents or foreigners.

It is expected that BI will be active in rupiah intervention since the country cannot afford to have a fluctuating Rp/US$ exchange rate. It is anticipated that there will be downward pressure on the rupiah in order to maintain Indonesia's export competitiveness.

CONCLUSION

Indonesia is one of the most attractive countries in Asia for investment. Three striking features, including the huge population, land mass and rising middle class income levels, have been responsible for economic growth and development in many Asian countries. Indonesia is no different. It has many business opportunities that can benefit an investor and the host country. Some of these opportunities are easily accessible within a short space of time while others take much longer. Although there could be legal complexities, and rightly so because of the diversity of this emerging economy, they are not insurmountable. Similarly, political uncertainty can be mitigated depending on the payback period of the investment.

REFERENCES

Asian Development Bank, *Business Opportunities*, February 1997.
Bank Indonesia, *Annual Report 1996*, Jakarta, 1996.
Bank Negara Indonesia, *Annual Report 1995*.
Lippo Bank, *Annual Report 1995*.
Merrill Lynch, *Country Report: Indonesia*, Jakarta, 1997.
Political and Economic Risk Consultancy, *Country Analysis: Indonesia*, Hong Kong, 1996.
The Association of Indonesian Private Commercial Banks, *Perbanas Financial Directory 1994–95*, Jakarta, 1996.
The Business Times, Editorial, 18 October 1994.

MARKETING

Chapter 10

The Indonesian Distribution System: Mastering the Maze*

BY
CHAN Huan Yong
Candace CHIA
CHONG Siok Chian
TEO Chin Chye

INTRODUCTION

ASIAN ECONOMIES ARE liberalising, booming and actively looking for foreign investments. The surging growth rates, expanding consumer base and rising private consumption expenditure provide extremely good opportunities to foreign investors seeking greater returns on their investments.

The outlook for economic growth and investment in Indonesia is very promising. The annual Gross Domestic Product (GDP) in 1995 was US$193.1 billion (Indonesia National Development Information Office (INDIO), 1996). The GDP is forecast to grow at about 7.5% per annum in 1996 (Bank of Indonesia, 1996). Although Indonesia started from a relatively low base, it is now one of the fastest growing economies in Asia as Figure 10–1 illustrates.

In fact, the Indonesian government has undertaken a series of deregulatory measures in 1994, 1995 and 1996 which are aimed at reducing taxes, import duties and simplifying investment requirements. As a result, the inflow of capital from multinational companies into Indonesia has increased tremendously.

* We appreciate the comments and assistance provided by Dr. Krishna Erramilli.

Foreign direct investment (FDI) in Indonesia has increased from US$8.1 billion in 1993 to US$39.9 billion in 1995 (Investment Coordinating Board, 1996). Total FDI from 1994 to November 1996 is US$92.25 billion and this has exceeded the total FDI from 1967 to 1993 of US$80.08 billion.[1]

FIGURE 10–1
GDP Growth of Selected Asia Pacific Countries

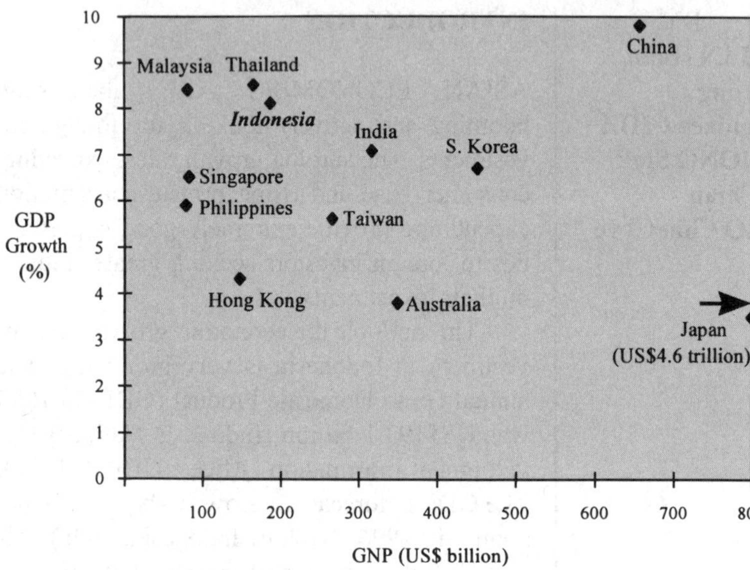

Source: Adapted from various issues of *Asiaweek*, 1996.

Indonesia is the fourth largest country (in terms of population) in the world and has a population of about 197 million (INDIO, 1996). High economic growth in recent years has "fuelled" the growth of an "emerging" middle class which is enjoying increasingly greater spending power. This has created a vibrant and ever-expanding retail sector in Indonesia. However, the country's geographic diversity, inadequate infrastructure, low education levels, inadequate human resource capabilities, and relatively low information technology has

---

1 Panel discussion with Ir. Sugihono Kadarisman, Deputy II, BKPM in Jakarta, on 10 December 1996.

posed major problems to foreign investors attempting to penetrate the consumer market in Indonesia.

There is little literature on the marketing and distribution system in Indonesia. Therefore, this chapter aims to bridge the knowledge gap of foreign investors and provide them with some practical insights into the distribution system in Indonesia. The focus is on the distribution of consumer products in the Indonesian market. The chapter first considers the structure and dynamics of the traditional distribution system in Indonesia. Next, the way in which the proliferation of modernised retailing outlets has revolutionised the traditional marketing channels is explored. Also, the challenges faced by foreign investors as well as the options available for entering the consumer market in Indonesia are identified. The final section of the chapter assesses the future trend of retailing in this vast archipelago.

Distribution of industrial products in Indonesia is not very different from that in other countries. They rely on authorised agents or dealers to sell directly to the end customers for their industrial use.[2] Some of the agents in Indonesia keep stock of spare parts or accessories but not the main products. The main products are usually delivered directly from the manufacturers' warehouses when customers place their orders. At the same time, the distribution of industrial products in Indonesia faces problems similar to those of consumer products. Examples of challenges to the distribution of these products are geographic diversity, inadequate infrastructure, government regulations and so forth which are discussed in detail in a later section in the context of consumer product distribution. Thus, no special attention is given to the distribution of industrial products in this chapter.

DISTRIBUTION SYSTEM IN INDONESIA

Typical Distribution System for Consumer Products

In the distribution channel, wholesaling is the first activity after the goods are produced. At this stage, the wholesaler resells the goods bought from the manufacturer to the retailer. Wholesalers are more efficient in distributing the goods to retailers than manufacturers be-

---

[2] Private discussion with Mr. Gunawan, President Director of P. T. Rutan Machinery Trading Company.

cause of their specialised skills, wide customer contacts and economies of scale. Furthermore, small and middle size manufacturers may have limited resources to carry out wholesaling activities while the large scale manufacturers may prefer to use their funds to expand their production operations than being involved in distribution activities.

Retailers are the frontline marketers who sell the goods directly to consumers for personal or non-business use. Retailers could take many forms including departmental stores, supermarkets or even small roadside shops and hawkers. Figure 10–2 shows a typical distribution system for consumer products.

FIGURE 10–2
Typical Distribution System for Consumer Products

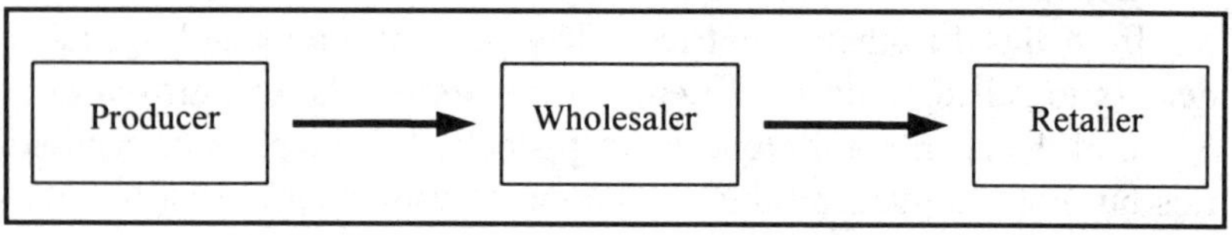

Distribution – The "Indonesian Way"

Foreign investors who are interested in distributing consumer products in Indonesia soon realise that the Indonesian way of distribution is quite unique. This is due to Indonesia's vast geographical span and widespread existence of traditional retail outlets.

The major problem faced by most foreign investors, especially those manufacturing fast moving consumer goods (FMCG), is the geographic diversity of the country. Due to the vastness of the country, nobody knows exactly how many distribution outlets there are in Indonesia. The estimated number of outlets varies from 200,000 to 1.5 million (Baldwin, 1994). According to the Economic Intelligence Unit (EIU), the traditional retail outlets in Indonesia account for 76% of the total value of goods transacted[3] (Baldwin, 1994). To ensure adequate coverage of such a large number of relatively small retailers, manufacturers and distribution companies have to set up numerous layers of distributorships and subdistributorships to ensure adequate coverage as shown in Figure 10–3.

[3] Based on 1991 figures.

An example of a foreign manufacturer of FMCG products doing its own distribution in Indonesia is P. T. Unilever Indonesia. Unilever manufactures Lux soap, Breeze detergent and Walls ice-cream among other products. It distributes all its products to 225 sub-distributors through five area sales offices and numerous stock points. The area sales offices are complete with warehousing facilities. The 225 sub-distributors, together with about 1,100 sales persons, are servicing approximately 400,000 retail outlets. Unlike Unilever, Beiersdorf, a German manufacturer of Handyplast and Nivea products, uses a national distributor, Ultramos Jaya, to distribute their products. Beiersdorf taps Ultramos Jaya's established network of about 60 sub-distributors throughout Indonesia and its experienced sales force. Both Unilever and Beiersdorf adopt a multi-layered distribution structure to achieve wide-spread coverage for penetrating the fragmented retail market.

FIGURE 10–3
Comparison of a Typical Distribution System and the Indonesian Distribution System

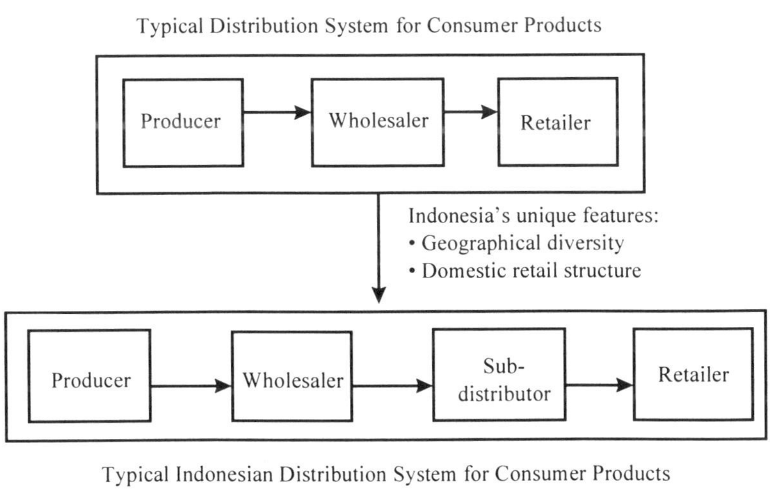

However, there are potential problems associated with a multi-layered distribution structure. First, pricing usually gets out of control at the retail level or even at the sub-distributor level. Due to intense competition, sub-distributors and retailers often resort to price wars to increase sales. Figure 10–4 shows an example of the selling prices and margins at each level of the distribution channel for a particular brand of cooking oil in Indonesia. Secondly, it is difficult to manage and maintain the image of a product when distribution and marketing of the product is widely spread to numerous parties. The image of the product will depend largely on the promotional efforts of the retailers. Although manufacturers can make use of broad based advertising e.g., television and radio advertising to influence the image of a product, very often, physical rack displays have a greater effect on consumers' perception of a product's image.

FIGURE 10–4
Example of Distribution of Cooking Oil in Indonesia

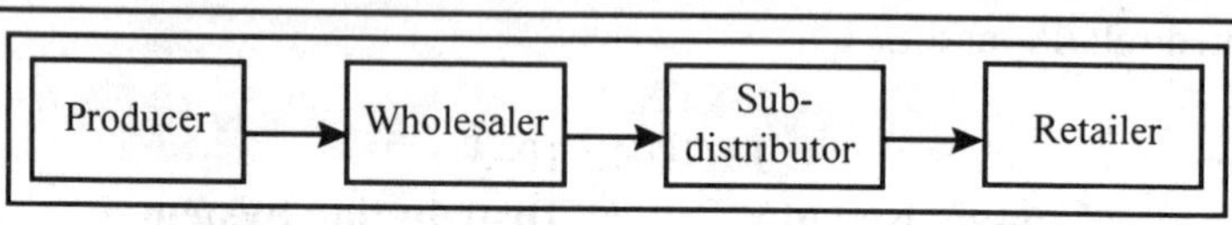

	Producer	Wholesaler	Sub-distributor	Retailer
USP:	Rp 1,000	Rp 1,150	Rp 1,225	Rp 1,400
EGM:		15%	6.5%	14%
ENM:		5%	3.5%	n.a.

USP – Unit selling price
EGM – Estimated gross margin
ENM – Estimated net margin

Selection of distribution channels is critical to the success of a product. Different distribution channels can help manufacturers or distributors reach different segments of the market and focus on the desired customer base. There are two main types of distribution channels in Indonesia: traditional retailing and modern retailing.

Traditional Retailing

Traditional retailing is one of the most important sectors of the Indonesian retail economy. In Jakarta, where modern retailing is thriving the most, traditional outlets account for about 99% of 302,912 retail outlets (Baldwin, 1994).

Another key feature of the Indonesian retail market is the relatively undeveloped modern retail outlets such as supermarkets and shopping centres. Even in an urban city like Jakarta, modern retail outlets in 1996 accounted for about 25% of the total value of goods transacted in the retail market and traditional retail outlets accounted for the remaining 75%. These percentages are more pronounced outside Jakarta where traditional outlets accounted for almost 95% of total sales (see Figure 10–5).[4]

FIGURE 10–5
Retail Market Structure in Indonesia
(value of goods transacted)

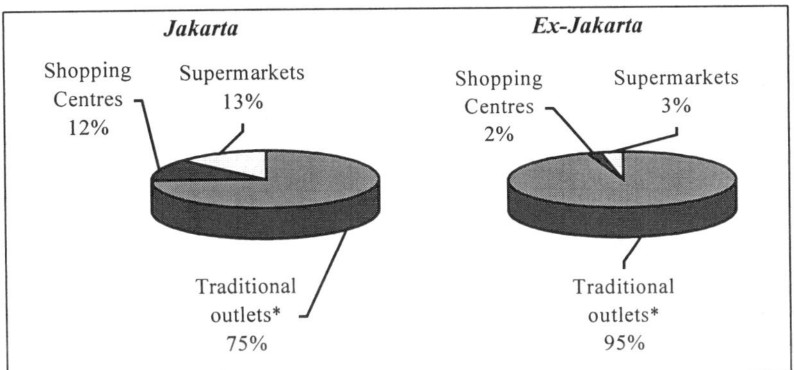

* Small shops and *warungs*.
Source: P. T. Schroders estimates, Jakarta, December 1996.

With traditional retail outlets still dominating Indonesia's retail industry, these small family-owned and family-operated shops continue to be the best way to penetrate the mass consumer market for certain products such as household products, personal products and groceries. However, it is interesting that within the retailer level there exists a hierarchical structure where a larger retailer (a *Toko* store) sometimes acts as a sub-distributor to the smaller outfits (the *warungs* or the *kaki limas*). Table 10–1 shows the number of traditional and modern retail outlets in Jakarta.

(i) ***Pasars or Markets***: These markets house a number of smaller stalls which sell a limited range of produce and locally manufactured goods such as fruits, vegetables, meat, fish and rice as well as household items. *Pasars* are found in all towns and cities

[4] These are figures estimated by P. T. Schroders, Jakarta, December 1996.

throughout Indonesia. In Jakarta alone, there are about 90,000 *pasars* (Baldwin, 1994). Nearly two-thirds of Indonesia's population buy from *pasars* and the total value of goods transacted at *pasars* each year is about US$2 billion. This has made *pasars* one of the most desired locations for distributing household goods.

TABLE 10–1
Retail Outlets by Type in Jakarta

Traditional Outlets	No. of Outlets
Kaki limas	152,000
Pasars	90,000
Shops (Tokos, P and D)	25,000
Warungs	20,120
Ansongan (street hawkers)	15,000
Boutiques	402
Furniture stores	137
Total	**302,659**

Modern Outlets	No. of Outlets
Supermarkets	140
Departmental stores	78
Convenience stores	15
Discount stores	10
Superstores	5
Warehouse stores	5
Total	**253**

Source: Baldwin (1994).

(ii) ***Tokos***: These are smaller shops situated along main streets and they are typically around 25 square metres in size. The shops normally have long counters in front and display shelves behind them placed against the wall. In this way, customers are unable to pick and choose what they want but have to call the shop owner to get the products they want from the shelves. The shop owner decides on the products to be displayed at customers' eye level, and the brand to sell and promote. Hence, *tokos* are quite powerful distribution channels in promoting new products and they have quite high bargaining power over the distributors. With higher stock capacity, some *tokos* also act as wholesalers and sell to village *warungs* and *kaki limas*.

(iii) ***P and D Stores***: These are large grocery shops selling a wide variety of food and household products. They can be imagined as an earlier version of modern convenience stores. In some Asian countries, these are commonly known as provision shops. The name *P and D* derives from the Dutch term *provisien en drinken* and refers to shops selling provisions and drinks. In contrast to *tokos*, *P and D* stores feature a browse-and-shop concept. Customers are free to move around to select the products they want. Hence, prominent display locations are critical to the sales of a product. Most distributors pay a price to "rent" these "eye-catching" rack or gondolas to display their products.

(iv) ***Warungs***: *Warungs* are small, semi-permanent roadside sheds specialising in selling certain products (*warung rokok* sells cigarettes and soft drinks and *warung makan* is an eatery). These places are where Indonesians have their daily meals and drinks during normal working days. Therefore, *warungs* are usually strategically placed at the entrances of office buildings and factories to serve these customers. *Warungs* normally carry less than ten product lines and they are limited to leading brands in the market.

(v) ***Kaki Lima or Street Traders***: *Kaki lima* literally translated means "five feet". This is the amount of pavement space a trader uses to set up makeshift stalls to display the stock of goods. At the end of the day, the trader bundles up all these goods and takes them home. *Kaki lima* can also refer to a movable cart, a peg stand or even the owner's two legs. In Jakarta, there are more than 150,000 *kaki limas* (Baldwin, 1994). Similar to the *warungs*, these street traders usually get their goods from the *tokos*.

(vi) ***Ansongan or Street Hawkers***: These are hawkers who sell goods to cars waiting at traffic lights or caught in traffic jams and passers-by. They carry the goods with them, usually in very small quantities, and go around on foot within a specific traffic area to solicit sales. The goods they carry are generally newspapers, magazines, fruits, cigarettes and drinks.

Modern Retailing

Rapid economic growth, high GDP and an emerging middle class in the 1990s have contributed to the rapid growth in modern retailing in Indonesia. A survey published by *The Asian Retail* in July 1994 mentioned that around 35% of Jakarta's residents do their shopping in supermarkets and departmental stores. This comes as no surprise since the per capita income of Jakarta's residents in 1995 was about US$3,000 which is much higher than the US$1,020 for all Indonesians (INDIO, 1996). With the entrance of major international players such as Sogo and Wal-Mart, shopping in up-market malls will become the way of life for most Indonesians in the near future. There is a growing trend in the development of modern, large scale shopping malls in the city centres as well as in the suburban residential areas. Many of the malls are incorporated into either commercial complexes or residential condominiums. Also, many up-market overseas brand names such as Gianni Versace, Emporio Armani and Hugo Boss can be found everywhere in the trendy shopping malls.

However, *Presidential Decree Number 31* of 1995 prohibits foreign equity ownership in retail trades. To overcome this barrier, foreign retailers have to find ways and means (through non-equity partnerships, franchising and technical assistance agreements) to collaborate with local partners and set up retail outlets carrying their trademarks. These modes of entering the Indonesian retail market are discussed in a later section.

(i) ***Supermarkets*** **and** ***Mini-marts***: Supermarkets are relatively new to Indonesia and they are rapidly emerging around major urban cities like Jakarta, Surabaya and Medan. Major players in this market include Hero, Makro and Gelael (see Table 10–2). These supermarkets are similar to those in the West. They carry a wide range of products and operate on a self-service basis.

It is estimated that as of 1995 there were around 350 supermarkets in Indonesia, about one-half of them in Jakarta (Baldwin, 1994). This number is rapidly increasing. The push for modern retailing by the larger retailers has fuelled the growth of smaller supermarkets or mini-marts in Jakarta and other cities. To stay ahead of increasing competition and to take full advantage of their retail expertise, market leaders like Hero Supermarket have recently shifted their energies to developing mini-marts. These outlets cater for quick purchases and provide convenience to consumers by locating near residential areas and in the suburban areas where large supermarkets are not commonly found.

There are several reasons for this type of strategy. First, the operation of supermarkets is heavily regulated by the government while mini-marts are not because they are considered small business units. The reason for regulating supermarkets is to protect the livelihood of local Indonesians engaged in the traditional retail trade. As a result, larger supermarkets such as Hero have been unable to obtain permits to build additional supermarkets. Secondly, the payback period for investments in mini-marts is shorter – less than one year as compared to two or three years for full size supermarkets (Wilianto, 1995).

TABLE 10–2
Profile of the Ten Largest Modern Retailers in Indonesia

Retailer	Number of Outlets	Market Share (%)
Matahari Putra Prima P. T.	70	15
Hero Supermarket P. T.	75*	12
Ramayana Lestari Sentosa P. T.	46	8
Pasayara Nusakarya P. T.	NA	6
Karabha Unggul P. T. (Makro)	4	5
Alfa Multi Retail	NA	5
Gelael Supermarket P. T. (Salim)	20	4
Panen Lestari Internusa P. T. (Sogo)	NA	3
Golden Truly P. T.	NA	3
Mitra Toko Discount (Hero)	NA	2
Others	NA	37

* Including 12 convenience stores.
NA – Not available.
Source: *Economic and Business Review Indonesia*, No. 220, 3 July 1996.

With a wide range of products for consumers to pick and choose from, supermarkets are the ideal outlet for sales promotion, product demonstration and education. As MBL-Consensus (a market research company) remarked, consumers expect new products to be launched at supermarkets before being rolled out to other retail stores. Hence, they usually carry additional money on supermarket visits just in case the new product launches and promotions are too tempting. From the experience in newly industrialised economies such as Thailand and Taiwan, supermarkets and shopping centres are destined to be an increasingly important part of the retail market in Indonesia.

(ii) ***Departmental Stores***: As the per capita income of people in major Indonesian cities grows, higher spending power is expected and this will lead to more demand for large departmental stores. Local departmental store chains, such as the state-owned Sarinah and privately-owned Matahari, are facing increasing competition as foreign retail giants such as Marks & Spencer, Wal-Mart and Sogo begin their foray into the local retail scene through franchising agreements with local companies. Table 10–2 shows the relative size and market share profile of the ten largest modern retailers in Indonesia.

(iii) ***Convenience Stores***: This is a new form of retailing in Indonesia. Convenience stores are smaller versions of mini-marts and they carry mainly groceries like drinks, breads, snacks and other consumer products including soap, shampoo and powder. Their competitive advantage is in operating 24 hours per day and they are normally located very near or within residential areas. Some of the international names, such as 7-Eleven, Circle-K and AM-PM, have started operating in major urban cities. The need for convenience stores is expected to rise in the future as more women join the workforce and their priority in shopping shifts from low price to efficiency and convenience.

DETERMINANTS OF DISTRIBUTION AND LOGISTICS

The promise of Indonesia's 197 million consumers can leave potential entrants to the retail market giddy with anticipation. But sizing up Indonesia's consumer market can be tricky. Its population is far flung and predominantly rural. While a middle class is gradually emerging, local market researchers feel that they are small in number and are geographically concentrated. This section examines some of the determinants of Indonesia's distribution system.

Geographic Diversity

Indonesia is the largest archipelago in the world, comprising the main islands of Java, Sumatra, Sulawesi, Kalimantan (western Borneo) and Irian Jaya (western New Guinea) as well as about 30 smaller archipelagos, with a total of 17,508 islands. However, only about 6,000 islands are inhabited. The total land area is approximately 1.91 million square kilometres and the terrain is varied (INDIO, 1996). Much of the country is mountainous and forest or jungle covers nearly two-thirds of the land.

The sheer size of Indonesia poses great challenges to foreign investors trying to reach out to the vast consumer market. Extensive transportation networks, such as roads, rail, air and sea transport, are extremely important in facilitating the efficient distribution of products, especially for perishable goods. In areas where the transportation infrastructure is not so well developed, it may be necessary to set up warehouses at strategic locations to serve the surrounding markets. Manufacturers of consumer products could consider setting up factories near the more populated cities and towns to capitalise on the ready market and minimise the need for extensive distribution.

There are a few other options available to companies in the distribution of their products. One is to appoint a sole national distributor which may have some sub-distributors in its network to effectively cover the country (multi-layered distribution system). Manufacturers then can rely on the extensive resources of these national distributors to achieve economies of scale. Another option is for manufacturers to do their own wholesaling and appoint several area distributors. This option, however, would require manufacturers to set up stock points or intermediate warehouses to support the area distributors. For example, Unilever has established this type of distribution system with over 250 area distributors assisting them in delivering goods to retailers. In supporting this distribution system, Unilever has set up 17 warehouses all over the archipelago.

Demographic Structure and Geographical Distribution of Consumers

As the fourth most populous nation in the world, the government has implemented a comprehensive family planning programme to control the population growth. The growth rate has fallen from 2.3% per annum in 1972 to around 1.6% per annum in 1996 (INDIO, 1996). About 59%, or 117 million of people, live on Java. And Jakarta accounts for nine million of Java's total population, making this island the most densely populated area in the world (see Figure 10–6). Just as the population density is unevenly distributed across the archipelago, so is the GDP contribution of various regions. Table 10–3 shows the percentage contribution to GDP of various regions for 1993 and the expected proportions for the year 2018.

FIGURE 10–6
Population By Major Regions

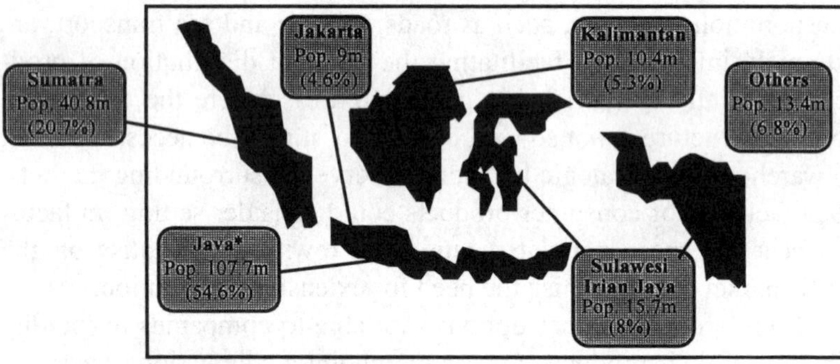

* Excluding Jakarta.
Source: INDIO (1996).

TABLE 10–3
Regional Contributions to GDP

Region	GDP Contribution 1993	GDP Contribution 2018	Average GDP Growth
Sumatra	22.15%	29.62%	8.8%
Java/Bali	61.19%	46.98%	6.6%
Kalimantan	8.68%	11.65%	8.7%
Sulawesi	4.08%	7.05%	10.0%
Other eastern islands	3.90%	4.70%	8.2%

Source: INDIO (1996).

With the majority of the population concentrated in Java and the island having the highest private consumption rate, a worthwhile strategy for firms may be to just focus their distribution efforts in Java. Unilever has sales offices and warehouses spread throughout Indonesia in proportion to the population on each island. However, competition in these densely populated islands is keen and companies need to search for "unserved markets" in order to gain a competitive edge.

Infrastructure Development

An efficient transportation system is vital to the effectiveness and efficiency of the country's distribution system. The logistics of transportation in Indonesia's archipelago require extensive development of roads, rail, sea and air transportation network. Due to the rapid economic growth, demand for transportation is high. Since the mid-1980s, the government has gradually opened the transportation sector to private investment. Almost all the restrictions on foreign investments in this sector were removed by June 1994. During *Repelita VI*, funds required for the development of infrastructure and transportation means are projected to be around US$13.7 billion and 65% of this amount is expected to be provided by the private sector in the form of business co-operation, management consultancy and operational contracts (INDIO, 1996).

(i) ***Rail***: The state-owned railway company, *Perum Kereta Api* (*Perumka*), has a total network of 6,362 kilometres and approximately 74% is on Java (INDIO, 1996). Prior to the 1970s, the rail network was neglected and not properly maintained, resulting in the substantial loss of passengers and freight traffic. Since then, major investments have been made and passengers are coming back as a result of the improved services and greater efficiency. But the rail network still faces stiff competition from the road network for the movement of freight. Rail transportation is the least popular because it is limited to Java and Sumatra. It takes more time and is more expensive to ship goods by rail than by trucks. Furthermore, with a total land area of 1.91 million square kilometres, the development of the railway system in Indonesia is clearly lagging. Therefore, roads and sea links play a greater role in Indonesia's transportation system. In the government's drive to deregulate, the railway company initiated a partial privatisation of its services by inviting private firms to operate joint services on a profit-sharing basis.

(ii) ***Roads***: The roads are best developed in Java, the northern and southern parts of Sumatra, Madura and Bali. Most of the major cities in Indonesia are well linked by highways or secondary roads. As of 1992, Indonesia (excluding Jakarta) had a total road length of 319,758 kilometres. Approximately 33.5% of the roads are in good condition, 29.9% are in moderate condition and 36.6% are classified as damaged or severely damaged (Economist Intelligence Unit, 1996). The poor road conditions create yet another hindrance for the transportation and distribution of goods. In *Repelita VI*, Indonesia plans to upgrade the road network capacity by including more than 26,000 kilometres of arterial and collector roads, 85,000 kilometres of bridges and 310 kilometres of new toll roads (INDIO, 1996).

(iii) ***Sea***: Being a vast archipelago, sea transport is of extreme importance to the integration of the Indonesia economy. The country's two most important international seaports are Tanjung Priok in Jakarta and Tanjung Perak in Surabaya. These seaports have highly diversified handling facilities including international container terminals for a variety of cargoes. As of mid-1996, there was a total of about 1,800 sea ports and small harbours in Indonesia and 133 of them are capable of handling foreign trade.

As of March 1995, the ocean-going fleet included 25 vessels with a total capacity of 322,000 dead weight tonnes (dwt) and the inter-island and local fleets comprised 526 and 453 vessels with total capacities of 936,000 dwt and 117,000 dwt, respectively. Inter-island and local fleets are significant in the conduct of domestic trade in Indonesia. The above data show that there are about three-fold more inter-island vessels than international vessels. This disproportionate number of vessels highlights the significance of sea transport for the physical distribution of goods throughout the Indonesia archipelago.

(iv) ***Air***: Indonesia has a well-developed air transport network. There are 26 registered airlines, five of which offer scheduled passenger services, while the remainder operate charter flights and cargo services. There are 72 airports in Indonesia although only six of them are capable of handling wide-bodied jets (Economist Intelligence Unit, 1996).

With greater emphasis on the development of air transport, a new airport is being built at Jakarta and several others are being modernised and expanded. Other airport projects, completed or currently under construction, include the new airports in the northern and western Sumatra provincial capitals of Medan and Padang. Though air transport provides fast and convenient distribution, the cost involved in air-freight is much higher than other modes of transportation. Furthermore, the current number of airports is insufficient to serve the more than 6,000 inhabited islands in Indonesia. Therefore, the sea transport network is relatively more important than air for the internal distribution of goods.

(v) ***Telecommunication***: The exigencies of Indonesia's vast and varied topography spreading out to more than 17,000 islands has presented the government with unique challenges in developing a comprehensive and effective communications system. To overcome this problem, Indonesia became the first nation among developing countries to establish a satellite communications system. Indonesia now has a well-developed satellite programme with ground stations linking all 27 provinces and 18 other centres (INDIO, 1996).

Communication services are provided by state-owned telephone companies (P. T. Telkom for domestic telephone and telegraph services; P. T. Indosat for international telecommunications; and P. T. Pos Indonesia for postal services). Recognising that an efficient communications system is a prerequisite to the achievement of economic goals, the Indonesian government has put in considerable effort to expand the existing system and an additional five million new telephone lines are to be completed by the end of this century.

Overall, the infrastructure in Indonesia ranks well among Asian countries. While lagging behind Singapore and Malaysia, it is ahead of countries like Thailand, the Philippines and China. Its relative position among select ASEAN countries is shown in Figure 10–7.

As can be observed from the Unilever experience, the road system is still the most commonly used means of transportation. This is followed by sea shipment and air freight. However, Unilever's experience is that the estimated damage to goods during sea shipment usually approximates 1% of total sales. This figure is quite substantial considering the low margins that distributors and retailers receive. On the other hand, air freight is quite expensive and, hence, shipment by sea is still by far the most popular means of distribution.

FIGURE 10–7
Infrastructure Ratings Among Selected ASEAN Countries

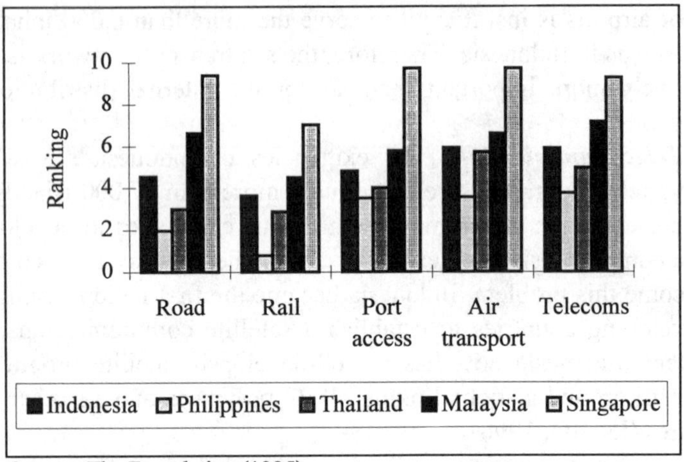

Source: The Foundation (1995).

Information Technology

The use of information technology has gained significant importance in recent years. The proliferation of home personal computers and the increasing access to the Internet has created new opportunities for product marketing and advertising. However, in Asia, the emerging economies have relatively low ratios of computer ownership compared to the developed countries. In fact, Indonesia has one of the lowest ratios among selected ASEAN economies as shown in Table 10–4.

The development of Internet shopping will take some time before it reaches a critical mass. Similarly, retailers that are considering advertising on the Net can expect to reach only a small segment of Indonesian consumers. On the other hand, the infrastructure vis-à-vis the relatively large number of service providers, provides a good foundation for the rapid growth in Internet usage given the low computer penetration rate.

Given the characteristics of retail distribution in Indonesia, it is definitely challenging for any company to distribute their products to consumers. The challenge is even greater for foreign companies as compared to their local counterparts. Some of these challenges are discussed in the next section.

TABLE 10–4
Availability of Computers and Accessibility to Internet

Country	Indonesia	Philippines	Malaysia	Thailand	Singapore
Internet service providers	7	4	2	2	4
Number of users of Internet	12,930	9,740	23,070	22,300	125,250
Computer penetration /100 people	0.3	0.5	3.3	1.2	15.3

Source: *Asia, Inc.*, September 1996.

SPECIFIC CHALLENGES FOR FOREIGN COMPANIES

Lack of Managerial Skills

It has long been recognised that one of the biggest obstacles facing the long term socio-economic development in Indonesia is the lack of trained human resources. Many multinational companies in Indonesia find that the skill levels and education standard of the average Indonesian may not match the "skill-set" required by multinational companies for their managerial and professional positions. As a result, recruiting, training and retaining managers and professionals represent a challenge to multinational companies. Salaries of managers and professionals are escalating so sharply that it is sometimes more effective (cost-skill comparison) to hire expatriates instead of locals for these positions.

The Indonesian education system does not produce sufficient graduates to meet the demands of the expanding economy. As shown in Table 10–5, only 1.7% of the total number of people in the age group from 19 to 24 are graduates as at the end of 1996. According to *The World Competitiveness Report* (The Foundation, 1995), Indonesia's public expenditure on education is one of the lowest in the world (see Figure 10–8). Indonesia's education system emphasises arts, social sciences and humanities rather than the more practical, vocation-oriented subjects. This focus may explain why Indonesia's education system is ranked as one of the least effective in meeting the needs of a competitive economy as shown in Figure 10–9. *The World Competitiveness Report* also shows that the ranking of Indonesia is quite low compared to other countries in the Asia region in terms of availability of competent senior managers and skilled workers (see Figure 10–10).

TABLE 10–5
Education Levels of Indonesians

	Unit	1968	End of 1994	End of 1996
Population (19–24 years)	'000	9,214.9	21,597.0	24,704.3
Senior secondary school graduates	'000	100.3	1,248.9	1,523.3
No. of students in tertiary education	'000	156.0	2,043.4	3,167.9
Postgraduate students	'000	-	8.0	15.2
Total number of graduates	'000	-	199.2	421.6
Graduates of Masters & Ph.D. Prog.	'000	-	2.0	3.9
Gross participation rate (GPR)	%	1.7	9.5	12.8
Continuation rate to higher education	%	25.7	41.0	49.4

* GPR: $\frac{\text{Total no. of students at primary school}}{\text{Total no. of population in 7 – 12 years age bracket}} \times 100\%.$

Source: INDIO (1996).

Recognising the role of human resources in maintaining growth and competitiveness of the country, President Suharto stressed the importance of developing a high quality education system in Indonesia in his budget proposal for 1997/1998 released on 6 January 1997. Out of the total development budget of 38.9 trillion rupiah (S$23.1 billion), about 12% will be allocated to education. The priority in education is to continue the nine-year compulsory basic education, expand vocational education and improve the overall quality of education in all types, levels and disciplines including higher education (*Business Times*, January 1997).

FIGURE 10–8
Public Expenditure on Education (1992)

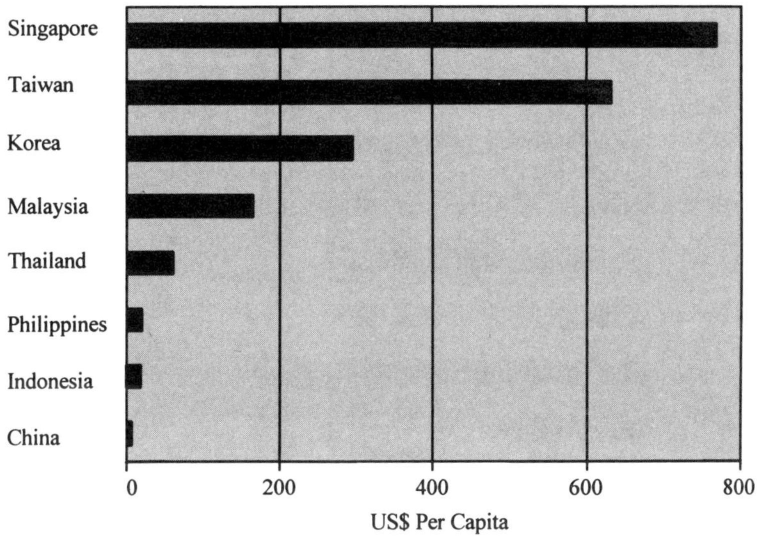

Source: The Foundation (1995).

The Potential for Conflict

Some independent distributors in Indonesia have nation-wide penetration such as Wickasana Overseas International, Indometra and Tigaraksa Satria. Many of these distributors are also part of a major business group (Indometra is part of the Salim Group, Indonesia's largest business group). Therefore, when foreign multinational companies engage these Indonesian distributors to handle their products, there could be two potential sources of conflict. First, the local distributor may be the distributor for another competitive product. Secondly, the local distributor, or a related company, may be manufacturing a similar product.

Wickasana and Tigaraksa are presently the two largest independent distributors. They handle a number of large multinational accounts. For example, Wickasana is distributing for BAT, Mead Johnson, Proctor & Gamble and Mars Australia; and Tigaraksa is distributing for Wyeth, Cadbury's, New Zealand Dairy Board and Johnson & Johnson. At the same time, each distributor has its own manufac-

FIGURE 10–9
Effectiveness of the Education System

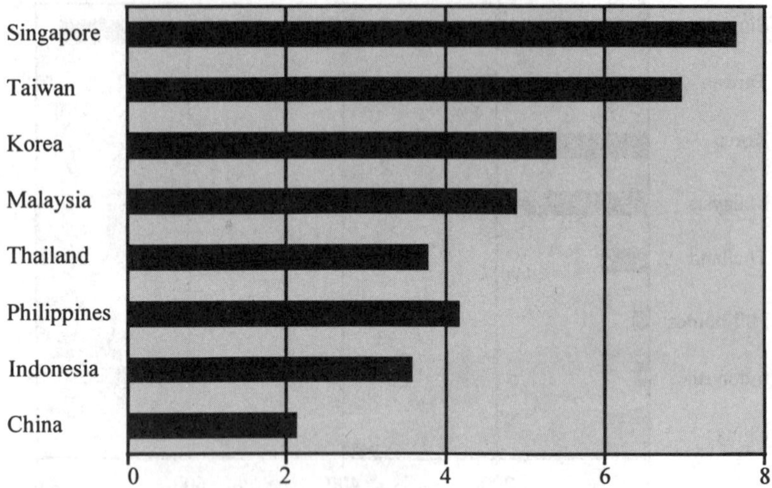

Ranking: Low – 0, High – 10
Source: The Foundation (1995).

FIGURE 10–10
Comparison of Availability of Human Resources

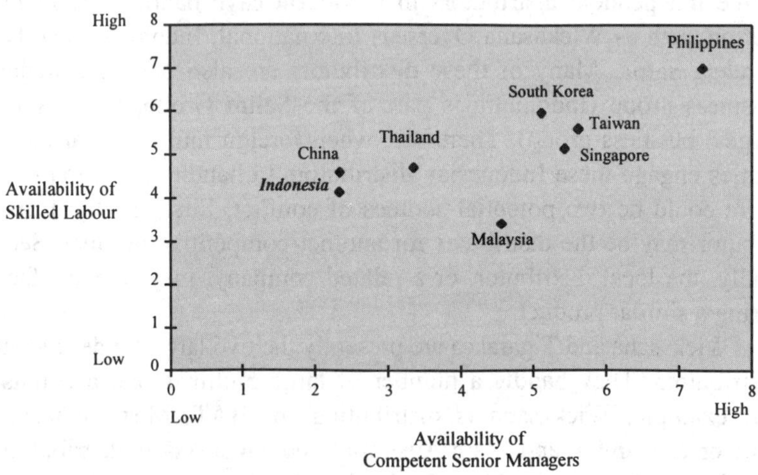

Source: The Foundation (1995).

turing arm. Wickasana produces pencils, toothbrushes, tea, electrical bulbs and instant noodles while Tigaraksa manufactures jeans and baby foods (P. T. Wickasana Overseas International, 1995; P. T. Lippo Securities, 1996). Other distributors are part of a business conglomerate. For example, Indometra belongs to the Salim Group which produces a variety of consumer food products including instant noodles, snacks and baby foods through its P. T. Indofood Sukses Makmur subsidiary (P. T. Indofood Sukses Makmur, 1995).

The case of Beiersdorf illustrates the problems arising from local distributors carrying competing brands. Suria Yozani, a subsidiary of Sara Lee, was appointed as the company's distributor in Indonesia. However, the distributor directed all its sales efforts towards its own primary product lines of Prodenta (a subsidiary of Sara Lee) rather than Beiersdorf's products. Eventually in 1990, Beiersdorf switched to another distributor, Ultramos Jaya, and has enjoyed significant growth since then (*Business Asia*, 1994).

To overcome or reduce the problem of potential conflict of interest, some principals such as Unilever have sought to restrict their distributors from distributing competing products. However, the effectiveness of this strategy depends on the relative bargaining power of the foreign company.

Vast Numbers of Distribution Outlets

The distribution system in Indonesia has generally been viewed as less efficient compared with other economies in the region (see Figure 10–11). This could be partially due the peculiar characteristics of the Indonesian distribution system, where the fragmented and long distribution channel has resulted in many small distribution outlets. There are no exact figures available for the total number of distribution outlets. Estimates range from 200,000 to 1.5 million, although 400,000 is the most commonly agreed upon figure (Baldwin, 1994).

As a distribution agent, there are several issues involved in dealing with small retailers. In particular, they may require credit financing or a longer credit period because of their small capital base. They also may prefer selling on a consignment basis due to the greater need to overstock as a result of the geographical diversity and transportation problem in rural areas.

FIGURE 10–11
Efficiency of Distribution Systems

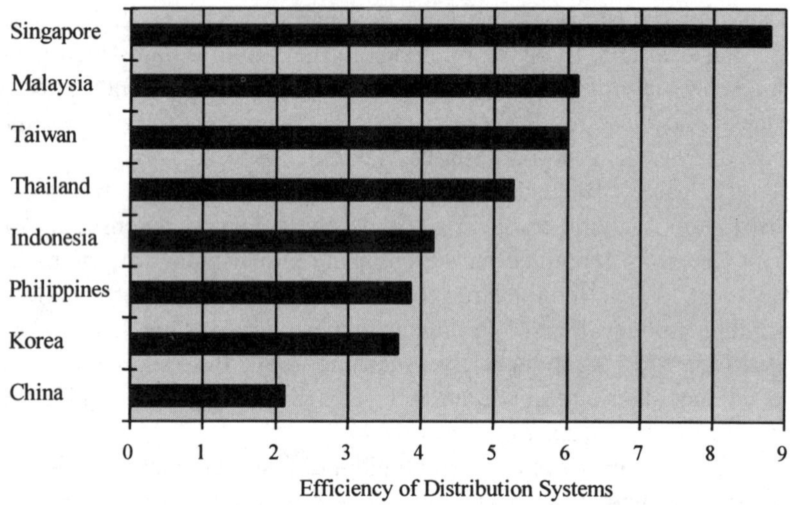

Ranking: Low – 0, High – 10
Source: The Foundation (1995).

These small retailers generally have very small shop space and quite often handle a large number of products. As a result, there may not be enough shelf space for display purposes, which is critical to product advertising and new product launches. The vastness of the country makes media circulation thin and segmented. Hence, the Indonesian market still relies heavily on in-store advertising.

The vast number of sub-distributors and retailers that a distribution agent has to control poses difficulties in monitoring and ensuring quality customer service, and efficient debt collection. Unilever has managed to minimise these risks by closely monitoring the sales volume of its distributors, capping distributors' stocks to a minimum level. Unilever is able to reduce its credit position by selling on cash terms or with collateral because of its strength and breadth of products in the Indonesian consumer market.

Governmental Regulations and Restrictions

As part of Indonesia's strategy to enhance competitiveness to attract foreign investment, several reform packages have been implemented to progressively deregulate and reduce burdensome bureaucratic procedures and substantive requirements for foreign investors. The major developments that have taken place in Indonesia in recent years are summarised in Table 10–6.

Foreign investors interested in distributing their products to the retail markets in Indonesia may face many uphill tasks. Currently, foreign companies or joint ventures with foreign shareholders are not allowed to distribute products in the domestic market unless they manufacture the products in Indonesia. Even for products manufactured locally, distribution is restricted to the wholesale level. All other types of retail distribution and sales must be handled by Indonesians or local firms. Given Indonesia's commitment to trade liberalisation in the context of the ASEAN Free Trade Area (AFTA), the Asia-Pacific Economic Co-operation (APEC) agreements and the World Trade Organisation (WTO), it is expected that foreign investors will benefit from further liberalisation and reforms in Indonesia in the years to come.

Price Controls

Pricing is usually difficult for manufacturers to control when independent middlemen are involved in the distribution channel. The task is daunting when the channel becomes longer and there are more layers of intermediaries to oversee. This is especially true in Indonesia with its unique multi-layered distribution structure. Very often retail prices in the cities are lower than those in the rural areas because of varying competitive conditions.

A fixed price policy can be difficult to enforce since producers, and even national distributors, have little control over the sub-distributors and retailers. To successfully ensure a fixed price, producers and national distributors must provide adequate marketing and promotional support at these levels.

Unilever has been implementing a fixed pricing policy for many years. Unilever passes down fixed retail price lists to the distributors and they ensure that it is passed down the line. The distributors' salespeople then ensure that the retailers strictly follow these prices. In return, Unilever provides distributors with strong advertising and marketing support. In 1992, Unilever spent nearly US$22.7 million on advertising which is almost double the second largest advertising expenditure of Konimex Solo at US$11.7 million (Baldwin, 1994).

At the distributor level, Unilever provides professional support in helping to set up the distribution network and sales forces. It promises the distributors a fixed net margin and works out the details with them. Thus, distributors are assured of a reasonable return, so there is no incentive for them to adjust the product prices.

TABLE 10–6
Major Regulations

Year	Event
1987	Indonesia enacted amendments to its copyright law which largely brought it into conformity with international standards for copyright protection.
1988	Foreign joint ventures may set up separate joint ventures to distribute their locally manufactured products up to the wholesale level.
1989	The U.S. and Indonesia signed an agreement to establish bilateral copyright regulations effective 1 August 1989.
1989	Foreign firms can hold a maximum of 55% ownership and qualify for the same treatment as domestic investments if 20% of their shares are offered on the capital market.
1993	A new trademark law came into effect which sets forth substantial civil and criminal penalties for trademark infringement.
1994	The government allows 100% foreign ownership of projects except sectors under the negative list and lifts capital divestment requirement.
1995	Foreign investors may enter a joint venture with Indonesians in advertising, without any specific Indonesian ownership requirement. Indonesia's applied tariff rates range from 5% to 30%. A number of products are subject to import surcharges as well. The May 1995 package laid out a scheduled process of tariff reform. Tariffs on items with protection (import duty + import surcharge) of more than 20% or lower will be reduced to 5% or lower. The government continues to reduce the number of items subject to import restrictions and special licensing requirements. The number of tariff lines has been reduced from a high of 1,112 in 1990 to 203 in 1996.
1996	Indonesia's first *Patent Law* took effect on 1 August 1991. The *Patent Law* and accompanying regulations include product and process protection for both pharmaceuticals and chemicals. In early 1996, the government made provisions in a new draft *Patent Law* to bring Indonesia into conformity with international norms.

Sales Force Structure and Policy

The unique distribution structure in Indonesia means that producers usually have restricted control over the structure of the distributors' sales force and their policies. Hence, these producers may have difficulties in ensuring that product brand image, sales activities and sales service are at satisfactory levels. Besides the physical capabilities and distribution networks, the strength and quality of a distributor's sales force are the most important criteria in distributor selection. The arrangement with a distributor should take into consideration the control that principals have over the distributor's sales force structure.

Sara Lee, for example, set up a joint venture company called Kiwi Distribution with a local partner to take over the distribution of all products manufactured by its Indonesian subsidiaries and to manage the distribution of its products in Indonesia. Sara Lee also acquired an equity stake in a local distribution company, Suria Yozani, which now handles all imported Sara Lee direct-sale products under the "House of Sara Lee" name. As Anthony Nowell, president director of Prodenta and managing director of Kiwi Distribution noted: "By having our own joint venture distribution company, we take direct management control and the company is run as part of the overall corporate structure. The foreign management team can now make all the decisions in respect of capital spending, human resources, information technology, etc." (Baldwin, 1994).

Smuggling and Parallel Imports

Smuggling and parallel imports are widespread in Indonesia because it is impossible to prevent products from landing along the vast archipelago coastline. Smuggled goods are mainly branded luxury products and they are highly priced even without import duties. These items are affordable only to higher income groups. Local investors do not view them as much of a threat since these brands cannot be advertised or promoted. Parallel imports, however, are another matter.

Parallel imports are brought in legally by an agent other than the one authorised. The targeted goods are usually well known brands with a high volume of circulation and large profit margins. This practice tends to be the result of pricing differentials between Indonesia and another country, making parallel imports attractive. To overcome this problem, companies must coordinate their regional pricing so that minimal price differentials exist among regional markets.

The regulations that influence options available to foreign companies in Indonesian's distribution system are complex and the permutations require careful examination by new entrants and established players alike. The following section presents the various options open to foreign investors.

WAYS OF ENTERING THE INDONESIAN MARKET

Indonesia has some of the most restrictive laws on foreign ownership of retail and distribution operations among the emerging Asian markets. Import/export and retail distribution have been reserved for Indonesian companies. However, with the tremendous economic growth and the surge in foreign direct investment in recent years, multinational companies have been putting tremendous pressure on the Indonesian Government to gradually open up the local market to foreign retailers.

To enter the Indonesia market, foreign companies can open a trade representative office in Indonesia with the permission of the Indonesian Department of Trade. This representative office may be an Indonesian company, an Indonesian individual or a foreign national. Each business is allowed to operate only one representative office. Through the representative office, foreign companies can then engage in market research, provide technical advice and engage in other promotional activities. But these representative offices are not allowed to sell directly to consumers. To overcome the problem of restricted distribution, there are several options available to foreign companies and they are described as follows.

Local Agents

Engaging an established and well-connected local distribution agent (a wholly Indonesian-owned distribution company) is a common option for foreign companies that want to expand their sales in Indonesia. The local agent can perform all trade activities and handle goods from all parties including those from third party manufacturers outside of Indonesia. It normally has offices throughout Indonesia, thereby allowing widespread distribution.

Since the end of 1980, Indonesian government agencies only deal with local agents when importing goods and services. This is part of the government's effort to boost the development of local enterprises. Therefore, foreign firms dealing with government agencies have a better chance of doing well if they appoint Indonesian firms as their distribution agents. Some of the leading nation-wide distribution agents include Wickasana, Indometra, Tigaraksa and Borsomig W. I.

After an agent is appointed and the trade representative office is established with a foreign employee, expatriate employees can be re-assigned to this agent. This arrangement allows for greater control over the marketing and distribution activities. Moreover, it meets Indonesia's legal requirements and effectively gives foreign firms a more direct hand in selling their products (U.S. Department of Commerce, 1996).

Captive Trading Companies

One option available to foreign investors is the establishment of a local private limited company (with zero foreign equity) through an Indonesian nominee. Foreign investors can then enter into management agreements to take *de facto* control of the business. Funding of the business activities can be done through loans made to captive trading companies. Some of the common types of management agreements are described below.

(i) ***Technical Assistance Agreement***: This agreement limits a foreign company to providing only technical assistance to an Indonesian company.

(ii) ***Management Agreement***: This agreement allows a foreign firm to manage an Indonesian company or a division of a company.

(iii) ***Management Agreement with Financial Agreement***: Under this agreement, a foreign firm not only manages an Indonesian company, but also finances its operations.

Using a captive trading company allows foreign investors into areas not open to direct foreign investments. Under Indonesian laws, only the nominee parties are recognised as beneficial owners of a company and foreign investors, having no equity interest, cannot exert full power and control over a company. Therefore, foreign investors are taking a risk if they enter into such arrangements. Having a loan agreement instead, could result in better protection to foreign investors because adequate securities can be required to support the loan.

Franchising

Franchising is a relatively new concept in Indonesia but it is becoming more popular. Franchising is governed by Indonesia's contract law. It involves a contractual relationship between a franchiser (which could be a manufacturer, wholesaler or service provider) and the franchisee. In a typical franchising agreement, a franchisee normally pays either the initial fees, the royalties on gross sales, the rental and lease fees for equipment provided by a franchiser, a share of the profits or a combination of these items to the franchiser. In return, the franchisee obtains the right to produce some unique products or use the service, method of doing business, a trade name, patent or goodwill that a franchiser has developed.

Franchising facilitates the transfer of technology and management expertise and it allows foreign companies to quickly establish a presence in the Indonesian market. In Indonesia, franchising is more prominent in fast foods, departmental stores and supermarkets. Table 10–7 lists some of the franchised operations with foreign retailers in Indonesia.

Joint Venture Distribution Company

Technically, it is possible for manufacturing *Penanaman Modal Asing* (Foreign Capital Investment, PMA) companies to form joint venture distribution companies to distribute goods made locally by their parent manufacturing PMA companies. So far, the *Badan Koordinasi Penanaman Modal* (Investment Coordinating Board, BKPM) has interpreted the edict on this type of permission fairly narrowly. A joint venture distribution company cannot distribute goods that are made solely by an Indonesian partner or imported by foreign investors (Baldwin, 1994).

There are several disadvantages in forming a joint venture distribution company. First, substantial investment is required to set up warehouses and distribution outlets throughout Indonesia and a critical sales mass is needed to make the investment a viable option. Secondly, there is the issue of control. Widespread distribution outlets make it difficult for foreign investors to control the marketing operations, the distribution outlets and the numerous salespeople. Although the same can be said about engaging local distribution agents, foreign companies have less control over how marketing is carried out by local agents.

Thirdly, many companies have a long standing relationship with their local distribution agents who are well established and financially strong. Companies may find that their manufacturing partner and distributor are the same entity and to sever the relationship could be expensive.

TABLE 10–7
Foreign Retailers with Franchise Operations in Indonesia

Retailer	Franchise Holder	Owner
Best Collection (Japan)	Pasaraya Nusakarya P. T.	Alatief
Body Shop (U.S.)	Monica Lestari P. T.	V. H. Santoso
Circle-K (U.S.)	Circle-K Indonesia P. T.	n.a.
Courts (U.K.)	Matahari Tatagriya P. T.	Matahari
FairPrice (Singapore)	Kopkas Fairprice P. T., Guardian Pharmacy	Sekar
Guardian Pharmacy (Singapore)	Rajawali Inti Retail P. T., JC Penney Collection	Rajawali
JC Penney Collection (U.S.)	Multipolar Laksindo P. T., Lotus Dept. Store	Lippo
Lotus Dept Store (Singapore)	Lotus Pertiwi P. T.	Gajah Tunggal
Makro (Dutch)	Karabha Unggul P. T.	T.P. Rachmat
Marks & Spencer (U.K.)	Mailkelindo Aneka P. T., Bahfet, Metro Dept. Store	Frieda ZA
Maruzen (Japan)	Pasaraya Nusakarya P. T.	Alatief
One Stop (Singapore)	Bahana Upaya Lestari P. T.	n.a.
Pro-Image (U.S.)	Manggala Pertiwi	Tantyo Sudharmono
Seibu (Japan)	Pasaraya Nusakarya P. T.	Alatief
Sogo (Japan)	Panen Lestari Internusa	Gajah Tunggal
Wal-Mart (U.S.)	Multipolar Perkasa P. T.	Lippo

Source: *Economic and Business Review Indonesia*, No. 220, 3 July 1996.

Before the economic reform in 1995, foreign investors that manufactured goods in Indonesia through joint venture companies (PMA companies) were not allowed to distribute them directly in Indonesia. They could distribute their products only through local distribution agents. With the change in regulations, PMA companies can now distribute locally produced goods up to the wholesaler level (i.e., dedicated buyers of large quantities).

FUTURE TRENDS

Development Trends in Other Regional Economies

In line with Indonesia's level of economic development, its retail sector is still in the infant stage of development. Small traditional outlets, such as *warungs* and *pasars*, are the main outlets for food and daily necessities. The future points to large scale retailing. The development of the retail sector in several Asian economies suggests the trends shown in Figure 10–12.

The life cycle of this development trend varies from country to country. Singapore, for example, raced through these developmental changes when its economy took off in the early 1970s. The per capita GDP soared from about US$3,000 to US$20,000 in about 20 years. Over the years, the development of departmental stores and supermarkets occurred at an extremely fast pace. At the same time, the concept of convenience stores began emerging when 7-Eleven entered the market in the early 1980s. By the early 1990s, large departmental stores and supermarkets began to spread out to the suburban residential areas. Franchised mini-mart chains have begun to replace the traditional retail outlets since then and, by 1992, 81% of the value transacted in foods and daily necessities was from mini-marts and supermarkets (Department of Statistics, 1992).

Similarly, retail development in Jakarta has been extremely fast because local retailers such as Matahari and Sarinah raced to set up departmental stores all over Jakarta at the rate of three to four stores each year. Competition became more intense when giant global retailers such as Wal-Mart and Marks & Spencer decided to enter the market in 1994, lured there by the tremendous potential all over Indonesia. Very soon, there will be further shifts towards more discount stores and factory outlets as consumers become more value conscious. As in the case of Singapore, large discount stores, including K-Mart, Wal-Mart and IMM stores, are appearing on the horizon already.

FIGURE 10–12
Development Trends in Asian Retail Markets

	Development	**Emerging NIE**	**NIE**	**Developed**
Countries	Indonesia Philippines	China Thailand Malaysia	Taiwan South Korea	Japan Australia Singapore
GDP Per Capita*	Around US$3,000	US$6,000–US$8,000	Around US$12,000	Around US$20,000
Retail Outlets Characteristics	• Small stalls/shops still prevail. For example, traditional outlets in Indonesia still account for about 90% of retail sales values. • Traditional markets are still the main source of food for lower income families. For example, 65% of Indonesians still buy in *pasars*, a traditional market place. • Major supermarkets are in early stage of development and mostly located in urban areas. For example, more than one-half of the supermarkets in Indonesia are in Jakarta.	• Small stalls/shops are still dominant features. • Development is towards discount stores (Makro in Thailand) and more established supermarkets (e.g., Cold Storage in Malaysia). • Convenience stores are emerging such as 7-Eleven in Thailand and Malaysia.	• Diminishing proportion of small stalls/-shops in the retail market (less than 30% in Taiwan). • Supermarkets and convenience stores are well established (Welcome and 7-Eleven in Taiwan). • Clear trend towards discount stores (Makro in Taiwan).	• Supermarkets and convenience stores are well established (NTUC FairPrice in Singapore). • Increasing popularity of speciality stores (Marks & Spencer in Singapore). • Store brands emerge and price discounting picks up pace (Daiei in Japan).

* *CIA World Fact Book* (1995).

Protection of Traditional Retailers

As the competition in large scale retailing heightens, small traditional retailers are facing the same pressure to upgrade. The retail association has taken a "watchdog" role in ensuring that the smaller retailers are protected from harsh competition. It has worked through the regulators to limit the competition from large modern retailers. For example, it forced modern outlets to close on Sundays and public holidays. The government helps local traditional retailers by keeping retailing on the "negative list" for foreign investment. Therefore, foreign participation in this area is mostly achieved through franchising agreements or via technical assistance cum loan agreements. Given the industry's crucial role in generating employment, the government will continue its negative listing at least until the year 2003.

Other Modes of Modern Retailing

Mail ordering and Internet shopping are likely to grow in importance in future. In Indonesia, this mode of shopping will take some time to develop for several reasons. First, there are cultural impediments since "Indonesian consumers are sceptical of transactions that are not face-to-face and do not have the merchandise in view" (Baldwin, 1994). Secondly, mailing lists are difficult to maintain and are costly to purchase from direct mail companies. Lastly, the comparatively lower proportion of ownership of computers at 0.3 computers for every 100 people, and the small number of Internet users, both limit the economies of scale in providing Internet shopping at the present time.

These modes of shopping will become more prominent as the Indonesian economy grows in size and the consumer market becomes more mature. Furthermore, the high departure tax on resident Indonesians will deter cross-border shopping and force them to rely more on mail ordering for luxury items such as jewellery, handbags, watches and so forth. The extensive telecommunication infrastructure will facilitate the growth in information technology development, and the increasing use and ownership of home computers. These factors should contribute positively to increased Internet shopping. In summary, the opportunities for foreign companies to master the challenging Indonesian distribution maze and to exploit the tremendous potential are substantial.

CONCLUSION

The discussion in this chapter suggests that the marketing and distribution system in Indonesia is different from conventional systems. Moreover, the geographical diversity presents a unique set of problems for retailing and distributing products. Potential investors face several challenges that have been addressed in the latter part of the chapter. Prudence suggests that they should carefully consider these factors as well as their mode of entry into the Indonesian market.

REFERENCES

Asia, Inc., "The New Asian Executive's Internet Map", September 1996.

Baldwin Peter, *Consumer Marketing in Indonesia: Harnessing Purchasing Power*, Economist Intelligence Unit, Hong Kong, March 1994.

Bank of Indonesia, *Economic and Monetary Development in 1996*, Economic and Monetary Statistics Department, Jakarta, 1996.

Business Asia, "Consumer Marketing in Indonesia – A Market Too Far", 14 February 1994.

CIA World Fact Book, "World Factbook Data on Indonesia", http://www. odci.gov/cia/publications/95fact/vm.html, 1995.

Department of Statistics, Ministry of Finance, Singapore, *Economic Survey Series – Wholesales and Retail 1992*, Singapore National Printers Ltd., Singapore, August 1994.

Economic and Business Review Indonesia, "The Race to Riches: Indonesia's Retail Renaissance", No. 220, 3 July 1996.

Economist Intelligence Unit, *Country Profile – Indonesia 1995/96*, London, 1996.

INDIO, *Indonesia Source Book*, Jakarta, Indonesia, August 1996.

Investment Coordinating Board (BKPM), *A Brief Guide for Investment*, Ministry of Investment, Jakarta, 1996.

P. T. Indofood Sukses Makmur, *Annual Report*, Jakarta, 1995.

P. T. Lippo Securities, *Indonesia Equity Review*, SBC Warburg Asia Limited, Jakarta, July 1996.

P. T. Wickasana Overseas International, *Annual Report*, Jakarta, 1995.

The Asian Retail, Editorial, July 1994.

The Business Times, "Indonesia's Election Year Budget", 8 January 1997.

The Foundation, *The World Competitiveness Report/EMF Foundation 1995*, Cologney/Geneva, Switzerland, 1995.

U.S. Department of Commerce, "Indonesia – Marketing US Products and Services", Washington, D.C., 1996.

Wilianto I. E., *Hero Supermarket*, P. T. Schroders, Jakarta, 19 September 1995.

Chapter 11

Indonesia's Advertising and Promotion Media: Some Recent Developments*

BY
Bernard CHEONG
CHUA Siew Beng
Shakander Singh CHAHAL
WONG Chew Wah

INTRODUCTION

THIS CHAPTER CONSIDERS recent developments affecting advertising and promotion media in Indonesia. It examines how various forms of advertising and promotion media are used to market products in the country and how the unique nature of the country shapes the development of advertising and promotions in Indonesia, both currently and in the future.

The chapter begins with an overview of advertising in Indonesia and provides an insight into important events that shaped the growth and distribution of advertising expenditures in the industry. Self-regulation, code of ethics and the various types of advertising agencies and support services are also discussed to provide a better understanding of the opportunities and constraints in advertising and promotion in the country. Various media used in Indonesia are then analysed and evaluated,

---

* The authors are grateful for the contributions from the following people: Mr. Yusca Ismail from Perwanal/DMB & B, Mr. Koes Pudjianto from P. T. Binamark Indonesia, Ms. Eleanor Modesto from Citra Lintas, Ms. Lalita A. Marjuni and Ms. Astari Herman from Indo-Ad, Mr. David Mackenzie from Batey Ads Singapore and for the guidance from the project supervisor, Dr. Krishna Erramilli.

which include broadcast media, print media, outdoor media and other common forms of media. Finally, a glimpse into future developments is provided.

During the research in Jakarta and Singapore, the authors received many useful insights into the industry from interviews with practitioners from the leading advertising agencies. Their frank views have given much depth to the understanding of the Indonesian advertising industry than would have been possible otherwise. Their comments have been incorporated throughout this chapter and touch on almost every issue that was discussed.

THE INDONESIAN ADVERTISING INDUSTRY

The advertising industry has been growing from strength to strength in the last few years. Advertising expenditure has increased from Rp 1,027 billion in 1992 to over Rp 3,335 billion in 1995! The proliferation of advertising in Indonesia is largely due to the government's efforts to deregulate the industry in the wake of its economic growth. The distribution of advertising expenditures from 1992 to 1996 (projected figures) over the different media is illustrated in Figure 11–1 (Subakti and Katoppo, 1996, p. 52).

FIGURE 11–1
Advertising Expenditures: By Type of Media 1992–96*
(Rp billion)

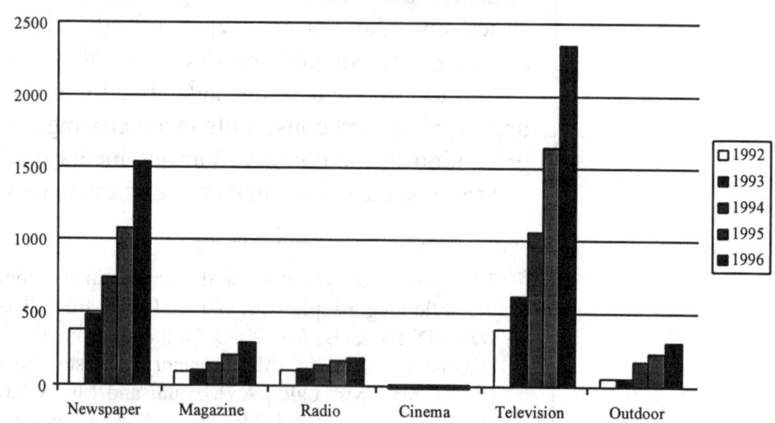

* Projected figures for 1996.
Source: Subakti and Katoppo (1996), p. 52.

Historical Perspective

The development of the advertising industry and the distribution of advertising expenditures in Indonesia are shaped by events that are politically and economically driven. For example, growth in advertising expenditure for television was very high in the four years from 1992 to 1995 (see Figure 11–1). This trend was fuelled by government policies implemented from 1981 to the early 1990s.

In January 1981, the government banned television advertising. The restriction took effect on 1 April 1981. Overnight, the first television station in Indonesia, the state-owned Televisi Republik Indonesia (TVRI), lost its estimated US$30 million annual advertising revenue. The fledgling television commercial production industry was torn apart (Geddes, 1990, p. 18).

The reasons for the ban vary. The most popular reason was that it was a pre-election year and the government sought to curb what it perceived as the undesirable development of consumerist sentiments among a population that could barely afford the bare essentials of life. Another reason was that the rapid development of consumerism in the world's largest Muslim country would speed a population drift from the countryside to the overpopulated cities.

The television ban deeply affected the marketing of mass products and newly launched goods for which coverage and reach are very important. However, media such as radio and print benefited from the ban, with an impressive increase in revenues of between 200% to 300% (Namis, 1982, p. 31). The billboard was another medium that grew rapidly then. The growth was so rapid that cluttering and visual "pollution" became an issue. This resulted in high taxes being imposed on billboards and strict government controls over where billboards could be put up.

By the early 1990s, there was deregulation in the air. In 1990, the government announced the establishment of private television stations. The Minister of Information, Mr. Harmoko, explained that the move was to allow wider access to information and knowledge vital to the public. However, the state-run TVRI would continue its policy of not running advertisements, and would receive a percentage of the revenue derived from advertising screened on commercial stations (Geddes, 1990, p. 18).

ADVERTISING CONTROLS AND CONSTRAINTS

A variety of self-imposed and externally imposed regulations guide the Indonesian advertising industry. These are discussed in the following sections.

Self-regulation

The Commission for Advertising Code of Ethics and Code of Practice was formed on 17 September 1981 as part of Indonesia's advertising movement to carry on the trend towards self-regulation in the industry. All major media, the press, cinemas, radio and television were represented in the Commission (Namis, 1982, p. 30). Thus, any problem that could not be resolved by an association may be filed with the commission for a decision. It was hoped that the Commission would become a clearing body for all advertising.

Advertising Code of Ethics and Code of Practice

The code of ethics and practice in advertising was formulated "in the interests of protecting the cultural values of the nation based on *Pancasila* and the Constitution of 1945 and in verifying its social responsibilities ..." (Subakti and Katoppo, 1996, p. 167). The general principles and guidelines in the code of ethics are based on one guiding principle known as SARA. This is an acronym for *Suku* (ethnic groups), *Agama* (religion), *Ras* (race) and *Antaragolongan* (political groups). All advertising agencies are sensitive to the needs and requirements of the four population groups in their advertising and promotion strategies.

The delicate balance advertisers have to maintain is largely driven by the uniqueness of the Indonesian culture. Approximately 87% of Indonesians embrace Islam as their religion (INDIO, 1996, p. 14) and the public is generally very sensitive to advertisements that are offensive to their culture and religion. Certain products that are forbidden by Islam will be considered *haram*. Examples of such products include those that contain pork or alcohol. In addition, food products must be certified *halal* to confirm that they meet the strict Muslim dietary requirements. For example, poultry and other animals must be slaughtered according to prescribed religious practices.

Any advertisements with sexual connotations are forbidden. An example was the Wrangler City Slickers jeans advertisement where an actress took off her jeans to put out a fire. It was considered offensive and was taken off the air when the audience protested.

Indonesians have a set of values called *Pancasila* which is unique to their country. The pride of the Indonesian traditional culture is embedded in this set of values. Themes such as *musyawarah untuk mufakat* (deliberation for consensus), *kebersamaan* and *kekeluargaan* (togetherness), *pembangunan manusia seutuhnya* (development of human beings in totality) are always reiterated not only by government officials at all levels but, also, by the mass media and general public (Rauf, 1995). It is thus important for businessmen to empathise with the Indonesians' penchant for seeking consensus. If these values could be exploited, then businesses could achieve "consensus" with the consumers on their choice of products. If it was handled improperly, then it could signify the death of the product in Indonesia. Since Indonesians value "togetherness", word-of-mouth publicity is a powerful channel of communication, be it positive or negative.

Due to Indonesia's political history, use of the Chinese language in the country is a sensitive issue. Thus, the display of any logo or trademark with Chinese characters has to be discrete.

Despite the seemingly restrictive nature of these religious and social inclinations, Indonesians are generally more tolerant to advertisements with Western influences when compared to Muslims in other countries such as Malaysia. For example, Triumph swimsuits are shown on both television and on huge electronic billboards in public. Similarly, even though the advertisement for Rexona deodorant shows the underarms of young girls in bath towels, there were no protests from consumers and the advertisement was even considered a success in Indonesia!

It is thus important for businessmen to respect *Pancasila* and the Indonesian value system in advertising and promoting their products. The unique culture is a double-edged sword. It could be an asset to businesses as well as a liability, depending on how it is handled.

Guidelines on Product Advertising

The code of ethics and code of practice provide guidelines on how advertisers should approach product advertising in Indonesia (MacKenzie, 1995). In a nutshell, the products covered are as follows:

(i) ***Alcoholic Beverages and Cigarettes***: Advertisements of these products should not influence or encourage the public to consume them by suggesting that they are good for health. The advertisements should not be directed at children under the age of 16 and/or pregnant women, nor portray them in any such advertisement. It is an unwritten law in the advertising industry that no one should be portrayed as enjoying smoking in advertisements.

(ii) ***Pharmaceuticals and Drugs***: Advertisements should be in accordance with the use of a drug as approved by the Indonesian Department of Health. Information on the safe use of a drug should be provided and health care professionals should not be featured in such advertisements. The Indonesian government imposed strict rules on medicine advertisements that are perceived to function as critical sources of health information, particularly to people in rural areas.[1]

(iii) ***Advertising for Children***: Children should not be portrayed in dangerous acts or those that are unseemly for children. Advertisements should not take advantage of the lack of experience and innocence of children. It is important to understand that no child should be seen endorsing a particular brand in advertisements. This policy is designed to discourage inculcating consumerism in children of a young age.

(iv) ***Commercial Production***: Foreign actors or locations are not allowed except for international non-consumer products. All television commercials must be of local production or from a joint venture and a production permit is necessary before shooting. However, as long as the models are Pan-Asian, or if the advertisement is part of an international campaign to promote a product, the government is flexible to allow the commercials to be aired.

ADVERTISING AGENCIES[2]

The socio-economic progress made by Indonesians has had much influence on the marketing arena. Today's better educated Indonesians, together with their growing affluence and spending power, have directly impacted advertising in the country. Improvements in advertising have resulted from the population becoming more advertising-literate and sophisticated.

Despite the fact that the Indonesian advertising industry is rela-

---

1 *Indonesia on Fast Track*, 28 June 1996.

2 This section is adapted from *Indonesia on Fast Track*, 28 June 1996.

tively young, some of the advertisements and commercials have succeeded in attaining respect at international advertising festivals. The progress is particularly evident by comparing print advertisements and commercials made in the 1980s with those produced over the last five years. Progress is evident in the many print advertisements and commercials composed of imaginative elements that prod interest while reflecting local traditions and tastes.

The progress in the creative dimensions of Indonesian advertising can be directly attributed to several factors. Firstly, there has been a rapid growth of the media. The proliferation of publications and TV channels poses challenges to advertising professionals to produce a wider variety of print advertisements and TV commercials. Secondly, the presence of foreign professionals has also been a significant factor. Expatriates, with their multinational agencies, have introduced new concepts and perspectives as well as sophisticated production equipment. They have provided access to their international network in terms of creative concepts and market research, besides bringing their regional accounts with them.

Advertisers would prefer, other things being equal, the same agency to handle their advertising work to ensure consistency of campaign concepts. In addition, affiliation by local agencies with such foreign firms helps to provide the former with the latest communication techniques that are being used in the more advanced markets. This exposure is very beneficial given the lack of industry training institutes. Thirdly, government deregulation in general, and deregulation of the advertising industry in particular, has resulted in many new entrants into the industry.

In trying to attract new talent into the industry as well as continuing efforts to improve the image of the advertising industry in general, the Indonesian Association of Advertising Agencies or *Persatuan Perusahaan Periklanan Indonesia* (PPPI), has organised an annual *Citra Pariwara* awards ceremony since 1990. This is the Indonesian equivalent of the Clio Awards.

Table 11–1 shows the total billings (1993–95) of leading advertising agencies. These are full-service firms that are able to provide a fully co-ordinated communications campaign. Citra Lintas, for instance, has kept pace with the high growth by supporting the growing needs of its clients. This action led the agency to develop an audio-visual department. It has diversified into three separate operating companies: Citra itself; Integrated Marketing Communications (IMC), specialising in accounts with integrated marketing communications requirements; and Initiative Media Indonesia (IMI), specialising in negotiating plans and being the buyer for the former two agencies.

Another agency, Indo-Ad, has diversified by opening its own public relations as well as direct marketing divisions, both in early 1990. It has formalised its relationship with a local graphic design company to extend the Artistree network (of Ogilvy & Mather) in Southeast Asia. This tie-up has helped Indo-Ad in the key area of technology transfer. In addition, this tie-up has enabled Indo-Ad to train its staff locally, regionally and internationally. This training is possible because Indo-Ad has linked up with Ogilvy & Mather's worldwide network, particularly in the new areas of public relations and direct marketing. The knowledge and expertise acquired as a result of these tie-ups ensures Indo-Ad of providing its clients with superior service in the range of communication disciplines.

TABLE 11–1
Growth of Top Agencies

	Rp millions		
Billings	**1993**	**1994**	**1995**
Citra Lintas	75,885	83,102	102,242
Matari Advertising	70,369	76,865	97,716
JWT Ad Force	49,643	66,500	82,895
Indo-Ad	43,095	48,984	62,626
Inter Admark	33,030	44,522	56,316
Fortune Indonesia	23,021	25,909	44,383
Perwanal/DMB & B	25,166	29,942	41,064
Kreasindo Ciptapariwara	-	-	39,033
Rama Perwira	-	-	35,349
Grafik McCann Erickson	19,680	26,632	35,233

Source: Subakti and Katoppo (1996), pp. 195–6.

Challenges

The ban that the Indonesian government imposed on the screening and production of commercials has impacted Jakarta's advertising production companies. The difficulties that these production houses are facing lies in their lack of up-to-date facilities, and lack of resources and expertise. For instance, while Video Disc Tara may be considered as one of the top post-production houses, it is not a full-service firm and can only handle off-line or on-line up to Betacam.

Some of the issues facing the advertising industry are fee undercutting, increased competition from small agencies and recruitment of experienced staff. It is possible that many new agencies that have been attracted to the industry because of more advertising expenditure, may eventually fold up for reasons of inadequate management, high costs and poor cash flows.

The lack of formal training institutes remains a setback. In addition, a negative image hampers the advertising business. "Advertising is coming under heavy attack from consumer groups who say that it creates false demands and is not truthful" (Andrei, 1995a, p. 20).

Another obstacle or challenge for advertising agencies and marketers, depending on one's viewpoint, is the February 1991 introduction of the broadcasting and production ruling. It states that advertisements must be locally produced, and the depiction of excessive aspirational lifestyles and Caucasian talent must be curtailed. In 1995, one multinational company, Coca-Cola, realised that international solutions do not necessarily work and introduced its first 100% locally produced campaign (through Grafik McCann Erickson) with the jingle performed by local star Indra Lesmana (Andrei, 1995a, p. 20). The lesson, then, is to be as local as possible and focus the advertising message along social, religious or tribal groupings. A touch of humour helps to gain viewer attention and loyalty. Most certainly, the message has to indicate clear and relevant benefits to the target audience.

The advertising industry of Indonesia is on the upswing, with an estimated 46% growth in spending for 1996. While this has created certain problems, such as poor client service and agent hopping, it has also offered opportunities. With a continued emphasis on investment in new technology, production houses will make sufficient progress such that the post-production of TV commercials will no longer have to be done in Singapore, Thailand, or Australia. The arrival of foreign professionals is timely because they can provide experience as well as expertise to the under-exposed advertising agencies of Indonesia. The learning may not necessarily be uni-directional. For instance, the first market research firm was formed in Indonesia in 1994. It later merged with A.C. Nielsen International, the world's largest market-research organisation, and has since been renamed Survey Research Indonesia (SRI). It continues to set high professional standards and provides a wide range of services, besides being the industry's innovator (Subakti and Katoppo, 1996, p. 216).

BROADCAST MEDIA

Television

TV spearheads the dramatic increase in advertising spending, growing 45-fold since the government lifted the ten-year ban (1981–1991) on TV advertising (see Figure 11–1). The expectation is for television's rampant growth to continue, capturing market share from other media.

One significant change that has led directly to the increase in TV advertising is the growth in the number of households with electricity. It has grown from 76% of total households in 1984 to 96% in 1994. Correspondingly, there has been an increase in the number of households with electrical appliances including television sets. About two-thirds of the population now have access to TV service, in part because of government installations in outlying rural areas as part of their programme to disseminate information across the country.

TABLE 11–2
Television Households: 1988 to 1992

	1988	1989	1990	1991	1992
Television households ('000)	17,300	18,500	20,000	20,350	21,350
% of households	45.6	47.5	50.4	51.1	53.4

Source: *Asian Advertising, Marketing & Media Handbook*, 1994, p. 144.

(i) ***Television Stations***: The Indonesian TV industry started in 1962 when Televisi Republik Indonesia (TVRI) was established as a state-owned and controlled operation providing non-commercial programmes. The Indonesian government has since licensed five additional private commercial television stations.[3]

TVRI operates the most extensive TV network in the country. It produces about 60 hours of television programmes per week. Aside from news and public service programming, it airs limited general entertainment shows of local and foreign origin nation-wide (Subakti and Katoppo, 1996, p. 25). TVRI is the only station broadcasting on the VHF band and it operates two channels: TVRI 1 and TVRI 2. All private stations broadcast on

[3] The five private television networks are: Rajawali Citra Televisi Indonesia (RCTI), Surya Citra Televisi (SCTV), Televisi Pendidikan Indonesia (TPI), Cakrawala Andalas Televisi (ANTEVE) and Indosiar Visual Mandiri (IVM).

the UHF band. Its two channels are on the air for nine hours per day (2.30 p.m. to 11.35 p.m.). TVRI does not televise advertisements because it is fully funded by licensing fees.

In 1989, Rajawali Citra Televisi Indonesia (RCTI) became the first private station to operate in Jakarta. Today, RCTI has national coverage and reaches major cities throughout Indonesia while providing 22.5 hours of airtime daily (5.30 a.m. to 4.00 a.m.). It is by far the leading TV network in terms of viewership (see Table 11–3).

TABLE 11–3
TV Share Per Day

	9 a.m. to 12 p.m.	12 p.m. to 4 p.m.	4 p.m. to 6 p.m.	6 p.m. to 9 p.m.	9 p.m. to 12 p.m.
RCTI	26%	59%	31%	31%	24%
TPI	37%	7%	3%	7%	31%
SCTV	27%	24%	26%	11%	3%
IVM	5%	4%	32%	40%	21%
ANTEVE	3%	4%	3%	3%	2%
TVRI 1	2%	2%	4%	7%	9%
TVRI 2	-	-	1%	1%	-

Source: *Media Guide 1995/'96*, 1996, pp. 22–3.

Surya Citra Televisi (SCTV) is another well-established private channel. It was first introduced in August 1990 and targeted Surabaya and the surrounding region. Today, it reaches 15 major cities in Indonesia, providing 21 hours of airtime daily (5.00 a.m. to 2.00 a.m.).

Televisi Pendidikan Indonesia (TPI), long considered the education channel, started operating in early 1991. It was the first to achieve a national broadcasting licence but is limited to educational and public service programmes. TPI reaches 47 cities throughout Indonesia and provides 19.5 hours of airtime daily (5.30 a.m. to 1.00 a.m.). Cakrawala Andalas Televisi (ANTEVE) has been broadcasting since 1993. It reaches 11 cities in Indonesia providing 21.5 hours of airtime daily.

Indosiar Visual Mandiri (IVM) started broadcasting in 1994. Today, it reaches ten cities, providing 10.5 hours of airtime daily. IVM is backed by Indonesia's biggest conglomerate, the Salim Group, and it is aligned with TVB of Hong Kong for technical expertise. IVM is considered the strongest challenger to RCTI.

In addition, pay-TV has made its appearance in Indonesia. Indovision, Indonesia's sole pay-TV licencee, offers the Discovery Channel, ESPN, HBO, CNN, Turner's TNT and Star TV. Indonesia's Palapa communication satellites enable urban centres to receive international broadcasts of non-Indonesian TV stations. This is done through the installation of parabolic (dish) antennae. There are about 700,000 parabola dishes receiving channels such as the Australian Television International (ATVI), Asian Business News (ABN), (Hong Kong), Radio Television Malaysia (RTM) and TV3 (Malaysia), Canal France International (CFI), GMA-7 (Philippines) and others (Subakti and Katoppo, 1996, p. 26).

The TV industry is regulated in several ways. First, all TV programming must be broadcast in *Bahasa Indonesia*. Secondly, private-owned TV stations are required to broadcast a minimum of one hour per day of government news supplied by TVRI. Thirdly, no more than 20% of the total broadcast time can be allocated to commercials. Fourthly, advertisements are not allowed to be offensive nor degrade religious faiths, moral ethics, tradition, culture, or be slanted toward any racial or ethnic group. Moreover, all local and foreign TV programmes and commercial content are subject to the approval of the Film Censorship Board (BSF) which is under the Ministry of Information (Subakti and Katoppo, 1996, p. 25).

(ii) ***Audience and Coverage***: TV is the most important medium through which marketers can reach their target audience. Each commercial TV station can reach approximately 60% of the available audience (six spots per week). The impact is greater considering that Indonesia's TV viewing population is steadily increasing (Subakti and Katoppo, 1996, p. 26). The top ten categories of TV advertising are as follows: beverage, food, cigarettes, toiletries, vitamins, medicine-others, candies and media (*Media Guide 1995/'96*, 1996, p. 14).

TV viewership among households is equally distributed between the sexes (*Media Guide 1995/'96*, 1996, p. 18). Viewership is dominated by the 20–29 age group (about 30% of all viewership), followed by the 30–39 age group at about 20%. By occupation, TV viewership is dominated by blue-collar workers (about 30% of viewership), followed by white-collar workers at 20% (*Media Guide 1995/'96*, 1996, p. 19). The programmes with the highest ratings are *sinetrons* (local drama series). They range from locally-produced shows to dubbed Chinese, Japanese, Filipino and Latin American titles (*Media Guide 1995/'96*, 1996, p. 15).

The main issue here is the growing need to generate better local programmes. TV stations have failed to carve out their own special niches. No TV station has developed its distinctive channel profile in terms of programme consistency. Instead, most channels feature the popular *sinetrons*, sitcoms, game variety shows, historical epics, music and talent shows, cartoons and kiddies shows, and old Indonesian movies.

ANTEVE has been working hard to shake off its earlier image as a youth channel but has failed to convince advertisers. It is consolidating its strength in sports and music programming, and marketing its appeal to a "younger", rather than young, audience from the middle and upper class.

While RCTI and SCTV share common owners, they have separated their management structure and now have different business strategies. RCTI is targeting a younger upscale audience while SCTV has a stronger following among housewives.

TPI is the country's education channel with 80% local content. It is the most focused among all stations. Its audience coverage is less than 20% in the four major urban centres (Jakarta, Surabaya, Bandung and Medan). Its core audience (mostly lower to middle class) is in the rural areas and these viewers are the target for many fast-moving consumer goods (FMCG) advertisers.

(iii) ***Evaluation***: The development of a competitive TV market is underway in Indonesia. The advent of private TV stations (RCTI, SCTV, TPI, ANTEVE and IVM) alongside the government's TVRI, has shifted the seller's market to a buyer's market (*Media Guide 1995/'96*, 1996, p. 15). Marketers now can negotiate and shop for flexibility in terms of meeting their target audience. With TV, the stakes are a great deal higher and the opportunity to create an impact is much greater. TV affords the ability to build long term awareness.

The entry of private national television channels has created enormous demand for creative advertising products. This has led to a marked improvement in sophistication for TV commercials in the last two years. More improvement lies ahead as the industry invests in training young people in basic technical skills. Currently, the agencies with international affiliations have greater TV expertise than do the station owners.

The advent of a strong TV market and the concurrent rise in

the number of TV stations has resulted in audience fragmentation and more expenditure on achieving media objectives. A local or international firm, therefore, needs to assess expenditure and determine whether it is sufficient in getting the message across to the target audience. Equally important is selecting the TV stations and programmes with the greatest access to the target audience.

Radio

Radio offers the most effective advertising medium in Indonesia. This stems from its ability to identify with individuals because it is more personal (intimate), portable and cheap as well as interacting with them more easily and understanding the target audience better. Because of Indonesia's topography and rural population density, radio continues to offer the most effective reach. There are about 40 million radio sets in Indonesia and approximately 36% are in the urban areas.

Despite its effectiveness, radio is the most challenging medium. Most clients and advertising agencies miss its powerful influence and creative opportunities. Radio is a medium that is not exactly high profile. However, in the 1995 *Citra Pariwata* creative awards, a radio spot won the Best of the Best award (*Media*, 5 July 1996, p. 2).

Radio as a medium comes with some restrictions. Commercial time is limited to a maximum of 25% of total airtime. Also, all private radio stations are required to air news reports produced by Radio Republik Indonesia (RRI).

(i) ***Radio Stations***: Radio is the most important source of information for a majority of the population. It reaches the whole socioeconomic spectrum and is listened to by all Indonesians at some time. There is a radio station in each of the 27 provinces and a total of 858 of them in Indonesia. Out of this number, 662 are privately owned, 50 belong to RRI and the remaining 146 are municipal government stations (Subakti and Katoppo, 1996, p. 26). This number far outstrips the six TV stations. With this imbalance, Indonesia is a country of radio stations that provide better national coverage when compared to TV since the latter is an urban phenomenon that is not very useful for reaching the rural population (*Media Guide 1995/'96*, 1996, p. 41).

About 35% of the radio stations have shifted from broadcasting on amplitude modulation (AM) to the frequency modulation (FM) band. This has facilitated stereo quality and more sophisticated programming (Subakti and Katoppo, 1996, p. 27).

(ii) ***Audience and Coverage***: Radio is listened to about equally by both sexes. The 20–29 age group provides the bulk of the radio audience (about 40%) followed by the 15–19 age group and the 40–49 age group (each account for 20%). Blue-collar workers are the majority audience (about 30%), followed by white-collar workers (about 20%) and then students (slightly less than 20%) (*Media Guide 1995/'96*, 1996, p. 42).

Indonesian pop music dominates the radio programmes (about 38%) followed by *Dang Dut* music (about 36%). The latter refers to the popular Indonesian music which has traces of Hindi (Indian) influence. Western pop music and religious programmes are not far behind at 24% and 22%, respectively (*Media Guide 1995/'96*, 1996, p. 43). The top categories of radio advertising are medicine–analgesic, medicine–others, medicine–traditional, household cleaners, toiletries, cigarettes, food, shampoos and hair treatments, cough medicine and cosmetics (*Media Guide 1995/'96*, 1996, p. 14).

Radio stations have been more successful than TV stations in developing distinct programme profiles to cater to a specific segment of the population. They have achieved this by being consistent in their programme content and by having a special appeal to their designated audiences. Radio is mostly listened to in the afternoon. It begins in the morning with religious programmes and then it provides drive-time rhapsody for the people commuting to work. (The same happens after working hours when they commute back to their homes.) Programmes aimed at housewives come on next and, in the afternoon, the younger generation is provided with its share of entertainment.

(iii) ***Evaluation***: There are about 300 ethnic groups speaking over 200 distinct languages in Indonesia and, so, radio offers an important avenue for local advertising campaigns (Subakti and Katoppo, 1996, p. 27). While radio is the second most effective form of national advertising medium after TV, advertisers regard it as being most effective for reaching rural audiences. About 80% of the rural population listens to the radio for entertainment and information, compared with 19% who watch television (Subakti and Katoppo, 1996, p. 27). The situation is different in urban areas where television dominates (73% for television and 63% for radio).

Radio should receive more attention as a vehicle for conveying messages. Due to Indonesia's largely rural and young population, radio is expected to remain significant. With its positive features of portability and inexpensive cost, radio is ideal for reaching young people, car owners and rural folks. Given these market segments, a marketer could use radio as a strong backup to TV despite the latter's growing dominance.

Radio stations are beginning to tap into the benefits of creating alliances. Smaller radio stations are now regrouping and consolidating into larger stations through ownership, management and marketing. These mergers will boost their financial strength as well as their ability to reach audiences over greater distances. Several examples of this trend in networking are the Kalimantan and Bali Network; the CPP Network with 30 radio stations in Java; and the KDS Group with 20 radio stations in East and Central Java (*Media Guide 1995/'96*, 1996, p. 41).

With keener competition between radio stations and greater segmentation among radio listeners, more radio stations are beginning to position themselves into specific marketing niches. Radio stations are catering to career women, housewives, young professionals and other groups. This effectively means that radio offers a more focused approach to the target audience than other medium. In addition to niche positioning, radio has a comparative advantage over TV in terms of low cost and localisation. All these factors are keeping radio competitive as an advertising medium (Subakti and Katoppo, 1996, p. 27). Currently, many radio stations are scattered in far flung towns and districts. But advertising agencies have focused on radio campaigns mainly in the major cities, primarily in the Jakarta area. The challenge, therefore, is to transfer these focused radio campaigns to the rural areas.

PRINT MEDIA

Newspapers

When television advertising was banned, newspapers naturally became the dominant medium. Even after the ban was lifted in 1991, newspapers continued to have a steady growth rate. In 1996, their projected share of advertising expenditure was 32.8% compared with television's 50.2% (Subakti and Katoppo, 1996, p. 53). But with television advertising costs rising faster than other media costs, print media is still cost effective.

The government has tight controls on the press. Under the 1966 *Press Act*, no foreign press can be established in the country. Publications must uphold and encourage the principles by which the country is governed. Media blackouts have occurred and issues or articles have been banned because of violations under this Act. In the last 15 years, no major newspaper has escaped temporary forced closures when they have dealt with controversial issues (*Asian Advertising, Marketing and Media Handbook*, 1994, pp. 17–8).

The Press Council sets the rules for the newspapers. It comprises the Minister of Information and appointed representatives from the media. For example, the number of pages in each edition is limited so smaller newspapers can flourish. This prevents the bigger players from gaining unfair advantage. The restriction is now 24 pages although permission for more is granted under special circumstances. The advertising content should not be more than 35% over one year.

(i) ***Audience and Coverage***: There are 165 newspapers (76 daily and 89 weekly) with a total circulation of 8.5 million copies. Over one-half of the daily newspapers are circulated in Java, mostly in Jakarta. The major dailies, *Kompas* and *Suara Pembaruan*, have significant circulation outside the Jakarta area. The largest circulation rates belong to *Kompas* and *Pos Kota*. The leading newspaper groups include *Gramedia* (national and regional newspapers), *Jawa Pos* (newspapers and tabloids for east Indonesia), and *Surya Pembaruan* (newspapers) (Subakti and Katoppo, 1996, p. 27).

There are three English language newspapers in Jakarta: the *Indonesian Times*, *Jakarta Post* and the *Indonesian Observer*. There is also a Chinese newspaper called *Harian Indonesia*. This group of newspapers is only meant to reach a small part of the population. The bulk of the revenue is earned from newspapers printed in the Indonesian language. Table 11–4 gives the readership numbers and the advertising revenue for the leading newspapers in 1994 and 1995, respectively.

Due to the poor distribution channels, outlying islands tend to have their own local papers. The influential regional papers include *Pikiran Rakyat* (Bandung: 150,000 circulation), *Suara Merdeka* (Semarang: 145,000 circulation), *Surabaya Pos* (Surabaya: 85,000 circulation) and *Analisa* (Medan: 75,000 circulation) (*Asian Advertising, Marketing and Media Handbook*, 1994, pp. 17–8).

TABLE 11–4
Newspaper Readership and Ad Revenue

Newspapers	Readership ('000s) 1995	Readership ('000s) 1994	% Change	Ad Revenue (US$ million) 1995	Ad Revenue (US$ million) 1994	% Change
Pos Kota	2,581	2,347	10	3.59	1.97	82
Kompas	2,065	1,798	15	39.84	29.90	11
Suara Pembaruan	836	734	14	13.19	11.30	17
Jawa Pos	748	901	(17)	9.53	6.42	48
Pikiran Rakyat	633	633	0	5.24	3.72	41

Source: Andrei (1995a), p. 20.

(ii) ***Evaluation***: Newspapers play an important role in complementing other media. An advertising campaign can use TV to introduce a new product, radio to increase the flow and newspapers to reinforce the message. The believability of the message is enhanced by the "credibility and news" properties of the medium. It can create the perception of "bigness of stature" and of being a "no nonsense" product (*Media Guide 1995/'96*, 1996, pp. 37–8). These considerations can be significant given the cultural background of the target audience.

Indonesia has achieved a literacy rate of more than 70% for people below 40 years of age and up to 95% for those of school age. This advance has fuelled an increasing trend in newspaper readership after a dip in 1992. Readership is targeted at the educated city dwellers who have more discerning tastes. Hence, most newspapers are produced to high standards, with the leading ones able to accept full-colour advertisements.

Newspaper advertising in Indonesia is one of the most expensive in the world due to the high cost of production and newsprint. A full-page colour advertisement in *Kompas* can cost about US$50,000 and, yet, there may be a six-month queue. To stay competitive, daily newspapers are more aggressively publishing supplements focused on business and financial issues, and various other recreational topics. These supplements can attract heavy advertisements (Andrei, 1995a, p. 21).

Some newly-established local papers were launched in response to TV. However, they had great difficulty in surviving and, subsequently, they merged with national publishing groups. Others have failed, partly due to mismanagement and partly due to their inability to position themselves as niche titles. Local and regional publishers such as the *Jawa Pos* Group, *Surya Persindo* and *Gramedia* have been buying up small newspapers around the country to enhance their outreach (*Asian Advertising, Marketing and Media Handbook*, pp. 17–8).

Electronic newspaper editions are appearing on the Internet. A recent search found web pages from *Kompas*, *Suara Pembaruan*, *Jawa Pos*, *Surabaya Post*, *Republika* and the *Indonesian Times*. They offer news stories, editorials and features, just like the paper version.

Magazines

(i) ***Audience and Coverage***: Magazines have become fully integrated into the lifestyles of the reading public. They are focused on specific niches and segments of the Indonesian population. There are about 125 consumer magazines (31 weekly, 46 fortnightly, 37 monthly, 2 bimonthly and 9 bulletins) with a total circulation of 5.5 million copies. Table 11–5 gives the readership and ad revenue of the leading magazines for 1994 and 1995, respectively. To attain a gross cumulative reach of 50% of the age group 15 years and above, around ten magazines are needed (Subakti and Katoppo, 1996, p. 27).

The magazine market is segmented by gender, age (children, teenagers and adults), socio-economic class (business, technology and computer) and special interest (sports, entertainment, health, home decoration and plants). Strong economic growth and increasing middle-class consumers are keeping the readership on an upward trend (*Media Guide 1995/'96*, 1996, pp. 34–6).

TABLE 11–5
Magazines Readership and Ad Revenue

Magazines	Readership ('000s)		% Change	Ad Revenue (US$ million)		% Change
	1995	1994		1995	1994	
Nova	1,816	1,081	68	3.93	3.05	29
Bola	1,271	1,069	19	1.38	1.10	26
Bintang	1,205	699	72	1.17	0.93	26
Femina	796	646	22	9.91	6.81	45
Kartini	782	641	22	4.21	3.41	23

Source: *Media Guide 1995/'96* (1996).

TABLE 11–6
Magazine Advertising Rates

Publication	Frequency	Circulation ('000s)	Readership Number ('000s)	Readership %	Rates Full Page Colour (Rp '000s)
Kartini	10 days	178	641	5	7,000
Femina	Weekly	120	646	5	6,800
Sarinah	Fortnightly	147	341	2	4,800
Nova	Weekly	427	1,081	8	17,100
Wanita Indonesia	Weekly	310	376	3	9,500
Bintang	Weekly	125	699	5	11,400
Citra	Weekly	239	445	3	9,500
Intisar	Fortnightly	141	516	4	4,050
Forum Keadilan	Fortnightly	47	226	2	3,000
Humor	Fortnightly	16	211	1	2,500
Higina	Fortnightly	74	36	-	5,000
Tiara	Fortnightly	47	46	-	3,000
Prospek	Weekly	10	38	-	5,600
Infobank	Monthly	40	139	1	5,000
Swasembada	Monthly	33	99	1	6,000
Eksekutif	Monthly	12	60	-	4,500
Economic & Business	Weekly	20	10	-	5,000

Source: MacKenzie (1995), p. 30.

The highest readership belongs to women's magazines. Advertisements for men's products appear in these magazines because they make up about 40% of the readers. The pass-on rates can be very high, averaging about 11 readers per copy. Family, friends and guests read the same copy before it is discarded. However, servants may retrieve the discarded copy and pass it on again (MacKenzie, 1995, p. 29).

A rapidly growing segment belongs to teen magazines that cater to the *Anak Baru Gede* (ABG) population. ABG are the highly sought after upper middle-class youngsters aged 10 to 15 years, representing a potential market of 15 million people. They are very brand-conscious but do not develop brand-loyalty. In emulating the fashionable richer upper-class, they are willing and able to pay for international labels. Teen titles such as *Gadis* (readership of 618,000) and *Hai* (readership of 354,000) claim to have doubled their advertising revenues since 1992. *Mode* (readership of 384,000) is another title with high growth (Andrei, 1995b).

(ii) ***Evaluation***: Magazine advertising expenditures show a growth rate of 36% which is only 6% of total expenditures. This medium is quite appropriate for penetrating the lucrative ABG and women markets. When matched with the right product, it can generate credibility and prestige for the top-end brand names, and provide high-quality colour reproduction that is so important in conveying the intended message.

Magazines can provoke government bans. In June 1994, the publishing licence of predominant news weekly *Tempo* was revoked along with two other leading magazines. The former then reappeared as the less controversial *Gatra* in November of the same year (Andrei, 1995a, p. 20).

OUTDOOR MEDIA

Billboards

There are more than 300,000 outdoor signs in Jakarta ranging from small neon signs to large billboards and many other billboards in larger cities. Billboards can provide effective advertising if they are located at strategic locations (*Media Guide 1995/'96*, 1996, p. 54).

After the ban on television advertising was imposed, there was a sudden growth in other media. Billboards began appearing everywhere since, like television advertising, they had visual appeal. However, the resulting clutter affected the aesthetics of city streets with billboards overlapping each other. City councils reacted by imposing punitive taxes to limit the number of billboards and boost the visual quality.

In 1989, Jakarta city authorities increased taxes for outdoor media by 3,000% making billboard advertisements very expensive. The tax can be as high as Rp 40 million in strategic places prompting agencies to choose lower tax hinterland areas. The billboard tax in the outskirts is only Rp 4 million to Rp 5 million (*EBRI*, 5 August 1995, pp. 20–1).

(i) ***Audience and Coverage***: Billboards can be found on almost every permanent structure in the streets where there is frequent pedestrian and vehicular traffic. In Jakarta, billboards can be seen on pedestrian bridges, bus shelters, community clocks, telephone booths and traffic police shelters at cross junctions. Large free-standing billboards are located at major junctions, and along roads and highways. Many billboards are exposed to passenger traffic at airports.

Regulations and taxes on billboards vary from region to region. Billboards are not allowed on several key roads and thoroughfares in major cities (Subakti and Katoppo, 1996, p. 27). However, this is not a constraint for advertisers willing to pay for a good spot. Advertisements from banks, property developers and large manufacturers are the most prominent.

(ii) ***Evaluation***: Billboard advertising will continue to be an important media given the recent improvements in quality. Advertising agencies prefer to subcontract the outdoor construction to external suppliers. But these suppliers lacked skilled artists in the past and the hand painting method was slow and expensive. Artistic talent has been improving and creating a more natural picture instead of showing crude paintings of advertised products. The use of vinyl skin enables a better picture reproduction and lowers the cost.

New technology has helped to rekindle interest in this media. The Q-Board is a computer-supported electronic billboard. Several kinds of billboards incorporating prism and light emitting diode (LED) technologies can be found in Jakarta. Prism technology allows three different views of a single flat billboard. Advanced lighting technology enhances the attractiveness of the presentation. All of these techniques, coupled with increased creativity, has enabled advertising agencies to make outdoor advertisements more lively and eye-catching (*EBRI*, 5 August 1995, pp. 20–1).

The billboard's impact will diminish over time. But the minimum rental period for most billboards is one year. To maximise the use of the space, different advertising messages can be rotated among billboards at various locations. A large consumer products manufacturer has done this by renting a few billboards and changing the advertisements every three months. Agencies have not yet co-ordinated this strategy among different advertisers.

Transit Advertisements

Two main forms of transit advertisements are bus panel and taxi rooftop advertisements. Bus panels can be placed either on single-decker or double-decker buses. In Jakarta, full body painting is available. Taxi rooftop panels are either double-sided or triple-sided, and they are displayed as stickers (MacKenzie, 1995, p. 32). Advertisements on taxis have been unsuccessful in Jakarta while full body advertisements on buses are very popular.

(i) ***Audience and Coverage***: Bus advertisements are most effective on the busy, and often jammed, roads in the big cities. Besides the high traffic flow, passengers in a slow moving vehicle cannot help but notice the colourful advertisements painted on buses. The message must be short and direct. Consumer product companies are using this medium to promote products such as detergents and ice-cream while others are using it to advertise cigarettes and hamburgers.

(ii) ***Evaluation***: Transit advertisements are challenging billboards as an alternative outdoor medium. Billboards are becoming very expensive due to high taxes and rental fees. A strategically located billboard can cost up to Rp 500 million per year. This is equivalent to placing the same advertisement at Rp 50 million each on ten buses. This is far cheaper for one bus and it can be very effective where there is a high concentration of people along the bus route. Bus operators have addressed concerns regarding the deteriorating quality of advertising displays arising from accidents or vandalism (*EBRI*, 30 October 1996, p. 19).

OTHER FORMS OF ADVERTISING MEDIA

In addition to the major advertising media discussed above, there are other forms that are peculiar to Indonesia, and some that have been introduced recently which have not gained public's acceptance yet.

Direct Marketing Media

New media such as direct mail, telemarketing and the Internet are restricted to a relatively small segment of the population. There are 16 telephone lines per 1,000 Indonesians with a successful call ratio of only 30% (*EBRI*, January 28 1995, p. 13). Clearly, these media are not viable for targeting a large segment. There are an estimated 30,000 Internet users in Jakarta, including a small number in Yogyakarta (Grocott, 1996) whose usage is mainly e-mailing. However, this coverage may change if the government's ambitious plan to wire up villages, announced in December 1996 by Jonathon Parapak, the

Secretary-General of Tourism, Post and Telecommunication, materialises (*Indonesia to Wire Villages for Internet*, 1996). The prospects for Internet as a medium are bright with the Indonesian Postal Service establishing its own Internet service provider, Wasantara-Net. Moreover, the public has access to computers at many larger post offices.

The use of direct mail to reach out to focus groups is also becoming popular in the Indonesian market. Mailing lists available from independent sources have been unreliable and, therefore, advertising agencies need to compile and maintain their own lists to ensure that their clients can reach out to target segments. These efforts can be quite costly at times. However in Indonesia, the use of rewards to entice responses is somewhat successful. Rewards such as sweepstakes or lucky draws are often offered in direct mail. An example was Pond's advertising campaign where the first 2,000 respondents received a token gift after they sent in a coupon. In addition to the reliability of mailing lists, efficiency of the public postal system is another factor to consider when using direct mail. Advertisers sometimes prefer to use private courier services to supplement the public postal system. However, this increases costs further.

Direct marketing via television is also new. ANTEVE was the first to accept this form of advertising in January 1995. It was reported that the response was good (*Asian Advertising & Marketing*, 24 March 1995, p. 2). Products are advertised and purchases can be made at certain outlets in various cities by calling in.

Cinema Advertising

Cinema patronage in Indonesia is relatively small, which adversely affects cinema advertisement demand and, in turn, advertising expenditure for this media. An interesting feature of Indonesian cinemas is their operation by a single entity called "the group of 21". A possible reason for declining advertising expenditure in cinema is that it has not considered advertising as an important source of revenue.

Indigenous Advertising Media

There is a lack of entertainment and amusement in the rural areas. Thus, people are often drawn by occasional events held in their vicinity. There are three types of travelling performances: the travelling musical band called *Dang Dut*, the outdoor cinema called *Lanya Tanchap* and the shadow puppet shows called *Wayang Kulit*. Not only do they provide entertainment, but they serve as advertising and promotion media for some consumer products. Small sachets of these products are handed out during the shows. Local radio stations are used to publicise these events.

FUTURE TRENDS IN THE DEVELOPMENT OF NEW MEDIA

The global advertising industry is continually influenced by technology. However, at national levels, demographic changes and political decisions tend to be the dominating forces. In Indonesia, dramatic changes in the advertising industry have followed changes in the state's policies balancing the need for openness and consequent negative effects.

Short Term Trends

The deregulation in the media industry is currently uncertain. The House of Representatives recently passed a bill on broadcasting giving the government the power to regulate the advertising industry and the use of new communications technology (*Jakarta Post*, 10 December 1996, p. 1). This will become Indonesia's first broadcasting law. Ironically, this is happening at a time when deregulation is a common buzzword. Reducing constraints in the broadcasting industry is an eventuality but it will be gradual so as to allow time for cultivating and building local talent. The industry is set to boom as the population becomes more educated, affluent and exposed to the outside world.

The current short supply of media space and slots should place upward pressures on costs. At the same time, agencies must be creative in maximising the effectiveness of available media. There are several media sources that have not been fully exploited; for example, transit advertising on taxis, sports event sponsorships and cinemas. Growth in these areas can be expected as the nation develops further.

Long Term Trends

It is said that Indonesia is in a hurry to develop. The current 25-year plan forecasts Indonesia to be the fourth largest world economy by the year 2010. The government is introducing changes and deregulating various sectors to meet a fully liberalised economy. At the same time, it is building infrastructure, a cohesive society, telecommunication networks and other essential bases to meet the challenges of an open economy. These changes are affecting many facets of society and the advertising sector is no exception.

Modern media, especially those that rely on telecommunications, should gain prominence. By April 1999, it is estimated that there will be 3.9 lines per 100 Indonesians with a successful call ratio near 70% (*EBRI*, 28 January 1995, p. 13). The information technology market is expected to be fully liberalised by the year 2005 (*The Straits Times*, 18 December 1996, p. 21), allowing Internet and telemarketing to be viable options. Another milestone affecting the advertising industry is the proposed liberalisation of the service industry by the year 2005. This should open up significant opportunities for foreign companies to enter the market.

CONCLUSION

Indonesia has many constraints but there are also plenty of rewarding opportunities. Before introducing any new means of advertising, it is important to consider the objectives of the government. Advertising and promotion media in Indonesia are experiencing steady growth from an emerging consumer market. This trend is expected to accelerate as the government further liberalises and opens up the economy to foreign participation.

Television has led this trend over the last few years subsequent to the ban on advertisements. Newspapers must find new ways to improve the distribution system and even venture into the Internet to find new channels. Magazines are well-positioned in niches to serve the special needs of the new upper middle-class which has expensive tastes and the money to afford it. Outdoor advertising has used creative talent and advanced technologies to recover from crippling taxes. Trends in new media like the Internet, e-mail, CD-ROM, telemarketing, interactive TV, video-on-demand, satellite and cable TV will exert their influence in Indonesia as well as the rest of the world.

REFERENCES

AdAsia, 1995, http://www.rad.net.id/republika/AdAsia/INDO-AD.HTM.html, 28 June 1996.

Andrei Anne, "Special Advertising Review, Indonesia", *Asian Advertising and Marketing*, Hong Kong, 21 April 1995a.

Andrei Anne, "Young, Cool and Privileged", *Asian Advertising and Marketing*, Hong Kong, 5 May 1995b.

Asian Advertising and Marketing, "Home Shopping Hops Channels", Hong Kong, 24 March 1995.

Asian Advertising, Marketing and Media Handbook, Euromonitor, London, 1994.

Economic and Business Review Indonesia (*EBRI*), "P. T. Telkom: Looking for More Private Participation", Jakarta, No. 146, 28 January 1995.

Economic and Business Review Indonesia (*EBRI*), "Outdoor Advertisement: Coming Back in from the Cold", Jakarta, No. 173, 5 August 1995.

Economic and Business Review Indonesia (*EBRI*), "Transit-ads: The New Look on the Streets", Jakarta, No. 237, 30 October 1995.

Geddes Andrew, "TV Ready for Ad Boom", *Media*, Hong Kong, 5 October 1990.

Grocott Mark, "Interactive Success Based on Ability to Evolve and Adapt", *Media*, Hong Kong, 5 July 1996.

INDIO, *Indonesia Source Book 1996*, Jakarta, 1996.

Indonesia on Fast Track, Advertising Growth, http://www.republika.co.id/adasia/indofast.htm.html, 28 June 1996.

Indonesia to Wire Villages for Internet, http://www.cnn.com/TECH/9612/31/cybersummary.reut/indonesia.html, 31 December 1996.

Jakarta Post, "House Passes Sweeping Bill on Broadcasting", Vol. 14, No. 223, 10 December 1996.

MacKenzie David, *The Batey Guide to Consumer and Media Information: Indonesia, 1995,* Batey Research and Information Centre (BRIC), Singapore, November 1995.

Media Guide 1995/'96, Initiative Media Indonesia, Jakarta, 1996.

Media, "Lintas Causes Stir at Citra Pariwara with Winning Radio Spot", Hong Kong, 5 July 1996.

Namis Muhammad, *Crisis Within a Crisis: Moving Towards Self-Regulation*, Asian Federation of Advertising Associations, Hong Kong, 1982.

Rauf Maswadi, "Cultural Development Towards the 21st Century: Indonesia Case", in *Cultures in ASEAN and the 21st Century Conference*, 21–24 August, Singapore, 1995.

Subakti B. and E. Katoppo, *Media Scene 1995–1996 Indonesia*, Persatuan Perusahaan Periklanan Indonesia (PPPI), Indonesia, 1996.

The Straits Times, "Indonesia Will Open up IT Market by 2005", Singapore, 18 December 1996.

Chapter 12

Doing Market Research in Indonesia*

BY
Eric CHIN Cheow Hiang
Clementine YAP Yaw Fung
Joanna FUNG Yuet Sim
LIM Yew Hoe

INTRODUCTION

EFFECTIVE RESEARCH IN Indonesia requires meticulous attention to methods of data collection, an ability to analyse information thoroughly, and sufficient knowledge of local conditions to be able to augment survey findings with marketing interpretation. This statement would be true of effective market research anywhere in the world. However, the underlying message is that an understanding of local conditions in Indonesia is the single most important element in distinguishing success from failure in conducting market research.

This chapter introduces the concept of market research and provides some insight and practical guidelines on the various aspects of market research in Indonesia. It is intended to give investors and businesses some ideas on what they can expect and some tips on conducting market research in Indonesia. In international business, doing the right things saves time and money, and differentiates success from failure. Market research, in particular, can help to establish what might be the right things to do. But to be effective, market research has to be done with full understanding of the local circumstances.

* We wish to thank Dr. Krishna Erramilli for his comments and assistance.

MARKET RESEARCH

The Components

Market research can be defined as the systematic gathering, recording, and analysing of data to provide information useful in marketing[1] decision making (Kotler, 1994). The market research process can be broken down into five steps.[2]

(i) ***Defining the Research Problem and Objectives***: This step involves establishing the key decisions that will be made using the market research outcome, the risk factors of the decisions to be made and the critical data requirements. The ability of researchers and decision makers to define the research problem and objectives accurately enhances the effectiveness of the market research outcomes.

(ii) ***Developing the Research Plan***: This step includes developing the way in which researchers collect secondary and primary data, as well as their research approach[3] and use of research instruments. It also includes the sample size, distribution and the methodology utilised for the data analysis.

In developing a research plan, local expertise is the most important factor. The objectives and problem definition identify the research direction. Essentially, the research plan charts out where and how to get the required information. For secondary data, knowing the right sources cuts down on time and enhances its accuracy.

(iii) ***Collecting the Information***: This stage is generally the most expensive and the most susceptible to error. Care must be exercised when establishing the method of data collection and when collecting the actual data. Errors may arise in the data source as a result of non-representative sample, biased questionnaires and so forth. No amount of expertise can be a remedy for poor data.

---

[1] There are many definitions of marketing but this is the one we prefer. Marketing is getting the goods and services to the right people at the right places at the right time at the right price with the right communications and promotion. See Kotler (1994), pp. 131–45.

[2] For details, see Kotler (1994), p. 33; Kotler *et al.*, (1996), pp. 154–71.

[3] There are basically four research approaches: observation, focus group studies, surveys, and experiments. For a more in-depth discussion refer to Kotler (1994), pp. 135–8.

Data sources may be classified as secondary and primary. Secondary data are obtained from published materials such as government publications, periodicals, the Internet, commercial data or from internal sources such as the balance sheet and other financial reports. On the other hand, primary data are obtained via surveys, observations and other forms of field work.

(iv) ***Analysing the Information***: Analysing information is generally coupled with advanced statistical techniques and decision models. This step precedes any discussion or interpretation of the research results.

(v) ***Presenting the Findings***: The objective of market research is to facilitate decision making. Presentation of the findings should be in a manner that benefits the audience. User friendliness is the key to a good report presentation coupled with valid and reliable interpretations.

The Need for Market Research

In today's business world, information is power. It is the top key component in developing successful marketing strategies. Information needs range from the general data required to assess market opportunities to specific market information for decisions about products, promotion, distribution and price. As an enterprise broadens its scope of operations to include international markets, the need for current, accurate information is magnified.

Generally, market research activities of foreign firms on Indonesia can be divided into three types based on information needs: (a) general information about Indonesia, and its main islands and cities; (b) information necessary to forecast future marketing requirements by anticipating social, economic and consumer trends; and (c) specific market information used to make decisions concerning products, promotion, distribution, prices and marketing plans.

Domestic firms generally focus on the third type but for foreign firms, a sound assessment of the Indonesian market requires an understanding of the macro issues surrounding the country. Hence, information about political stability, diverse cultural attributes and spatial geographical characteristics is required.

UNIQUE FACTORS AFFECTING MARKET RESEARCH IN INDONESIA

The Myths

Similar to new markets in other developing nations, there are many myths about Indonesia, but especially on doing business there. Some of the myths imply that Indonesia is a closed economy; business is done with gut feel; Indonesians are generally poor; information on the market is generally not available; and it is very difficult to conduct any sort of market research in Indonesia due to its topography, many different ethnic groups and languages. Perhaps some foreign firms may never venture into Indonesia because of these myths. And some companies see Indonesia only as a low cost manufacturing base for re-export. Nevertheless, it is important to recognise the unique factors that may affect doing market research in Indonesia.

Geographic Dispersion

Indonesia consists of 17,508 islands, stretching 3,200 miles from Sumatra in the northwest to Irian Jaya in the southeast. The physical terrain is marked by rivers, swamps, mountains and lowlands and, together with the high rainfall, they pose logistic and communication problems. Many hinterland areas are still inaccessible despite the construction of trans-highways such as the Trans-Seram Highway where 330 kilometres have been completed and the 651 kilometres Trans-Flores Highway. Over 390 large and small ports link towns via the sea (*The Straits Times*, 20 August 1996).

Ethnic Diversity and Languages

Although most Indonesians are of Malay descent, there are about 360 tribal and ethnic groups and 260 dialects and languages (Business Monitor International, 1996). *Bahasa Indonesia*, the national language, is not spoken by the largest ethnic group, which are the Javanese. Adopting a non-majority language as the national language is the Indonesian way of maintaining racial harmony.

Although *Bahasa Indonesia* can be used with little difficulty in the cities, the same is not true in rural areas. If research is done in the rural areas, then caution must be exercised because of the high illiteracy rate. Indonesia's adult literacy rate was 82.5% in 1992, and for females it was 10% lower than the national average (Business Monitor International, 1996). Therefore, questionnaires developed in *Bahasa Indonesia* are suitable for urban use but not for rural use.

Cultural Characteristics

When people talk about Indonesian culture it is not something given by nature but an historical development. Indonesians have indigenous traits from being part of the larger Malay-Polynesian culture group. There is Hindu influence, a very big Islamic influence, a smaller influence from Christianity and 300 to 400 years of Dutch colonial rule. These influences all contributed to creating what is now Indonesian culture (Mann, 1996).

The issue of ethnic diversity does not end with language. The various ethnic groups are different in their value judgements. For example, the Javanese are extremely polite and courteous, potentially hiding their true feelings from the words they say. For some Javanese, saying no to someone's request or question is simply not acceptable especially if they perceive that they have been slighted.[4]

Communications Infrastructure

For communications, there is not much problem in the cities. However, the communications infrastructure in rural areas may not be as conducive to the process of data collection. Telephone lines are available to only 58% of all Indonesian villages or a total of about 38,000 villages (*The Straits Times*, 20 August 1996, p. 34).

Concentrated Population in Java

The distribution of population among the various provinces and islands is not uniform. About 59% of the population is concentrated in Java, and Jakarta has the majority share of city dwellers with over 12 million people. Whether a survey is nation-wide, confined to major cities, or just limited to Jakarta is a function of the research issue and an understanding of local conditions, including the characteristics of the company's products.

---

4 A guide in Jakarta recounted an anecdote about two brothers. The first brother who refused to carry out his father's impossible request was scolded for being unfilial. The second brother said yes to the same request in front of his father's company. His father rewarded him even though he subsequently reneged because he had given his father face. The important point is that one must avoid causing Indonesians to lose face.

Cross Cultural Surveys and Language

If the surveys are part of a corporate worldwide survey involving cross cultural issues, then language barrier is the common problem. Differences in idiomatic expressions and the difficulty of exact translation create problems in eliciting the specific information desired and in interpreting the respondent's answers. Equivalent concepts may not exist across local languages.

QUALITY, RELIABILITY AND DEPENDABILITY OF SECONDARY SOURCE DATA

Many Western managers, including expatriate executives, share the view that Indonesia lags behind countries such as Singapore or Hong Kong in terms of accessibility of information, the reliability of information, as well as the reliability of forecasts (Lasserre and Schütte, 1995). The general perception with regard to Indonesia is that information is kept within a relatively small circle, or that obtaining information is costly, or the information is not accessible.

For businesses where specific market information is more important than macroeconomic details, Indonesia is lagging behind other countries. Both aggregated and disaggregated market statistics decomposed into smaller geographical areas and sub-sectors of the economy may not be available from official published materials. Generally, information is provided on major economic sectors as well as major geographical zones.

Detailed data on the number of wholesalers, retailers, manufacturers, facilitating services, population and income are not readily available. Indonesia does not have government agencies that collect secondary data on a regular basis. To gather disaggregated secondary data, a marketer must initiate the research or rely on private sources. Disaggregated information is not available due to the vast geographical span and the high cost of doing census surveys. However, large amounts of information are made available through private and government agencies at little cost.[5]

A caveat is necessary, however. The availability of information does not mean that the task of a market researcher is easier. Accept-

---

[5] For a more detailed discussion, see the section on Strategies for Minimising Problems.

ing information at face value is dangerous. One may get different figures for the same question depending on who one goes to. One example is the number of islands comprising Indonesia. One may get figures ranging from 14,000 to over 17,000. This is not a phenomenon specific to Indonesia. It is a fact that many developing countries have to work with less than precise information. But information must still be verified since the facts presented are a matter of perspective from different points of view. Since Indonesia is a developing country, it may be prone to optimism which reflects national pride rather than the real situation in reporting economic data.

Checking the consistency of secondary data with comparable data of known validity is an effective way of judging its usefulness. As a practical guide, the following questions should be asked to effectively judge the reliability of data sources: (a) Who collected the data? (b) Would there be any reasons to misrepresent the facts? (c) Why was the data collected? (d) How was the data collected? (e) Is the data internally consistent and logical in light of known data sources or market factors?

Current and comparable data are other shortcomings faced by foreign marketers in Indonesia. Information can be dated and irrelevant to current needs. Historical data series may not exist which compromises any comparisons. Secondary data may be rendered unreliable or outdated very quickly due to population shifts. For example, Indonesian youths have the tendency to move from the villages to the cities in search of jobs and better lives. The number of transient residents in Jakarta, such as expatriates, may have implications for consumer research. In Indonesia, the government policy of "transmigration" has moved 7.2 million people from Java, Bali, Madura and Lombok to 2,600 villages in the outer islands of Irian Jaya and Kalimantan (*The Straits Times*, 22 November 1996, p. 34). It has been estimated that one-third of the 110 million Javanese will be resettled eventually (*The Sunday Times*, 10 November 1996, p. 2). In 1970, over 60% of Indonesia's population was under 24 years old. By 1990, almost one-half of the population was in the 15 to 44 age group; and, by 2020, the population will be more evenly distributed with less than 40% of the population under 25 (Tripathi, 1994, p. 64). This kind of information is not only useful for sampling distributions among the various demographic groups but, also, in setting future strategies.

PROBLEMS IN GATHERING PRIMARY DATA

A company doing market research in Indonesia should anticipate some problems in gathering primary data. The major considerations to bear in mind are discussed below.

Sampling

Given inadequate and inaccurate demographic information, sampling in Indonesia becomes more complex and generally less reliable. Therefore, research companies like Frank Small and Associates normally have their own sampling maps. For example, Jakarta is broken down into many small areas and surveys are done by approaching a specified number of respondents from each area on a random basis.[6]

Ability to Communicate Opinions

The level of literacy among Indonesians impedes many foreign marketers' efforts to enlighten them about the usefulness and value of any product or service. It is difficult for any respondent to formulate needs, attitudes, or opinions about the nature of products if they lack the knowledge. One example is ice-cream which became popular only after Walls marketed this product in Indonesia. Ice-cream is difficult to describe to Indonesians because the common ice-associated treat is shaved ice mixed with flavoured syrup. Hence, the more complex the product, the more difficult it is to design research that aids the respondent in communicating meaningful opinions and reactions.

Willingness to Respond

Cultural differences and the level of literacy are the main causes for the unwillingness or the inability of most Indonesians to respond to any surveys. Most companies that conduct surveys offer the respondents a small token gift such as household items. This strategy works well in Indonesia.

Survey Method

For industrial surveys, telephone interviews can be used since most companies have phone lines. But for consumer surveys, a face-to-face

---

6 Based on an interview with Mr. Iwan Murty, Project Manager, Frank Small and Associates Jakarta, Indonesia, December 1996.

interview is the norm because most homes, particularly in the rural areas, are not connected to the phone network. It has been estimated that that there are only 2.5 telephone lines per 100 Indonesians (*The Straits Times*, 20 August 1996). A comprehensive census survey requires significant field research and involves higher costs. The trade-off is a smaller survey sample at a lower cost versus a larger, more reliable sample which incurs a higher cost. One encouraging point to note is that in Indonesia, people generally read their mail and respond accordingly, especially since junk mail is not so much a phenomenon in Indonesia.[7]

Analysis of Information

The difficulties in analysing collected data are magnified by factors such as a "courtesy bias" which arises when Indonesians provide information that they perceived is desired by the researcher.[8] Generally, Indonesians still retain certain traditional attitudes such as reluctance to give offence (Mann, 1996). The results obtained need to be adjusted.[9] The accuracy of assigning this adjustment factor depends on the researcher's experience and knowledge of the Indonesians.

Female interviewers

It is common practice to use female interviewers almost exclusively in consumer interviews in the West (Kaynak, 1984). However, the geographically dispersed population in Indonesia, the stigma of women travelling alone or making evening calls, accessibility, and political unrest in East Timor, Aceh and Irian Jaya, would preclude the use of female interviewers in Indonesia.

STRATEGIES FOR MINIMISING PROBLEMS

One who has done any form of market research before can understand

---

7 Mr. Iwan Murty, *op. cit.*

8 Mr. Iwan Murty, *op. cit.*

9 While a researcher can conduct many rounds of pilot surveys to get the sample size that will take care of the courtesy bias, time may not be on the researcher's side. It may be necessary to adjust the responses downward. For example, if a question asks for a response on a Likert-type five-point scale (1 – very satisfied, 2 – satisfied, 3 – neutral, 4 – dissatisfied, 5 – very dissatisfied), then the responses for 1 and 2 must be adjusted by a ratio of, for example 0.8.

how difficult it is sometimes to get the right information from the right source. The following sub-sections outline some strategies to minimise these problems.

Secondary Source Research

A company may begin its preliminary research on Indonesia by referring to books and articles in international journals.[10] English editions of books on business practices in Indonesia which were originally published in *Bahasa Indonesia* are readily available. Consultants recognising the demand for such books have written various reports of interest for foreign investors.

For updates of recent events and for economic and investment figures, one can refer to, among others, the Internet under the websites of the many government agencies as well as private organisations.[11] But one problem a person may have with surfing the sites is that they are normally busy and information downloading can be slow. The trick here is to surf the websites after Indonesia's midnight hour.

The journey to obtain information and understanding on government policies, rules, regulations, and other requirements for doing business in Indonesia should start in the home country of the incumbent. Visits to the Indonesian embassy may be fruitful as there are staff such as economic counsellors and commercial attaches to provide assistance. For private consultation or advice, it is necessary to draw on local contacts, business associates or friends. Table 12–1 provides a summary of resources available for preliminary information prior to embarking on an in-depth study of Indonesia. Further clarification of the information obtained in the home country can be done on arrival in Indonesia. Table 12–2 provides a list of some of these resource centres in Indonesia.

---

[10] Books on Indonesian business practices which are published in *Bahasa Indonesia* are increasingly being translated into English. These translations include *Guide for Investors* and *Sectorial Reports on the Economy*. Some consultants have also published English reports for the benefit of foreign readers.

[11] See Indonesia General Information – Indonesia Business Centre Online, or simply search using key words "Indonesia" and "Information".

TABLE 12–1
Resource Centres for Secondary Data on Indonesia While in the Home Country

Resource Centres	Examples
Official representatives of the Indonesian government	Commercial Attaché, Embassy of the Republic of Indonesia
Government bodies with memorandum of understanding with Indonesia	Trade Development Board and Economic Development Board in Singapore
Universities	Nanyang Technological University
Business associations	Chamber of Commerce
Business contacts	Banks or other businesses with branches or representative offices in Indonesia
Consultancy agencies	Retired diplomats, A .T. Kearney Pte. Ltd., Sreekumar-Siddique and Co. Pte. Ltd., and others listed in the yellow pages

Market Research Firms

There is no shortage of credible research agencies in Indonesia. In the May 1995–96 *Jakarta Commercial and Industrial Guide*, there are about 45 firms listed under various categories of market research and survey consultants.[12] The list of firms includes foreign and domestic agencies. Major international research firms, such as the Survey Research Group (under the local name Survey Research Indonesia) and Frank Small and Associates (Fakta Sarana Ampuh) are located in Jakarta. The latter has been in Indonesia since 1981, and the former has been there even longer. There are other firms with research experience in Indonesia.

---

[12] See *Petunjuk Industri dan Niaga – Petunjuk Telefon Jakarta, Mei 1995–1996*, 1995, pp. B-570–1.

TABLE 12–2
Resource Centres for Secondary Data on Indonesia on Arrival in Indonesia

Resource Centres	Examples
For investment-related matters	The Investment Coordinating Board (BKPM)
For statistics on demographics, economic employment and other such information	Pusat Data Business Indonesia – Indonesia Business Centre On-line (PDBI) and Badan Pusat Statistik (BPS) or the Statistics Bureau
For general information as well as economic indicators	Indonesia National Development Information Office
For research on Indonesia	Centre for Strategic and International Studies on Indonesia

Sector Information

Specific information on certain sectors is made available for a fee by research consultants who carry out sample surveys on a wide range of marketing issues over different cities as well as rural areas. Survey Research Indonesia (SRI) is one of the leading companies in this area.[13]

What Can Research Firms Do?

The corporate brochures of the leading market research firms in Indonesia offer a whole range of services as shown in Table 12–3. The scope of information gathering activities by these firms is comprehensive and covers the entire chain of marketing activities from pre-sales to post-sales.

It is common for foreign market research firms to have expatriates stationed in Indonesia who have been there for a long time. More locals who are graduates from overseas are joining the market research field and they are quite proficient in English. They are a great asset in conducting market research in Indonesia because they are ca-

[13] Among other things, SRI publishes *The Indonesian Consumer1995, Food Report Indonesia 1996* and *Rural Data*, three publications based upon surveys among consumers as well as environmental scanning. These publications contain information not provided by the various publications of the government agencies.

pable of applying Western techniques of market research to the nuances of the Indonesian culture.

TABLE 12–3
Services Offered by Indonesian Market Research Firms

1. Omnibus survey/consumer scope studies and syndicated surveys
2. Focus group and corporate image studies
3. Media index and TV ratings
4. Retail audit and market monitors
5. Customised market surveys
6. Advertising concept and development research
7. Product and brand development/mapping
8. Packaging research
9. Market modelling, evaluation and forecasting (i.e., segmentation, etc.)
10. Industrial research
11. Consumer usage and attitudes studies
12. Various opinion surveys
13. Ad-hoc surveys with data published for sale

Cost

Certainly market surveys cannot be conducted without a budget limit. So just how expensive is it to conduct market research in Indonesia compared to the rest of the Asia Pacific region? A study done on Coca-Cola indicates that the cost of such an exercise in Indonesia is below average, with an index of 66 as compared to 13 other Pacific Rim countries, including Japan which was the most expensive with an index of 269 against an average index of 100.[14] In other words, it costs four times more to conduct market research in Japan than in Indonesia. The Indonesian advantage is probably due to the lower labour cost for interviewers and local field personnel.

Market Research – Where It Should Be Done?

Market research activities in Indonesia are typically concentrated around the major cities such as Jakarta, Surabaya, Bandung, Yogyakarta, Semarang and Bali island where the critical mass of the population are found. The urban population is mainly concentrated in Java which has four cities of over 1 million (Jakarta at 10 million, Sura-

[14] For details see Mohn (1994) or Kotler *et al.* (1996).

baya at 2 million, Bandung at just under 2 million, and Semarang at 1 million). Outside of Java, the biggest city is Medan in Sumatra with 1.4 million people. As Indonesia modernises, urbanisation is expected to grow by an estimated 3 million people per year. This is supported by the increase of its urban population from 18% of the total population in 1973 to 30% in 1990 as well as the development of satellite towns such as Serpong, just outside Jakarta (Business Monitor International, 1996, p. 25).

Some Success Stories

There have been a number of well documented examples of successful foreign companies, such as Coca-Cola, Honda and Unilever, which have used market research and clever marketing to penetrate the market and increase market share. Even among local companies, market research has been used extensively. The most celebrated marketing successes of local companies are Sampoerna, the local cigarette company, and Astra, the distributor for Toyota in Indonesia. When Sampoerna's low tar, low nicotine cigarette *A Mild* was launched, brand attitude tracking was conducted extensively for three months. The results showed that 65% of smokers tried the cigarette but almost all of them rejected it for being too light. However, the survey also showed that people use this brand because of the low tar and low nicotine (health reasons). The company realised that they had a good product but the positioning and the communication programmes needed to be improved. Then came the marketing strategy which positioned *A Mild* as the cigarette with the lowest content of tar and nicotine (15 mg and 1.1 mg respectively in each cigarette). The catch phrase "How Low Can You Go?" attracted the young and the health conscious. The brand became an instant success, creating a trend among them. From an initial sale of 5 million sticks per week, it sky-rocketed to 90 million sticks per day as of the first quarter of 1995.

Astra, which distributes Toyota, operates the Auto 2000 workshops which service and repair Toyota cars. Through surveys, Astra identified that customer service in workshops was one thing lacking in Indonesia's car retail scene. So quality service became the positioning strategy for Astra. In addition, it conducted satisfaction surveys among its customers and continued to improve the ratings given by customers. The quality service programme was extended to its subsidiary TSM which distributes BMW. Repeat customers of 35%

was reported among the purchasers of new BMWs.[15] This trend shows that market research is relevant, and more companies will join the ranks of those companies doing market research in order to compete successfully.

Opportunities

The basic reason for doing business in a foreign country is to make money, and the reasons for conducting market research are to ensure that investments are in the right market and the right strategies are used. Given the usefulness of soft data based upon local knowledge and conditions, relative to hard data, there may be a tendency for foreign investors to adopt a less painful approach and establish strategic alliances with local firms. The value of a local partner far exceeds any dilution in profit margin. It is an expedient way to learn about the local business climate and the market. It also provides a direct pipeline to important local contacts and immediate convenience in dealing with various agencies. In return, local firms benefit from the sophisticated marketing knowledge of the foreign partners and the potential for utilising previous market research experience. However, this option is not necessarily available for smaller investors and, therefore, they must undertake their own research with all of the above guidelines in mind.

CONCLUSION

The diversity of Indonesia should be viewed as an opportunity rather than a problem. The marketing research process can identify various market segments based on the needs and requirements for certain attributes in a product or service, an estimation of purchasing power capabilities, geographical locations, and buying attitudes and practices. Researchers must evaluate both primary and secondary data carefully to ascertain their reliability and comparability. Collected information must be validated before proceeding to the next stage of the marketing process. Government policies tend to favour capital investments by multinational companies but smaller enterprises are not excluded. Therefore, research efforts should take full advantage

---

[15] For details and more cases on marketing success, see Wibowo *et al., 36 Kasus Pemasaran Asli Indonesia*, 1996. The book is written in *Bahasa Indonesia*.

of those government agencies which are set up to provide information on the country, its people, rules, regulations, and secondary data on various industries and other relevant statistics.

With growing competition from more foreign companies, market research may be the winning advantage. Given more income, consumption patterns are likely to change. Therefore, market research based upon a good understanding of the market place will be essential for foreign businesses entering the Indonesian market.

REFERENCES

Business Monitor International, *Indonesia 1996–98: Annual Report on Government, Economy, the Business Environment, Capital Markets and Industry, with Forecasts Through End-1998*, London, June 1996.

Cateora Philip, *International Marketing*, Irwin, Burr Ridge, IL, U.S., 1993.

Frank Small and Associates, *Target Market*, Vol. 1, 1996.

INDIO, *Indonesia Source Book 1996*, Jakarta, August 1996.

Kaynak Erdener, *International Marketing Management*, Praeger Publishers, N.Y., U.S., 1984.

Kotler Philip, *Marketing Management: Analysis, Planning, Implementation and Control*, Prentice Hall, Eaglewood Cliffs, N.J., U.S., 1994.

Kotler Philip, Swee Hoon Ang, Siew Meng Leong and Chin Tiong Tan, *Marketing Management: An Asian Perspective,* Prentice Hall, Singapore, 1996.

Lassere Philippe and Hellmut Schütte, *Strategies for Asia Pacific*, Macmillan, London, 1995.

Mann Richard I., *The Culture of Business in Indonesia*, Gateway Books, Indonesia, 1996.

Mohn Carrol N., "Pacific Rim Prices", *Marketing Research*, Vol. 6, Winter 1994, pp. 22–7.

Petunjuk Industri dan Niaga – Petunjuk Telefon Jakarta, Mei 1995–1996, P. T. Elnusa Yellow Pages, Indonesia, 1995.

Tabalujan Benny, Minter Ellison, and Makarim & Taira S., *Doing Business in Indonesia*, Minter Ellison, February 1996.

The Indonesian Quarterly, Vol. 24, No. 3, Third Quarter 1996, Centre for Strategic and International Studies, Indonesia, 1996.

The Straits Times, "Five-Year Plans have Produced Growth, Social Justice for Indonesians", Singapore, 20 August 1996.

The Straits Times, "Indonesian Graduates Blamed for Being Jobless", Singapore, 18 November 1996.

The Straits Times, "Indonesia to Resettle 80,000 Families Next Year", Singapore, 22 November 1996.

The Sunday Times, "Indonesia Looks East for New Growth", Singapore, 10 November 1996.

Tripathi Salil, "The Anxious Archipelago", *Asia, Inc.*, Vol. 3, No. 5, May 1994.

Wibowo A. S., V. Elisawati and H. Kartajaya, *36 Kasus Pemasaran Asli Indonesia*, P. T. Elex Media Kamputindo, Indonesia, 1996.

Chapter 13

Marketing in Indonesia: Separating the Myths from Reality

BY
M. Krishna ERRAMILLI

INTRODUCTION

MOST FOREIGN COMPANIES perceive Indonesia as an intimidating marketing challenge. Who would not be intimidated on being told that the country is a vast archipelago made up of more than 17,500 islands, populated by 200 million people, earning relatively low incomes, split up into 360 ethnic groups, and speaking more than 260 languages and dialects? Add to this list of challenges, problems of inadequate infrastructure, serious restrictions on promotion and distribution activities, and protective government policies, and you get the marketing equivalent of Godzilla. It is enough to scare away the bravest of marketers. But as the three chapters in this section have demonstrated, marketing in Indonesia is not Mission Impossible. Overwhelming as the above facts are, many of the concerns about Indonesia are just myths. In what follows, an attempt is made to separate the myths from reality by presenting answers to some frequently asked questions about Indonesian marketing.

DISTRIBUTION IN INDONESIA

Is it true that promoting and distributing consumer products in an archipelago with more than 17,500 islands represents a daunting challenge?

It is true that Indonesia has about 17,500 islands, with a land area of 1.9 million square kilometres. But closer inspection reveals that almost 90% of the population is concentrated on just five islands: Java, Sumatra, Kalimantan, Sulawesi and Irian Jaya. These islands also account for close to 95% of Indonesia's GDP. Java alone accounts for close to 60% of the population and 61% of the GDP. So, for most foreign marketers, the challenge dramatically diminishes to serving a handful of islands, perhaps even to just one.

Does the underdeveloped infrastructure turn physical distribution and logistics into a veritable nightmare?

For a nation so geographically diverse, infrastructure is indeed lagging. Rail transport is confined to two islands. The road transportation network of about 320,000 kilometres is apparently not even close to covering the 1.9 million square kilometres of land area. A significant percentage of these roads (almost 36%) are in a poor state. These aggregated facts, however, hide the reality of doing business in Indonesia. While much of the country does suffer from infrastructure problems, Java, which accounts for much of the Indonesian market, enjoys an excellent road and rail network. Moreover, a great deal of the inter-island traffic occurs by sea and air, both of which are reasonably good. A little known secret about Indonesia is that it was the first among developing countries to employ satellite technology to knit its thousands of islands together into a communication network. The Indonesian government has placed high priority on developing infrastructure, so this sector should improve in future. It may surprise a lot of people to know that the 1995 World Competitiveness Report rated Indonesia's infrastructure higher than that of other Asian countries, like Thailand, the Philippines and China.

How does the Indonesian distribution channel for consumer products differ from the channel systems employed in the West? Why is this so?

Typical consumer product channel systems in the United States and other industrial countries tend to have one level of wholesalers and one level of retailers. In many cases, even the wholesale level is being eliminated, and manufacturers deal directly with large retail chains. So channels generally tend to be quite short. In Indonesia, the channel is often long, with two or even three levels of wholesalers intervening between producers and retailers. This is because of the intense fragmentation of Indonesian retailers. There exist anywhere from 200,000 to 1.5 million retailers, most of whom are small and geographically dispersed. To cover such a huge number of retailers dispersed over a large land area, consumer product marketers employ two or more layers of wholesalers. It must be emphasised that, compared to the West, even the wholesalers tend to be small and provide less market coverage. Typically, there is a major distributor who sells to a subdistributor who, in turn, distributes to retailers. For example, Unilever employs five area sales offices which distribute to 225 subdistributors who, in turn, service about 400,000 retailers.

What are the different types of retailers available for distributing consumer goods in Indonesia?

Small traditional outlets represent a huge portion of the value of goods sold in Indonesia, accounting for 75% in Jakarta and 95% outside of it. These are typically family-owned and family-operated stores located very near places of residence and work. They come in various shapes and forms (*kaki lima, pasars, tokos,* P & D stores, *warungs, ansongan* and so on), distinguished from each other mainly in product assortments carried and services provided. Modern retail outlets, such as supermarkets, convenience stores and departmental stores, are increasingly appearing in major cities like Jakarta. International retailers, such as Sogo and Wal-Mart, have made their appearance, and shopping centres and malls are springing up everywhere. These modern outlets are still largely confined to major cities.

Is it true that foreign companies cannot engage in distribution activities in Indonesia?

Foreign manufacturers or joint ventures with foreign shareholders are not allowed to distribute products in Indonesia unless they manufacture these goods in the country. Even local manufacturers cannot engage in distribution activities beyond the wholesale level. Retail sales must be entirely handled by Indonesian-owned companies. Foreign retailers are not allowed to have equity ownership of retail outlets.

If this is so, then how do foreign retailers, such as Sogo and Wal-Mart, operate in Indonesia?

Foreign retailers operate mainly through franchising, or management and technical assistance agreements. Such arrangements are allowed by Indonesian law.

With the fragmented multi-layered distribution system in Indonesia, involving hundreds of wholesalers and thousands of retailers, do the manufacturers not lose control over their marketing activities?

This is indeed a serious problem. One of the biggest complaints is that manufacturers lose control on pricing at the retail level and even at the sub-distributor level. Sub-distributors and retailers resort to price wars in areas where competition is high and charge above the recommended prices when it is low. This could affect the image of the company's brands. The standard response by foreign multinationals to this problem has been to integrate as much as is legally possible.

Unilever, for example, distributes to sub-distributors through its own area sales offices (thus effectively owning the primary wholesale level). Sara Lee set up a joint venture company called Kiwi Distribution to wholesale its Indonesian products. Such ownership control of wholesaling provides a significant degree of control to the company. Of course, this strategy is available only if the products are made locally in Indonesia. Other ways to forward integrate are through service and support. For example, Unilever is able to motivate sub-distributors to maintain fixed prices by providing them with strong advertising and marketing support, assistance to set up their own distribution networks and training their salespeople.

What are the different ways a foreign firm can enter Indonesia and distribute its products there?

Many foreign companies initially establish a representative office. This allows them to undertake some initial market research, provide technical advice and engage in promotional activities. However, representative offices are not allowed to distribute products in Indonesia. Therefore, many multinationals hire local distribution agents (which are wholly Indonesian-owned distribution companies) with good nation-wide coverage. Wickasana, Indometra, Tigaraska and Borsomig W. I. are all examples of leading agents. To maintain some control, foreign firms can arrange for their representative (typically an expatriate) to be employed by these agents.

Another option is to establish a captive trading company that is 100% owned by an Indonesian party but with which you can enter into management, technical assistance and financial agreements. As mentioned before, franchising is also an available avenue. Many Japanese, American and British retailers have taken advantage of this arrangement to enter Indonesia.

Finally, it is also possible for the manufacturing PMA companies to form joint venture distribution companies to distribute locally made products. The joint venture distribution company, however, cannot distribute goods that are imported or made solely by the Indonesian partner or the foreign investors.

Is it true that there is very little direct distribution activity in Indonesia today?

It is generally true that very little direct distribution exists in Indonesia. Direct mail distribution is not common yet because mailing lists are difficult to buy and maintain. More importantly, Indonesian consumers are sceptical of transactions not involving face-to-face dealings and merchandise display. However, there are rapid changes underway. The economy is growing more prosperous and sophisticated. Telecommunications, computers and the Internet are growing in importance and are bound to fuel increased direct distribution activity. The high departure tax on resident Indonesians will further deter cross-border shopping and force them to rely more on mail ordering for luxury items like jewellery, handbags, watches and so forth. Most indications, therefore, point to increased direct distribution activity in the future.

ADVERTISING AND PROMOTION

What do foreign advertisers find unique about Indonesian advertising?

Indonesian advertising is driven primarily by three forces. One is SARA, the Indonesian advertising industry's code of ethics which is really an acronym for *suku* (ethnic groups), *agama* (religion), *ras* (race) and *antaragolongan* (political groups). Advertising must be sensitive to the needs and requirements of these four groups. The second force is, of course, religion. In a country that is 87% Muslim, advertisers must be extremely sensitive to the "dos" and "don'ts" of Islam. Although many advertisers find Indonesia to be more liberal than other Muslim countries in South and West Asia, it is important to be sensitive in this regard. Finally, advertisers must be guided by the set of five national values enunciated in the *Pancasila.* For example, the ideas of achieving consensus, togetherness and total human development are important values to be emphasised in advertising campaigns.

Are there any specific regulations and restrictions on advertising that foreign companies should be aware of?

The advertising industry is largely self-regulated, although with strong direction from the government. Regulations affect certain types of products. For example, there are many restrictions on the advertising of alcoholic beverages, cigarettes and pharmaceutical products. Advertising directed at children is another area closely monitored and regulated. There are also restrictions on advertisements created outside Indonesia and on foreign models used in advertisements. The best advice that can be provided to foreign advertisers is to employ an Indonesian-based advertising agency to develop their campaigns.

What about media? Do advertisers have free access to a variety of media?

Advertisers have access to a variety of traditional advertising media such as television, radio, newspapers, magazines and billboards. Modern methods of communicating with markets, such as telemarketing, direct mail and Internet, are only now being developed. The government has recognised that the development of the media must mirror the nation's economic development and it has taken steps to deregulate the television industry during the early 1990s. To date, these attempts have resulted in making television a viable medium for advertising.

However, there remains some uncertainty about the extent of deregulation. Recently, the government passed a law that gives it powers to regulate the advertising industry and the use of new communications technology. The implications of this law are not clear yet. Also, industry observers will be keenly watching the government's efforts to liberalise the information technology and service sectors of the economy by the year 2005. For most companies at present though, availability of advertising media is not a serious problem.

Is it true that radio is the most important medium for advertising in Indonesia?

The radio is not the most important medium for advertising in Indonesia. The general perception of Indonesia as a less developed and less educated country naturally gives rise to images of radio as being the most important commercial medium. It is true that radio is perhaps the medium which reaches the most number of people in Indonesia. A country with 75% rural population spread over a large number of islands naturally finds radio to be an effective medium for news and entertainment. However, it may shock some people to know that television is by far the most important medium in Indonesia in terms of total advertising expenditure. More than two-thirds of the population have access to television. Television advertising has been growing at an incredible pace since deregulation in the early 1990s. Equally surprising, radio is not even the second biggest medium for advertising expenditure. It is newspapers. Radio, magazines and outdoor media are all nearly similar in advertising expenditure but they are much smaller than the other two media. Cinema has a very small and insignificant following.

How effective are these media in reaching specific target markets? Is it true that Indonesian media are more geared to the mass market than to specific demographic groups?

Commercial television, which is still a young industry in Indonesia, does not yet deliver to very select audiences. Although Indonesia has five commercial TV stations, none of them has developed a distinctive channel profile in terms of programme content. However, the situation is changing. TPI is devoting itself to educational programmes, ANTEVE is trying to consolidate its strengths in sports and music programmes, RCTI is targeting an upscale young audience while SCTV seems to have a stronger following among housewives.

There are more than 850 radio stations in Indonesia, the majority of them are privately owned. They service audiences grouped ethnically and geographically. It is a good medium for local advertising campaigns in a country with nearly 300 ethnic groups, and 200 languages and dialects. There are 165 daily and weekly newspapers which are read nationally and locally. They are published in different languages as well. Magazines are perhaps the most selective of all media. Indonesian magazines cater to a variety of demographic groups (teenagers, women, men and so forth), occupations (business, computing and so forth) and hobbyists (sports, entertainment and so forth). To give an idea of the selectivity of Indonesian magazines, several teen magazines now cater to a rapidly growing group of more than 15 million affluent teenagers called the "ABG" (*Anak Baru Gede*). In many ways, the Indonesian media are offering increasingly specialised vehicles to reach a variety of specific audiences.

What about the supporting industries such as advertisement agencies, production houses, and training institutes?

The ban on television commercials during the 1980s had a crippling impact on all of the support infrastructure, particularly production houses. An inadequate number of formal training institutes remains a hurdle as well. The advertisement agency support is not too bad. The management and artistic talent may not be comparable to what advanced-country multinationals are used to. But there are quite a few affiliates of multinational agencies, such as Lintas and McCann Erickson, which brought new advertising concepts into Indonesia. In addition, advertisers can choose from a fairly large number of local agencies. Overall, this sector is not as poor as perceived but Indonesia needs to develop this type of infrastructure. The requirement to produce all commercials locally should give impetus to this effort.

MARKET RESEARCH

Businesses need good quality information to make sound decisions. It is generally believed that such information is hard to come by in Indonesia.

There is a strong perception outside that information is inadequate and unreliable for decision-making in Indonesia. Much of the published secondary source data that one takes for granted in more advanced countries is not available. Information that is published is usually quite aggregated and not good enough to make specific decisions. Available data may be outdated or not easily comparable with published data from other countries. To make matters more complicated, market research to generate primary source data is quite difficult due to the ethnic, religious, geographic and linguistic diversity characterising the population. The infrastructure necessary for such research (e.g., sampling frames, mailing lists, telephones and so forth) is also generally sub-par. This is not intended to convey the impression that this is the dark ages. Far from it. There are 45 market research firms in Jakarta alone, some of them affiliates of multinational agencies such as the Survey Research Group. Most of them can undertake a full range of studies, from surveys to focus groups, to generate specific product and market type information. So, despite the difficulties, it is possible to generate some hard data on which to base decisions.

If hard data (published and primary source data) is so difficult to generate, how can foreign businesses cope in Indonesia?

By complementing hard data with soft data (i.e., experiential knowledge gained through personal visits and discussions with local distributors, business partners, customers and suppliers), foreign businesses can cope in Indonesia. Decision makers sitting in New York will make disastrous decisions unless they personally visit and soak in the environment of Indonesia. A joint venture partner or alliance partner who knows the Indonesian market is probably an extremely valuable source of soft data as well.

What is the key to marketing success in Indonesia?

There are undoubtedly unique challenges for novices entering Indonesia. However, patience, improvisation, good local partners and a long-term outlook will help most companies accomplish their objectives in Indonesia.

FOREIGN INVESTMENT REGULATIONS AND PETROLEUM SECTOR

Chapter 14

Foreign Direct Investment and Related Issues*

BY
NG Seng Huat
Roger GOH
Brian LAI
LIM Hock Leng

INTRODUCTION

INDONESIAN HISTORY INCLUDES 300 years as an European colony, the declaration of independence, a left-wing takeover and socialist policies leading to massive inflation and unemployment that resulted in a military takeover. By opening its doors to foreign investment, Indonesia prospered in the 1960s and 1970s as an oil producer but then experienced a debt crisis precipitated by a fall in world oil prices. Subsequently, Indonesia mounted a vigorous non-oil export policy (Halverson, 1991).

For more than 100 years, oil has played an important role in the development of Indonesia. By the early 1980s, the oil and gas sector accounted for 25% of the country's Gross Domestic Product (GDP), more than 65% of government revenues and 80% of merchandise exports. In 1983, the government introduced a policy reducing the economy's dependency on the petroleum industry. The collapse of oil prices in 1986 led to a sharp reduction in the contribution of oil and gas revenues to the fiscal budget and, hence, the balance of payments (World Bank, 1996).

* The authors thank Dr. Austin Pullé for his comments and guidance.

Indonesia's GDP grew at an average annual rate of 6.8% during the first 25-year Development Plan, from 1969 to 1994. The industrial sector share of GDP increased from 9.2% in 1969 to 23.9% in 1994. GDP grew 8.1% in fiscal year 1994/95, reaching over US$200 billion.

A wide ranging programme of deregulation has been pursued since the early 1980s, with emphasis on the banking and financial sectors. Investment spending has been exceptionally strong but Indonesia needs an investment of approximately US$370 billion to attain its targeted GDP growth of 7.1% annually from 1994 through 1999. The private sector is expected to fund about 77% of this investment. Indonesia is committed to supporting the Asia-Pacific Economic Co-operation (APEC) objectives charted in the 1994 *Bogor Declaration*. These include strengthening the open multilateral trading system, enhancing trade and investment liberalisation in Asia Pacific, and intensifying Asia Pacific development co-operation.

This chapter discusses the investment opportunities available in Indonesia. It focuses on the deregulation process that has been taking place. The deregulation process has resulted in its enactment of the new *Company Law* and new *Capital Law* of 1996. Foreign direct investment (FDI) has increased with the relaxation of investment-related policies. It will also review the foreign investment issues and legalities involved for a foreign entity investing in Indonesia.

FOREIGN DIRECT INVESTMENT IN INDONESIA

Importance and Motivation of FDI in Indonesia

The benefits of FDI to Indonesia are the provision of technology, managerial and marketing skills, and greater real income per capita. The government has attracted billions of U.S. dollars in FDI involving hundreds of investment projects. FDI in manufacturing has helped Indonesia to re-orient its economy and mitigate its vulnerability to world oil prices. Economically weakened by the soft market for oil in the 1980s (particularly the sudden drop of world oil prices in 1986), Indonesia changed its economic policy to boost non-oil exports. By liberalising trade flows and encouraging foreign investment in manufacturing, Indonesia has succeeded in tripling its non-oil exports as a percentage of total exports, from 20% in 1982 to 60% in 1990 and to 77% in 1995 (INDIO, 1996b). It welcomes labour intensive industries which can reduce unemployment and more capital goods industries to alleviate the current high level of imports.

Foreign Investor Profile

From 1967 through 15 October 1996, Japan had the largest cumulative share of investment (excluding oil and gas and the financial sectors) with US$34.4 billion. The U.K. ranked second with US$29.9 billion followed by Hong Kong with US$18.6 billion, Singapore with US$14.3 billion and the U.S. with US$12.5 billion. Table 14–1 shows the cumulative foreign investment approvals for the top ten investing countries over this time period (Investment Coordinating Board, 1996a).

TABLE 14–1
Cumulative Foreign Investment by Country: 1967 to 15 October 1996

Countries	Total Investment		
	Projects*	US$ million	%
Japan	908	34,399.6	20.06
U.K.	214	29,935.0	17.46
Hong Kong	356	18,567.1	10.83
Singapore	583	14,301.0	8.34
U.S.	258	12,466.0	7.27
Netherlands	157	10,787.5	6.29
Taiwan	501	9,306.9	5.43
South Korea	415	7,770.8	4.53
Australia	244	6,260.4	3.65
Germany	98	5,079.1	2.96
Others	1053	22,582.5	13.18
Total	**4787**	**171,455.9**	**100.00**

* Including 423 joint projects with other countries.
Source: Investment Coordinating Board (1996a).

The data in Table 14–1 reveal a high proportion of FDI flowing from Indonesia's East Asian neighbours. Japan has committed more investment than any other Asian country. Meanwhile, Hong Kong, Taiwan, South Korea and Singapore have been progressively increasing their investments by relocating manufacturing facilities to combat cost-push inflation that is diminishing investment returns in their respective countries. The overall trend in foreign investment has led to high growth in Indonesia's manufacturing sector which comprises nearly 66% of the cumulative FDI from 1967 to June 1996. As of July 1996, this sector employed 8.6 million people which is approximately 11% of the workforce (INDIO, 1996b).

Impact of FDI

Indonesia enjoys one of the more impressive records of FDI in the developing world. From 1967, when the *Foreign Capital Law* was enacted, through 15 October 1996, FDI commitments (excluding financial and oil and gas sectors) totalled US$171.4 billion over 4,787 projects (see Table 14–1). FDI approvals exceeded US$8 billion in each year from 1990 to 1993, reached US$23.7 billion in 1994, a record of US$39.9 billion in 1995 and was US$27.6 billion for the period January to 15 October 1996 (INDIO, 1996b).

FIGURE 14–1
Trend of Foreign Investment Approvals
1990 to 15 October 1996

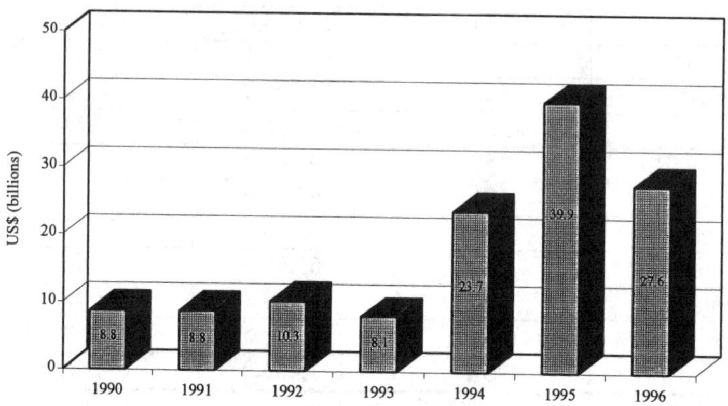

Source: Investment Coordinating Board (1996a).

In 1995, Japan and the U.S. were Indonesia's main source of FDI, accounting for 79% of total foreign investment. While the U.S. is Indonesia's largest investor, the vast majority of its investment is in the petroleum sector. However, in line with Indonesia's strategy to reduce its dependence on oil revenue coupled with a conducive investment climate, non-oil exports have exceeded oil exports since 1987. In 1995, they accounted for nearly 77% of total export value and the manufacturing sector contributed over 64.5% of this amount, thus leading to significant jobs creation (INDIO, 1996b).

Tax Holidays Reinstated

The Indonesian authorities are aware of the difficulties and high costs involved in establishing industries and enterprises throughout Indonesia. In June 1996, they announced the revival of tax holidays for new foreign and domestic firms establishing operations in designated sectors. The Special Assistant to Investment Minister, Sanyoto Sastrowardoyo, stated that the move to revive the incentive 13 years after it was abandoned was part of the government's efforts to accelerate industrial development, ensure that Indonesia remained competitive and attractive to investors, and encourage a greater focus on eastern Indonesia (Jacob, 1996).

A five-man ministerial team is to determine specific sectors and investments that will benefit from tax breaks which could be up to 12 years in some cases. New foreign and domestic firms can enjoy exemptions from corporate tax and tax on dividends paid to foreign-based shareholders for up to ten years. Furthermore, those firms locating in areas other than Java and Bali can enjoy these exemptions for a further two years (Jacob, 1996).

LEGAL REGULATIONS GOVERNING FDI

The Investment Coordinating Board (BKPM)

BKPM was established in 1983 (INDIO, 1996b) to assist the President in formulating government policies with respect to investment; to evaluate and approve investment proposals, and licences from both foreign and domestic interests; and to supervise investment implementation. The domain of BKPM covered all sectors except for oil and gas, and financial services. In addition to BKPM, there are regional investment coordinating boards (BKPMD) in every province which organise regional permits for location, land rights, land cultivation rights, construction and work permits for expatriate employees (Investment Coordinating Board, 1996a).

BKPM acts as the prime regulator of foreign investment in Indonesia under the *Foreign Investment Law No. 1* of 1976 and domestic investment under the *Domestic Capital Law*. The chairman of BKPM reports directly to the President. BKPM is responsible for the planning and administration of investment and assisting investors in finding feasible investment projects and suitable local partners. With the tremendous growth in FDI and the deregulation packages announced on 4 June 1996, BKPM ensures that FDI is consistent with government objectives (Investment Coordinating Board, 1996b).

Government Policies on Foreign Investment

Indonesia's strong pro-business administration and political stability have created an environment for business investment. Sweeping free-market reforms have opened the private sector to world trade and economic competition. Indonesia's deregulation measures, which started in 1983, have opened the floodgates to foreign investments. In an effort to increase the level of investment and capital formation, to boost exports and strengthen both the current account and balance of payments, the steps taken have included streamlining approval procedures, reducing initial capital requirements and opening more sectors of the economy to private investment. These can be seen in the most recent three trade deregulation packages announced in May 1995, January 1996 and June 1996, respectively.

Collectively, the packages have provided for further reductions in tariffs. These have cut Indonesia's unweighted average tariff by seven percentage points, from over 19% prior to May 1995 to 12.2% with the implementation of the June 1996 measures. In addition, the packages abolished non-tariff barriers, eliminated a number of surcharges and assimilated the remainder into the base tariff code (a step consistent with the new *Customs Law* of 1995 which does not recognise the concept of surcharges). Finally, they have provided a clear timetable for future tariff reductions and provided businesses with improved scope for future planning (INDIO, 1996c). Key trade features of the deregulation packages and a schedule of tariff reductions can be found in Tables 14–2 and 14–3, respectively.

For investors who injected capital directly into production and business facilities, trade reforms have made them more competitive and increased their profits. The private sector is now providing the greater part of direct investment in production activities, and expanding financial and other services significantly. This outcome is because the government has reduced its role substantially, particularly in production activities. Furthermore, foreign investors have generated significant employment opportunities. State investment has

TABLE 14–2
Key Trade Features of the May 1995, January 1996 and June 1996 Deregulation Packages

May 1995

- Reduced tariffs on 96% of items in code with rates above 5%, thereby lowering the unweighted average tariff by four percentage points, from over 19% to under 15%.
- Trade barriers eliminated on 81 items, reducing the number of non-tariff barriers by 30%.
- Provided broad eight-year timetable for future tariff reductions, whereby all tariff rates of 20% or less will be gradually reduced to a maximum of 5% by the year 2000; and those of 20% or more will be reduced to a maximum of 20% in 1998 and 10% by the year 2003.
- Import surcharges and tariffs divided into separate categories.

January 1996

- Import tariffs reduced by between 5% and 20% on 428 items, chiefly capital goods and raw materials used directly and indirectly in production of exports.
- Rebate of duty paid on imported materials and components used not only in the production of direct exports but also those sold to bonded zones and export processing entrepots for further processing into exports.
- Wholly-owned foreign firms allowed to establish exporting houses and to set up import firms solely importing goods for further processing and re-export.
- From April 1996, private firms allowed to develop and manage bonded zones, previously the prerogative of state firms.
- Removal of VAT on importation of fishing and other commercial vessels (except yachts and cruise ships) and on shipping related services; aimed at boosting the capacity of national shipping firms in both inter-island and international freight.

June 1996

- Reductions on 1,497 tariff items, including 385 capital goods items; unweighted average tariff further lowered to 2.2%.
- Detailed timetable for future tariff reductions (see Table 14–3).
- A number of surcharges eliminated; the remainder assimilated into base tariff structure in line with the 1995 *Customs Law*.
- NTBs further reduced by allowing private general importers to import certain capital goods (including electric motors and generators, industrial stoves, displacement and rotary pumps, tractors and soy meal) previously restricted to licensed firms importing such goods for their own production purposes.
- Pilot project announced aimed at boosting key export categories (textiles and related products, shoes, electronics, wood/rattan products, and leather goods, which between them account for some US$15 billion, or around one-third, of non-oil exports) through special tax, customs and banking facilities.
- Establishment of special Ministerial Anti-Dumping Committee to investigate and recommend response measures to dumping by foreign firms.

Source: INDIO (1996c).

shifted from production activities to the provision of supporting physical infrastructure and human resource development. Although state-owned enterprises continue to play a major role in a number of sectors, the government has emphasised their commercial operation and partnership ventures with private firms, particularly for large projects and programmes. It is expected that the government's privatisation programme will further reduce its presence in the commercial sector. Recognising that good infrastructure attracts investment, the government has opened up a number of strategic sectors, largely public-owned, to offshore investors. These are ports, shipping, railways, power generation, airlines, water, telecommunications and atomic energy. The idea is to attract more private equity capital into infrastructure development which will ease the financing burden of the government and be more efficient (INDIO, 1996c).

Table 14–3
Schedule of Tariff Reductions

Before May 1995	1995	1996	1997	1998	1999	2000	2001	2002	2003
5%	*	*	*	*	*	Max. 5%			
10%	5%	*	*	*	*	Max. 5%			
15%	10%	*	5%	*	*	Max. 5%			
20%	15%	*	10%	*	5%	Max. 5%			
25%	20%	15%	*	10%	*	*	*	*	Max. 10%
30%	25%	20%	*	15%	*	10%	*	*	Max. 10%
35%	30%	25%	*	20%	*	15%	*	10%	Max. 10%
40%	30%	25%	*	20%	*	15%	*	10%	Max. 10%

Source: INDIO (1996c).

Impact of Recent Government Policies on FDI

Since deregulation began in June 1994, foreign investment approval in 1994 surged to US$23.7 billion from just US$8 billion in the previous year, to US$39.9 billion in 1995 and to US$20.1 billion from

January to 15 June 1996 (INDIO, 1996b). The more open climate created by deregulation is a partial reason for the surge in private investment demand, both domestic and foreign. Of course, higher investment demand creates more production and employment, and solidly supports medium term growth in the economy.

The easing of restrictions on foreign ownership and relaxing divestment rules for foreign investors have had a major impact on sentiments in the investment community. Indonesia has become one of the world's most open capital markets despite its higher interest rates and inflation, and the lure of other Asian markets such as China, Vietnam and India. "Indonesia is now extremely competitive in all of the sectors open to offshore investors" according to James Castle of the consulting group Business Advisory Indonesia (*Institutional Investors*, August 1995).

Negative Impact of Recent Government Policies on FDI

Although the central government has announced plans to reduce red tape, regional licence requirements and other levies can make investing difficult. The Indonesian president must personally approve every individual foreign investment project. In practice, this means that approval of investment applications can be delayed with little or no explanation (Indonesian Investment, 1996).

While foreign investment approvals have soared for the past few years, with impressive figures, foreign bankers note that only about one-third of them are realised (*Institutional Investor*, August 1995). The explanation given is that in some instances projects are withdrawn by the promoters themselves; and in other cases, approval is revoked because projects do not proceed within the agreed upon timescale or fail to meet other approval requirements. Apart from this, projects are allowed to proceed with less (usually) or more (rarely) capital outlay than initially proposed. In addition, figures for realised investments over a given period cannot be directly compared with approvals for the same period since projects take time to come on stream – sometimes several years if they go ahead at all. This is particularly true for large capital-intensive projects, such as oil refineries and cement plants. The BKPM currently has on its books between US$15 billion and US$20 billion of approvals for ten oil refineries whereas only four or five are likely to be required. A number of approved cement facilities are having difficulty raising capital funds and are taking longer than anticipated to proceed (INDIO, 1996c; World Bank, 1996).

The Indonesian government recently revised its estimate of the 1995 economic growth rate to 8.1% from 7.5%. Some economic observers considered a growth rate of 7.5% to be too high hence running the risk of the economy becoming overheated. One of the World Bank's suggestions is to increase the price of fuel. However, increases in fuel prices always trigger price increases in consumer goods and eventually lead to more acute inflation which would be traumatic for Indonesia. An atmosphere of panic could prevail if the inflation rate approaches 10% (World Bank, 1996).

Indonesia's trade balance may deteriorate due to the tremendous increase in foreign investment. The balance of trade is projected to register a deficit in 1997/98, something which has not occurred before. Normally the balance of trade is boosted by a surplus in the oil and gas trade balance. But because the surplus in the trade balance is dropping, the 1995/96 current account is estimated to have a huge deficit of US$6.9 billion in comparison with the 1994/95 figure of US$3.5 billion. Some observers, both within Indonesia and overseas, are dubious about this figure. An overseas consulting company has estimated the deficit in the current account for 1995/96 at US$9 billion and some have even mentioned US$13 billion. The main source of the deficit in the current account continues to be the high deficit in the balance of services which is always higher than the surplus in the trade balance. This situation is exacerbated because the balance of trade is now moving towards a deficit position.

The main source of the deficit in the balance of services is the payment of interest, transportation costs and the transfer of profits by foreign companies. For example, in 1994/95 Indonesia transferred US$5.6 billion in interest payments, US$3.4 billion in transportation costs and US$0.6 billion in profits from overseas companies. This deficit would have been even greater had it not been for the injection of a surplus of US$2.9 billion from the tourism sector and US$0.5 billion from Indonesians working overseas. It is likely that the deficit in the balance of services will increase in the next few years, particularly due to increases in interest payments and transportation costs. The World Bank has also warned that such a high deficit in the current account could reduce investor confidence and, thus, eventually complicate efforts to maintain a high level of economic growth (World Bank, 1996).

In the midst of optimism about Indonesia's economic development, there are various external constraints. The first is the uncertainty in the price of commodities on the international market. For example, the balance of trade and the current account will be better only if the price of oil rises as anticipated. Fluctuations in the price cycle of non-oil and gas primary commodities also could create problems since 40% of the non-oil and gas exports still consist of primary commodities and industrial products made from them. There is the possibility that the exchange rate of the U.S. dollar relative to the yen could drop again, creating yet other problems for Indonesia because the overseas debt burden would increase. Approximately 50% of Indonesia's debts are in yen while most of the export earnings are in U.S. dollar (World Bank, 1996).

Despite the deregulation policies launched by the government, including the acceleration of scheduled cuts in tariff and non-tariff barriers that formalised the scheduled cuts in 1994 and 1995, the World Bank still believes that the deregulation agenda is unfinished. The unfinished agenda includes: the removal of tariff protection on vehicles; the opening up of strategic industries to import competition and the removal of their domestic subsidies; the removal of export taxes on forest products; and the removal of non-tariff barriers on the agricultural commodities imported by the Board of Logistics (BULOG) which has the sole right to import rice, fertiliser and sugar (World Bank, 1996).

According to the World Bank, Indonesian trade policy still has some anti-trade bias. For import competing activities, this means domestic production is favoured over imports while for export-oriented activities, domestic sales are favoured over exports. Import protection tariffs and non-tariff barriers account for two-thirds of the anti-trade bias and export restrictions account for the remainder. The World Bank further disclosed that the anti-trade bias disadvantages the outer islands. Elimination of the anti-trade bias, therefore, would raise efficiency in import-competing industries, stimulate non-oil exports and enhance the quality of growth. The World Bank disclosed that the tariff cuts announced in May 1995 should reduce the anti-trade bias by one-third. There would be three principal tariff rates, i.e., 0%, 5% and 10% and the average rate would be 7% (World Bank, 1996).

The unfinished agenda for reducing import protection consists mainly of removing non-tariff barriers, notably those on rice, sugar, wheat and soybeans, and the associated restrictions that protect wheat flour milling. BULOG is granted the sole right to import these items. In addition to BULOG's sole right to import the above items, other agricultural products protected by restrictive import licensing include milk and dairy products, onions, garlic and cloves. There are also some industrial items that are also protected by restrictive import licensing which include alcoholic beverages, salt, iodised salt, fertilizers, polypropylene copolymers, printed matter, hand tools, motor vehicles, motorcycles and keyboard instruments in a completely knocked down condition.

Although Indonesia needs increased exports, they remain subject to considerable restrictions which cover one-half of total non-oil exports affecting nearly 2,000 products. The export restrictions take four forms: export bans; regulated exports whereby products can only be exported by exporters approved by the Ministry of Industry and Trade; supervised exports which require approval by the Ministry of Industry and Trade; and export taxes. Most of these restrictions are directed toward agricultural products, including coffee, rubber, palm oil and copra. Trade associations have affected the marketing of some agricultural commodities because they demand fees, and determine prices and quotas. This was the situation and climate before the *4 June 1996 deregulation package* launched by the government (World Bank, 1996).

By the June 1996 deregulation, the government raised the maximum value of exports not covered by the PEB (Export Declaration Document) from Rp 10 million to Rp 100 million hoping that exports by small enterprises will significantly increase. The deregulation abolishes the compulsory examination of export commodities by P. T. Sucofindo, a surveyor, which was formerly applicable to rattan products, crude palm oil, timber products and rubber products. However, the deregulation in exports also remains unfinished because it does not cover the export restrictions applicable to some essential commodities as noted by the World Bank. Some essential obstacles still remaining include monopolies and oligopolies, restrictions on imports and exports of certain goods, wrong incentive targets, high interest rates, and the high value added tax (World Bank, 1996).

Seeking Redress for Investment Disputes

Indonesia is a party to the 1965 *Washington Convention for the Settlement of Investment Disputes between States and Nationals of Other States*. Based on the *Convention*, disputes among foreign investors, or locally incorporated foreign investment companies, and the Government of Indonesia may, with the written consent of the parties, be submitted to arbitration. These cases are heard under the auspices of the International Center for Settlement of Investment Disputes (ICSID) in Washington, D.C., in the U.S. Several of Indonesia's bilateral investment protection agreements, including those with Belgium, France, the Netherlands, and the U.K., contain ICSID arbitration clauses providing for arbitration of certain investment disputes between Indonesia and nationals of the treaty countries. Many foreign investment applications for capital investment in Indonesia contain ICSID arbitration clauses which become binding upon the government's written approval of the application (Hornick, 1991).

Apart from the ICSID, the government has sometimes agreed to the inclusion of arbitration clauses in commercial contracts, particularly with foreigners. For example, many of its oil production sharing contracts between foreign contractors and the state-owned oil company, Pertamina, provide for International Chamber of Commerce (ICC) arbitration of disputes. In addition to the ICSID arbitration clauses, the *Foreign Investment Law* provides for the arbitration of disputes regarding compensation for nationalised investments. The mechanism consists of two party-appointed arbitrators and a neutral third arbitrator appointed jointly by the parties. The *Foreign Investment Law* does not specify what rules will govern the arbitration, or where the arbitration should be held or how the neutral arbitrator should be designated in the event of a deadlock (Hornick, 1991).

THE COMMERCIAL LAWS OF INDONESIA

Political and Legal Framework

Indonesia's political system and constitution concentrate significant power in the President. Since independence in 1945, Indonesia has had two presidents, Sukarno (1945–1967) and Soeharto (1967 to the present). The nation has undergone some remarkable political *variations* in the past half-century: from colonial control by the Dutch to Japanese occupation in the 1940s; from parliamentary democracy to Sukarno's "guided democracy" in the 1950s; and from chaos and crisis in the 1960s to Soeharto's "New Order" democracy of today.

The army and the Chinese play dominant roles in the cooperation between the government and business. The role of the armed forces has been described by the term *dual funksi* which requires it to participate in the political life of the country in addition to its traditional role of defender of the country. This has led to its procurement of licences and involvement in key sectors of the economy. The Indonesian Chinese have dominated the entrepreneurial sector for generations, dating back to early Dutch colonial rule nearly three centuries ago. The Indonesian political environment is often described as a triangular partnership among President Soeharto, the armed forces and the Chinese ethnic entrepreneurs. However, this partnership has been altered by the growth of *pribumi* (indigenous Indonesian) conglomerates during the last few years.

The existing legal system in Indonesia is a mixture of traditional customary law (*adat*), Islamic law (*syariah*), old Dutch laws and modern legislation enacted since independence. Although the enactment of legislation is the responsibility of the Indonesian parliament (*Dewan Permusyawarantan Rakyat*, or DPR), in practice most of the regulations leading to the implementation of laws are created by government departments. The President frequently issues decrees and instructions which effectively operate as law. The language of these laws are general and require clarification from the respective ministries. Consequently, many laws are implemented by government decree and administrative policy. Therefore, it is prudent to consult government officials for explanations of the policies and laws on a particular matter (Investment Coordinating Board, 1996b).

The development of the legal system has been slow compared with the nation's economic growth. In the current Five-Year Plan the government is focusing on developing the legal framework. One of the milestones was the enactment of *Company Law* to replace the company law provisions that were found in the 1847 Dutch-based *Commercial Code*. Provisions which impose stricter responsibility on company officers and protect the rights of minority shareholders are among the more important changes made by the *Company Law* which came into effect in March 1996. Companies established prior to March 1996 are required to revise their Articles of Association (AOA) to bring them into compliance with the *Company Law* (Mills, 1996).

Prior to *Law No. 1* of 1967, which is Indonesia's basic foreign investment law, no foreign interests could own property or businesses in the country, nor own shares, nor act as directors or other management in an Indonesian company. The enactment of the *Foreign In-*

vestment Law changed these terms. It permitted foreign interests to own shares and appoint foreign directors in them subject to government approval. It was originally enacted in 1967 and amended in 1970. Pursuant to the authority under these laws to make further regulations, the government has periodically liberalised investments under "packages", taking into account the World Bank's recommendations and competition from other Asian countries. These packages relate to the initial percentage of foreign investment permitted in a company and the time limit for divestiture to Indonesian majority interest. The former has been gradually increased and the latter decreased with each deregulation package. By mid-1994, foreign ownership in Indonesian companies was permitted to a maximum of 80%, which had to be reduced to a maximum of 49% within 20 years of the commercial operation. These regulations do not apply to certain major infrastructure projects (Mills, 1996).

Indonesia's *Foreign Investment Law*

Under *Article 6* of the *Foreign Investment Law*, foreign investment is prohibited in certain fields of activity for national strategic reasons. These include the production of arms, ammunition, explosives and other military equipment. Other industries deemed important to the economy cannot have complete foreign ownership. These include harbours, shipping and railways, telecommunications, aviation, drinking water, atomic energy and the mass media (Mills, 1996).

Article 7 of the *Foreign Investment Law* designates other fields of activity where foreign capital cannot be invested. Pursuant to *Article 7*, the government promulgated a Negative List for capital investments but it is not exhaustive. Certain areas not specified in the *Foreign Investment Law* and not on the Negative List are banned to foreigners because of specific government policy and include drilling, mining in Java, and professional services such as legal, medical, tax and financial consulting (Mills, 1996).

The only alternative that used to be available for foreign ownership in Indonesian companies was a government-approved foreign investment joint venture company known as a PMA (*Penanaman Modal Asing*), regulated by the Investment Coordinating Board (*Badan Koordinasi Penanaman Modal*, BKPM). However, on 19 May 1994, *Government Regulation No. 20* (PP20) was issued. PP20 and its implementation guidelines permitted 100% foreign ownership by corporate entities and individuals in BKPM-regulated PMA companies and the purchase of up to 95% of the shares in Indonesian limited liability companies (Mills, 1996).

Article 7 of the *Company Law* dictates that the company shall be established by two or more persons using a notarial document written in the Indonesian language. It strips a company of limited liability status if it is owned by a single shareholder for more than six months. *Articles 14, 15* and *16* provide for company statues to be changed with the concurrence of the shareholders. Certain changes to the company statutes do require prior approval by the Minister of Justice of the Republic of Indonesia (Mills, 1996).

Indonesia's New *Capital Law* of 1996

In January 1996, the long awaited new *Capital Law* came into effect and, with it, a number of other government regulations designed to improve the efficiency of the Indonesian capital market. The regulations include licensing, registration and approval of both institutions and individuals operating in the stock exchange, clearing and settlement institutions, mutual funds, securities companies, investment advisory services, administration, custodian and support services (Tabalujan, 1997).

The capital market is assuming a strategic role in Indonesia's national development. It is an important engine of economic growth and funding for the business community. The new *Capital Law* was enacted to provide legal certainty for all participating parties in the capital market and to protect the interests of the investor community against harmful practices.

Article 1 decrees that the Securities Administration Bureau shall be the legal party operating the system and facilities of the Stock Exchange. All members of the Stock Exchange (Securities Trading Brokers) must obtain the required business licence from the Capital Markets Supervising Agency (*Padan Pelaksana Pasar Modal*, Bapepam) before they are allowed to practise. Bapepam functions as the policing arm for the Minister of Finance of Indonesia, providing guidance, regulatory and day to day supervision of capital markets activities (The Limited Liability Company, *Law No. 1*, 1995; Tabalujan, 1997).

FOREIGN INVESTMENT ISSUES

Wages across Indonesia vary and they have to be considered in conjunction with fringe benefits which average about 30% of the wage. A mandatory insurance scheme, plus accident and disability insurance are required. There is only one official union in Indonesia, the All Indonesia Workers Union (Serikat *Perburuhan Seluruh Indonesia* – SPSI). Under government regulations, any industrial disputes must be reported to the Department of Manpower which negotiates with the parties involved. Negotiation is typically based on Indonesia's preferred consensus system.

The employment of expatriates is governed by *Regulation No. 4* of 1995 which states that a company wishing to employ expatriate labour must submit a plan of training for Indonesians who will later assume the relevant position. The regulation also outlines the work permit process. Some industries are closed to foreign workers, while permits are easy to obtain in exporting, marketing and tourism. In the manufacturing industry there are three levels of employment: the working and supervisory class where foreigners cannot be employed; technical staff where there is usually a three-year limit for foreign workers; and jobs requiring expatriates such as in consultancy. In each case, a sponsorship letter is required from the employer or government agency. Under the current tax regulations, a company is not allowed to deduct non-salary benefits granted to an expatriate such as housing, club memberships and children's schooling. An expatriate is not taxed on these benefits as personal income.

Since mid-1994, there are three options for establishing a business. The first option is to team up with an Indonesian partner and establish a foreign investment PMA joint venture company (through BKPM and regulated by BKPM). The foreign investor is allowed to own up to 95% indefinitely. The second option is to establish a wholly-owned PMA FDI company (through BKPM and regulated by BKPM). In this case, the investor must divest at least a nominal portion of the shares to Indonesian interests within 15 years. The third option is to purchase up to 95% of an existing Indonesian company. It is not regulated by BKPM although approval is required (Mills, 1996).

Purchase of Shares in Non-PMA Companies

Foreign individuals and corporations have been permitted to purchase up to 95% of the shares of existing non-PMA Indonesian companies since 1994 provided that the latter's objectives meet the regulations. Prior approval by the Ministry of Justice (MOJ) and the BKPM are required to complete this type of purchase (Mills, 1996; Investment Coordinating Board, 1996b).

New regulations issued in late 1995 permit foreigners to act as directors of non-PMA Indonesian companies. However, these do not guarantee automatic entitlement to residence visas and work permits as is the case for foreign directors of PMA companies. Another disadvantage is that fiscal incentives available to PMA companies are not available to non-PMAs. The principal advantage to the latter option is that of not waiting for government approval. There is no supervision of the amount of capital that must be invested. Although new regulations theoretically have done away with the minimum capital requirement for PMA companies, it may be difficult to obtain approval for a non-PMA company if the BKPM deems the investment insufficient (Investment Coordinating Board, 1996b).

Approval Procedures for Investment in PMA Companies

Government approval is required for the establishment of a PMA company. BKPM reviews the applications before forwarding them to the appropriate ministries and the State Secretariat for review and approval. The final step involves presenting the approval letter to the President for his ratification. The approval letter signed by the President functions as the official provisional approval of the project. The final approval will be awarded once the PMA company commences complete commercial operation, or production, and invests its full authorised capital in compliance with the terms of its application and approval letter (Investment Coordinating Board, 1996b).

The procedure for application involves completing a simple official form. All ancillary documentation (see Table 14–4) must be attached and multiple copies of the application form must be submitted. BKPM redistributes these copies to various ministries and departments for review.

Joint Venture Agreement

Where a corporate joint venture between a foreign investor and an Indonesian partner to establish a PMA company is envisaged, the applicants must submit a copy of the agreement as a part of the application. There is no fixed format for joint venture agreements and those in English are routinely accepted by the BKPM. Amendments to such agreements need not be submitted. The joint venture agreement stipulates the contractual relationship concerning subscription shares, divestment and preemptive rights of purchase of existing or newly issued shares, rights in the composition of management, voting and decision-making rights, and alterations to the Articles of Association of the joint venture company (Mills, 1996). The joint venture agreement needs to set out any other relationships and any ancillary agreements required for licensing, distribution or technical assistance agreements. Thus, the scope of the joint venture agreement must cover all relationships over their entire duration.

TABLE 14–4
Ancillary Documents

1.	Power of attorney to sign/submit and execution of the application.
2.	Certificates of incorporation and articles of association of both foreign and Indonesian companies.
3.	A flow chart of the production process with an explanation of materials used if in the industrial sector, or an explanation of business activities if in the service sector.
4.	Tax Registration Code Number Identification Card (NPWP) for the Indonesian company or individual person(s).
5.	Joint Venture Agreement in complete form (each page initialised by both partner(s) and Technical Assistance Agreement (if applicable).

Source: Investment Coordinating Board (1996b).

Articles of Association (AOA)

AOA are the formal constitution of a company apart from being a contract among the shareholders. They are a public document that is accessible to third parties and specifies the rights and obligations of shareholders in the company. They regulate the voting rights, management, powers and authority, and meetings of the company. Specific to Indonesian law, AOA must govern the conduct of the company and their provisions will prevail in the event of any inconsistency with other agreements including the joint venture agreement. It is important to review carefully the AOA prior to their engrossment in notarial form so as to ensure that the Indonesian version faithfully reflects the English draft that was agreed to by the parties (Mills, 1996).

Capital

The 1994 deregulation measures eliminated the minimum capital requirement for a foreign investment project. Prior to that, a minimum investment of US$1 million was required in most cases. In practice, however, few approvals have been issued for projects where the investment is less than US$250,000, or in fields requiring little fixed capital such as the service industries (Mills, 1996).

The composition of the total investment commitment may consist of a combination of equity and loan capital. The percentage of equity capital specified as the initial contribution in the application must be paid up prior to the AOA approval by the Ministry of Justice. In the application, an estimated commencement date for full commercial operations must be stated. The full amount of authorised capital must be paid in no later than this date. The final investment approval is issued at this time and the time limits for the investment licence and divestment, if any, begins from this date. The BKPM suggests that a start-up period of up to 36 months from the issuance of government approval to the commencement of commercial production is an acceptable timeframe. There is no time limit within which the loan capital must be taken up or invested nor are the parties required to demonstrate that such loans are available (Mills, 1996).

PMA Approval and Formation

Indonesian regulations state that the BKPM has six weeks from the date of receipt to accept or reject a foreign investment application. In practice, this usually takes approximately eight weeks. Upon receipt of the approval letter, the applicant may establish the PMA as a limited liability Indonesian company before a notary public. Indonesian *Company Law* does not permit the establishment of single shareholder limited liability companies (Mills, 1996; Investment Coordinating Board, 1996b).

The notary reads out the AOA to the parties and the duly authorised shareholder representatives sign the original on a revenue stamp which is affixed to the document. This original is kept by the notary in the master files as property of the government. Official copies, executed and stamped by the notary, are delivered to the parties within a few days together with the receipt for the filing with the MOJ. The notary submits the AOA for approval to the MOJ. When the MOJ approves the AOA and the AOA is published in the government gazette, the company is fully incorporated. During the time between the execution of the articles and their approval by the MOJ there is no legal impediment to the company transacting business. Since the directors at this stage are not properly authorised to represent the shareholders in binding the company, the shareholders should countersign any important third party agreements, or have such agreements re-executed or ratified, after the MOJ approves the AOA (Mills, 1996).

Administrative Matters

The life of an Indonesian company is usually 75 years. The *Foreign Investment Law*, however, dictates that the duration of a foreign investment licence cannot exceed 30 years from the commencement of commercial operations. According to the 1994 deregulation package (PP20), a renewal of the licence for an additional 30 years is permitted if the business is continuing in operation and it is beneficial to the Indonesian economy (Investment Coordinating Board, 1996c).

Upon receipt of the approval letter, applicants are encouraged to submit a "manpower plan" and a "master list" of capital goods to be imported. BKPM will then arrange for the issuance of any relevant tax facilities, such as exemption from import duties on equipment or supplies for certain projects. BKPM will assist in obtaining approval for residence visas and work permits for required expatriate personnel as specified in the application and the manpower plan. It will further assist in applying for business licences, expatriate work permits, a tax registration number, an import identification number and customs clearance for capital goods and raw materials. There are no exchange control regulations or restrictions on the repatriation of after-tax profits (Mills, 1996).

Real Property Rights

A PMA company has similar options to a domestic company regarding ownership of land. In Indonesia, only citizens are entitled to own land through *Hak Milik* title which is equivalent to freehold. There are several other levels of title available to Indonesian or foreign companies. These levels consist of different land rights for fixed but renewable periods of 10 to 35 years. A PMA foreign investment company may hold one of the following three land rights: (a) *Hak Guna Bangunan*, or the right to build on the land, which is generally valid for 30 years and is renewable for 20 years if the land is properly utilised; (b) *Hai Pakai*, or the right to use the land, which is generally valid for 10 years and is renewable for 10 years at a time; and (c) *Hak Guna Usaha*, or the right to conduct business on the land, which is generally valid for 35 years and can be renewed twice, each time for 25 years to a maximum of 85 years (pursuant to a 1992 *Presidential Decree*).

Incentives

A PMA foreign investment company is accorded certain financial incentives which are not available to companies that are not regulated by BKPM. These incentives include: (a) exemption from, or reduction of, import duties on machinery, equipment and spare parts imported for use in production; (b) exemption from, or reduction of, import duties for up to two years on raw materials or components used in production; and (c) easily obtainable work permits and residence visas for expatriate personnel.

For PMA companies engaged in manufacturing for export, additional incentives available include: (a) restitution of import duty and surcharges on imports of goods and materials used in the manufacturing process of goods for export; (b) accelerated refunds of value added tax (VAT) and luxury tax paid on goods and materials purchased domestically to be used in the manufacturing process of goods for export; and (c) permitted raw material imports required in the manufacturing process of goods for export regardless of the availability of comparable domestic products.

CROSS CULTURAL MANAGEMENT

Managing cultural differences has become an integral part of multinational corporations (MNCs) adjustment to doing business in Indonesia. With increased globalisation, MNCs are focusing on transfer of technology, general operations and management. Managing high growth businesses and joint ventures requires an examination of different management styles including cross cultural management issues.

Understanding the Indonesian Culture

Indonesia has been influenced by several foreign cultures. Early influences came from India with Hinduism, followed by Buddhism. These were followed by Arabs with Islam and, finally by the Dutch with Christianity around the end of the sixteenth century. All of these influences occurred through successive waves of traders. The Dutch trading activity resulted in more than 300 years of colonisation. Several popular nationalist independence movements had started by the early twentieth century and came to maturation with the Japanese occupation during World War II. Two days after the surrender of the Japanese on 15 August 1945, Indonesia declared independence although the Dutch did not concede sovereignty until 1949. In addition to being ethnically diverse, Indonesia is religiously diverse, encompassing Islam, Hinduism (mostly on the island of Bali), Christianity and Buddhism (primarily among the ethnic Chinese population). Although the country is predominantly Muslim (88%), it is not an Islamic state. The government has devoted much attention to separating state from religion.

Managing Cultural Diversity in Indonesia

Fundamental to business success is the management team, control processes, interpersonal management skills and successful integration of management processes. Several cultural dimensions in Indonesia require careful attention in setting up business and they are discussed below.

(i) ***Power Distance***: Hofstede (1980a) defined power distance as a measure of the extent to which less powerful members of organisations accept the unequal distribution of power. Indonesians rank high on the dimension of power distance and this characteristic is crucial in analysing the way decisions are made. High power distance means inequalities in status and roles that are formalised in superior–subordinate relationships. Indonesian managers tend to be more status conscious than their Western counterparts. In more hierarchical cultures, according to Hofstede (1980a), only senior managers make decisions and lower level personnel implement them. This is the case in Indonesian society. Lower level Indonesian employees would question the competence of a superior who consulted them on routine decisions. The majority of Indonesian managers prefer an autocratic style of management. More than four times as many Indonesian managers as American managers agreed with the statement, "It is important for a manager to have at hand precise answers to most of the questions that his subordinates may raise about their work" (Laurent, 1995).

Indonesian managers do not delegate responsibilities to their staff. Empowerment is not common in Indonesia and foreign managers wishing to delegate responsibilities to lower level staff must be cognitive of the discomfort which they may experience.

(ii) ***Time Orientation***: American businessmen have a tendency to make quick decisions but Indonesian culture downplays time and urgency. Indonesians place more value on decisions that require more time to make. Western businessmen may believe that Indonesians lack interest or sincerity in doing business because their decision making takes longer. Ironically, Indonesian businessmen will think that their western counterparts do not place enough importance on the deal since they are unwilling to commit more time in making the decision. Clearly, the time related to processing decisions is a crucial dimension in understanding Indonesian business behaviour. Indonesians do not like relating time to group or organisational decision making. They tend to regard time as an abstract phenomenon and, therefore, deadlines are always flexible and punctuality is not the norm (Adler, 1991).

The Indonesian attitude towards time impacts on the effectiveness of traditional Western management practices such as management by objectives, deadlines and detailed schedules. However, an increasing number of Indonesian middle managers have a professional background and education from Western business schools. Therefore, current management styles are in the process of transition but still require prudent handling.

(iii) ***Uncertainty Avoidance***: Hofstede (1980a) defined uncertainty avoidance as a measure of the extent to which people in a society feel threatened by ambiguous situations and the extent to which they try to avoid these situations. Indonesian managers have low levels of uncertainty avoidance, or little anxiety about future events and, also, low individualism reflecting the importance of collectivism and community in Indonesian society.

(iv) ***Motivation***: Maslow (1943, 1954, 1962), an American psychologist, suggested that human beings' five basic needs form a hierarchy: from physiological, to safety, to social, to esteem, to self-actualisation needs. According to Maslow, the higher order needs (i.e., esteem and self-actualisation) only become activated and, thus, motivate behaviour after lower order needs have been satisfied. However, in applying motivation theories in Indonesia, one must be conscious that Maslow's hierarchy of needs does not hold in all countries. In countries high on uncertainty avoidance as compared with lower uncertainty avoidance, security motivates most employees more strongly than does self-actualisation (Hofstede, 1980b). Employees in high uncertainty avoidance countries tend to consider job security and life-time employment as more important than holding a very interesting or challenging job. Workers in more collectivist countries, such as Indonesia, tend to stress social needs like cultivating good relationships over the more individualistic ego and self-actualisation needs.

(v) ***Communication***: Culture strongly influences and, in many cases, determines a person's interpretations (Adler, 1991). Certain concepts do not have a one-to-one correspondence. For example, "power" in the Javanese context is very different from the western context (Djajadiningrat-Nieuwenhuis, 1987). In the West, individuals strive for power and then use it when it is required. For a Javanese, it is an ascribed characteristic, one either has power or no power and it is futile to strive for it. There is only one Indonesian concept to convey the two English concepts of power and authority. As another example, Indonesians differentiate between an agreement in principle and a signed agreement. The English word "agreement" is ambiguous to them.

(vi) ***Relationships and Contacts***: Indonesians believe in cultivating long-standing relationships with their partners which underscores the importance of its diffused culture. The investment in building relationships is as important, if not more so, as the deal itself. This contrasts sharply with a western management-by-objectives style of business.

Negotiating with Indonesians

Indonesians use an affective approach to negotiating. They counter opponent's arguments based on emotional appeal rather than confrontation. Since they value long term relationships with their bargaining partners, they are more willing to make concessions throughout the bargaining process. Indonesians give a great deal of thought to both the contract and the contracting party before signing any document (Adler, 1991).

Indonesians are quite flexible during the course of negotiations. Terms are expressed in general form but they are held no less strongly. Throughout the negotiations, proposals are offered rather than argued, and emphasis is placed on establishing a good working relationship. Faced with a strong assertion, the non-confrontational Indonesian will express respect by replying indirectly.

Once concessions have reached a limit, Indonesians will not force a further concession. If the counterpart makes a concession, then Indonesians recognise the effort and respect the person. From their standpoint, a concession by either side is evidence of strength; and it becomes a basis for subsequent reconciliation and co-operation rather than being perceived as a sign of weakness (Adler, 1991). It is difficult for Indonesians to commit to long term contracts where the stakes are high because they tend to be less certain of controlling the future than Western managers. It is even more difficult for Indonesians to commit if they do not trust the other party.

Managing Successful Joint Ventures

Studies indicate that forging successful joint ventures requires more than a contractual agreement. Investors need to understand different cultural behaviours. Studies on cross-national joint ventures have suggested five barriers and facilitators that affect the outcome of a successful joint venture and these are discussed below (Calingo, 1994).

(i) ***Goal Compatibility***: A successful joint venture enables both parties to strike a win-win situation in achieving goals. Prior to the alliance, each party's motivations must be made known and both short term and long term goals must be compatible.
(ii) ***Strategic Advantage***: The parties must provide complementary resources that are value added. Synergy should emerge when the partners pool their resources, work closely together, reinforce one another's strengths and formulate better ideas for managing the business enterprise.
(iii) ***Interdependence***: A joint venture performs better if strategic decisions are made jointly by both parties. Both parties should participate actively in board meetings and strive for consensus on major strategies and policies of the company.
(iv) ***Commitment***: Linking long term cash incentives to wealth creation can foster closer relationships and commitment among key personnel in a joint venture. Struggling joint ventures seldom possess the level of management commitment enjoyed by those that are successful.
(v) ***Communication and Conflict Resolution***: The joint venture agreement should be comprehensive and cover all major aspects of the business, including how and under what circumstances it will end. Constant communication is essential so that disputes can be resolved expeditiously.

CONCLUSION

The Government of Indonesia has taken progressive steps to improve the investment climate in Indonesia to attract more FDI. The current consensus is that recent deregulation measures are conducive to FDI, but for them to be truly effective, the government needs to focus on political stability. The introduction of the new *Company Law* affirms Indonesia's commitment to the business sector and this will continue to add confidence to potential investors and attract more funds into the country, especially from other ASEAN nations.

REFERENCES

Adler Nancy J., *International Dimensions of Organizational Behaviour*, PWS-Kent, London, 1991.

Calingo Luis Ma. R., "The Organization and Management of successful Cross-National Joint Ventures: Lessons from Southeast Asia", keynote speech delivered at the Conference on "Modernization of Vietnam's Economy: Industrialization Momentum and its Implications for Vietnam", organised by the Ho Chi Minh National Political Academy of the Socialist Republic of Vietnam and sponsored by the Hanns Seidel Foundation, Hanoi, Vietnam, 14–15 September 1994.

Djajadiningrat-Nieuwenhuis Madelon, "Ibuism and Priyayization: Path to Power", in *Indonesian Women in Focus*, Elsbeth Locher-Scholten, editor, Foris Publications, Dordrecht, Holland, 1987.

Halverson Karen, "Foreign Direct Investment in Indonesia: A Comparison of Industrialized and Developing Country Investors", *Law and Policy in International Business*, Vol. 22, 1991.

Hofstede G., *Culture's Consequences: International Differences in Work Related Values*, Sage Publications, Beverly Hills, 1980a.

Hofstede G., "Motivation, Leadership and Organization: Do American Theories Apply Abroad?", *Organizational Dynamics*, Summer 1980b, pp. 42–63.

Hornick Robert N., "Indonesia Arbitration in Theory and Practices", *The American Journal of Comparative Law*, Vol. 39, 1991.

INDIO, *Indonesia Economic Brief*, Indonesia National Development Information Office, Jakarta, February 1996a.

INDIO, *Indonesia Facts*, Indonesia National Development Information Office, Jakarta, July 1996b.

INDIO, *Indonesia Source Book 1996*, Indonesia National Development Information Office, Jakarta, August 1996c.

"Indonesia – Greater Emphasis on the Private Sector", *Institutional Investor*, Vol. 28, No. 12, December 1994.

Indonesian Investment, *1996 National Trade Estimate*, Jakarta, 1996.

Institutional Investor, "50 Years of Achievement", Vol. 29, August 1995.

Investment Coordinating Board, *A Brief Guide for Investment*, Ministry of Investment, Jakarta, 1996a.

Investment Coordinating Board, *Investment Procedures in Indonesia*, Ministry of Investment, Jakarta, 1996b.

Investment Coordinating Board, *Regulations on Foreign Direct Investment*, Ministry of Investment, Jakarta, 1996c.

Investment Coordinating Board, *Statistics on Investment – Up to 31 October 1996*, Jakarta, 1996.

Jacob Paul, "Indonesia Looks East", *The Sunday Times*, 10 November 1996.

Laurent Andre, "The Cultural Diversity of Western Conceptions of Management", *International Studies of Management and Organization*, Vol. 13, No. 1–2, 1995.

Maslow A. H., "A Theory of Human Motivation", *Psychology Review*, July 1943, pp. 370–96.

Maslow A. H., *Motivation and Personality*, Harper & Row, New York, 1954.

Maslow A. H., *Toward a Psychology of Being*, Ven Nostrand, Princeton, N.J., 1962.

Mills Karen, "Indonesia's Ongoing Deregulation of Direct Foreign Investment", *East Asian Executive Report*, 15 January 1996.

Minter Ellison, *Doing Business in Indonesia*, Jakarta, 1996.

Tabalujan Benny S., "Indonesia's New Capital Market Law", *Asia Business Law Review*, No. 15, January 1997.

World Bank, *The World Bank's Report*, Edition No. 197, Geneva, 10 June 1996.

Chapter 15

Oil and Gas Industry in Indonesia*

BY
Djajadi SUSASTRA
Coleman YEE Kang Wen
LIM Poh Guan
HUANG Ming Hong

INTRODUCTION

INDONESIA IS ATTRACTIVE to investors because of its natural resources, political stability and economic potential. The petroleum industry plays a significant, although diminishing, role in its economy. This is partly due to the Organisation of Petroleum Exporting Countries (OPEC) production ceiling of around 1.5 million barrels of crude oil per day and the government's intention to produce just enough for the domestic and export markets. Another reason is the rapid expansion of the manufacturing sector due to recent deregulation efforts.

After China, Indonesia is Asia's largest producer of oil and gas. Only 36 of its 60 known basins have been explored. Estimated recoverable crude oil reserves located in 14 out of the 60 sedimentary basins is approximately 48 billion barrels. Daily production peaked at 1.558 million barrels of oil per day in 1992 and decreased slightly in 1993 and 1994. In addition to oil production, Indonesia is now one of the major gas producers in the world. Indonesia's total gas reserves are over 115 trillion cubic feet and are located in northern

* We wish to thank Dr. Austin Pullé for his guidance and helpful comments.

Sumatra, East Kalimantan and the offshore Natuna field. Gas production peaked at 7.42 million cubic feet per day in 1993 (Barnes, 1995).

Petroleum refining is carried out by the state oil firm, Pertamina. The government has announced proposals for further expansion of domestic refining and processing capacity. The objective is to eliminate crude oil exports, replacing them with refined petroleum products and petrochemicals exports.

Indonesia is increasing production and exports of liquefied petroleum gas. It has a ten-year export agreement to supply 1.95 million tonnes of butane and propane each year to Japan, making Indonesia the second largest supplier of liquefied petroleum gas (LPG) to Japan after Saudi Arabia. Indonesia's proven natural gas reserves are estimated at more than 80 trillion cubic feet. Pertamina has the sole ownership rights in Indonesia's gas reserves.

The oil and gas industry requires huge investments of capital, technology and know-how. There is provision for the participation of foreign investors through the Production Sharing Contract (PSC). Unlike concession arrangements in a PSC, Indonesia retains all rights to its petroleum resources including their ownership after they are removed from the ground. The PSC system has enabled Indonesia to enlist vitally needed foreign participation in its quest for economic expansion and stability.

New foreign investment in oil exploration and production is negotiated through Pertamina. The activities of foreign contractors are coordinated and administered by the Foreign Contractors Guiding Board (BPPKA), a division of Pertamina. The Directorate General of Oil and Gas (known as MIGAS) oversees the operations of all contractors and Pertamina. MIGAS licenses companies to operate in oil and enforces safety and environmental regulations. Downstream industries and supporting industries are coordinated by both Pertamina and the BKPM, investment coordinating board.

This chapter focuses on Pertamina, related industries and relevant policies. First, given the important role of Pertamina in Indonesia's oil and gas industry, the next section gives an overview of Pertamina's corporate profile and main activities. Secondly, business arrangements for exploration and development are described. Thirdly, the main activities of upstream and downstream industries are examined. Fourthly, government policy in environmental issues that affect the exploration and development of oil and gas are analysed.

Finally, the opportunities available to potential investors in the oil and gas industry are highlighted.

PERTAMINA

The Indonesian Constitution vests in the state the sole ownership of oil, gas and mineral resources. With respect to oil and gas, this monopoly power is exercised through Pertamina, a company solely owned by the government. Established in December 1957, Pertamina began realising its full potential as an instrument of national development in 1967 when laws enacted under the New Order Government attracted significant foreign investment in Indonesia's oil and gas industry. Pertamina has expanded significantly in recent years and it has earned a new image in the world oil community and in OPEC (Pertamina, 1996a).

Pertamina has been a catalyst for national development through exploration, production and marketing of Indonesia's energy resources for over three decades. The company supervises the activities of more than 100 domestic and foreign oil and gas contractors. Indonesian law charges Pertamina with supplying petroleum to the domestic market. The company concentrates much of its activity on downstream oil activities. Pertamina sells crude oil, petroleum products and natural gas abroad through subsidiary and joint venture operations.

Corporate Profile and Organisation

Under *Law No. 8* of 1971, Pertamina is directed and managed by a board of directors, headed by a president director appointed by the President of the Republic of Indonesia. In accordance with *Presidential Decree No. 11* of 1990, six senior vice president director positions were established to head and represent a directorate with special tasks and duties. The board of directors is responsible to the Government Board of Commissioners for Pertamina. Pertamina's organisation chart is shown in Appendix 15–1.

Main Activities

Pertamina explores and produces oil and gas on its own account. It operates a number of fields and is responsible for putting new areas up for bid as PSCs. It also operates ten refineries. These activities are administered through five regional offices.

Pertamina's Domestic Marketing Division coordinates the delivery of petroleum products from terminals throughout the country. It is expanding and upgrading existing facilities to meet demand through eight regional marketing organisations. The General Affairs Directorate controls the overall administrative direction of Pertamina. A major focus of the directorate is the international marketing of oil and liquefied natural gas (LNG). Included in this directorate are the sub-directorates of planning and methods, development, foreign marketing and logistics. Pertamina is responsible for domestic and foreign distribution of its crude oil and petroleum products which it implements through the Directorate of Shipping and Telecommunication. The vessels under its control are ocean going tankers, tankers and lighters used to transfer crude and other products for domestic consumption and smaller inter-island boats for servicing offshore facilities and regional distribution centres.

BPPKA manages the PSCs. After a foreign or domestic firm has signed a PSC with Pertamina, BPPKA reviews the contractor's budgets, annual work programmes and recommendations on awarding contracts for projects. BPPKA ensures that contracts are awarded on price and product quality and not on subjective factors. It makes final decisions concerning the commercial viability of oil and gas discoveries.

The Foreign Marketing sub-directorate is in charge of selling various crude products from Pertamina's own operations and the government's share of contract production. This sub-directorate is also responsible for marketing LNG. The company participates in a number of petroleum-related activities through wholly-owned subsidiary companies and joint ventures.

EXPLORATION AND DEVELOPMENT BUSINESS ARRANGEMENTS

Production Sharing Contract

Under the 1945 Constitution (UUD, 1945), mineral deposits in Indonesia are owned by the government; therefore, extraction of oil and gas can only be undertaken by the state. In 1966, the government introduced PSCs so that foreign investors could participate in the exploration and production of oil and gas in Indonesia.

The PSC is a contractual arrangement between Pertamina and a foreign investor, usually a foreign oil company, whereby the latter acts as a contractor for Pertamina and bears the financial risk of exploration in return for a share in the production off-take in the event the exploration is declared commercially viable under the PSC. If an exploration agreement fails to reach commercial production, then the contractor absorbs all the costs of the unsuccessful exploration (American Embassy, 1995). On the other hand, if the exploration is declared commercially viable, the contractor is allowed to recover certain agreed upon costs from the proceeds of oil sales and, thereafter, sharing of the production between Pertamina and the contractor begins.

A PSC is usually granted for 30 years. However, a contract can be relinquished after six to ten years of unsuccessful exploration as stipulated in the initial contract. To assure a reasonable rate of return to investors, the government is aware that the terms and conditions of PSCs must be modified from time to time to take into account the dynamics of the world economic situation. This contingency is reflected in the four incentive packages introduced since 1988 and these are discussed in subsequent sections. Although the details of PSCs vary from one agreement to another, they share some common characteristics which are listed in Table 15–1.

In 1995, production sharing contractors were responsible for producing 526 million barrels of crude oil and condensate, over 96% of total production. The most important condition in a PSC is the profit sharing agreement on extracted oil or gas. In most oil contracts, the distribution of net income is 80% to the government and 20% to the contractor while for gas contracts the distribution is 70% and 30%, respectively. Another important cost to the contractor is the signature bonus which varies across PSCs. A PSC signed with Overseas Petroleum and Investment Co. on 8 May 1996 specified bonuses to Pertamina as shown in Table 15–2.

Other Types of Arrangement

(i) ***Joint Operating Agreements (JOAs)***: A JOA is a form of a PSC which was introduced in 1977. JOAs require the formation of

Joint Operating Bodies (JOBs) between Pertamina and the contractors.

TABLE 15–1
Common Characteristics of Production Sharing Contracts

- Pertamina is responsible for the management of the operations.
- Contractor is responsible for the execution of the operations in accordance with agreed work programmes.
- Contractor provides financial and technical assistance required to conduct petroleum operations.
- Contractor bears the risk of the operating cost in return for an interest in the development of petroleum deposits in the contract area.
- Contract allows 6 to 10 years for exploration and 30 years' total term if commercial production is established.
- Contractor prepares annual work programmes and operating budgets to be approved by Pertamina.
- All equipment purchased by the contractor become the property of Pertamina when brought into Indonesian territory.
- Pertamina retains title to all data obtained from the operations.
- The remaining production after provision for the recovery of operating costs is shared between Pertamina and the contractor.
- Contractor is subject to pay income tax in Indonesia and Pertamina will reimburse contractor for the other taxes paid in conducting the operations.
- Contractor is obligated to supply Indonesia's domestic requirement for crude oil, called the domestic market obligation (DMO).
- Pertamina may demand that a 10% undivided interest in the contract be offered to itself or to an Indonesian entity at the time that the first petroleum discovery can be produced commercially.
- Costs incurred in one contract area are not recoverable from the operations of a block under separate contract.
- Contractor pays a non-recoverable signature bonus to Pertamina upon signing of the PSC.

Source: Pertamina (1996b).

These are designed to reduce Pertamina's exploration costs while opening previously explored low-risk areas to foreign firms. In a JOB, Pertamina is the operator and it is assisted by a contractor. A Joint Operating Committee (OPCOM), whose members are from Pertamina and the contractor, supervises the arrangement and approves the work programme, budget and policies. JOAs require contractors to invest an amount equal to what was previously spent by Pertamina or a foreign contractor on exploration in the area. All expenses are borne by the contractor for the first three years and, thereafter, they are shared equally with Pertamina. Production is shared equally, with the contractor's share dealt with in accordance with the negotiated terms of standard PSCs. A summary of important terms is shown in Table 15–3.

TABLE 15–2
Specific Bonuses Payable to Pertamina upon Signing of PSC

Types of Bonus	Amount (US$'000)
For receiving information, payable within 30 days of the signing of the contract.	750
Assistance to Pertamina in the form of equipment or services.	100
For the cumulative production of oil and gas of 25,000,000 barrels of oil equivalent.	4,000
For the cumulative production of oil and gas of 50,000,000 barrels of oil equivalent.	5,000
For the cumulative production of oil and gas of 100,000,000 barrels of oil equivalent.	5,000
For the cumulative production of oil and gas of 150,000,000 barrels of oil equivalent.	5,000
For the cumulative production of oil and gas of 200,000,000 barrels of oil equivalent.	5,000

Source: *Petrominer*, June 1996.

TABLE 15–3
Terms of a Joint Operating Agreement (JOA)

- Pertamina holds a 50% participating interest.
- Contractor's 50% is subject to the same terms and split as used in current PSCs.
- Pertamina is the operator assisted by the contractor in the form of a Joint Operating Body (JOB) which is responsible to, and supervised by, a Joint Operating Committee (OPCOM) whose members are from Pertamina and the contractor.
- OPCOM approves Work Programme and Budget (WPB) and policies.
- Contractor advances Pertamina's shared expenses in exploration and development stages.
- A 50% uplift is applicable to the amount of repayment by Pertamina to the contractor.
- Pertamina sunk costs are recoverable.

Source: Pertamina (1996b).

(ii) ***Enhanced Oil Recovery (EOR) Contract***: EORs were first introduced in 1979 and they form a specific type of PSC applicable to recovery programmes aimed at boosting production from existing fields. The primary oil production profile of each production zone is agreed on prior to contract signing. A contractor only receives a share in any oil produced in excess of the primary oil production. Cost and incremental oil produced are governed by the same terms as the JOA, except that a 65% cost recovery ceiling is applied. Costs incurred by Pertamina downstream are chargeable to an EOR operation on a pro-rata basis. The initial two contract years are allowed for the pilot phase and, thereafter, the full EOR project commences. A summary of important contractual terms is shown in Table 15–4.

TABLE 15–4
Terms of an Enhanced Oil Recovery (EOR) Contract

- The scope encompasses the pilot phase, the injection of water and fluid handling and treating facilities, drilling/workover of injection and production wells, injection system, flowlines until the connecting flanges to the manifold inlet of Pertamina's gathering stations.
- Incremental oil production determined for each production zone and agreed to prior to contract signing.
- Each cost and incremental oil produced are governed by the same terms as the JOA, except that a 65% cost recovery ceiling is applied.
- Cost incurred by Pertamina downstream are chargeable to EOR operation on a pro-rata basis.
- The initial two contract years are allowed for the pilot phase. Thereafter, the full EOR project will commence.

Source: Pertamina (1996b).

(iii) ***Technical Assistance Contract (TAC)***: TACs are another type of production sharing arrangement applicable to areas which have already been producing oil. Under a TAC, a contractor takes over the operation of a producing field from Pertamina. The cost of equipment and services for the primary crude oil becomes part of the operating cost which is limited to a maximum of 35% of what is extracted. After cost recovery, the contractor's net share is 35% while 65% goes to Pertamina. There is a domestic market obligation (DMO) contribution of US$0.20 per barrel from a contractor's production share. The contractual terms are summarised in Table 15–5.

TABLE 15–5
Terms of a Technical Assistance Contract (TAC)

- The contractor is entitled to share in the shareable crude (crude other than the primary).
- Cost of equipment and services for the primary crude will become part of the operating cost.
- The operating cost is a maximum of 35% of total shareable lifting.
- Out of contractor's share of shareable crude there is an obligatory DMO contribution valued at US$0.20/bbl.
- After the cost recovery, contractor's net share is 35% and 65% for Pertamina.

Source: Pertamina (1996b).

Government Incentives

Analysts of the Indonesian oil industry have predicted that Indonesia would become a net importer of petroleum within the next decade. Decreasing oil production combined with increasing domestic consumption could lead to net imports of crude and petroleum products. Although oil production increased in 1994 and imports of oil products declined (American Embassy, 1995), Indonesia becoming a net importer remains a strong possibility. To prevent this outcome, the government needs to maintain production levels, decrease imports and spur exploration to bolster dwindling levels of proven reserves.

Indonesia produced an estimated 1.61 million barrels per day (bpd) of crude oil and condensate in 1994 which was 5% higher than in 1993. Nonetheless, analysts foresee declining production. Few new major oil field discoveries have occurred in the last several years. In 1994, the number of exploration wells drilled and the discoveries made were fewer than in 1993. Reduced earnings by major energy companies as a result of lower oil prices has meant fewer dollars available for exploration. Moreover, areas such as the former Soviet Union, Vietnam, Myanmar and China have been attracting scarce exploration dollars (TDB, 1994). Thus, the government released its fourth exploration incentive package in August 1993. The details are shown in Table 15–6. Several conditions apply to the incentives. They are shown in Table 15–7.

TABLE 15–6
Summary of 1993 Petroleum Incentive Package

Terms and Conditions	Conventional	Frontier Area
Depreciation of capital costs (oil)	Depreciation is calculated using accelerated (double declining balance) method.	Same as for conventional area.
Depreciation of capital costs (gas)	Depreciation is calculated over 50% of the assets' useful life irrespective of the size of the reserves.	Same as for conventional area.
Amortisation of intangible drilling costs	Recovery of intangible costs of drilling exploratory and development wells can be made directly in the year.	Same as for conventional area.
Tariff on income tax and tax on interest	48%. Any other taxes such as value added tax, duties and other levies on import shall be borne by the government.	Same as for conventional area.
Split equity after tax	Oil: 85/15; Gas: 70/30	Oil: 65/35; Gas: 60/40
Split equity for pre-tertiary rocks (oil)	Incremental; 0–50,000 bpd: 80/20; 50,000–150,000 bpd: 85/15; > 150,000 bpd: 90/10	Same as above.
Split equity for marginal field (oil)	80/20	Same as above.
First tranche petroleum	20%	15%
DMO price (after first five years)	15% export price.	25% export price.
Investment credit	17% unconditional.	None.
Investment credit for pre-tertiary rock	Oil: 110%; Gas: 110%	None.
Extension of contract	1 × 4 years.	1 × 4 years.

Source: American Embassy (1995).

TABLE 15–7
Conditions of the Fourth Incentive Package: August 1993

- The 1993 incentive package must be applied as a whole; no individual item may be applied independently.
- Existing operators have the option to apply either the 1993 incentive package or the previous incentive packages to frontier terms.
- The 1993 incentive package is also aimed at promoting economies of discoveries which were not feasible to be developed under previous incentive packages. Therefore, it is applicable not only to new contracts but, also, to the existing non-producing contracts.
- Frontier areas are defined as:
  - Eastern Indonesia: all areas excluding Bintuni, Salawati and Seram basins.
  - Western Indonesia: offshore areas in West Sumatra, offshore areas in South Java and any offshore areas with water depth of more than 200 metres, Intramontane basins of Sumatra, West and Central Kalimantan.

Source: American Embassy (1995).

The new package has not provided encouragement for investors to accelerate investment in exploration in the high risk, high cost eastern Indonesian oil province. Pertamina attributes the drop in exploration to factors beyond government control including reduced earnings by major energy companies, lower oil prices and fewer dollars for exploration. Oil companies based in Indonesia claim that the major reason for not committing resources to Indonesia is because of a fiscal regime which remains unattractive despite the improvements implemented in 1993 (American Embassy, 1995). They favour improvements that would reduce the cost of exploration. For example, eliminating the "ring fence" provision would allow expenditures in non-producing PSC areas to be offset against revenues in producing areas through tax consolidation. At present, taxable income is determined on a contract area by contract area basis, an arrangement referred to in the industry as the "ring fence". Indonesian tax law allows other industries outside the petroleum and minerals sectors to consolidate statements from subsidiaries for determining tax income. In addition, many other oil producing countries which are competing with Indonesia for exploration dollars allow tax consolidation.

Although this change would probably decrease government revenue initially, it would be a powerful incentive for exploration activities. The expected increase in exploration and production would lead to higher revenue through the development of new discoveries.

Tax deductions would effectively reduce the cost of dry holes by one-half, thus encouraging companies to drill in risky and high cost areas. Industry sources note that about 75% of current exploration takes place in producing areas where companies can deduct costs which would not otherwise be allowed from cost consolidation.

Tax consolidation, however, will not be implemented soon. The government is reluctant to permit consolidation since the cost of a dry hole is difficult to verify. Secondly, the government is afraid of losing revenue. The Minister of Mines and Energy, Ida Bagus Sudjana, believes that further incentives will be held back because foreign investment is still sufficiently high. To maintain crude production level, Pertamina will increase co-operation with existing oil companies instead.

UPSTREAM INDUSTRY AND SUPPORTING ACTIVITIES

The upstream industry involves the exploration and production of petroleum. Activities start with the signing of a PSC contract. This is followed by supporting activities which include a geological survey, drilling rigs, logging and testing services, downhole equipment, tubular (casing and tubing), wellhead and completion equipment, pipe line, mechanical and electronic gages, cementing, acidising, platform construction, and other activities related to exploration and production. The industry is characterised by cyclical activities depending on the international price of oil and gas. If oil prices are predicted to go up, then exploration and development spending both increase which results in more activities for the supporting industry.

In the upstream industry, American companies have played a major role in the exploration and production of oil and gas in Indonesia. Tables 15–8 and 15–9 show the top five producers of crude oil and gas in 1994. In supporting activities, American companies also dominate the market, with the exception of tubular (casings and tubings) where Japanese companies dominate the market. Some local companies have entered the market in low technology areas such as drilling supplies, cementing and testing.

Government Regulations

All oil companies buy equipment and services under Pertamina guidelines. Pertamina's Migas and BPPKA set the guidelines of tender and make the final decision on large purchases. Unlike traditional manufacturing, oil and gas equipment and services must be purchased through a local limited liability company. As such, foreign companies wanting to sell equipment and services relating to the oil and gas industry must set up a local company either by themselves or with a local joint venture partner to sell the products. They may also appoint a local company to act as their local agent. These companies may sell direct to Pertamina or its production sharing contractors without a distributor (*Petrominer*, August 1996b).

TABLE 15–8
Top Five Producers of Crude Oil in 1994

Company	Crude and Condensate Production (thousands of barrels/day)
Caltex (Riau, central Sumatra)	696.7
Maxus (southeast Sumatra)	132.7
Conoco (Natuna/Irian Jaya)	110.6
Arco (northwest Java)	100.7
Mobil Oil (North Sumatra)	91.8

Source: American Embassy (1995).

TABLE 15–9
Top Five Producers of Gas in 1994

Company	Natural Gas Production (millions of cubic feet)
Mobil Oil	1,217,066
VICO	585,539
Total	309,846
Arco	240,576
Pertamina	222,769

Source: American Embassy (1995).

The decree of the Pertamina Board of Directors, No. Kpts.108/-Coooo/94-50, provides guidance for the procurement of goods and services within the periphery of Pertamina and its PSCs. Of importance to the supplier is the requirement of local content detailed in the decree. The local content is one of the most important factors in determining who wins a bid. The formula used to calculate the local content is the finished product price minus imported raw material, components, and engineering, divided by the finished product price. The higher the local content, the more favourable is the bid. As such, equipment and service suppliers with a local joint venture (JV) partnership in Indonesia will be favoured by Pertamina and its PSCs.

The Suppliers

Potential investors have several options in participating in the business of oil-related and gas-related products and services. One option is for a foreign company to establish a temporary relationship for a specific sale or purpose. This provides high flexibility with the lowest risk. However, this arrangement increases the difficulty of becoming established in the market. A second option is an agency arrangement whereby one sole agent represents one or more foreign companies. This form of agency provides continuity and presence.

A third option is direct investment. Since the equipment and services are open to direct investment, this arrangement requires a large investment. The present law, government regulation No. 20/1994 and *Decree on the President of the Republic of Indonesia* No. 31/1995, allows 100% foreign direct investment (FDI) for 15 years after the commencement of commercial operations. A percentage of the shares must be sold to the government or the stock exchange after this period. The law does not specify the percentage and it is up to the investor to divest. Regulation No. 20 has attracted many foreign direct investors. Sources in FMC Santana have indicated that if the company, a joint venture wellhead and christmas tree supplier, had the opportunity to invest again in a manufacturing plant, then it would invest in a 100% equity plant. This would permit better control over operations.

A fourth and commonly practised arrangement is the JV. The law specifies that at least 5% of the total paid up capital must be owned by the Indonesian partner upon establishing the JV. A minimum paid up capital of US$1 million investment is required for investment by hardware suppliers and US$500,000 for investment by service providers.

A final option is investment through a local company. Since the local company generally lacks technical expertise, it usually forms an alliance with a foreign company or hires consultants to run its operations. These companies have a low cost advantage which is favoured by Pertamina but not the foreign oil companies because the former's service and equipment are not of the same quality as those of the multinationals.

Integrated Services

Integrated services are turnkey services which package multi-service and equipment supply into one source. It is also called an EPCI (engineering, procurement, construction, and installation) contract. The advantage is that it prevents a multi-tender process for service and equipment. This results in simpler project management, reduces the project time, and lowers the cost of the oil companies and the suppliers. One example is Schlumberger which can offer a drilling rig complete with wireline, cementing, measurement-while-drilling (MWD) and mud logging into one package. For a typical contract, each service or product has to be evaluated and the oil companies need to write the technical specifications for the service or product. The EPCI approach, however, is not common even though it is preferred by the oil companies. EPCIs tend to lessen the chance of local companies winning a contract since large multinationals are experts in the process.

Bidding

According to sources in FMC Singapore, the bidding process with production-sharing contractors is conducted in the following manner. For the supply of goods or services, an oil company evaluates the technical package first. This is followed by an evaluation of the commercial package. The lowest priced bidder does not necessarily win since the company also evaluates the local content, speed of delivery and past performance of the supplier. After considering these factors, an oil company normally invites the suppliers for technical and commercial presentations. Only at this time does an oil company announce the winner of the bid. The appointment of the supplier must be approved by Pertamina's BPPKA. If the value of the bid exceeds Rp10 billion (approximately US$4.5 million), then BPPKA must obtain the approval of the Coordinating Minister of Economy.

According to various sources, one important tactic used by oil companies to lower the bid price is the re-tender. After the suppliers' prices are revealed, they are forced to lower their prices in the second round.

The following factors determine who wins a bid:

(i) ***Technical Capability and Price***: Technical capability can be built into a tender specification favouring one specific supplier. This works by the supplier approaching the oil company to convince it of the supplier's technical superiority. This can result in tender specifications that includes the supplier's peculiar product design features and project management capabilities.

(ii) ***Price, Speed of Delivery and After-sales Support***: These are critical factors when all the suppliers competing for a bid have similar technical capabilities. According to sources in FMC Singapore, on-time delivery has proven to be a deciding factor in winning bids.

(iii) ***Presence***: A customer generally feels more comfortable when the salespeople and service personnel are available when needed. As noted by the experience of FMC Santana, the quality and presence of service personnel are just as important as the quality of a product. Once a product is shipped, service personnel installing the equipment charge between US$450 to US$850 per day. Typical field assignments last about seven days. The revenue from servicing a product can amount to 20% of a product's sales price.

(iv) ***Local Content***: As required by Pertamina, any bid must include the necessary local content. A high local content can be achieved by having a JV plant in Indonesia.

(v) ***Preliminary Price Quotation***: Before an oil company invites a formal bid, it will request for rough-order-of-magnitude (ROM) pricing from suppliers for internal budgeting purposes. During this period, suppliers must ensure that the oil company receives high quality service. Good supplier performance during this initial period will be taken into account favourably during the formal bid evaluation.

(vi) ***Personal Relationships***: In most instances, good personal relationships with the oil companies help a supplier to win a bid.

Setting up the Equipment and Services Supply Agency

A JV arrangement provides a supplier with the strongest local presence. Selecting a partner has to be done carefully. In many cases, local partners allow a foreign supplier a free hand in running the day-to-day operations. Local partners may only provide some capital. The JV usually takes the form of a P. T. (*perseroan terbatas*) which is a private limited company. FMC Indonesia selected P. T. Kodel as its partner since FMC's chemical division had a long term agency co-operation agreement with them in marketing pest control and grower chemicals in Indonesia.

It is important to protect the assets after a JV company is formed. This can be done by ensuring that equipment, land and other assets are registered under the company. A foreign investor should structure the JV agreement to have a majority vote in the company. This way, the investor's assets will not be acquired by the partner during economic downturns.

DOWNSTREAM INDUSTRY

Oil Refining

Crude oil refineries are currently geared to Indonesia's domestic fuel demands. Petroleum products are exported only if there is an over supply in the domestic market. Products for domestic consumption are mainly the middle distillates. The more common refined products include aviation fuel, kerosene, gasoline, diesel, fuel oil, naphtha, asphalt and coke. Some of these refined products, such as naphtha, are used as feedstock for chemical plants.

Indonesia has nine producing refineries with a combined design capacity of 990,000 barrels per day (bpd). The refineries are Pangkalan Bradan, Dumai, Sungai Pakning, Musi, Cilacap, Cepu, Wonokromo, Balikpapan and Balongan. Balongan in West Java is the first export-oriented refinery with a design capacity of 125,000 bpd.

(i) ***Current Refinery Projects***: The Balongan refinery is a US$2 billion investment and it was brought on stream in mid-1995. It processes 125,000 bpd of domestic crude oil to produce 136,000 metric tons of liquefied petroleum gas (LPG) per year, 186,000 metric tons of propylene per year, 54,500 bpd of gasoline, 10,437 bpd of kerosene, 24,500 bpd of automotive diesel fuel, 14,890 bpd of industrial diesel fuel and 7,200 bpd of decant oil, as well as 27 metric tons of sulphur per day.

The Musi refinery upgrading project combined the Royal Dutch Shell and Stanvac refineries into one refinery. The main purpose of the US$270 million upgrading is to improve the quality of the products, especially the middle distillates. Pertamina is considering raising the refinery's throughput but first it must find an economic means of transporting more crude oil up the heavily utilised Musi river.

De-bottlenecking the Cilacap refinery will increase plant capacity from 300,000 bpd to 348,000 bpd and is scheduled for completion in 1999. Output will include 45,000 metric tons of LPG per year, 50,000 metric tons of gasoline per year, 175,000 metric tons of lubricating base oil per year, 205,000 metric tons of asphalt per year, 350,000 metric tons of naphtha per year and 425,000 metric tons of low sulphur waxy residue per year.

The Balikpapan upgrade project will cost US$407 million. In addition to increasing production capacity from 45,000 bpd to 65,000 bpd, it will enable the refinery to process a wider range of crude so that it can process the Middle East crude in addition to the declining Kalimantan output.

The pipeline supply in the Jakarta region is on a build-operate-transfer (BOT) basis. A 221-kilometre pipeline carries petroleum products from the Balongan refinery to the Jakarta region where there is a demand for gas, oil for vehicles, generating electricity and home cooking fuels. The pipeline's capacity is seven million kilolitres of fuel per year. There are plans to expand this pipeline, and the Cilacap to Yogyakarta and Bandung product pipelines. Plans also include a 120-kilometre pipeline from Balongan to Tasikmalaya, a 60-kilometre pipeline from Sukabumi to Padalarang and another 40-kilometre pipeline from Rewulu to Semarang.

The Sorong "mini-refinery" has a US$75 million budget in Irian Jaya. It will process crude from sites near the facility. The refinery has a maximum capacity of 15,000 bpd and is scheduled for completion by the end of 1997.

(ii) ***Proposed Refinery Projects***: As of October 1996, 36 companies applied for licences to build new refineries in Indonesia and 13 have received permission to build facilities.[1] However, none of these proposed projects are in the construction stage. It is unlikely that any of these refineries will be built until Indonesia deregulates the downstream sector which is currently under review by the Ministry of Mines and Energy.

Under the *Pertamina Law* of 1971, the marketing and distribution of petroleum products may be undertaken only by Pertamina. The government sets the product prices. Until these conditions are changed the proposed refineries will not be able to give their owners an acceptable return on their investment. A summary listing these proposed projects is found in Appendix 15–2.

Petrochemical Industries in Indonesia

In the last few years, Indonesia's petrochemical industry has grown robustly. It now covers almost all branches of the industry including aromatics, olefins and natural gas-based petrochemicals. Its market size has grown at an average annual rate of 12.3% in the last five years due mainly to the increasing number of downstream petrochemical plants built in the country. This trend has shifted Indonesia's domestic reliance on imports for petrochemical products.

(i) ***Aromatics***: Pertamina's aromatic plant located at Plaju in southern Sumatra was completed in 1988. It is now producing 225,000 tons per year of purified terephthalic (PTA) and the Bakrie group also produces 250,000 tons of PTA a year, thus securing the domestic textile industries of raw material for polyester. In conjunction with Mitsui Petrochemical Industries, Amoco is constructing a 350,000 tons per year PTA plant at Merak, West Java, which began production in July 1997.

Pertamina's plant in Cilacap, Central Java, produces 120,000 tons a year of benzene and 270,000 tons per year of paraxylene, which is being used as feed stock for the Plaju aromatic plant. P. T. Humpuss Aromatic, a 70,000 bpd condensate processing and aromatics petrochemical facility near the Arun LNG plant in Aceh, is currently under construction. The facility will have the

[1] Source: Sugihono Kadarisman, Deputy Chairman for Promotions, BKPM, December 1996.

capacity to produce 370,000 tons per year of paraxylene and 160,000 tons per year of benzene when it is completed.

(ii) ***Olefins***: This sector has experienced extraordinary growth over the last five years because of the operation of new plants in the downstream industry. Some of these projects are shown in Table 15–10.

Prior to the operation of P. T. Chandra Asri in 1994, upstream olefin products were entirely imported. Now the Chandra Asri plant has a capacity of 522,000 tons per year of ethylene and 243,000 tons per year of propylene.

(iii) ***Natural Gas-based Petrochemical Industry***: The natural gas-based petrochemical industry was the pioneer of Indonesia's petrochemical industry. Natural gas is used as a basic ingredient in the production of methanol, urea and ammonia. It has a stable market size because the demand for its downstream products such as urea fertilizer and adhesives has been relatively stable. Since 20% of Indonesia's GDP is from agriculture, urea fertilizer demand has been high.

TABLE 15–10
New Plants in the Olefins Sector

Company	Product	Capacity (tons per year)
Tri Polyta Indonesia	Polypropylene	320,000
JGC Corporation	Polypropylene	100,000
P. T. Pusaka Warna	Polypropylene	140,000
P. T. Polypropylene Perkasa's	Polypropylene	200,000
P. T. Polytama Propindo	Polypropylene	100,000
P. T. Indotara Semesta	Polypropylene	180,000
P. T. Petrokimia Nusantara's	Polyethylene	400,000
Chandra Asri	Polyethylene Polypropylene	300,000 80,000

Source: American Embassy (1995).

The government has opened the fertilizer industry to the private sector but there has been little interest due to price controls by the government and the need to meet domestic demand first before exporting any products. The government subsidises the price of urea for farmers by setting the price of natural gas feed stock at a low level of US$1 per million BTU. The list of urea and ammonia or fertilizer producers is given in Table 15–11.

Marketing and Distribution

Retailing petroleum products in Indonesia is presently closed to private investment because of *Law 44* of 1960 which states that only state enterprises may exploit petroleum and natural gas, and because of the *Pertamina Law* of 1971 which restricts the marketing and distribution rights of petroleum products to Pertamina. Although the Ministry of Mines and Energy is exploring the feasibility of deregulation, the outcome is still uncertain. However, investment opportunities in the marketing and distribution of petroleum products are not completely closed to foreign investment as joint venture companies with manufacturing facilities are now allowed to market their products through local distributors.[2] Figure 15–1 shows the distribution channel for lubricant products prior to the opening of the market to foreign investment.

TABLE 15–11
Urea and Ammonia Producers

Producer	Location	Urea Capacity (tons/year)	Ammonia Capacity (tons/year)
Pupuk Sriwidjaya	Palembang, South Sumatra	2,280,000	1,500,000
Pupuk Kaltim	Bontang, East Kalimantan	1,841,000	1,320,000
Pupuk Kujang	Cikampek, West Java	570,000	396,000
ASEAN Fertilizer	Aceh, Sumatra	684,000	380,000
Pupuk Iskandar Muda	Aceh, Sumatra	656,000	396,000
Petrokimia Gresik	Gresik, East Java	462,000	446,000

Source: American Embassy (1995).

2 Source: Sugihono Kadarisman, Deputy Chairman for Promotions, BKPM, December 1996.

FIGURE 15–1
Old Distribution Channel for Lubricant Products

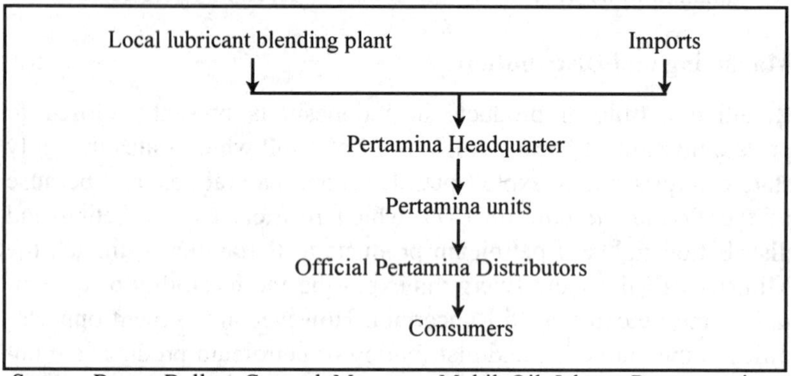

Source: Bryan Dellar, General Manager, Mobil Oil Jakarta Representative Office, December 1996.

With the deregulation of the marketing and distribution of lubricants applicable to joint venture companies with manufacturing facilities in Indonesia, the new distribution channel assumes the structure shown in Figure 15–2.

FIGURE 15–2
New Distribution Channel for Lubricant Products

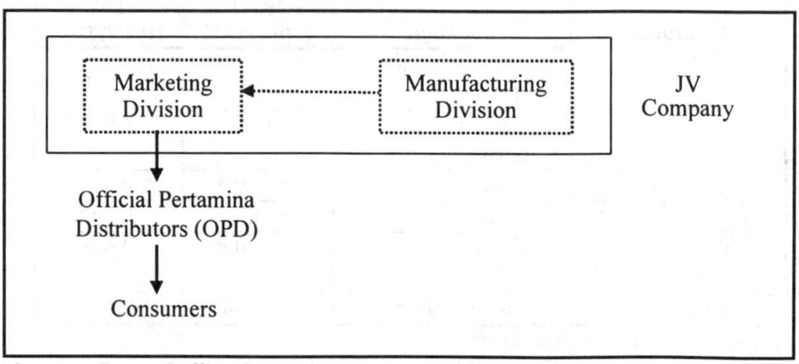

Source: Bryan Dellar, General Manager, Mobil Oil Jakarta Representative Office, December 1996.

In the interim wait for a JV's manufacturing facilities to be completed, it can engage in pre-marketing by acquiring supplies from

Pertamina.[3] With further deregulation of the industry expected by 2003, JV companies will be able to sell to consumers directly.

In summary, Pertamina sells and distributes petroleum products, and investors are allowed to sell their products only through Pertamina. Investors may produce the products in their local manufacturing plants or import them. Pertamina may allow foreign investment in marketing and selling of petroleum products on a case by case basis.

Power Generation

The Indonesian government is encouraging the private sector to use geothermal sources and gas for power generation to reduce the dependency on oil. At present, oil provides 58% of Indonesia's energy needs, gas 25%, coal 9%, hydropower 6% and geothermal 2%. The supply of electricity has been scarce, especially in Java, where the growth in demand has out-paced its supply. Consequently, the government is encouraging private investment in geothermal powered infrastructure.

Natural Gas

Indonesia's natural gas production increased 10.5% in 1994 to 2,942 billion cubic feet (bcf) which is 2.6% of world output or 8.2 bcf per day. This is an energy equivalent of 1.39 million barrels of oil per day, or slightly less than the country's oil and condensate production. Pertamina has predicted that gas production will exceed 3,200 bcf by 1999 in response to the increase in domestic and export demand. Approximately 75% of the natural gas will be converted into LNG, 10% for fertilizer plants and 4% for power generation.

LNG for export comes from the Arun field in northern Sumatra and Bontang in eastern Kalimantan. The LNG is exported mostly to South Korea, Taiwan and Japan. In August 1995, two agreements worth US$20.3 billion were signed with Japan and Korea for an extended 11 and 8 years, respectively.

The future Natuna gas development project is estimated at US$35 billion to US$40 billion and Exxon, Mobil and Pertamina are

---

3 Source: Bryan Dellar, General Manager, Mobil Oil Jakarta Representative Office, December 1996.

the partners. Requests for budget estimates on the equipment for the project have been released to bidders by the consortium which is expected to start operating before the end of 1997.

ENVIRONMENTAL ISSUES

As Indonesia becomes more developed economically, attention is being focused on environmental issues. In January 1996, Environment Minister Sarwono Kusumaatmadja, in a seminar on implementing the 14000 series of the International Organisation of Standards (ISO), urged Indonesian companies to obtain international environmental standards certificates.[4] The ISO 14000 series is aimed at increasing the efficiency and quality of environmental management systems. The impact of these international standards for trade and services in the international markets is significant since 55% of Indonesian products are for export. It is especially important for the oil and gas industry since 24% of all exports come from this sector. Indonesian laws will require the use of unleaded gas by the year 1999.

With export going to countries that have strict environmental requirements as well as vocal local non-governmental organisations calling out for environmental protection in Indonesia, oil companies will need to implement comprehensive environmental management systems. Implementation of their action programmes will have a direct impact on the costs of their operations. Since the safety, health, and environmental (SHE) issues are voluntary, the government must depend on the moral obligations of the oil companies. Fortunately, multinational oil companies are under tremendous pressure at their central headquarters to apply a comprehensive SHE programme. Caltex Pacific Indonesia (CPI), for example, has an SHE audit every three years and it hires a third party to conduct the audit and develop a programme to improve its performance (*Petrominer*, October 1996a). A reliance on such social obligations of the oil and gas companies has not protected the environment sufficiently. Discharging drilling cuttings and biological waste into the sea is widely

---

[4] Source: Internet URL, http://www.newsindonesia.com, News and Views Indonesia, 1996.

practised even though it is illegal under the Convention on Dumping of Wastes and Harmful Materials in the U.S.

OPPORTUNITIES

Oil and Gas Exploration and Production

The government plans to maintain the total crude production at about 1.5 million barrels per day, which is the OPEC production ceiling for Indonesia (see Table 15–12). To sustain production, there will be steady activities in the upstream and supporting industries and dried wells will be replaced by producing ones.

Gas production is much more promising since it is not subject to an OPEC production ceiling. The market for gas is huge as evidenced by the long term contracts of LNG supply to South Korea, Japan and Taiwan. The needs of fertilizer plants and power generating plants enhance this market. Given these opportunities, Mobil Indonesia, the biggest gas producer in Indonesia, bought the Ampolex concession[5] and a 26% equity in the Natuna gas development from Pertamina (*Petrominer*, September 1996). It hopes to keep its commitment of gas supply for LNG exports to Pertamina.

TABLE 15–12
Five-Year Plan for Oil Production
(in '000 of barrels per day)

	1994/95	1995/96	1996/97	1997/98	1998/99
Primary	968.0	855.5	738.0	650.3	584.4
EOR	358.6	394.3	507.3	602.3	655.0
New	0.6	3.9	16.9	26.9	39.4
Total crude	1,365.8	1,357.1	1,352.2	1,360.0	1,354.4
Condensate	164.2	162.9	162.9	150.0	145.6
Total oil	1,530.0	1,520.0	1,515.0	1,510.0	1,500.0

Source: American Embassy (1995).

5 Source: Bryan Dellar, General Manager, Mobil Oil Jakarta Representative Office, December 1996.

ARCO, the fourth largest oil and gas producer in 1994, has been increasing its offshore oil and gas production in northeast Java and the Kangean blocks. This gas production has been feeding a fertiliser factory, a cement factory and an electric generator east of Java. ARCO's investment as of August 1996 was over US$9 billion. To date, PSCs operated by ARCO have generated revenue of US$23 billion with the government receiving 53% of this amount. Recovery costs have amounted to 34% of revenue, with 13% going to ARCO. An additional US$15 billion of revenue is projected over the next ten years. Recent gas discoveries in the Wiriagar and Berau blocks in northern Irian Jaya promise additional revenue of US$21 billion with US$11 billion going to the government.

ARCO recognises the risk in oil exploration and production. When ARCO secures a PSC, it forms a partnership to limit its share accordingly. To reduce its development cost, ARCO contracted with a third party to build a pipeline for transmitting the gas from Pagerungan island to Gresik in East Java. ARCO pays a fee for each unit volume transmitted through the pipeline.

Geothermal

The government has been encouraging the private sector to utilise geothermal energy for electricity because it is a non-polluting energy source that reduces the dependency on diesel fired power generation. Demand for electricity is growing at 15% per year. During the next decade, 20,000 megawatts (MW) of capacity will be added to the existing 13,000 MW. Peak demand in Java, where the availability of the geothermal energy is abundant, is projected to reach 21,000 MW by the year 2000.

Equipment Refurbishment

Oil exploration and drilling equipment may last longer than the well itself. Wellheads and christmas trees, for example, are designed for a 20-year life. After an oil well is depleted, the wellhead and christmas tree can be removed and refurbished for resale.

Other

Indonesian regulations require the use of unleaded fuel by 1999. Local refineries have to be upgraded and this presents good business opportunities for both local and foreign companies.

TABLE 15–13
ARCO's PSCs in Indonesia

PSC	Year	ARCO's Share (%)	Ult. Rec.[4] Reserves MBOE[2]	Explora-tion Wells	Current Production MBOEPD[3]
Producing					
ONWJ[5]	1967+	46	1,985	327	156
Malacca	1970–93	33	185	53	30
N.E. Kalimantan	1970–84	25	40	17	54
Kangean	1980+	54	470	18	54
Subtotal			**2,680**	**415**	**294**
Non-producing					
N.E. Irian	1970–76	50	-	-	-
KBSA	1989–92	28	-	2	-
Seram	1985+	53	100[1]	3	-
Kalosi	1991+	50	-	1	-
Babo	1993+	40	-	1	-
Wiriagar	1993+	80	380[1]	1	-
Berau	1995+	48	880[1]	3	-
Sepanjang	1995+	54	5[1]	1	-
Subtotal			**1,365**[1]	**12**	-
Grand Total			**4,045**	**427**	**294**

Legend:

1 Known, potentially commercial.
2 Million barrels of oil equivalent.
3 Million barrels of oil equivalent per day.
4 Ultimate recoverable.
5 Offshore northWest Java.

Source: *Petrominer*, August 1996a.

CONCLUSION

With a large domestic market and a liberalised investment and fiscal policy, Indonesia offers opportunities to investors who understand the system and are able to work within it. For example, Exxon has successfully negotiated with the government in the Natuna development for a favourable corporate tax rate and equity interest. An investor has to ensure that any proposed projects are in line with strategic government policies in order to enjoy any special incentives. As Minister of Trade and Industry, Tunky Ariwibowo, noted in January 1996, “Incentives will be given to those after a very specific, case by case, company by company, and product by product evaluation” (*The Straits Times*, 7 January 1997).

Oil exploration has been relatively successful as shown in Table 15–14. The relatively high success ratio suggests that Indonesia is one of the most attractive places to invest in oil and gas.

Changes in the downstream industry have favoured private investors in the last few years. Success in the industry depends on the resourcefulness of investors in finding opportunities within the system and the ability to negotiate with Pertamina. This was demonstrated by Mobil Indonesia in its project to erect a lubricant plant. Furthermore, the government is in the process of replacing current laws so that traditionally closed sectors, such as the distribution and marketing of fuel oil will finally be opened.

TABLE 15–14
Oil and Gas Success Ratio

	Oil	**Gas**	**Dry**	**Total**	**Success Ratio**
1993					
Wildcat	11	14	46	71	35.2
Appraisal	16	13	14	43	67.2
Total	**27**	**27**	**60**	**114**	**47.3**
1994					
Wildcat	7	13	32	52	38.0
Appraisal	7	12	8	27	70.0
Total	**14**	**25**	**40**	**79**	**49.0**

Source: American Embassy (1995).

APPENDIX 15–1
Pertamina Organisation Chart

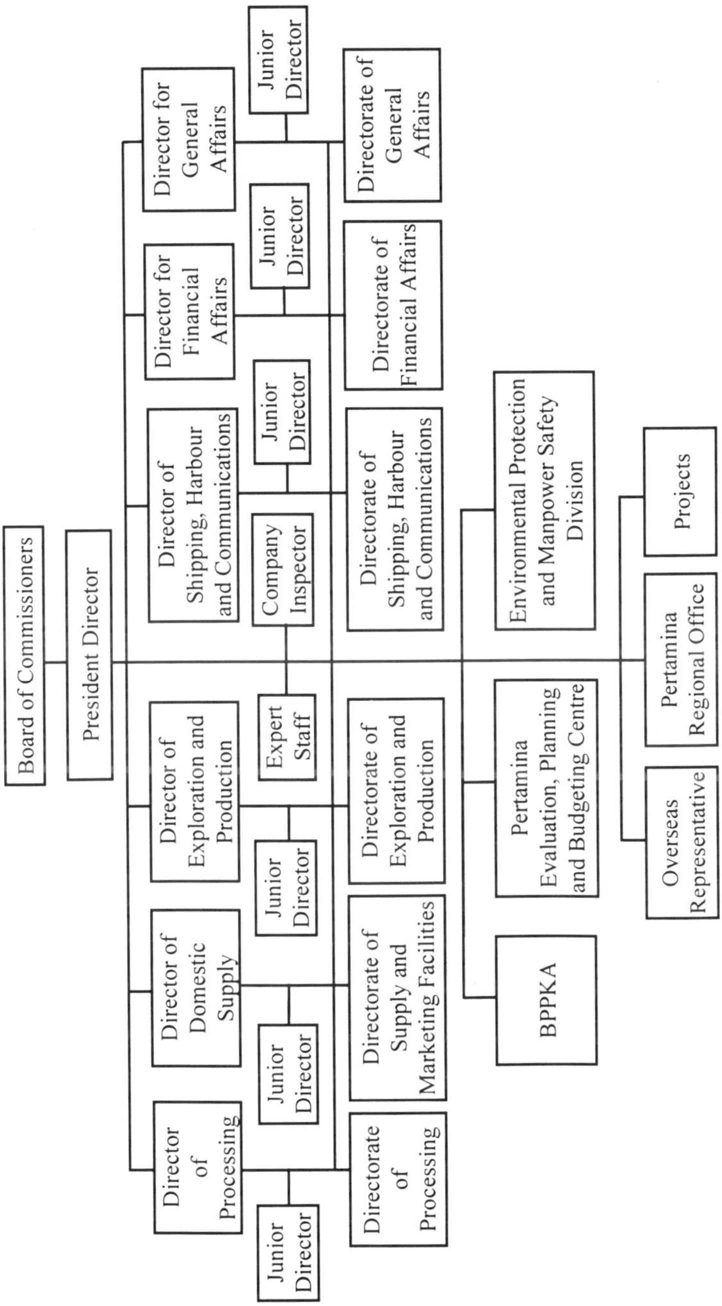

APPENDIX 15–2
Proposed Oil Refinery Projects

No.	Company/Location	Capacity (bbl/day)	Investment (US$m)	Status
1	P. T. Sabang Oil refinery, Aceh	N/A	1,588	Awaiting BKPM approval
2	P. T. Tanjung Uban refinery (U.K.), Riau	120,000	1,500	Approved November 1992
3	P. T. Asia Pacific Petroleum Ltd. (Hong Kong), Situbundo, East Java	300,000	1,096	Approved July 1994
4	Wisertech Limited (Hong Kong) & P. T. Ganda Buana Perkasa, Probolinggo, East Java	300,000	3,500	Approved July 1994
5	P. T. Sumber Catur Daya Nusantara Corp, Pare-pare, South Sulawesi	125,000	1,320	Approved November 1994
6	P. T. First Indra Corp. / P. T. Indo-Xo Ltd., Sorong, Irian Jaya	175,000	2,000	Approved February 1995
7	P. T. Norco Internusal / FWB Wheeler (Australia), Gresik, East Java	125,000	1,800	Approved February 1995
8	P. T. Paras Refining Company, East Java	125,000	3,000	Approved July 1995
9	P. T. Hadirindo Wanajaya Ltd., Serang, W Java	125,000	2,000	Approved May 1995
10	Pare-pare Refining Corp., South Sulawesi	125,000	1,600	Approved July 1995
11	P. T. Asia Pacific Petroleum (Hong Kong), Bontang, East Kalimantan	N/A	N/A	Approved July 1995
12	P. T. Tujuh Belas Augustus Ltd., South Sulawesi	N/A	800	Plan
13	P. T. Nusamba / Mitsubishi Corp., Lombok	N/A	1,341	Plan
14	P. T. Arvesco Handayani, Sorong, Irian Jaya	N/A	2,000	Plan
15	P. T. Mercu Buana / Spie Botgolles (France), Pangkalan Berandan, North Sumatra	N/A	1,562	Plan

APPENDIX 15–2 (cont'd)
Proposed Oil Refinery Projects

No.	Company/Location	Capacity (bbl/day)	Investment (US$m)	Status
16	P. T. Bimantara Group, Balongan, West Java	N/A	2,073	Plan
17	P. T. Nias Oil refinery, North Sumatra	N/A	1,414	Plan
18	P. T. Bakrie Group, Cilacap, Central Java or Pare-pare, Sulawesi	N/A	3,500	Plan
19	P. T. Chinese Petroleum Corp. (CPC-Taiwan), East Java/Lombok/Palu	N/A	1,600–2,000	Plan
20	P. T. Citic Chemical Co. Ltd. (RRC)			
	– Refinery, P. Sambu, Riau	N/A	N/A	Plan
	– MTBE plant, Plaju, S. Sumatra	N/A	N/A	Plan
	– Asphalt plant, Tanjung Uban	N/A	N/A	Plan
21	P. T. Barito Pacific Group, Cilegon, West Java	N/A	N/A	Plan
22	P. T. Percaminesa, P. Sambu, Riau	N/A	N/A	Plan
23	P. T. Menara Bumi Indonesia, P. Sambu, Riau	N/A	N/A	Plan
24	P. T. Tri Sakti Agung Indonesia, P. Sambu, Riau	N/A	N/A	Plan
25	P. T. Mentari Kumala Utama	N/A	N/A	Plan
26	P. T. Archacitra Internusa	N/A	N/A	Plan
27	P. T. Aquanur Indonesia	N/A	N/A	Plan
28	P. T. Biliton Referindo Indonesia, P. Belitung	N/A	N/A	Plan
29	P. T. Himpurna Roba Indonesia, Pare-pare	N/A	N/A	Plan
30	P. T. Mataram Agung Surya Mandiri	N/A	N/A	Plan
31	P. T. Minnai Corp W.L.L. (Malaysia)	N/A	N/A	Plan
32	P. T. Pacific Shinde Utama, Indonesia	N/A	N/A	Plan

APPENDIX 15–2 (cont'd)
Proposed Oil Refinery Projects

No.	Company/Location	Capacity (bbl/day)	Invest-ment (US$m)	Status
33	P. T. Teroden Holding Sdn. Bhd. (Malaysia), East Kalimantan	N/A	N/A	Plan
34	P. T. Terrasea Ltd. (Germany), East Kalimantan	N/A	N/A	Plan
35	P. T. Delila Petro Indonesia	N/A	N/A	Plan
36	P. T. Refindo Samasan Handayani, Burru, South Sulawesi	N/A	1,700	Plan

Sources: Various issues of *Petrominer*, 1996.

APPENDIX 15–3
Domestic Fuel Consumption
(million kilolitres)

	1989	1990	1991	1992	1993	1994	1995
Transportation	11.85	13.31	14.39	15.27	16.07	17.99	19.64
Industry	5.96	6.70	7.09	8.12	8.86	9.19	9.93
Household	7.41	7.85	7.99	8.46	8.53	8.80	9.14
Electricity	3.42	4.32	5.26	5.87	6.83	3.83	2.97

Source: Indonesian Petrochemical Industry (1996).

REFERENCES

American Embassy, "Petroleum Report Indonesia 1995", U.S. and Foreign Commercial Service, Embassy of the United States of America, Jakarta, November 1995.

ARCO, "Subsea Trees and Associated Running Equipment for Pagerungan PGC Development, Drill Through, Mudline Suspension Equipment, and Surface Wellhead Equipment", Arco Bali North Inc., Tender Specification number 6941118-36-A, Revision 2, September 1994.

ASEAN, *Trade and the Environment: Issues and Opportunities*, ASEAN Secretariat, Jakarta, 1995.

Barnes Philip, "Indonesia, the Political Economy of Energy", Oxford University Press for the Oxford Institute of Energy Studies, 1995.

FMC Santana, "Pagerungan Subsea Development", Quotation number JQ 94/0606R1, 4 January 1995.

INDIO, *Indonesia Source Book 1996*, Jakarta, August 1996.

Indonesian Petrochemical Industry, Internet URL, http://www.ntu.ac.sg/ntu/lib/jakarta/julaug/petroch, Indonesian Petrochemical Industry Home Page, 1996.

Internet URL, http://www.worldenergy.com, World Energy Home Page, 1996.

Internet URL, http://www.newsindonesia.com, News and Views Indonesia, 1996.

Pertamina, *Indonesia Oil and Gas Ventures 1996*, Pertamina Directorate of Exploration and Production, Jakarta, 1996a.

Pertamina, Internet URL, http://www.catalog.com/pertamina, Pertamina Home Page, 1996b.

Petrominer, "Pertamina Signs Two Production Sharing Contracts", June 1996.

Petrominer, "Indonesia to Issue New Oil and Gas Law", July 1996.

Petrominer, "Tax Consolidation Capable of Attracting Investors?", July 1996.

Petrominer, "ARCO in Indonesia", August 1996a, pp. 66–7.

Petrominer, "Government Regulations", August 1996b.

Petrominer, "P. T. PLN Always Ready as a Buyer", August 1996c, pp. 26–7.

Petrominer, "Pertamina to Ask Exxon to Reduce Stake in Natuna", September 1996.

Petrominer, "Environmental Auditing in P. T. Caltex Pacific Indonesia", October 1996a.

Petrominer, "Indonesia Stretching Its Limit", October 1996b.

Seda Maria, "Environmental Management in Asean: Perspectives on Critical Regional Issues", Institute of Southeast Asian Studies, Singapore, 1993.

TDB, *TDB Report on Indonesia*, Trade Development Board of Singapore, Singapore, 1994.

The Straits Times, "Indonesia Considers Tax Breaks for Strategic Industries", 7 January 1997.

Chapter 16

Dispute Resolution in Indonesia*

BY
C. G. DE SOUZA
M. A. KAROLEWSKI

INTRODUCTION

FOREIGN DIRECT INVESTMENT in Indonesia is regulated by the Indonesian government and normally takes the form of an equity joint venture with an Indonesian business partner. Among the many things which a potential investor must prepare for is the possibility of a dispute with joint venture partners, an employee, a local supplier or contractor, or government agencies. Such disputes can occur because of the alleged failure of one party in a joint venture or contract to honour its obligations; they may also arise from unanticipated circumstances such as the dissolution of a business or changes in government policy. This chapter reviews the main avenues for commercial dispute resolution in Indonesia from the perspective of a foreign businessman or entrepreneur. The main areas of focus are Indonesia's system of justice, the structure of the courts, recent developments in Indonesia's commercial law and, finally, arbitration.

---

* The authors wish to express their gratitude to Mr. Hotman P. Hutapea (Partner, Makarim and Taira S., Jakarta) for his assistance in providing information on legal issues relating to business disputes. Also, we appreciate the efforts and guidance received from Dr. Austin I. Pullé.

REVIEW OF INDONESIAN BUSINESS LAW

Sources of Law

During the colonial period, Indonesia's civil, commercial and criminal laws were codified and premised on the Dutch model (Hooker, 1978). Even today, the Dutch civil, commercial and penal codes remain applicable. Consequently, Indonesia's civil law system is code-based (Gautama and Hornick, 1983).

From the earliest days of colonial rule, Indonesia's population has been divided into different racial groups, each retaining their own applicable laws which were recognised by the Dutch authorities. The main population groups were: Europeans, Asian foreigners (such as the Chinese) and native Indonesians. The native Indonesians followed customary laws or *Adat* (unwritten, customary laws pre-dating the Dutch arrival) which are extant. For all the groups, Dutch-made legislation supplemented existing laws (Hooker, 1978).

Indonesian law is organised around the following five sources: (a) the *Pancasila* (five pillars) of Indonesian state philosophy; (b) the 1945 Indonesian Constitution; (c) *adat* (customary) law; (d) laws enacted by Parliament; and (e) Presidential and ministerial regulations supplemented by *ad hoc*, unwritten government policy. The first two items (i.e., (a) and (b)) rank as the highest sources of law (Hooker, 1978).

Principles of *Adat* Law

When the Dutch arrived in the East Indies in the seventeenth century, they discovered that the legal systems of the various states consisted of a blend of indigenous, Indian and Islamic laws. Thus, for example, some of the Islamic laws were incorporated into the *adat* of Muslims (Hooker, 1978).

European lawyers and administrators had difficulty in understanding the true nature of the *adat* stemming from the indigenous people of the Dutch colonies. *Adat* law defined the laws, customs, mores and institutions of a particular community and, in turn, it was defined by them. *Adat* law is customary and unwritten, and is more a pattern of observed behaviour than a system of regulation. The indigenous legal systems differed markedly from those of the Netherlands. The Dutch colonial authorities never intended to replace the indigenous laws with their own, nor were they prepared to be subjected to them. This dichotomy resulted in the establishment of a system of legal pluralism in the Dutch East Indies whereby the Dutch and native populations lived under different legal orders.

Adat law is only important nowadays to the businessman to the extent that it permeates the Indonesian collective consciousness and shapes the perception of abstract notions such as justice and fair play. But it may be relevant in determining the capacity of some Indonesians to give guarantees and to transfer their property because of community property restrictions.

Comparison of *Adat* and Western Contract Laws

Contracts are one of the most frequent sources of conflict between western and *adat* law. These two systems differ on how a contract is formed, who bears the risk of loss and what remedies are available for breach (Gautama and Hornick 1983).

An example of their difference is that there is no distinction between real and personal rights in *adat* law. If a *bona fide* purchaser buys goods from someone who is not the actual owner of the goods, then there is no certainty that the owner can recover the goods from the purchaser. Recovery depends on the judge's evaluation of the relative hardships which would result if one or the other party were denied their claim.

There is no distinction in *adat* law between private and public law. Under *adat*, contracts for the sale of land come under public law because the vital interests of the community are intimately affected by the use of land. Hence, because of these differences, *adat* contract law is only meant for the closed, rural community and is ill-suited for the native Indonesians who are engaged in international trade and commerce. For these people, western contract law based on the Dutch Civil and Commercial Codes is more appropriate.

Contracts under western law are regulated by Book III of the *Civil Code*, entitled the *Law of Obligations*. Contracts are the most important sub-category of the obligations contained in Book III.

Civil Code Contracts

Although the *Civil Code* contains general provisions on contract obligations, and special articles pertaining to specified contract types, the discussion here only considers sales agreements and agency contracts since they are the most common contracts entered into by foreign businessmen. Joint venture agreements are discussed under the scope of the new business laws in the next section.

(i) ***Sales Agreements***: Under the Indonesian *Civil Code*, a contract for the sale and purchase of goods creates an obligation to sell and buy but it does not automatically result in any transfer of the item being sold. Because of the peculiarity of the *Civil Code*, it is possible that a particular item can be sold to more than one buyer. A transfer, derived from the Roman law concept of *traditio*, is necessary to complete the sale. To illustrate, suppose that X sells a car to Y, and then sells the same car to Z, a bona fide buyer, and follows this up with a formal transfer to Z instead of to Y. This makes Z the lawful owner of the car. Y thus has an action against X for breach of contract but Y cannot reclaim the car from Z.

In the absence of any agreement to the contrary, the customary practice is that expenses incurred in the sales agreement, such as stamp fees, notarial fees and transportation, are borne by the purchaser. The seller bears the transfer costs such as the risk of loss of the goods borne by the purchaser from the moment of sale as long as the goods are specific or can be ascertained.

The *Code* offers protection to the buyer in that the seller to the buyer (a) warrants title to the goods and (b) warrants against latent defects. Warranties (a) and (b) are not unlike sections 12 (title) and 14 (merchantable quality), respectively, of the English *Sales of Goods Act*. Although it may be possible for the parties to waive warranty (b), it is not permissible to waive warranty (a).

(ii) ***Agency Contracts***: According to the *Code*, the “mandate” (*pemberian kuasa*) is a contract where the principal/mandator gives to the agent/mandatory the power to execute a juristic act in his name. There are no formal requirements to create a mandate. A power of attorney (*kuasa*) can be given and accepted by authentic deed or private signature, either by letter (*surat kuasa*) or orally.

The mandatory has three obligations: to execute the mandate, to compensate the principal if he fails to do so and to account for his acts. The obligations of the principal are also threefold: to indemnify his mandatory, to remunerate him and to execute all obligations contracted on his behalf by the mandatory. The principal is liable for all torts committed by the agent in the course of agency duties. Termination of agency can be effected in any of the following ways: (a) revocation by the principal; (b) renunciation by the mandatory; (c) death of the principal or agent; (d) bankruptcy of the principal or agent; (e) interdiction of the principal or agent; and (f) the marriage of a female principal or agent (Gautama, 1995).

Business Law Reform

The enactment of *Law No. 1/1995* in March 1995 was a major reform of the Indonesian *Commercial Code* and, consequently, of the Indonesian system of economic law, particularly in the area concerning limited liability companies. This reform adopts the new *Company Law* and was deemed necessary to reduce the costs and risks of entering into private transactions, and to reduce the barriers to entry and mobility of domestic or foreign investment. *Law No. 1/1995* is a positive step towards meeting these objectives. The translation of *Law No. 1/1995* into the English language makes it readily accessible to the international business community (Dunstan and Carr-Gregg, 1995; Pakpahan, 1995).

Only a brief overview of the new *Company Law* is provided here and foreign businesses need to examine *Law No. 1/1995* directly and consult professional advisors. The 1995 reforms make the administration of Indonesian business law more predictable than before. The new law has more articles (129) and covers many areas that were not dealt with by the old law. For example, the former law made no reference to mergers, minority shareholder rights or classes of shares. Some of the significant features of the new law are: (a) it does not permit a single shareholder in a limited liability company (there must be at least two shareholders); (b) a company must have a minimum authorised capital of 20 million rupiah; (c) a company may repurchase its own shares and reduce its capital; (d) the potential liability of directors is now tightened; and (e) it creates rights for minority shareholders.

Under the old law, if a company's losses were 75% of its authorised capital, then it automatically would be dissolved. This requirement is not consistent with modern business needs. Under the new law, dissolution can be effected only by a court order, or by expiration of the duration stated in the Articles of Agreement, or by a shareholder vote. Under the new law, the procedure for registration of a company has been simplified and freed from excessive administrative discretionary controls and expense.

Further reforms of Indonesia's economic laws are anticipated in the coming years. Several Indonesian governmental agencies are now actively collaborating with international bodies to encourage the development of modern economic laws in Indonesia in international and domestic contracts, company law, competition, secured transactions, capital markets, intellectual property, negotiable instruments, bankruptcy and arbitration. For example, the Economic Law and Improved Procurement Systems (ELIPS) project is a collaboration between the U.S. Agency for International Development (USAID), the Office of the Coordinating Minister for Economics, Finance and Development Supervision (EKKU), the National Law Development Agency of the Department of Justice (BPHN), the State Secretariat (SEKNEG), the Department of Finance (DEPKEU) and the Law School of the University of Indonesia (UI).[1]

Insolvency Legislation

The Indonesian insolvency rules are mainly found in the *Bankruptcy Ordinance* (*Undang-Undang Kepailitan*, or UUK) enacted by the Dutch in 1905 (Tabalujan, 1996). Due to Indonesia's pluralistic legal system, the UUK applies only to Europeans and foreign Orientals (e.g., Chinese). It is not applicable to indigenous Indonesians unless they voluntarily submit to its jurisdiction.

On 7 March 1996, a new law on limited liability companies (*Undang-Undang tentang Perseroan Terbatas*, or UUPT) came into force. The difference between these two laws is that the UUK deals with the bankruptcy and insolvency of individuals and various business entities (including partnerships and companies). Limited liability companies, however, must comply with both laws. The UUPT provides three grounds for the dissolution of a company: (a) by a resolution of the general meeting of shareholders; (b) when the period of existence specified in the company's Deed of Establishment expires; and (c) by a court order. The most common ground is by an order of the court. In practice, the UUK bankruptcy provisions rarely have been applied in business. Whether the UUPT provisions for limited liability companies will change this situation remains uncertain.

---

1 Contact: Professor Theodore Parnall, Chief of Party – ELIPS Project, Gedung PAIK, 12th Floor, Dep. Keuangan, Jl. Lapangan Banteng Timur 2, Jakarta 10710; Fax: (6221) 386-6113.

Judicial Power and Jurisdictions

(i) ***Indonesian Courts***: There are four classes of courts in Indonesia: general courts, military courts, religious courts and administrative courts (Ball, 1981). Only the general courts are of concern to foreign businesses. The general courts have general jurisdiction in both civil as well as criminal matters. These courts are three-tiered and comprise the district courts (*Pengadilan Negeri*), high courts (*Pengadilan Tinggi*) and the Supreme Court (*Mahkamah Agung*).

The main characteristic of civil proceedings in Indonesia is their simplicity (Setiawan, 1993). This has been made possible by *Law No.2/1986* concerning the general courts (*Undang-Undang Peradilan Umum*). Under Article 24 of the *1945 Constitution*, judicial power is vested in the Supreme Court and such subordinate courts as may be established by law. The language used in the Indonesian courts for both oral proceedings and written submissions is *Bahasa Indonesia.*

(ii) ***District Courts***: A district court is the ordinary court of first instance in civil and criminal matters. This court is managed by a chairman, vice-chairman and several judges. Theoretically, every court session requires three judges to be present (Ball, 1981). However, the law gives the chairman the discretion to establish one-judge courts and, in practice, this is the norm. Three-judge panels are reserved for complex cases. A district court is the daily court for all strata of Indonesian society, and is found in every major city. This court examines and decides all civil disputes without any limitation whatsoever. *Ex-parte* petitions can also be applied through these courts. In Jakarta alone, there are five district courts.

(iii) ***High Courts***: High courts do not hear cases in the first instance but only have appellate jurisdiction, in both civil and criminal matters. Hence, cases heard earlier in the district courts may be appealed to the particular territorial high court which has the power to review questions of law as well as of fact. In addition to their appellate functions, high courts also supervise the administration of district courts within their region.

(iv) ***The Supreme Court***: The Supreme Court has original and exclusive jurisdiction in the following cases: (a) all jurisdictional disputes between courts of different spheres; (b) all jurisdictional disputes between high courts; (c) all jurisdictional disputes between district courts located in different regions; and (d) all jurisdictional disputes between, or involving, courts not belonging to one of the four preceding spheres. It is empowered to annul or quash decisions of the high courts. Petitions for annulments may be brought by any of the parties in a civil action. Annulments may be made for any of the following reasons: (a) if a procedural mistake was made by a litigant when appealing from a lower to a higher court; (b) when a lower court has exceeded its jurisdiction; or (c) when a lower court has either wrongly applied or evaded legal regulations (Ball, 1981).

Besides resolving disputes, the Supreme Court provides non-binding opinions and advice about legal matters requested by the government. The English doctrine of binding precedent is non-existent in the Indonesian judicial hierarchy. Earlier judgements of superior courts are only persuasive, and not binding, on the inferior courts. There are no law reports which are made available to the public. Therefore, lawyers have to keep abreast of legal developments by attending law seminars and by "keeping their ears open".

DISPUTE RESOLUTION PROCEDURES

Causes of Disputes

The main causes of commercial disputes between an Indonesian national or business entity, and a foreign individual or business entity are: (a) agency disagreements; (b) disputes within a joint venture company; and (c) employer-employee disputes. Examples of an agency disagreement are a foreign principal wanting to terminate the agency agreement because of unsatisfactory performance by the agent, intentions to establish his own representative office in Indonesia or because he desires to enter into a joint venture business agreement with another Indonesian partner. Problems in joint venture companies typically arise because minority shareholders disagree with the management policy of the foreign directors. Employer-employee disputes are commonly due to wrongful dismissal or ill-treatment of Indonesian employees.

Whenever a dispute arises, the parties concerned can choose to have the matter litigated in the courts or, alternatively, they can attempt to settle the dispute by alternative methods such as negotiation, mediation or arbitration. The cheapest and quickest way to resolve disputes is by negotiation or mediation whenever possible. However, if the parties cannot reach an amicable settlement by these means, then they have no choice but to pursue the issue in the courts or refer it to an arbitrator. Arbitration is possible only if this is provided for in the contract that is the subject of the dispute, or if the parties to the dispute mutually consent to arbitration after the dispute has arisen.

Law of Procedure and Dispute Settlement

The legal grounds of Indonesian *Civil Procedural Law* are contained in the *Revised Indonesian Regulation* (*Reglemen Indonesia Yang Diperbaharui,* abbreviated as RIB), *State Gazette 1941 No. 44*. This Regulation pre-dates Indonesian independence but it remains valid on account of Article II of the *Transitional Provisions* of the 1945 Constitution. For historical reasons, the procedural provisions of the revised Indonesian civil proceedings in Indonesia are conducted orally. Since it is not compulsory to engage a lawyer before any court of first instance, the judge has to actively conduct the proceedings. After the conclusion of proceedings, the judge initiates the enforcement proceedings.

In accordance with Indonesia's state philosophy, *Pancasila*, the court acts as a *pengayom*, or "giver of the feeling of justice". This feeling of justice includes the recognition by both parties that the judge of the case has been able to settle the dispute wisely and flexibly. Procedural matters are considered secondary to this objective. For the same reason, a case cannot be ruled to be invalid just because of a procedural error. The judge has an important role to play in ensuring the smooth conduct of court proceedings and in making efforts to settle the case amicably at every stage of the proceedings. He is expected to render advice, as necessary, to both litigants on legal remedies and to take the initiative to provide any other useful information.

Steps in Civil Proceedings

A civil action commences with a plaintiff submitting a request to the chairman of the district court located in a defendant's domicile to summon a defendant. If an oral claim is filed, then it will be converted to writing by the chairman of the district court. The plaintiff then is required to register the civil suit with the district court's deputy registrar. The registration fee is approximately Rp 75,000. Upon such registration, the deputy registrar is required to issue a letter of summons to a defendant at least three days prior to the first court hearing. There is no pre-trial conference (Setiawan, 1993).

If a defendant fails to appear at the first hearing, then a summons is issued for a second hearing and, if necessary, one is issued for a third hearing. If a defendant has not made an appearance by the third hearing, then the court has the discretion to issue a default judgement (*Putusan Verstek*). A default judgement is subject to an appeal.

Where both parties appear at the first hearing, the judge is obliged to encourage them to reach an amicable settlement or conciliation. There are no formal conciliation procedures to be followed, nor is the judge required to make a formal finding that the conciliation has not been successful, before the legal proceedings may commence. In practice, informal conciliation procedures are not successful in the majority of cases.

If the informal conciliation process has not been successful, the first court hearing is then devoted to receiving a defendant's statement and to certain administrative matters. As stipulated by the *Indonesian Revised Regulation* (RIB), the judge should begin the examination of a case by reading out the claim. However, in practice (particularly in big cities) this procedure is not followed. The judge, instead, clarifies the basic grounds of the claim to a defendant.

The judge is empowered to give directives to the parties regarding the evidence and legal alternatives available. The main arguments raised during the course of the trial are presented in the form of written submissions to the court. Next, a defendant files a reply arguing on the merits of the case, or on the court's jurisdiction, or on other matters. The defendant may file a counter-claim against a plaintiff's claim only at this point. The counter-claim may be for an amount which is the same, higher, or lower than the amount claimed by a plaintiff.

The court then adjourns for a period of time during which a plaintiff is permitted to file a counter plea (the *Replik*). The filing of the *Replik* triggers the commencement of a second period of time during which a defendant is required to file a rejoinder or response to the *Replik* (the *Duplik*). After both of these written submissions have been filed at the court, another session is scheduled to examine them.

After the written exhibits have been properly examined by the judge, a subsequent court session is scheduled to hear the witnesses for the plaintiff and the defendant. Indonesian procedural law requires a plaintiff to produce at least two witnesses. The witnesses for a plaintiff are heard first and, then, the witnesses for a defendant are heard. Each witness is examined by the lawyer calling the witness and may be cross-examined by the opposing lawyer and, then, re-examined by the first lawyer. The judge is entitled to question the witness. The burden is on the party who has submitted an argument to furnish the relevant proof. A written record of the testimony is made by a court official and given to the judge. Usually counsel for both parties approach the court official to review the record and, subject to the judge's approval, to correct any errors.

In the next court session, final written submissions (*Kesimputan*) from each party are accepted. Upon receipt of these final submissions, the judge usually adjourns the court for two to three weeks in order to review the submissions carefully and to render a decision. At the final court session, the judge issues the decision. The time lapse from commencement of legal proceedings at the district court level to rendering a judgement is rarely less than six months, and is often a year or more.

Appeal to the High Court

The legal remedy of *verzet* is to oppose a decision which was made in the absence of a defendant. By way of this remedy, the case is examined from the beginning as if the prior decision had never existed. The burden of proof rests throughout with a plaintiff (Setiawan, 1993).

An appeal to a high court can be made either by a plaintiff or by a defendant who is dissatisfied with a district court's judgement. Such an appeal is normally lodged with a high court by an appellant within 14 days from the date of issuance of the decision. However, if an appellant is domiciled outside Java or the Madura Islands, an appeal must be filed within 30 days. If an appellant is absent from the final session of the district court, then the time to lodge an appeal (14 days) is calculated from the time an appellant received the notice of the court's decision.

An appellant has to file an appeal with the deputy registrar from the same district court which rendered the initial decision. An appellant must sign the deed of appeal (*Akta Banding*) and pay the appeal fee. However, no legal grounds justifying an appeal need to be included in the *Akta Banding*, apart from an expression of dissatisfaction with the lower court's decision.

An appeal to a high court may ask for a review of the facts and the law, and is based on written submissions made on behalf of each party. Normally, an appeal has the effect of staying an enforcement of a court judgement, except where the judgement has explicitly forbidden such a stay whilst an appeal is still pending. This judgement is known as a *keputusan serta merta* (settlement on the spot). The deliberations of a high court may require a year or more before a final judgement is made.

Appeal to the Supreme Court

The losing party in a high court may appeal to the Supreme Court. The application for appeal and an executed deed of appeal have to be filed with the original district court within 14 days from the time the losing party received the notice of decision. Within 14 days of an application for appeal being filed, the *Memori Kasasi*, which is the statement containing the reasons for an appeal, must be submitted by an appellant to the Supreme Court. A respondent may submit a counter-statement, the *Kontra Memori Kasasi*, within 14 days of receipt of a copy of the *Memori Kasasi*. The Supreme Court, however, only hears appeals on points of law and on whether the lower courts have been incompetent or exceeded their jurisdiction. An appeal to the Supreme Court may require three years or more before a final decision is issued.

Enforcement of Judgements

If a plaintiff prevails at a district court, a high court or the Supreme Court, then an attachment order in respect of a defendant's assets (*conservatoir beslag*) is issued. If a court decision is final and binding, then the attachment order is changed to an execution order whereby the judge notifies the defendant that there is an outstanding order. If the defendant fails to satisfy the obligations thereunder, then the judgement is enforced by a public auction of the defendant's possessions. A public auction is effected by a special administrative board (*Juru Lelang*) under the jurisdiction of the Ministry of Finance. A public auction is preceded by a notification published in a local newspaper (at a cost of approximately Rp 1 million). Police assistance may be called upon to encourage a recalcitrant defendant to release property which is the subject of the auction (Setiawan, 1993).

Another method of enforcement is eviction of a defendant. Under Indonesian law, it is possible in some circumstances to obtain an execution order even though there is still an appeal pending. A high court's approval is needed by a district court before issuing such an order. Indonesia has not yet entered into any reciprocal agreements with other countries for the enforcement of foreign judgements. However, foreign arbitral awards can now be enforced under the Supreme Court's *Regulation No. 1, Year 1990*, provided they are from countries that are members of the *1958 New York Convention on the Recognition and Enforcement of Foreign Arbitral Awards*.

Court Fees and Legal Costs

The statutory court fees for registering a claim in a district court are between Rp 75,000 to Rp 100,000 while an application for an injunction against an opponent costs about Rp 3 million to Rp 4 million (less than US$2,000). These administrative costs are trivial. However, depending on the quantum of the claim, the nature of the dispute and the duration of the trial, a litigant who engages an established lawyer (charging typically US$250 per hour) for representation in a commercial dispute at a district court should be prepared to incur around US$25,000 to US$50,000 in legal costs. With the addition of other hidden costs, the legal and court fees may well approach US$100,000. The total court and legal fees can escalate further if the case is appealed to a high court or the Supreme Court.

A characteristic feature of Indonesian litigation is that a losing party only pays the court fees and not an opponent's legal costs. This principle applies to a first instance hearing as well as to appeals. Indonesian defendants of limited means may be entitled to subsidised or free services from the legal aid office at any district court. The Ministry of Justice pays Legal Aid Post lawyers Rp 200,000 (US$85) per case on behalf of a defendant if a judge approves their representation (*The Jakarta Post*, 12 December 1996).

DOMESTIC ARBITRATION

Background

Arbitration as a means for the settlement of business disputes has been practised in Indonesia since the Dutch colonial period, and was legitimised by Articles 615–650 of the *Dutch Code of Civil Procedure* which are extant. The following account of contemporary arbitration procedures draws especially on the work of Gautama (1990, 1991, 1993, 1995). Hornick (1991) summarises the legal basis and scope of arbitration in Indonesia.

Emphasis is placed on those aspects of arbitration which need to be understood by foreign investors in Indonesia. These include both domestic and foreign arbitration: domestic arbitration refers to arbitration taking place in Indonesia whereas foreign arbitration refers to arbitration taking place outside Indonesia.

The most important body for arbitration in Indonesia is the *Badan Arbitrase Nasional Indonesia* (BANI, known in English as the Indonesian National Board of Arbitration). BANI was established by the Indonesian Chamber of Commerce and Industry in 1977 and deals with disputes in the areas of trade, industry and commerce. Smaller bodies exist for the purpose of settling claims in specialised areas such as insurance.

BANI has been involved in settling commercial disputes arising between foreign individuals, or corporations, and Indonesian parties. Approximately 10% of BANI's cases fall into this category. In commercial agreements which involve foreign investors, it is normal practice to stipulate that disputes be referred to an arbitration body outside of Indonesia. This is done because foreign investors believe that they are at a disadvantage in settling their claims in a jurisdiction which may be more sympathetic to an Indonesian party, or because they believe that foreign arbitration proceedings will be more competent, less costly or less dilatory than domestic arbitration. However, few cases have been submitted for arbitration overseas to test these beliefs.

Procedure

A precondition for dispute settlement by arbitration is the existence of a written agreement by both parties to use arbitration. This agreement can be subsequently repudiated only with the consent of both parties. Under Indonesian law, all disputes of a purely commercial nature may be submitted to arbitration. Indonesian courts have the authority to determine the validity of an arbitration agreement but not to interpret the terms of the corresponding contract. The latter is deemed to be the role of the arbitrators. The place of arbitration may be decided by the disputing parties, or by the arbitrators if the former fail to reach an agreement.

An arbitral clause need not specify the method of appointing arbitrators although it would normally do so. Arbitrators must be nominated in odd numbers. Members of the judiciary are expressly disqualified from acting as arbitrators but, otherwise, there are few restrictions. Cases submitted to BANI are normally heard by a tribunal consisting of the respective nominees of the disputing parties and one presiding individual nominated by BANI.

Arbitral proceedings are carried out according to the rules specified in the arbitration agreement. The BANI rules specify a detailed procedure for initiating an arbitration hearing, including the respective responsibilities of claimant and respondent, and a timeframe for the hearing (BANI, 1979). Under normal circumstances, arbitrators are expected to reach a decision within six months of accepting a case but this does not always happen. Unlike court cases, BANI hearings are closed to the general public. Both written and oral submissions are normally invited. However, the disputing parties are not required to appear at the hearing in person but may be represented by a lawyer instead. The cost of bringing a case before BANI is based on a sliding scale which is typically 2% to 5% of the amount claimed. The apportionment of arbitration costs, other than legal expenses incurred by the disputing parties, is determined by the arbitrators.

Enforcement and Appeals

Arbitral awards determined by BANI normally require legal enforcement unless there is voluntary compliance by a losing party. The enforcement of an award made as a result of an arbitral decision by BANI (or other domestic arbitration centre) can be carried out by a district court after the original documents containing details of the award have been filed with it according to standardised procedures. The President of the court examines the basis of the award and circumstances surrounding it, and grants an *exequator* (order for enforcement of the award) provided that the award is deemed to be valid and not contrary to public policy. The *exequator* has a force comparable to that of a civil law decision, and should be quickly implemented in urban centres.

It is normal practice for the parties to an arbitral agreement to waive their right to appeal. If they have not done so, then an arbitral award may be appealed to the Supreme Court. An award may be rejected because of procedural irregularities, or because the arbitrators have exceeded their terms of reference, but not because the decision on which it is based is deemed to be incorrect.

Arbitration Cases

There are no systematic compilations of commercial disputes arbitrated through BANI. Hornick (1991) summarises several representative cases which involved single arbitrators or unanimous tribunals. One feature of these cases is the lack of consistency in the way the arbitrators presented their findings and explained their awards.

A foreign party who loses a dispute may feel that the decision is capricious if the basis of the award is not explained in detail. It is here, however, where an implicit knowledge of Indonesian culture becomes valuable. In disputes involving foreign businesses, a majority of the arbitrators are normally Indonesian nationals and their decisions will be rendered in accordance with Indonesian perceptions of justice. Arguments based on technical points that might succeed in a western arbitration setting are much less compelling in Indonesia.

FOREIGN ARBITRATION

Applicable Conventions

In order to be recognised in Indonesia, foreign arbitration must have been carried out in accordance with the provisions of international conventions to which Indonesia is a signatory. There are presently two such conventions: the *1958 New York Convention on the Recognition and Enforcement of Foreign Arbitral Awards* (dealing with commercial disputes) and the *1968 Washington Convention* which established the International Center for Settlement of Investment Disputes (ICSID) (dealing with investment disputes between foreign investors and the host government). Most foreign investment agreements made in Indonesia under the provisions of the *Foreign Investment Law of 1967* include an arbitration clause referring disputes to arbitration under the rules of the *Washington Convention.*

Trade agreements involving a foreign entrepreneur and an Indonesian party normally include a provision for settlement through international arbitration under the UNCITRAL rules and, for enforcement, by recourse to *the New York Convention.* The designated place of arbitration should be a recognised centre such as the International Court of Arbitration (Paris) or the London Court of International Arbitration.

Procedure and Enforcement

Indonesia ratified the *1958 New York Convention* in 1981 (Presidential Decree No. 34/1981). However, the applicability of this convention was cast in doubt in 1984 following a controversial ruling in the *Bulgare* case by the Supreme Court of Indonesia. The court determined that foreign arbitral awards made under the *New York Convention* were not enforceable yet in Indonesia because of the government's failure to develop the legislative framework needed to implement the judicial process (Hornick, 1985).

It was not until 1990 that the Supreme Court issued regulations confirming that Indonesia was bound by the *New York Convention* and specifying the procedures for obtaining an enforcement from Indonesian courts (Gingerich, 1990). Under these regulations, a foreign arbitral award must meet a number of conditions before it can be enforced in Indonesia.

The award must have arisen as a result of a commercial dispute in a country which is a signatory to the *1958 New York Convention*, or which has a comparable bilateral agreement with Indonesia. The scope and definition of a commercial dispute apparently is left to the discretion of the Supreme Court. The party seeking enforcement is required to obtain an *exequator* from the Supreme Court. The *exequator* is issued only if the Court is satisfied that enforcement of the award does not contravene either "public policy" or the "basic principles of the entire legal system". However, the practical consequences of these wide ranging exclusion clauses have not been established. In the worst case, the process of enforcing an arbitral award can be as complex as the process of litigation. Recognition and enforcement of a foreign arbitral award can be refused by the Supreme Court on various grounds as stated in the articles of the *Convention*.

Application for an *exequator* in connection with a foreign arbitral award is made in the first instance to the Supreme Court via the Central Jakarta district court. The latter is the only court authorised to handle issues relating to foreign arbitral awards. The *exequator* is issued by the Supreme Court to the Central Jakarta district court which subsequently executes it (in Jakarta) or forwards it to a district court of the appropriate jurisdiction for execution.

The application for the *exequator* must include the following documents: (a) authenticated duplicates and translations of all documents relating to the foreign arbitration award; (b) authenticated duplicates and translations of the commercial agreement on which the award was based; and (c) a statement from the Indonesian diplomatic representative in the foreign country which confirms that the foreign country is reciprocally bound to enforce arbitral judgements originating in Indonesia.

The cost of enforcement includes general legal expenses, expenses for the issuance of the *exequator* (Rp 250,000) and any expenses incurred by the district court responsible for the enforcement. Under Indonesian civil law, a party whom the award is enforced against may be compelled to pay the official court costs but does not have to bear the cost of the opponent's lawyers. Once the award is recognised by Indonesian courts, no appeals for annulment are allowed.

Only one arbitration case involving the Indonesian government has been referred to the ICSID under the *Washington Convention* (Hornick, 1985). One notable feature of this case, which arose after the cancellation of a foreign investment licence, is that it lasted 12 years and involved four rounds of arbitration proceedings. This case is considered further in the following section.

The Amco Indonesia Case

This well-known case arose in 1980 out of a dispute between the Indonesian government and an Indonesian subsidiary of a company based in Hong Kong (Amco). The basis of the dispute was: (a) the repossession of a hotel built by Amco a decade earlier, and operated by it supposedly under a 30-year lease; and (b) the subsequent revocation of Amco's investment licence by the Foreign Investment Board. The Indonesian government claimed that Amco had reneged on its investment obligations by investing US$0.6 million less than the amount of US$3 million stipulated in the licence.

In 1981, the case was referred by Amco to the ICSID for arbitration. In 1984, a judgement was rendered by the ICSID tribunal in Amco's favour. However, the arbitral award was annulled on procedural grounds in 1986 by an ad hoc ICSID committee formed at the request of Indonesia, and the case was resubmitted for consideration by another tribunal. The decision of the second tribunal was given in 1988, again, largely in Amco's favour. However, both parties rejected the tribunal's assessment and the final round of review proceedings involving another ad hoc committee (which upheld the previous award) was not completed until 1992.

CONCLUSION

The preceding discussion indicates that it can be costly and time-consuming to pursue dispute resolution by means of litigation or arbitration. A defendant in a case often has little to lose from prolonging the dispute through the appeal process. The principal advice for foreign investors doing business in Indonesia is that they should plan carefully prior to entering into any business contract. This is crucial for anticipating and avoiding potential disputes. Several factors are worth remembering.

First, an effort should be made to learn the Indonesian language and understand the Indonesian culture, philosophy and way of life (*Pancasila*). This knowledge can prevent needless misunderstandings when dealing with Indonesian partners or employees. A business relationship with an Indonesian partner based on mutual respect will rarely result in dispute. On the contrary, poor human resource practices of disaffected expatriate managers are a potential source of employer-employee disputes.

Secondly, the business contract should be carefully drafted. Here the services of a good Indonesian lawyer are indispensable. All too often, contracting parties insert clauses stipulating that a law other than Indonesian law should apply in case of dispute. This practice creates problems of enforceability in an Indonesian court where a judge is likely to apply only Indonesian law as the curial law (de Seriere, 1987).

Thirdly, investors should know their Indonesian partner(s) well. If they do not, then the integrity and credibility of the partner(s) should be thoroughly investigated. Negotiations should be carried out in the Indonesian language to ensure that the local partner(s) can express any misgivings or doubts in a culturally acceptable manner before entering into a contract which may later be regretted or reinterpreted according to local norms.

Finally, as an alternative to the complexities and expense of litigation, foreign businesses operating in Indonesia may consider referring all routine disputes with domestic providers of services, office equipment and rental space to arbitration by BANI. However, it is inadvisable to agree to any settlement of major disputes by arbitration because of the uncertainties that currently surround the enforceability of arbitral awards.

REFERENCES

Ball John, *Indonesian Law Commentary and Teaching Materials*, Faculty of Law, University of Sydney, Sydney, 1981.

BANI, *Arbitration in Indonesia and International Conventions on Arbitration*, Penerbit Alumni, Bandung, 1979.

de Seriere R., "Offshore Lending to Borrowers in Indonesia: Recent Supreme Court Judgements Highlight Enforceability Problems", *International Lawyer*, Vol. 21, 1987, pp. 883–93.

Dunstan Jim, and John Carr-Gregg, *Indonesia's New Law on Limited Companies*, International Bar Association, London, 1995.

Gautama Sudargo, "Some Legal Aspects of International Commercial Arbitration in Indonesia", *Journal of International Arbitration*, Vol. 7, 1990, pp. 93–105.

Gautama S., *Hukum Dagang dan Arbitrase Internasional*, Penerbit Pt. Citra Aditya Bakti, Bandung, 1991.

Gautama S., "An Overview of the Indonesian Legal System (with Special Reference to Foreign Investments)", in *Business and Investment Laws in Indonesia, Proceedings of the First Indonesia-Singapore Law Seminar*, National University of Singapore, 26–27 February 1993, Singapore, 1993.

Gautama S., *Indonesian Business Law*, Penerbit Pt. Citra Aditya Bakti, Bandung, 1995.

Gautama Sudargo and Robert Hornick, *An Introduction to Indonesian Law: Unity in Diversity*, Penerbit Alumni, Bandung, 1983.

Gingerich D. J., "Indonesia to Enforce Foreign Arbitral Awards", *East Asian Executive Reports*, June 1990, pp. 9–20.

Hooker M. B., *Adat Law in Modern Indonesia*, Oxford University Press, Kuala Lumpur, 1978.

Hornick R. N., "Indonesia – Foreign Arbitral Awards Are Not Enforceable", *East Asian Executive Reports*, Vol. 7, 1985, pp. 11–3.

Hornick R. N., "Indonesian Arbitration in Theory and Practice", *American Journal of Comparative Law*, Vol. 39, 1991, pp. 559–81.

Pakpahan Normin S., *Introduction to the New Company Law of Indonesia: An Overview of Law No. 1 of Year 1995 on Limited Liability Companies*, ELIPS Project, Jakarta, 1995.

Setiawan S. H., "Civil Proceedings, Litigation, Enforcement of Judgements and Other Remedies", presentation at Indonesia-Singapore Law Seminar, Marina Mandarin Singapore, 26–27 February 1993, unpublished.

Tabalujan Benny S., "Insolvency Laws in Indonesia", *Asia Business Law Review*, No. 14, October 1996, pp. 34–7.

The Jakarta Post: "Many Do Not Have Legal Council [*sic*]", 12 December 1996, p. 8.

Chapter 17

A Time of Transition, a Time of Turbulence?

BY
Austin I. PULLÉ

INTRODUCTION

AS INVESTORS WATCHED in horror, tests of ore samples confirmed their worst suspicions. The Busang field in Kalimantan, Indonesia, promoted as the biggest goldfield in the world, was exposed as the biggest gold-mining fraud in history. Investors in the shares of the Canadian company, Bre-X, lost more than US$2.5 billion. Meanwhile, the complaint by Japan to the WTO about Indonesia's national car project is pending. Just after the Busang fiasco, the financial media reported on pressure being put on Newmont Mining by the Indonesian Ministry of Mines to surrender a part of its interest in the Sumbawa mine to certain powerful domestic interests despite the fact that this would be a violation of a signed Contract of Work that Newmont has with the Indonesian Government. These events have refocused the attention of the global investment community and media on Indonesia.

Indonesia's sheer geographical expanse from the northern tip of Sumatra to the eastern tip of Irian Jaya, its abundant resources, a legal system and bureaucracy that has not kept pace with a modernising economy, its 75-year-old president who has not chosen a successor, and a burgeoning population of 200 million make the country, at present, the most dominant as well as the least predictable economy in Southeast Asia.

Observers of the archipelago have noticed a more confident and assertive Indonesia as exemplified by its President who ordered his ministers to discontinue negotiations with Japan, Indonesia's largest aid donor and source of investors, on the national car dispute when the latter filed its WTO complaint. This confidence has also manifested itself in sweeping deregulation measures. After 50 years of independence, the country has, at last, confronted the sclerotic laws and rules that applied to the primary economic actor of a modern society, the limited liability company. While the recent regulatory and corporate law reforms were long overdue they are as yet untested. Because they will be tested in the courts that cannot draw upon an existing jurisprudence, no one can predict how broad and general rules will be given specific content. The additional factor, the lack of a tested structure to cope with an orderly and peaceful presidential succession, makes Indonesia a country in the throes of a transition. Investors and political analysts speculate on whether the transition would be smooth or turbulent. A violent transition similar to that of 1965 would have repercussions both for the region as well as for the investment community.

Chapters 14, 15 and 16 discussed the salient features of foreign direct investment, the oil and gas industry, and dispute settlement in Indonesia. This chapter addresses specific issues arising from recent reforms that concern foreign investors and others doing business in Indonesia and the impact of the new *Company Law* on foreign investors.

THE DYNAMICS OF FOREIGN INVESTMENT REGULATION

In 1965, when the New Order government of President Suharto replaced the government of Indonesia's first president, Sukarno, the Indonesian economy was in shambles and inflation was rampant. The New Order government changed course with pro-business policies largely overseen by a technocratic group within the government, the so-called "Berkeley Mafia". The main thrust of this change of course was to alter the approach to foreign investment. With the enactment of *Law No. 1 of 1967*, Indonesia constructed a relatively liberal foreign investment regime while many of its newly independent Asian neighbours were mired in the socialist dogma that accompanied their independence. Despite its formal pro-business tilt, the government found it difficult to realise the full benefits of a market economy because of excessive regulation and vestiges of anti-business attitudes that continued to linger in powerful sections of a nationalistic bureaucracy. Thus, the economic history of the New Order government can be seen as a history of a constant tussle between various conflicting forces. Foreign investors and capital exporting countries, supported by donor institutions such as the World Bank, have lobbied for deregulation and more transparency. Local conglomerates, the beneficiaries of lucrative monopolies, sweetheart contracts, and protectionist policies, resisted dismantling some barriers but lobbied for incentives to make Indonesia's economy more export driven. During its existence, BKPM (the institution that regulates and oversees foreign investment in Indonesia) has unveiled "investment packages" that have opened various sectors of the economy to foreign investment. These packages also contained various incentives that were designed to stimulate foreign investment. As China, India, Vietnam and other Asian countries adopt pro-foreign investment policies, it may be expected that BKPM will continue to respond to such competition by calibrating its policies to attract more foreign investment.

REFORMS AND THE NEW COMPANY LAW

During the past few years, Indonesia has begun to take a more prominent role in regional and global forums such as APEC. She has demonstrated a commitment to integrate herself fully in the global economy. The momentum generated by WTO dictated reduction of trade barriers, competition for the investment dollar, and demands from both the local and foreign investment communities also stimulated the Indonesian government to undertake a series of legal reforms in the areas of company law, mortgage law, and related areas. Until March 1996, Indonesia's company law was based on a handful of articles found in the Indonesian *Commercial Code* that was inherited from the Dutch. These provisions were unsuitable for a modern economy. The new law replaced these rudimentary provisions with a set of detailed articles. However, the content of many articles dealing with subjects critical to the foreign investor is vague and awaits clarification by the Indonesian courts. Several articles of the *Company Law* regulate the relationship among shareholders in the company. Hitherto, foreign investors had addressed these issues in joint venture agreements with their local partners. Most joint venture agreements provided for arbitration of shareholder disputes. However, under the *Company Law*, ultimate jurisdiction is vested in the courts on such matters. This jurisdiction may not be ousted by shareholder agreements.

ESTABLISHING FOREIGN INVESTMENT COMPANIES

All foreign direct investment in Indonesia must be in the form of shares in an Indonesian company. (Foreigners undoubtedly "invest" and take a risk in the extractive industry sector. The production sharing contract and the contract of work, the principal vehicles for foreign companies to take interests in oil and gas and mining ventures, respectively, take the format of a contract with an Indonesian government instrumentality.) This is a requirement mandated by the foreign investment law. The original regulations required a foreign investor to associate in a joint venture with a local partner. A foreign investor was permitted a maximum ownership of 80% of the shares of the company and was required to divest shares to the local shareholder after ten years of commercial production. The maximum amount of shares that a foreign investor was allowed to own after this ten-year period was 49%. This system was obviously unsatisfactory. Often, the local shareholder in the joint venture had the legal privilege of receiving the divestment but claimed that he lacked the funds required to pay the asking price for the shares. BKPM procedures for share transfers effectively precluded a foreign investor from selling the divested shares to a third party over the objection of his local partner. The local joint venture partner had to support the share transfer by executing a consent to share transfer, the *Modal III* form. This, the local joint venture partner would naturally decline to do. As a result, the local partner could buy the shares at an undervalued price and the resulting friction would damage the joint venture. Also, foreign investors were reluctant to commit the capital necessary for the joint venture to expand because of the constraint on indefinite foreign majority ownership.

Responding to foreign investor complaints, BKPM relaxed its rules in important respects. First, it allowed foreign investment companies to list on the Jakarta Stock Exchange. This allows a company to obtain fresh sources of capital and encourages sound management of the foreign investment companies. Second, BKPM has relaxed its limits on foreign ownership of shares and has extended the divestment deadlines.

However, there are still sectors that are closed to foreigners. BKPM retains a "negative list" that lists the sectors that are closed to foreign investment. These relate primarily to areas such as national security, service industries, environmentally sensitive sectors and smallholder sectors.

With respect to the sectors open to foreign investment, the current rules and practices appear to offer more incentives to a foreigner. A foreigner is allowed to own 100% of the shares in most sectors of the economy and a divestment of 5% of the shares is required only after 15 years of commercial production. In the case of infrastructure and plantation projects, the maximum shareholding can be 95%. Shares of a company established under the *Foreign Investment Law*, where such companies are frequently referred to as a P. T. PMA company, can be listed on the Jakarta Stock Exchange. Although foreigners are allowed to own 100% of the shares of certain enterprises, the usual practice is to invite an Indonesian national as a shareholder. In addition to creating desirable synergies, an Indonesian partner is able to facilitate many approvals and lobby for government contracts and indulgences on behalf of a company before the authorities more effectively than his foreign counterpart. The directors of a company may be foreign. P. T. PMA companies are also eligible to hold titles to buildings and industrial lots. The land title, known as HGB, is granted for a period of 30 years and can be extended to a maximum period of 20 years.

In addition to P. T. PMA companies, foreigners may also directly invest in so-called PP20 companies. These are companies which previously were owned solely by Indonesian nationals. However, by *Peraturan Pemerintah* (Government Regulation) *No. 20 of 1995*, foreigners were allowed to own shares in such companies without the need for such companies converting their status into that of a P. T. PMA company. As a matter of policy, BKPM allows this facility to apply only where a company had the status of a fully domestic investment company or PMDN company.

Although BKPM is the regulatory institution that oversees investment, it has no authority to approve a foreigner's investment application. This is the prerogative of the President of Indonesia. The President will not approve any application unless it has first been reviewed and recommended by BKPM and forwarded to the President through the State Secretariat (*Sekneg*). Approval of the President is contained in the *Surat Pemberitahuan Persetujuan Presiden* or "SP3". The SP3 also serves as a temporary business licence for a PMA company. Once a company commences commercial production, it will obtain a permanent business licence (*Izin Usaha Tetap*) which will replace the SP3.

A NEW, BUT UNTESTED, COMPANY LAW

Unlike companies established in common law countries that provide for two sets of documents, the Memorandum of Association and the Articles of Association, Indonesia provides for a single document that is called the "Articles of Association". This document, which must be in the Indonesian language, is in the form of a deed (*Akte Pendirian*) drawn up before a notary who, unlike the common law counterpart, is a quasi-judicial officer and a senior lawyer. Once the Articles of Association has been subscribed to, the notary's office will obtain the NPWP (*Nomor Pokok Wajib Pajak*) which is an income tax registration number for the company. Upon receipt of the tax registration number, the notary's office will submit the Articles to the Ministry of Justice for review and approval. It is only when the Ministry of Justice approves the articles and these approved articles are published in the State Gazette that the company achieves limited liability status. The company is also required to register with the company register maintained by the Department of Industry and Trade. At this time, the company must obtain the PPKP (*Pengukuhan Pengusaha Kena Pajak*) that certifies the company's ability to issue creditable VAT invoices and the permanent business licence (*Izin Usaha Tetap*) which will replace the SP3. The local BKPM office, known as the BKPM Daerah, issues the permanent business licence.

THE COMPANY LAW AND FOREIGN INVESTORS

The Indonesian *Company Law* that replaced the earlier *Commercial Code* provisions came into effect in 1996. There are several features of this law that are relevant to foreign investors. The two new features, as yet untested in the courts, are the range of liability of the directors and the rights of minority shareholders. Investment advisors await with interest the meaning that the courts would attach to sections dealing with these topics, especially in the context of foreign and local shareholder disputes. However, before these are discussed, the two-tier system of corporate governance will be examined.

Even prior to the enactment of the *Company Law*, Indonesian practice allowed for a two-tier system of management. The senior tier, known as the Board of Commissioners (*Komisaris*), took no active part in the management of the company but had supervisory powers, the most important of which was the right to examine the books and records of the company. It was, however, the Board of Directors

(*Direksi*) that had the authority to manage the affairs of the company. Exceptionally, the Board of Commissioners could manage the company when the directors were incapacitated or dismissed. The *Company Law* makes the two-tier system of management mandatory. In other words, every Indonesian company is now required to have these two boards.

As an organ of corporate governance, the Board of Commissioners has limited value. In the normal P. T. companies, (i.e., companies that are fully owned by Indonesian nationals) the members of the Board of Commissioners tend to be relatives or close friends of the directors. As a result, the balance of power that is supposed to exist rarely becomes a reality. On the other hand, the requirement that such dual boards are necessary simply increases the transaction costs of a company. Most foreign investors would be unable to spare additional expatriate staff to function on these boards. The costs associated with placing additional expatriates such as housing, travel, medical and schooling for children are not deductible expenses of the P. T. PMA company under current Indonesian tax practice.

Directors' Duties under the Company Law

One of the more dramatic features of the *Company Law* is the section dealing with the duties of directors. Prior to its enactment, the duties of directors were hazy and undefined. By bringing in a chapter on directors' duties, the law introduces a level of uncertainty. In the common law world, the subject of directors' duties has been regulated by statute and clarified as well as developed by judicial decisions. Consequently, there is a high degree of predictability with respect to proposed actions of the directors.

Indonesia, as a civil law jurisdiction, does not have a doctrine of binding precedent, hence, there has not been a comparable body of law developed by the judges. Neither does Indonesia have a tradition of scholarly annotation that prevails in many continental European countries. The new law appears to have imported various concepts on directors' duties from common law jurisdictions. Absent a larger context of judicial interpretation, these duties appear to be vague and are susceptible to being interpreted in inconsistent and unfamiliar ways. It will be seen from an examination of such duties that directors, especially foreign directors, who may be used to the wide range of powers granted them in common law jurisdictions, may be prone to overreach themselves in managing an Indonesian company.

Article 85(2) makes the directors personally liable if they are found to be negligent in performing their duties or if they wrongfully exercise their powers. Article 85(3) then provides that shareholders representing 10% of the voting rights may, on behalf of the company, bring an action against directors for wrongful acts or negligence that harm the company. Article 54(2) permits a shareholder to sue the company for any loss caused by corporate action that is considered unfair and without reasonable ground taken pursuant to a general meeting of shareholders or board of directors' decision.

Article 1(4) of the *Company Law* vests in the board of directors the full responsibility of managing the company and representing the company both before a court as well as with third parties. Article 82 reflects the position in many jurisdictions that the directors owe these duties to the company and not to the individual shareholders. Article 85(1) requires that the directors act in good faith and discharge their duties in the operation of the business in the interests of the company. These provisions by themselves are unexceptionable. It is when the enforcement of these duties becomes a privilege of the shareholders, who are given standing to sue, that these duties, or at least the method of enforcement, become problematic.

Article 90(2) and (3) impose joint and several liability on the directors, where by reason of their fault or negligence, the assets of the company are insufficient, in the event of a company liquidation, to cover the liabilities of the company. Directors may escape liability by showing that they did not commit any wrongful or negligent act and that other factors caused the insolvency of the company.

Finally, Article 1365 of the Indonesian *Civil Code* could be used to justify a tort claim against directors. The basis of the tort would be that the directors, acting in violation of their duties under the Indonesian *Company Law*, have caused harm to the shareholders.

Although the *Company Law* has been in existence for over a year, these provisions against directors have yet to be tested in a court. For foreign directors, these provisions could prove troublesome as the Indonesian courts lack the experience of their common law counterparts of allowing directors a large discretion in handling the business affairs of the company but intervening when certain lines are crossed. Directors nominated by foreign parties may wish to be indemnified by the foreign shareholders against personal liability. The costs of such indemnity insurance would probably have to be borne by the foreign shareholder as it cannot be charged to the expenses of the P. T. PMA company. If the Indonesian courts favour a more interventionist approach and are receptive to shareholder complaints against alleged director mismanagement, the uncertainty caused and the exposure of foreign directors to personal liability, sometimes orchestrated by aggressive local attorneys to include criminal liability, could erode Indonesia's attractiveness as an investment location.

Minority Protection

Another area in the *Company Law* that would interest foreign investors is the protection accorded to minorities. It is arguable that minorities had some rights under the pre-existing *Commercial Code* provisions. The *Company Law* explicitly recognises minority rights as worthy of protection and provides for redress to an aggrieved minority shareholder.

The *Company Law* provides to both majority and minority shareholders a right of pre-emption or first refusal in respect of shares that are to be sold. The law requires that the price of the share be "reasonable". Moreover, the law requires that the company itself guarantee that the price is "reasonable". It is unclear how the company would discharge this "guarantee". Would it refuse to recognise a share transfer from the majority shareholder to a third party when the minority shareholder complains that the price was excessive and that such minority shareholder should have had the opportunity to purchase at a lower "reasonable" price? If so, then how would the directors who presumably would be nominees of the majority shareholder, respond to such a complaint? By the same token, the minority shareholder could exercise his rights of sale and may be able to convert the present right effectively into a put option whereby the majority shareholder should pay a "reasonable" price. The components of what it would take to make a price "reasonable" are unstated. A net asset value computation would not be regarded as unreasonable. However, if "reasonable" takes in certain intangibles such as the future earnings prospects of the company as well as the actual cost of the selling shareholder's investment, then this provision could effectively insure the shareholder against a loss in the investment.

Article 66(2) of the *Company Law* allows shareholders representing at least one-tenth of the voting shares the right to request that a general meeting be convened. If the boards of directors or commissioners fail to bring an action, the requesting shareholders may apply to a district court which will convene the meeting.

Shareholders representing a tenth of the voting shares are also allowed to bring a derivative action on behalf of the company against directors or commissioners who, through their mistakes or negligence, have caused a loss to the company (see Articles 85(3) and 98(2) of the

Company Law). In common law countries, directors are able to discharge quite easily the duties of diligence. Should the Indonesian courts impose industry specific standards of diligence and require high standards of care, it is likely that directors and commissioners may have to defend themselves in such derivative actions.

Shareholders have a right to information and data besides a right to inspect the shareholder register. If they are denied this right, then shareholders representing a tenth or more of the voting shares are permitted to petition the District Court (Article 110.2) for the appointment of an investigator to examine the records of the company to ascertain if the directors or commissioners have committed acts contrary to the law.

Article 54(2) grants to any shareholder the right to bring an action against the company by reason of injury suffered as a result of the action of the company that a shareholder claims is unfair or unreasonable and which was taken in consequence of a general meeting resolution or a meeting of the directors or commissioners.

The *Company Law* appears to have taken a strong tilt towards the shareholders in the familiar corporate conflict between shareholders and management. It remains to be seen whether this strong tilt towards the shareholders will prove to be disruptive to management. These provisions may also impale a foreign investor on the horns of a dilemma. Although allowed to own 100% of the shares in most P. T. PMA companies, the conventional wisdom dictates that a prudent investor will bring on board an Indonesian national as a minority shareholder in order to facilitate the operations of the company. The moment that such a person becomes a shareholder, this person becomes entitled to a wide range of privileges provided for under the *Company Law*. A foreign investor must ensure that such a minority shareholder does not turn out to be a Trojan horse.

INTERESTING TIMES

In globalised portfolio and direct investment markets, investors are skittish and do not react well to surprises. Despite the lack of bright line rules in Indonesia during the past decades, investors found stability in the very lack of change. The yet untested legal reforms and the tectonic changes portended by presidential succession may well prove to be too turbulent to investors in a time of transition. Then investors will understand the full meaning of the ancient Chinese curse, "May you live in interesting times!"

CONCLUSION

Chapter 18

Factors Shaping Indonesia's Investment Future

BY
John J. WILLIAMS

INTRODUCTION

EARLIER CHAPTERS HAVE presented a set of themes which overarch Indonesia's determination to sustain economic growth and create a vibrant climate for investment opportunities. As noted therein, economic reform and deregulation efforts have been remarkable and they have filled a fiscal space dedicated to basic economic fundamentals for competing in the global markets of the 21st century. Notwithstanding these achievements, Indonesia, like any country, remains vulnerable to worldwide market forces and must deal with the ongoing dynamics of its domestic economy. In the process of completing earlier chapters, a major political election, new reforms and currency crises in Southeast Asia have permeated the investment scene. The implications of these events on business opportunities in Indonesia are addressed in the following sections.

ASIA'S CURRENCY CRISES

Speculators could not have asked for more. Thailand was in the throes of monetary difficulty in the early part of 1997. The country was spending more than it earned which, in simple terms, put pressure on the current account deficit – equalling 8.5% of the gross domestic product (GDP) at one point (Bacani and Shameen, 1997). Unfortunately, a weak banking sector, in need of reform, had provided capital for an overheated real estate sector where values had escalated beyond economic reality. The economy was sluggish because of cheaper goods in the region, notably from China, and real estate developers began to renege on their bank loans. The Thai baht, meanwhile, remained trading at around 24 to the U.S. dollar. However, the Thai government did not have the foreign reserves to continue propping up the baht. Like sharks, the currency speculators moved in for the kill which sent the baht tumbling. On 2 July 1997, Thailand's first devaluation in 14 years happened as the Bank of Thailand allowed the currency to fall to 30 baht to the dollar, a 16% decline in value which could be the start of a downward spiral.

The next target was the Philippine peso and currency speculators challenged Manila, which had vowed to support the peso at any cost. However, after ten days, foreign exchange reserves were down over US$1.6 billion. For Manila, this was serious because it meant that the Philippines central bank, Bangko Sentral, had less than US$10 billion of reserves which translated into approximately three months of imports. Despite overnight interest rates of 50% to prevent selling pesos for dollar purchases, the central bank allowed the peso to free-float against the U.S. dollar and it dropped 12% instantly (Saludo and Lopez, 1997). A similar scenario humbled the Malaysian ringgit in the latter part of July 1997 and even the safe haven Singapore dollar fell to over S$1.50 to the U.S. dollar by mid-August 1997.

The End of the Rupiah Trading Band

Earlier chapters in this book discussed the reforms unfolding in Indonesia's banking sector to make it more competitive as well as the government's policy to depreciate its currency by 4% to 5% annually against the U.S. dollar through a widening rupiah trading band. On 11 July 1997, Bank Indonesia widened the intervention band for the rupiah from 8% to 12% amidst the turmoil of the Thai baht and the Philippine peso while the rupiah traded at 2,450 to the U.S. dollar (*The Straits Times*, 12 July 1997).

But by 13 August 1997, the rupiah breached the lower limit of the band and sank to a historic low of 2,684 rupiah to the U.S. dollar

(Chan, 1997a). The following day, Bank Indonesia bowed to market pressures and allowed the rupiah to float freely. In doing so, Bank Indonesia Governor, Sudradjad Djiwandono, indicated that a trading band for the rupiah would no longer be posted (Sim, 1997a). The rupiah promptly fell to a record low of 2,805 per dollar which translates into a decline of nearly 18% since the beginning of the year.

However, the worst was yet to come as the rupiah plunged still further to 3,005 against the U.S. dollar the following day. At the same time, the Jakarta Stock Exchange's Composite Index declined 3.9% to its lowest level of 1997. Of course, part of the reason for the stock market's fall was the potential damage to the earnings' of big corporations which had not fully hedged their dollar denominated debts (Sim, 1997b). This very possibility was the reason for addressing hedging alternatives in Chapter 8. Many investors did not do this because much of their debt is in offshore loans at interest rates under 10% compared to domestic rupiah loans of 18%.

Implications of the Rupiah's Decline

There is a negative and a positive side to the rupiah's plunging value against the dollar. On the positive side, exports become cheaper and, thus, export growth should remain strong. Combined with other fundamentals, including foreign bank reserves of US$20 billion, Indonesia should be able to sustain its forecasted economic growth of 7.5% for 1997. In addition, Bank Indonesia has taken action to increase the capital adequacy requirements of commercial banks. Plans are also in progress to consolidate Indonesia's seven state banks into a smaller number with more demanding loan requirements. Despite a current account deficit of US$8.82 billion in 1996/97, the World Bank expressed confidence that Indonesia could sustain its financing (*The Straits Times*, 23 June 1997).

However, the downside of the rupiah's fall will be felt by those companies with U.S. dollar-based debt, banks and retailers that import into Indonesia. The dollar denominated debt, of course, is more expensive since more rupiah are required per dollar of debt repayment. Retailers are hit hard because the rupiah's decline for importers translates directly into reduced profits. In turn, domestic prices can be expected to increase and this will put upward pressure on inflation which the government is trying to hold at 6% for the remainder of 1997.

Project financing is especially vulnerable to a falling rupiah. Existing projects are subject to cost overruns and the viability of these projects is problematic because the banks are holding the debt. If the banks in question do not survive, the projects will be stalled. Moreover, many projects which have been approved, but have not been started, will be put on hold and, perhaps, retrenched in the future.

In summary, Indonesia's financial sector is continuing to implement reforms to support the country's drive towards global competitiveness. Although the Jakarta bourse has been jolted by the recent currency upheaval throughout the Southeast Asian economies, it is the only one in the region which posted gains in the first six months of 1997. While bourses in Thailand, the Philippines, Malaysia and Singapore all fell, share values increased 26.8% to US$110.5 billion in the first half of 1997 on the Jakarta Stock Exchange (Chan, 1997b).

NEW DEREGULATION MEASURES

On 7 July 1997, the Indonesian Government continued its policy of promoting further economic reforms. At stake were measures to strengthen the monetary sector, trade regulations involving imports and exports, and investment and tax incentives (Sim, 1977c). The new measures are the first since June 1996. In the monetary sector, real estate developers will not have access to new credits for land purchases or improvements. This action is tantamount to a ban on property loans of any kind including guarantees on property-related securities. Effectively, land value cannot be used as collateral to obtain bank loans and credit extensions for property development are restricted to cases of land ownership or legal proof supporting the right to use the land. The one exception to this ban are developers of low-cost houses which is consistent with government policies for upgrading the poor and needy. This new measure should allay to some extent investors' concerns that the experiences of Japan and Thailand will be repeated in Indonesia.

On trade issues, import tariffs were reduced on 1,600 items covering mostly manufactured goods and sugar mills now can circumvent the National Logistics Board's monopoly by importing raw sugar directly. Also, second-hand cargo and fishing vessels can be imported. This measure is a critical reform pertaining to domestic regulations which substantially enhances inter-island equity, thus supporting one of the World Bank's recommendations. Turning to exports, the limit for exporting without custom documents was tripled to Rp 300 million while a value added tax was placed on crude palm oil exports. These measures should enhance economic efficiency as well as strengthen Indonesia's commitments to the World Trade Organisation (WTO), ASEAN Free Trade Area (AFTA) and the Asia-Pacific Economic Cooperation (APEC). The tariff reductions mean that 62.55% of all tariff codes are in the range of zero to 10%.

Also significant were new measures limiting the power of regional governments and requiring them to obtain the approval of the Ministry of Home Affairs before levying any taxes. Moreover, all non-tax payments received by government departments must be deposited with the State Treasurer. These reforms address recent concerns expressed by the World Bank that deal with the high cost of doing business arising from special payments to ministries (Pereira, 1997a). Finally, there is now equal treatment for all investors that import capital goods and raw materials.

ASSESSING INDONESIA'S INVESTMENT CLIMATE

Short Term Challenges

In June 1997, the World Bank released its report entitled *Indonesia: Sustaining High Growth with Equity* praising Indonesia as a "model developing economy". In fact, it placed Indonesia in the top 20 world economies by the year 2005. At the same time, however, the report predicted that growth of 7.5% per annum combined with current inflation of approximately 6% only could be sustained if the government proceeds with deregulation measures and tackles social inequities.

The latest deregulation package is a positive step towards promoting the export sector which fell from 18% for the year ended April 1996 to 3.1% for the year ended April 1997. Some economic observers suggest that the deregulation measures are not the solution because the problem lies in a restructuring of the labour-intensive manufacturing industry (Pereira, 1997a). But this is precisely where foreign investors can supply new technology to bolster the efficiency of the internal economy. Assuming that the rupiah exchange rate stabilises relative to foreign currencies, foreign investment should remain very attractive. In addition, limiting the powers of provincial authorities to impose taxes and levies on products is a bold move by the government to reduce the high cost of doing business in Indonesia.

The World Bank's reference to economic expansion with equity is aimed at Indonesia's widening income gap and the need to further the interests of small and medium-sized enterprises (SMEs). This is a monumental task and the Indonesian Government should be applauded for taking serious remedial action. Of course, the market bias towards big business cannot be altered overnight but the recent deregulation package does address the interests of small business. Furthermore, President Suharto has directed ministers to formulate a partnership plan between large business giants and the SMEs (Periera, 1997b). Not only would the former have to link up with SMEs to help eradicate poverty but, in addition, large retailers and franchises in the urban centres would be restricted from expanding unilaterally into other areas. There is ample opportunity, therefore, for foreign investment initiatives to support this strategy.

Longer Term Challenges

With the exception of Singapore, Indonesia in not unlike other developing and newly industrialised economies in Southeast Asia. To advance its domestic quality of life and compete in global markets, Indonesia historically needed a lot of everything – from infrastructure development, employment opportunities, domestic growth, education and technological advancement, to skilled human resources for higher value added productivity. Indonesia's economic performance over the last decade is amazingly good but serious challenges remain. Accompanying the incredible growth rates in the economy are a current account deficit in excess of US$8 billion and recent attacks on the currency which have cost the government over US$1.5 billion in foreign reserves. Naturally, the government must carefully consider its future fiscal plans, and monitor infrastructure development and investment in the overheated real estate market.

Indonesia requires more intellectual property and less real estate development. Moreover, increased high-level technical and managerial skills are necessary in order to shift the country's economic profile to higher value added products. It is estimated that 40% of Indonesia's exports are low value added products (Khanna, 1997). Given the gigantic push from China in this category of products, Indonesia needs investors that can contribute to human resource development, enhance soft infrastructure, and move the banking system and financial sector toward greater stability to support innovation and entrepreneurship. Foreign investment sentiment in this respect should be bolstered by the World Bank's commitment to make equality of education and health services in Indonesia the number one priority for the next five years.

Intra-ASEAN Relations

Indonesia is a dominant member of ASEAN (now comprising nine countries) and its acumen in foreign policy matters was exemplified in ASEAN's handling of the recent political crises in Cambodia. In this respect, Indonesia reflects the solidarity of purpose underpinning the ASEAN economies. More importantly for investors, this cohesive attitude spans the entire spectrum of trade and cooperation throughout the region. Most experts agree that Southeast Asia still remains a critical engine of global economic trade growth. Since over 40% of Indonesia's trade is tied to intra-regional partners, its prosperity is geared to the performance of the whole region. In terms of trade, ASEAN is the third largest regional grouping in the world with a population of 415 million people and a combined GDP of US$536 billion (Soh, 1997).

Indonesia's economic relationships with neighbouring countries are manifested in several emerging growth triangles and these have positive implications for business opportunities. One is the Southern Growth Triangle which includes Singapore, the state of Johor in Malaysia and Riau Island in Indonesia. Another is the Northern Growth Triangle which covers the northern part of Peninsular Malaysia, northern Sumatra and southern Thailand. A third one is the East ASEAN Growth Area covering Brunei; Sarawak, Sabah and Labuan in East Malaysia; East and West Kalimantan and northern Sulawesi in Indonesia; and Mindanao in the Philippines. Directly, these growth triangles enhance competitive advantages and, indirectly, offer a second wave of investment opportunities via Indonesia.

Political Stability

The general elections held in May 1997 were the culmination of months of controversy and tension throughout the diverse Indonesian archipelago. Some individuals are not happy with the structure of Indonesia's electoral system but the ruling Golkar party took 74% of the vote followed by the Muslim-oriented United Development Party (PPP) with 23% and the Indonesian Democratic Party (PDI) with 3%. This victory gave Golkar 324 seats in the 500-member House of Representative, with 75 members appointed from the military (Lee, 1997).

For investors, this election result means continuity and a preservation of the status quo. Golkar's decisive win at the polls will ensure solid support for President Suharto's seventh five-year term in the 1998 presidential election. Although a future successor remains unknown, investors have the benefit of assessing the strengths, and the flexibility in pursuing modernisation, emanating from the same leader who has steered Indonesia to its miraculous achievements over the past 30 years.

REFERENCES

Bacani Cesar and Assif Shameen, "Devaluation 101: A Layman's Guide to the Turmoil", *Asiaweek*, 25 July 1997, p. 47.

Chan Wee Chun, "Indonesian Rupiah Falls to New Low as Speculators Turn on Heat", *The Straits Times*, 14 August 1997a.

Chan Wee Chun, "Weak First Half for ASEAN Bourses as Turnover Tumbles", *The Straits Times*, 12 July 1997b.

Khanna Vikram, "Markets' Message", *The Straits Times*, 19 August 1997.

Lee Kim Chew, "Golkar Win Promises Continuity", *The Straits Times*, 7 June 1997.

Pereira Derwin, "Glowing World Bank Report Card for Indonesia", *The Straits Times*, 16 July 1997a.

Pereira Derwin, "Suharto Orders Plan for Business Partnerships", *The Straits Times*, 4 July 1997b.

Saludo Richard and Antonio Lopez, "Eye of the Storm", *Asiaweek*, 25 July 1997, pp. 43–5.

Sim Susan, "Indonesia Allows Rupiah to Float", *The Straits Times*, 15 August 1997a.

Sim Susan, "Rupiah and Equities Dive Further on Heavy Selling", *The Straits Times*, 16 August 1997b.

Sim Susan, "Indonesian Govt Cuts Tariffs, Curbs Land Speculation", *The Straits Times*, 8 July 1997c.

Soh Felix, "ASEAN in the Next Millennium", *The Straits Times*, 14 August 1997.

The Straits Times, "Jakarta Out to Make Banking Sector More Competitive", 23 June 1997.

The Straits Times, "Indonesia Widens Rupiah Trading Band", 12 July 1997.